TIME AND MIND:
Interdisciplinary Issues

TIME AND MIND:

Interdisciplinary Issues

The Study of Time VI

Edited by J. T. Fraser

INTERNATIONAL UNIVERSITIES PRESS, INC.
Madison, Connecticut

ISBN 0-8236-6542-9
ISSN 0170-9704
LOC 79-640956

Manufactured in the United States of America

To the memory of

Nathaniel M. Lawrence (1917–1986)

who taught the wonder of the moral law within
and of the starry heavens above

Table of Contents

Contributors

Jacob A. Arlow, M.D. Clinical Professor of Psychiatry, New York University Medical Center; past President of the American Psychoanalytic Association; past Editor-in-Chief of the *Psychoanalytic Quarterly*.

Richard A. Block, Ph.D. Professor of Psychology, Montana State University; editor, *Cognitive Models of Psychological Time*.

Kenneth G. Denbigh, D.Sc., F.R.S. Professor Emeritus and Honorary Research Fellow, King's College, London; thermodynamicist; author of *Three Concepts of Time* and other books.

J. T. Fraser, Ph.D. Founder of the International Society for the Study of Time, author of *Time, the Familiar Stranger*, of *Time, Passion, and Knowledge* and other works, and editor of *The Study of Time* series.

Janet L. Jackson, Ph.D. Lecturer in Cognitive Psychology, Institute of Experimental Psychology, The Netherlands; Secretary of the European Society for Cognitive Psychology; editor with John A. Michon of *Time, Mind, and Behavior*.

Albert Mayr Professor of Experimental Music, Conservatorio L. Cherubini, Florence; composer and theorist; coordinator of the project "the music of times and tides."

Frederick T. Melges, M.D. Deceased. Formerly, Professor and Vice Chairman, Department of Psychiatry, Duke University Medical Center; author of *Time and the Inner Future*.

John A. Michon, Ph.D. Professor of Experimental Psychology and Traffic Science, University of Groningen; Fellow of the Royal Netherlands Academy of Arts and Sciences, editor with Janet L. Jackson of *Time, Mind, and Behavior;* past President of the International Society for the Study of Time.

Helga Nowotny, Dr. iur., Ph.D. Professor of Sociology, Institut für Wissenschaftstheorie und Wissenschaftsforschung, University of Vienna; Chairperson, Standing Committee for the Social Sciences, European Science Foundation, Strasbourg.

David Park, Ph.D. Professor Emeritus of Physics, Williams College; author of *The How and the Why;* past President of the International Society for the Study of Time.

Jann Pasler, Ph.D. Associate Professor of Music, University of California, San Diego; Editor, *Confronting Stravinsky;* author of research articles on aesthetic and sociological issues in 20th-century music.

Albert Shalom, D. ès L. Professor of Philosophy, McMaster University; formerly Chercheur,

CNRS (Paris); among other publications, *The Body/Mind Conceptual Framework and the Problem of Personal Identity;* corresponding member of l'Institut de France.

Charles M. Sherover, Ph.D. Professor of Philosophy, Hunter College/CUNY; author of several books and articles in the philosophy of time, social and political philosophy, and Kant and Heidegger studies.

Marlene Pilarcik Soulsby, Ph.D. Assistant Professor of German and Comparative Literature, Pennsylvania State University; publications in East-West literary relations, German literature, and foreign language pedagogy.

Robert J. Thornton, Ph.D. Associate Professor of Anthropology at the University of Cape Town; author of *Space Time and Culture among the Iraqw of Tanzania,* and articles on eastern and southern Africa, ethnographic methods, and history of anthropology.

Gerald J. Whitrow, M.A., D.Phil. (Oxon) Emeritus Professor of the History and Applications of Mathematics in the University of London and Senior Research Fellow of the Imperial College of Science, Technology and Medicine; author of *The Natural Philosophy of Time, What is Time?, Time in History,* among other works; past President of the International Society for the Study of Time.

Acknowledgments

I am much indebted to Professor Mary W. Lawrence for her assistance in editing this volume.

I also wish to thank those who helped, over and above the call of their duty, in the critical revision of the papers: Jacob A. Arlow, M.D., Professor Richard A. Block, Professor Robert Brumbaugh, Dr. Kenneth G. Denbigh, F.R.S., Professors Lawrence W. Fagg, George H. Ford, Barry Glassner, Francis C. Haber, Jon Hendricks, Jonathan D. Kramer, David Park, Albert I. Rabin, Lewis Rowell, Barry Schwartz, Albert Schmidt, and Charles Sherover.

The Editor

Foreword

Events are paradoxical entities: they allow time to happen but easily perish in it. The only way to prevent events from drowning in the very stream they generate is to make them outstanding and therefore memorable in terms of both content and context.

The Sixth Conference of the International Society for the Study of Time (ISST) easily qualifies as an outstanding event. Both its content, its program, and its context, the highly attractive surroundings offered by Dartington Hall in Totnes, Devon, England, have contributed to the "distinguished eventhood" of the meeting.

The theme of the conference, "Time and Mind," was certainly a very difficult and, therefore, an appropriate one to our meeting. The topics time and mind taken separately are complex enough; we may expect nothing less from their conjunction.

The theme succeeded in bringing to light a gratifying amount of topical convergence among issues related to time and to mind. For example, there is a renewed interest among physicists and cosmologists in the conscious observer, which is one of the mythical beasts quietly grazing on the meadows of psychology and physiology. Also, psychology and the social sciences have begun cultivating territories they share with the humanities, such as the structural and functional aspects of narrative. Although no full-grown theory of time and mind emerged, the conference will have surely inspired many of its participants by demonstrating that progress toward a coherent study of time and mind is possible and that, in fact, some coherent regions of interdisciplinary understanding are already emerging.

With its conference at Dartington Hall, the International Society for the Study of Time completed the second decade of its existence.

Upon this occasion, I wish to congratulate Dr. J. T. Fraser, Founder and, currently, also the Secretary of the Society. To an overwhelming degree he is the person responsible for what the Society has been and has become. He must feel the pride and perhaps also the relief parents feel when their child attains adulthood. While straight from the inception of the Society there have been others who helped develop ISST, there is no doubt that Dr. Fraser has been the architect, the contractor, the interior decorator, as well as the concierge of this condominium of scholars and scientists.

I shall refrain from calling all the important contributors to mind, but I wish to make an exception for the Distinguished Lecturer of the Conference, Dr. G. J. Whitrow, whose involvement reaches back to the very earliest moments of the Society's existence.

Focusing now on the present conference, may I remind you that meetings such as this do not just happen. Preparations are time-consuming and involved, and this one was no exception. The first to realize that such is the case are of necessity the members of the Conference Committee. I wish to thank Dr. Kenneth Denbigh, F.R.S., Professor George H. Ford, Professor Jonathan Kramer, Professor Lewis Rowell, and Dr. Masanao Toda for their valuable contributions.

It is tragic that a distinguished member of that Committee did not live to participate at the conference. In Professor Nathaniel Lawrence many of us lost a good friend and the Society lost one of its most prominent members.

As has been the case on previous occasions, the local organization of the conference was put into the hands of a single person. I have always found this unbelievable. Now that in the past two years I have observed Dr. Gordon Bevans at work, I wish to declare gratefully that I have seen a miracle happen. We are deeply indebted to the local organizing "committee." Finally, under Dr. Bevans's guidance, Arianne Boon and Jos van Berkum of the University of Groningen took care of the innumerable details that required attention; their competent assistance helped in the smooth unfolding of the events that made up the Sixth Conference of our Society.

But organizing a conference is not yet the same as running it. I wish to thank all those who helped transforming our plans into an actual event, but I can name only a few. I thank Michael Lord Young of Dartington whose support before and during the conference clearly revealed his interest in the study of time. The staff of Dartington Hall, represented by Mr. Robert Jones is to be thanked for its masterly handling of the infrastructure of the meeting.

John A. Michon
President, 1983–1986

I

The Many Dimensions of Time and Mind: An Epistemic Jigsaw Puzzle Game*

J. T. Fraser

Abstract This chapter suggests a framework for an interdisciplinary dialogue on the theme, time and mind.

The advanced functions of the mind include the generation of symbols that represent possible and impossible events, structures and feelings. The skill of manipulating these symbols instead of actual objects and happenings makes possible the comprehension of the world in terms of noetic time.

To be able to construct its symbols, the mind separates in its interpretation of sensory inputs those elements it judges beinglike, predictable, and hence nameable, from those it perceives as becominglike and unpredictable. This is not a passive recognition of preexistent conditions but a creative act with irreducible biological, cognitive, and social dimensions. It follows that the theme of this volume is necessarily multidisciplinary.

Basing its arguments on the hierarchical theory of time, chapter 1 reasons that the human brain represents boundary conditions to biologically achievable complexity. It follows that those brain functions that are ordinarily ascribed to the mind are also delimited, although the delineation of its boundaries is difficult because of the hierarchical organization of languages and logics. The best tactic that suggests itself for getting around the difficulty is one of interdisciplinary reality testing, described in the chapter as the epistemic jigsaw puzzle game.

Fields of learning that concern themselves with matter, life, mind, and society play the game differently; they employ different methods for seeking knowledge and different criteria for legitimizing truth. As a result, there are families of views on time and mind distinguished by their methodological preferences, metaphysical assumptions, and the personalities of the people who work in physics, biology, psychology, sociology, and the arts and letters.

Using as an illustration the changing rate of time's experienced flow, the paper concludes with remarks on what might be expected of a multidisciplinary approach to inquiries concerning time and mind.

*The Founder's Lecture, July 5, 1986.

This chapter proposes, discusses, and illustrates a conceptual framework for an interdisciplinary dialogue on time and mind.

Timing and Minding

The noble art of change ringing consists in the ringing, according to a law of permutations, of a set of tower bells of different pitches. A set of rings is called a change, a complete set of changes is a peal.

When one listens to a peal, the mind is continuously searching in the rush of sound for a stable melodic pattern, but finding none, its search goes on. The experience suggests the Heracletian view of reality as flux: "Upon those who step in the same rivers, different and different waters flow. . . ." A dedicated listener may nevertheless succeed in identifying an unchanging law beneath what he hears and expressing it in a mathematical formula. Such a labor reminds one of the Parmenedian *Way of Truth* that assigned reality only to whatever was permanent.

All living organisms know how to distinguish in their umwelts (or species-specific realities) between patterns that are permanent and those that are not. The capacity to employ this distinction in the control of behavior is the *timing* ability of life.

But only our species has the further capacity to enlarge the biological know-how of timing by means of a universe of symbols and to employ those symbols in the control of behavior; for example, through imagining possible and impossible futures and pasts. I will call this capacity *minding*.

The verbal nouns—timing and minding—are intended to stress that I am speaking of two generalized and inherently uncompletable processes of which time and mind are reified representations.

The copresence in our self-awareness of the feelings of change and permanence is the source of an unresolvable conflict, an existential stress that informs all human actions in both their individual and collective dimensions. I believe that this stress has been responsible for the chronic state of restlessness which characterizes our species. It has been a source of insecurity that may be lessened, though only in a transient manner, through a ceaseless expansion of the horizons of noetic reality.

The Multidisciplinary Dimensions of Timing and Minding

In terms of the cosmos as it is understood today, the world may be thought of as one gigantic peal of innumerable bells, each ringing under the control of a hierarchy of governing principles. The spectrum of bell frequencies extends from gamma rays to the vast exhalation of the expanding universe, across thirty-eight orders of magnitude or, in the language of musicians, 126 octaves. Across this wide band of ringing, the separation of the permanent from the fleeting is carried on by the life process, by people's minds, and by society.

In biology, permanent forms and functions useful for the survival of the species are retained by natural selection and deposited, as a cumulative residue, in the programs and structures of the material that carries biological inheritance. This knowledge is then passed on as the behavioral traits and structural features of subsequent generations of living organisms. The programs and structures of the genetic material thus constitute the memory of whatever has been collectively learned of permanence and change.

The rigid and slowly growing biological memory storage expands in man into a versatile, rapidly enlargeable know-how, employed by the brain in its task of minding the body. This new skill uses the symbols of language, art, and artifact; it makes them stand for events, feelings, and structures that may or may not be present, and manipulates them instead of the actual events, feelings, and structures. Thus, these created worlds constitute the cumulative residue of what has been collectively *and* individually learned of permanence and change.

The symbols of human communication may pertain not only to actual or possible, but also to impossible events, feelings, and things. Through this freedom they have made possible the creation of the great cultural continuities of mankind.

Trying to discover the rules (permanent patterns) that govern the peals of a world that includes ourselves among its ringing bells, is necessarily a many-tiered process. It follows that the theme of our conference—timing and minding— involves issues far beyond questions in psychology: we must seek insights from physics, biology, social science, history, and the arts and letters.

As our instrument of search we propose to use our brains. They are organs of unique and curious historiography, for whereas in our bodies earlier somatic structures have been superseded by later ones, our brains have retained, without replacing, certain modified forms of the stages of their own evolution.

These stages, differing in neural organization and chemistry, correspond to the three main layers of the human brain. They have been described as the reptilian, the paleomammalian or limbic, and the neomammalian systems. The three layers share the same cranial cavity; they are, so to say, on speaking terms, but the older brains speak simpler languages (see Figure 6.1 on p.111).

The reptilian and paleomammalian brains concern themselves only with the immediate future and past; theirs is a biotemporal world. The world of the much younger neocortex is the nootemporal umwelt: its reality, in addition to the immediate future and past, includes long-term futures and pasts as well.

How may the laws of the nootemporal world (one of vast temporal horizons) and those of the biotemporal world (one with limited horizons) be integrated? How may these integrated laws be further integrated, in their turn, with the temporalities of the physical world, in which nothing at all corresponds to our idea of the present, and hence of future and past and, therefore, to the flow of time?

The most broadly held view is summed up in the second edition of G. J. Whitrow's classic, *The Natural Philosophy of Time*. It states that "at all levels time is essentially the same, although certain aspects of it become increasingly significant the more complex the nature of the particular object or system studied (p. 375). On this view, various aspects of time may be discovered as they make themselves manifest, but they have been there, as it were, all along. Time is then ontologically prior to the structures and functions through which its various aspects disclose themselves.

If it is assumed that the ultimate sources of passing time are independent of all objects and systems—including life, mind, and society—then the most appropriate discipline through which those sources could be discovered must be physics.

A few years ago Roger Penrose set out to seek an answer "to one of the long-standing mysteries of physics: the origins of the arrow of time" (Penrose, 1979, p. 581). Forty-five pages of careful arguments and 114 bibliographical references later, all of them entirely from physics, he concluded that, "Some readers might feel let down by this. Rather than finding some subtle way that a universe based on time-symmetric laws might nevertheless exhibit gross time asymmetry, I have merely asserted that certain laws are not in fact time-symmetric—and worse than this, that these asymmetric laws are not yet known." (Penrose, 1979, p. 635).

The reasons for the negative outcome of his search are implicit in a paper by P. C. W. Davies, entitled, "What Is Time?" Professor Davies writes that, "Psychological images are not usually considered good physical science and by invading our thoughts, language and actions, mental time at best inhibits our understanding of physical time, and is at worst in direct conflict with it" (1979, p. 18).

The claim, I believe, is backward. Psychological images, among which we must include all events and structures of the future and past, do not inhibit but rather make possible the understanding of the temporalities of life and of nonliving matter. Furthermore, carefully argued views of time and mind cannot remain in conflict with each other because that would imply inconsistency in nature. But insights into the nature of time gained through physics, biology, psychology, the social sciences, and the arts and letters may appear incompatible if the hierarchically nested character of temporalities goes unnoticed.

Professor Penrose could not identify the roots of the arrow of time precisely because he failed to consult biology, psychology, and sociology. The reason he did not do so, in my view, lies in the parochialism implicit in Professor Davies' remarks and in those of Professor Penrose as well. Both men insist that the sources for the arrow of time, come what may, must necessarily be found in physical science.

Let me examine what happens if one attempts to understand the flow of time through an integration of insights gained through several intellectual disciplines. To be able to do so, we need an epistemic framework. I propose to sketch such a framework, derived from the theory of time as conflict (Fraser, 1975).

The Nested Hierarchy of Presents

It is an axiom of the theory of time as conflict that nature comprises a number of stable organizational levels along a scale of increasing complexity. Each level is seen as governed by a set of level-specific principles, expressible in level-specific languages, and using level-specific logics. The governing principles of each organizational level incorporate and are, therefore, restrained by the principles that govern the levels beneath it; each adds to the nested hierarchy new structures and functions and with them, new degrees of freedom. The dynamics of each integrative level determines its specific temporality. These different and distinct temporalities

I have called the *canonical forms of time*. As a family, the canonical forms of time constitute an open-ended, nested hierarchy along a scale of increasing potential creativity.

Let me give an illustration of the hierarchy of temporalities by describing what the theory teaches about the nature of the "now."

As I mentioned, there is nothing in the physical world to which the idea of the "present" could correspond. According to the hierarchical theory of time, what we know as the "now" first emerged only with the *organic present* of life. The organic present, as I shall explain, is a manifestation of the capacity of living organisms for maintaining their internal coherence from instant to instant.

For an organism to remain alive it is necessary that certain biochemical changes do, and certain others do not, take place simultaneously. These demands for simultaneities by copresence, and by exclusion are maintained as long as the organism is alive. If we turn the reasoning around, an organism remains alive only as long as the internal coordination that creates its organic present is maintained. Since future and past must always refer to a present, it was only with biogenesis that futurity and pastness were born. And, since the metaphor, "the flow of time" means future becoming past, it was only with life that time's flow could acquire reality. This interpretation of the origins of our experience of passing time eliminates the need for an appeal to a moving cosmic present. To establish the flow or direction of time, therefore, human consciousness is not necessary but the life process is.

Jumping over the mental present, let me turn from the organic present of life to the "now" of human communities. For a society to remain viable, it is necessary for those events that ought to take place simultaneously to do so and for those that ought not, not to. As long as a group of people forms a society these demands of simultaneities by copresence and exclusion are maintained through communication via biological and cultural channels. Turning it around, one can speak of a viable society only if, and only as long as, its social present is maintained. It is with reference to the social present that collective futures and pasts acquire meaning. The social present and the flow of social time thus emerge as phenomenal manifestations of the autonomy of a society, and may be thought of without an appeal to a necessary cosmic "now."

I submit that the creation and maintenance of the organic present is a necessary as well as a sufficient criterion of life, and that the creation and maintenance of the social present is a necessary and sufficient criterion for regarding a group of people as a society.

Let me now return to the *mental present*. The mental present is seen by the hierarchical theory of time as the manifestation of the capacity of the human brain and central nervous system for maintaining its viability from instant to instant. For the living human brain to discharge its functions of minding the body, it is necessary that certain biochemical and electrical events do, while others do not, happen simultaneously. The integrity of minding is maintained only if, and as long as, the necessary simultaneities of physiological events are maintained. It is with respect to the mental present that our hopes and fears about the future and our memories and regrets about the past, can acquire meaning.

I have spoken thus far about a hierarchy of nested presents: the organic, the mental, and the social. Associated with these presents the hierarchical theory of time identifies biotemporality, nootemporality, and sociotemporality, with their increasingly broader range of temporal domains.

It is not only temporalities that are seen to form a nested hierarchy: so are complexities, languages (taken in the generalized sense as the rules and modes of communication), and causations. Let me now turn to these: the hierarchy of complexities and languages.

The Human Brain: A Boundary to Biological Complexity

The notion of complexity is intuitively obvious but it is difficult to express that intuition in the form of a measurable variable. Nevertheless, I attempted a few years ago to do just that (Fraser, 1982, pp. 154–156). I defined the complexity of an integrative level as equal to, and measured by, the number of distinct, stable structures that belong or belonged in that level.

For the physical world these numbers are easy to find. The number of stable objects that belong in the atemporal level of speed-of-light particles (where none of our ordinary notions of time apply) is three: photons, neutrinos, and gravitons or perhaps only two or only one.

The number of stable objects that belong in the prototemporal level of elementary objects (where time is discontinuous and exact locations of instants have no meaning) may be equated to the number of long-lived particles. That number is a few hundred and growing. But, since in the prototemporal world, space and time are not yet sufficiently distinct and hence processes and structures are often interchangeable, it is not clear which of the several hundred particles, alias waves, or, sometimes, resonances, should be included. For the purposes of my reasoning, I used the conservative figure of 250.

I took the number of stable objects that belong in the eotemporal level of macroscopic objects (where time is continuous but does not yet have a direction) as equal to the number of the stable chemical compounds we know of or can justify. After making some reasonable assumptions, one arrives at the figure 10^7, take or leave an order of magnitude.

When we step an organizational level higher, that is, to life, the number of stable, distinct organisms that ever existed is not easy to estimate. The problem is not that it is awkward to count the heads and tails of all the living and the dead, then divide the number by two, but that as one leaves the sexually reproducing species and even the world of metazoa, it becomes increasingly difficult to declare what is to be meant by a distinct organism. But the kind of absolute identity which exists among particles of the same species does not exist among living organisms, and, for that reason, the notion of distinctness may be defended. Again, making some reasonable assumptions, one arrives at the broad range of 10^{30} to 10^{40}. The vast margin of uncertainty is of no consequence because the complexities, measured according to the prescription proposed, go up first by one, then by five, then by another twenty-five to thirty orders of magnitude, making the distinctness of the levels clear.

In trying to obtain a figure for the complexity of the human brain I followed others who, using learning theory, hierarchy theory, and sociobiology, also attempted to obtain numerical indices to brain capacities (Fraser, 1982, pp. 165–168). I assumed with some of them that each distinct element of thought— whatever that may mean—corresponded to a different configuration of neuronal interconnections. With several caveats, the figure of 10^{10^9}, that is 10 to the one billion, obtains.

In rounded-out logarithms, the complexities of the organizational levels of nature may, therefore, be characterized by the figures 0, 2, 6–7, 30–40, and 10^9.[1]

The suggestion comes to mind that the human brain may represent a limiting condition, that its organization is the upper boundary to complexity possible for an aggregate of identical cells—neurons—so connected as to be able to maintain concerted functions.

The jump of a billion orders of magnitude in complexity from the biological to the mental might well account for the unique position of noetic time in the hierarchy of temporalities.

Limiting or boundary conditions are not new to science; physics has already identified a number of them. There is an absolute zero and possibly also an upper limit to temperature; we know of the smallest possible objects and of the largest single one; there is an upper limit to density and an upper limit to the speed at which information may be transmitted.

These boundaries have certain properties in common.

- Each of them may be approached along a continuous path from the human-sized world.
- The principles that govern each are limiting forms of the principles that govern the same processes in the human-dimensioned world.
- The laws of the boundary conditions, however, are not predictable from their garden-variety forms because each of the boundary domains has its peculiar language and logic, different from those of everyday experience.

If the complexity of the human brain does represent a boundary condition to nature, then the specifications which hold for the other boundary conditions are likely to apply to minding as well. Specifically:

- An understanding of the mind should be achievable by progressing along a path of analysis from what we know of nonliving and living matter.
- The principles that govern minding and the noetic sense of time should be

[1]The universe has many more identical components than does the human brain. But they are not so interconnected as to be able to define *simultaneities of necessity*. Coincidences in the physical world are always *simultaneities of chance*. This is also the reason why the physical world cannot define a present, hence future and past, hence an arrow of time.

coherent with what we know about the laws that govern the biotemporal world.

- None of the principles that are specific to minding could, however, be predictable from the world of biology, much less from that of physics. In other words, the laws peculiar to psychology will have to be discovered independently of the other sciences, through methodologies peculiar to psychology.

- Finally, the sciences of the mind would be expected to possess a distinct language and logic, as if minding were something independent of the rest of the world, even though it is not. We might then expect the eventual establishment of continuity between psychology and biology and physical science only ex post facto, provided we can begin with a self-consistent body of psychological knowledge, developed in its own right.

These remarks on the epistemic status of minding and timing, obtained by inductive reasoning from what we already knew about nature, carry a degree of plausibility. Certainly, conscious awareness, selfhood, fantasy, or the feeling of free will are out on a limb of the tree of animal behavior. As humans, our bodies do not place us anywhere close to the natural boundaries of temperature, size, or speed, but by having evolved the human brain, our species has reached the cutting edge of biological complexity.

The Effectiveness of the Mind: Boundaries to What Is Knowable by an Individual

If the complexity of the human brain does represent a boundary condition to nature, I would expect that minding also has its rationally delineable boundaries of effectiveness. This, I believe, is the case, even though those boundaries are difficult to identify. Attention to the nested hierarchy of logics and forms of laws that control the stable integrative levels of nature will help us to identify the reasons for the difficulty.

To develop the argument, I want to point first to an isomorphism between the hierarchy of principles governing the stable integrative levels of nature on the one hand and, on the other, a liberalized form of Russell's hierarchy of types. I take my lead from John von Neumann who remarked that:

> In the complicated parts of formal logic it is always an order of magnitude harder to tell what an object can do than to produce that object. The domain of validity of a question is of a higher type than the question itself. . . . The feature is just this, that you can perform within the logical type that is involved everything that is feasible, but the question of whether something is feasible in a type, belongs to a higher logical type [1969, pp. 47–48, 51].

Let me assume that these remarks on the hierarchy of types are valid for the level-specific laws and logics of nature, in other words, that each integrative level is capable of creating and maintaining structures and processes feasible under the control of its principles; but the question of what is feasible in that integrative level can only be answered in the language of a higher integrative level.

A corollary claim would say that the higher order language is, in some ways, broader than the ones beneath it; that the higher order principles are not expressible in, and therefore remain unrecognizable by, the lower order ones. To state it again differently, each integrative level possesses new and unforeseeable degrees of freedom.

Von Neumann also noted that the hierarchy of types is isomorphic in its structure with Gödel's famous principle of undecidability. This principle teaches that in mathematics, even at the simplest formal level, it is possible to formulate legitimate propositions which may be true or false, but whether they are true or false can only be decided in the formalism of a more complex mathematical system.

According to my reasoning, the laws and languages of the stable integrative levels of nature are also isomorphic in their structure to the hierarchy of types and to Gödel's principle of undecidability. I am even prepared to turn the argument around and maintain that the hierarchically nested structure of nature is ontologically prior to the mathematical and logical relationships identified by Russell, Gödel, and von Neumann. They only formulated in symbols what the immense journey of organic evolution has taught us. Be that as it may, how does the hierarchically nested progressions of complexities and undecidabilities translate into the hierarchy of temporalities?

The chaos of the atemporal world may be recognized as such only in contrast with the minimal ordering represented by the statistical character of time in the prototemporal world. One can talk about total confusion only in comparison with a modicum of order.

Going one step higher, the absence of continuity in a prototemporal universe may only be recognized in comparison with the continuity of time in an eotemporal one. And again, the absence of a "now" and of directed time in the eotemporal world may be so seen only in comparison with the biotemporal world with its definition of a present and a directed time. And once again, the narrow horizons of future and past—the hallmarks of the biotemporal world—may only be recognized in comparison with the broad horizons of nootemporality.

Along these consecutive steps of increasing freedom, it has been the case that the principles of the higher levels remained inexpressible in the lower level languages. Let me assume that this asymmetry holds between any two adjacent integrative levels, and that organic evolution is open-ended.

It will then follow that, among the many propositions which have been made about time and mind, there must be some whose truth or falsehood is undecidable in the languages appropriate to the noetic world at the current level of social complexity, but may be decidable in the language and logic of a next higher integrative level. That new organizational level is, I believe, in the making. It is the level of the society of a time-compact world with its narrow global present, with the graying of its calendar, with the interpenetration of its economic, ideological, and military empires, and with the shift of responsibilities for planning and history to small, specialist groups (on the time-compact globe see Fraser [1987, pp. 310–353]). I would imagine that the language and logic appropriate to that level are parts of a collective, rather than an individualistic artificial intelligence.

If my reasoning about the languages of the stable integrative levels is correct, it would then follow that there is no way of telling which of the many propositions about time and mind that have been made, and remain undecided, may eventually be answerable in the languages appropriate to the noetic world, and which must await the possible development of the language and logic of a time-compact global society.

The Principle of Time Measurement

From an examination of the boundaries of the mind, and the difficulties of identifying these boundaries, let me turn to an issue concerning timing and minding that lends itself well to interdisciplinary exploration. I will pose a question, then attempt to answer it, using the hierarchical theory of time as my guide. The exercise will lead us to a number of general questions concerning the interdisciplinary study of time.

For a statement of the time and mind problem I want to examine, I turn to the domain of letters. We learn from Shakespeare's *As You Like It* that,

> Time travels in diverse paces with diverse persons.
> I'll tell you who Time ambles withal, who Time trots
> withal, who Time gallops withal, and who he stands withal.
>
> [III:2:328]

The speed-of-time metaphors in their many guises are immediately intelligible to mature, English-speaking persons. They may also be translated into many other languages where they carry the same immediate self-evidence.

What is the basis of the great power of that metaphor?

Consider first that no clock can in itself be fast, slow, or right. To have a speed its readings must be compared with those of at least one other clock, in which case it might be said to have run slower or faster than, or at the same rate as, the other clock. Time itself can only be said to pass as a result of comparisons between the readings of at least two clocks..

The *principle of time measurement* asserts that every time measurement must involve at least two clocklike processes, as well as a belief or theory that validates the comparison between their readings. In everyday use one of the clocks and the idea or theory that connects the two readings become matters of convention and go unnoticed, like wallpaper music. In scientific work, however, the connecting principles are formalized as laws of nature, expressed in equations, and the identity of the clocks made obvious.

The speed-of-time metaphor reports on a comparison that has been made between certain clock readings. In search of the reasons for the effectiveness of that metaphor, let me attempt to identify the clocks or clocklike processes which, when compared, give rise to the experience of time having a speed, of time passing. I plan to do so through an appeal to the natural philosophy of time and, specifically, to considerations that derive from the hierarchical theory of time.

I want to consider the task of time measurement along the hierarchy of the stable integrative levels of nature.

Let us begin at the integrative level of inorganic matter with the illuminating clock problem of relativity theory. Two clocks in relative motion or two clocks in different gravitational fields will generally show different amounts of elapsed time between the same two events. Which clock measures the correct time? They both do, provided their readings may be mutually transformable through the instructions of an acceptable theory. In the case of relative motion those instructions even have a name: They are called Lorentz Transformations.

From the nonliving, let me step up to the living and consult our colleagues in chronobiology. Every living organism is a clockshop of billions of clocks, kept coordinated and coherent in the organic present. In innumerable ways, however, they can get out of step. Some of them, then, may be said to be fast with respect to some others, and vice versa. The resulting dysrhythmia often manifests itself as an ailment of some kind.

From the biotemporal world, let me move to the nootemporal one, the domain of psychology. In the hierarchically nested organization of time the nootemporal umwelt subsumes the biotemporal and the physical worlds; it also adds new and unique degrees of freedom to what is available to living, but mindless, matter. Let us see how this works out for time measurement when we consider the human brain.

The concerns of the reptilian and paleomammalian levels of the human brain, as already mentioned, are those of immediate satisfaction. The furnishings of their reality is that of concrete objects and goals. In their worlds selfhood cannot be defined because their capacities for the formation of symbolic continuities are poor or nonexistent.

In contrast, as we learn from neurologists, long-term planning and memory, conscious experience, selfhood, and concern with abstract and symbolic causes populate the umwelt of the neocortex. The two umwelts amount to two different ways of perceiving time, with the nootemporal subsuming the biotemporal. Our colleagues in psychology might note here that it is possible to act on the basis of emotions without much or even any rational thought, but it is not possible to reason without an emotional underpinning. Our philosopher friends may remind us of Rousseau: "I felt before I thought: this is the common lot of humanity."

Encouraged by these remarks we may then permit ourselves to associate the older and newer ways of assessing time—the temporalities of the older and newer parts of the human brain—with the ideas of time felt and time understood.

I submit that the experience of time traveling at diverse paces originates in comparisons in our minds between the older and the newer perceptions of reality weighted, from instant to instant, by the biological, psychological, and social factors that mediate those comparisons.

I propose, furthermore, that the reason we have experiences which may be described, to begin with, as those of the flow of time, ought to be sought in the hierarchical organization of the human brain. For an understanding of the effectiveness of the metaphor, "time passes," we should not look to presumed comparisons between an internal sense of temporal passage and a presumed external passing of cosmic time—for such an external passage of time does not exist—but rather should consider the functions of the human brain and nervous system and their archaic and more recent assessments of external reality.

Whenever the higher brain functions are short-circuited, as in sleep, the metaphor, "the passing of time," ceases to be meaningful. This does not mean that dream umwelts may be properly called timeless—traditional beliefs notwithstanding—but that they are mixtures of the lower temporalities, with noetic ordering introduced only when the dreams are reconstructed in the waking state.

Noetic temporal ordering is projected not only upon the dream world but also, and probably for similar psychological needs, upon the physical world, despite the fact that the equations of physics tell us that nothing in that world corresponds to the experience of flowing time. These projected schemes, known as narrative cosmologies, open up the speed-of-time issue to contributions by one and all who ever asked questions about the universe at large.

In scientific measurements of time (the comparison of two clock readings!) the clock selected as the reference clock is usually the one judged more reliable. By being "more reliable" is usually meant that the processes constituting that clock are better understood than those constituting the other one. This is the reason why we measure rat time by the clock on the wall and the earth's rotation time by atomic clocks, and not the other way round.

I am going to assume that in our brains a continuous comparison is being carried on among the various "clock readings," that is, among the different assessments of reality. On this view, the minding process includes, from instant to instant, the selection of a reference clock. This is the clock—this is the assessment of the world—whose reality is invested, at an instant, with the most mental and emotional energy, because its functions are most relevant to the task at hand. That clock may be said to be "better understood" at that moment. It is in terms of the cathected assessment of time—the assessment invested with the most psychic energy—that the other readings are then evaluated.

My speculative conclusion is that what emerges into consciousness is the end product of an intricate process of such weighted comparisons. That end product is the feeling of time passing slowly, rapidly, or not at all. These feelings, in their turn, give rise to the infinite variety of metaphors our languages use to describe the passing of time.

Many learned papers have been written to inform us that time does not "really" flow. Indeed, time's flow is a metaphor. But, I believe with John Michon that "metaphors are not arbitrary but rather derive from structural properties of the human mind. This actually amounts to the position that . . . metaphors cannot take just any conceivable form, but instead, display considerable morphological stability (Michon, 1985, p. 290).

Through appeals to a many-sided understanding of time, my reasoning has illustrated an interdisciplinary approach to an elucidation of the metaphor, "the flow of time," and to an explanation of why the metaphor has such a great morphological stability.

Let me now sum up some of the claims I have made.

- I defined, *timing* as the ability of living organisms to separate permanence from change in their species-specific realities and use that distinction in the control of their behavior.
- I defined, *minding* as the ability of members of our species to enlarge their biological know-how of timing into a universe of symbols, representing possible and impossible futures and pasts, and to use those symbols in the control of their behavior.
- *Time* and *mind* then emerged as reified representations of the timing and minding processes.
- The study of time and mind turned out to be a necessarily multidisciplinary task. To hold the different contributions together, I directed attention to the conceptual framework of the hierarchical theory of time, invoking its account of the nested hierarchy of presents, temporalities, complexities, and languages.
- An examination of the hierarchy of complexities suggested that the human brain forms a boundary to the complexity achievable through biological means.
- An examination of the hierarchy of languages suggested that not all legitimate propositions on the nature of time and mind may be decidable, as to their truth or falsity, in the currently available languages and logics.

The Epistemic Jigsaw Puzzle Game

My attempt to integrate views from different fields of knowledge was guided by the hierarchical theory of time. That theory permitted us to play the epistemic jigsaw puzzle game. This game consists of fitting together, for a special purpose, various pieces of knowledge, derived from intellectual disciplines that differ in their methodologies, their proofs of acceptable evidence, their logics, and their languages. It is a difficult game because the pieces change while they are being assembled, and the answer sought is not single-valued. Yet, if carefully played it leads to sensible intellectual structures.

The broadest and most concise statement why this is so is due to an anonymous reviewer of one of the earlier volumes of The Study of Time series (Fraser, Lawrence, and Haber, 1986). He or she remarked that "Epistemologies of time, however idiosyncratic, sum to a cultural universal" (*The Key Reporter*, 1987, p. 7).

But what I have sketched was only one example of possible interdisciplinary work on a single, though many-sided problem related to time. In a more general way, can we hope to be able to combine in a nontrivial, constructive manner different answers to time-related inquiries, considering that the opinions of people from different intellectual disciplines represent different (usually tacit) assumptions concerning the nature of reality, different scales of values, different ways of handling evidence, and different professional temperaments?

In *Brave New World*, Aldous Huxley, taking his cue from Hamlet, made Mr. Savage define a philosopher as someone who dreamed of fewer things than are in heaven and earth. A timesmith cannot permit himself or herself to be so limited. Those who wish to study the nature of time must be able to dream, in a disciplined way, of more things than are in the haven of their special training. Some of the technical issues of the study of time have been identified and discussed in earlier communications (Fraser, 1981a, pp. xxv–xlix; Fraser, 1981b, pp. xiii–xxii). The primary need now is for scholars and scientists, such as the readers of this volume, who are able and prepared, to inform themselves on a professional, rather than a journalistic-popular, level of the details of time-related issues debated outside their own fields of learning.

As in all jigsaw puzzles, so it is in the epistemic one. The sequence of putting down the pieces does not matter: one begins with whatever is easiest to recognize. In this volume on time and mind the most easily recognizable pieces are those of time in psychology..

References

Davies, P. C. W. (1979), What Is Time? *The Sciences*, 19:18–23. .

Fraser, J. T. (1975), *Of Time, Passion and Knowledge*. New York: Braziller.

———— (1981a), Toward an integrated understanding of time. In: *The Voices of Time*, 2nd ed., ed. J. T. Fraser. Amherst, MA: University of Massachusetts Press.

———— (1981b), A backward and a forward glance: The uses and problems of the study of time. In: *The Study of Time*, Vol. 4, eds. J. T. Fraser, N. Lawrence, & D. Park. New York: Springer Verlag.

———— (1982), *The Genesis and Evolution of Time*. Amherst, MA: University of Massachusetts Press.

———— (1987), *Time, the Familiar Stranger*. Amherst, MA: University of Massachusetts Press.

————Lawrence, N., & Haber, F. C., eds. (1986), *Time, Science, and Society in China and the West* (*The Study of Time*, Vol. 5). Amherst, MA: University of Massachusetts Press.

The Key Reporter (1987), Review of J. T. Fraser, N. Lawrence, & F. C. Haber, eds. Time, science, and society in China and the West. The Key Reporter, 52:7.

Michon, J. A. (1985), Temporality and metaphor. In: *Time, Mind and Behavior*, eds. J. A. Michon & J. L. Jackson. Berlin: Springer Verlag.

von Neumann, J. (1969), *Theory of Self-Reproducing Automata*, ed. & completed A. W. Burns. Urbana, IL: University of Illinois Press.

Penrose, R. (1979), Singularities and time asymmetry. In: *General Relativity*, eds. S. W. Hawking & W. Israel. Cambridge: Cambridge University Press.

Whitrow, G. J. (1980), *The Natural Philosophy of Time*. Oxford, U.K.: Clarendon Press.

I

Cognitive Psychology

2

Timing Your Mind and Minding Your Time*

John A. Michon

Abstract In this chapter I present an information processing view of the relation between time and mind. Coping with the temporal contingencies of the world around us is to a large extent based on partly innate, partly learned "attunements." Such "tuning" to the course of events does not necessarily involve any conscious awareness of time as an explicit dimension or property of reality. When circumstances prevail for which no "attunements" are available in the physiological or behavioral repertoire of the human organism, conscious strategies are required for coping with these circumstances. In such cases explicit mental representations of time need to be generated; for this purpose several metaphors are used. Among these the spatial metaphors are particularly suitable since they allow some form of formalization or quantification of temporal relations.

Prologue in Hell

Since we humans find the problem of time perplexing and the problem of the mind excruciatingly difficult, it is safe to say that the problems born from the conjunction of time and mind, the subject of this volume, are simply diabolical. So let us go to Hell for illumination. And let our guide be that latterday Dante Alighieri, Stanley Elkin, whose masterly *The Living End* offers a revealing view of life after death (Elkin, 1979).

Burning in Hell is Lesefario, a man to whom, as the author tells us, "life had not signified." But Lesefario has changed. He wants to make something of his death. He now strives for mortality, whatever that may mean for a man in his position. Thinking of ways to achieve his goal in the midst of all the senseless suffering that is surrounding him, the truth suddenly dawns upon him: "The meaning of death is how long it takes!" Drawing the only possible conclusion from this insight, Lesefario begins to count time, and soon he finds himself followed by the billions of other denizens of Hell.

*Presidential Address, July 4, 1986.

17

Meanwhile at God's in Heaven there is a garden party. Being in a really relaxed and talkative mood, the Lord begins explaining to His guests what the universe is all about. He reveals, among other things, what the *real* causes of inflation are, and why dentistry is a purer science than astronomy. At that point the counting from down below attracts His attention. And instantly realizing the trick Lesefario has been playing on Him, He pronounces Doomsday and the Last Judgment, in the process annihilating the universe with everything that is in it.

Now, the point of this allegory of almost apocalyptic allure is not an *absence* of time in Hell. We are actually told that "they had time; they had minutes, seconds, hours, years." However, what they did not have was structured time. And so, when Lesefario came to recognize the significance of duration, Hell and suffering became meaningful and, consequently, vanished.

In my view this infernal episode epitomizes the fundamental relation which exists between time and mind. It points out the distinction between a nonreflective, if not passive, adaptation to the course of events on the one hand and a deliberate effort to make events "signify" on the other; the distinction between damnation and redemption; the distinction between being and becoming; or indeed, between *timing your mind* and *minding your time*.

Time, Reality, and the Mind

That there is a relation between time and mind is rarely denied, although most discussions have been phrased in exclusive terms: time is real and, therefore, in principle at least, a property of the physical world, independent of the presence of a natural (or supernatural) spectator; or it is "all in the mind" and therefore, in principle at least, unreal. The simplest way to avoid the dilemma of a physical as opposed to a mental origin of time is to acknowledge that there is a fundamental duality and to look at both aspects as complementary but equally important manifestations of the structure of reality.

Although most philosophers of time have attempted, somehow, to accommodate both aspects, the problem took a more serious turn when Immanuel Kant closed the gateway to an uncorrupted knowledge of the world around us. The inaccessibility of the world-in-itself might not have caused so much epistemological distress as it actually did, had Darwin been around at the time when Kant formulated his *Critique of Pure Reason*. Evolution, Kant would certainly have agreed, must have tuned us to the world as it really is, or we would not be here and now. Although we may not have direct access to the world-in-itself, we are structurally tuned to it, just as my radio is tuned to the electromagnetic spectrum in such a way as to make it a radio. Similarly, *time is real although it requires a mind to be aware of temporal relations*.

Time and Mind as a Psychological Problem

Leaving aside these ontological concerns, I simply note that time is a prominent and variegated feature of human experience and that it is, therefore, the task of psychology to provide an explanation for both that prominence and the various appearances of time. This, however, is not yet a workable formulation of the problem; it all depends on what is meant by "explanation." Just what this task actually entails became clear to me during a workshop on "Scientific Concepts of Time in Humanistic and Social Perspectives," convened by Dr. Fraser in 1981, at the Study Center of the Rockefeller Foundation on Lake Como. One afternoon, David Park and I, while walking the gardens of the Villa Serbelloni, discussed what psychology might contribute to what he saw as a fundamental problem of time in physics: defining the characteristics of a conscious observer in a not quite deterministic universe.

It was then that I realized that with respect to time, psychology is essentially facing a design problem, namely, and here I quote from my notebook, how to demonstrate that the human mind operates in such a fashion that it can cope with the sequential contingencies of its natural and self-created (cultural) environment and at the same time produce the experiential appearances (phenomenology) of time which conscious reflection reveals. The latter includes such aspects as the conscious experience of the present, pastness, or the subjective flow of time, and such pathological phenomena as déjà-vu. Some of these products of experience may themselves serve as strategies of negotiating the temporal contingencies of the world outside.

What I distilled from our discussion was that one should eventually be able to provide the design specifications for an intelligent system that, by dealing with a dynamic environment, could succeed in timing its mind and also, by explicitly manipulating its temporal experience, might be said to be minding its time.

A Psychological Frame of Reference

At this point I feel it is necessary to make a slight digression into psychological theory. It is common, nowadays, to consider the human mind–brain as an information processing system (Reed, 1982; Reed and Jones, 1982; Anderson 1985). Whatever the exact nature of this system, a distinction must be made between two functionally different and complementary ways of processing information: *automatic* (or habitual) and *controlled* (or conscious) processing. Examples of automatic information processing include, in the first place, such largely innate abilities as maintaining an upright position, recognizing a hand when you see one, or scratching an itch; and in the second place learned automatic behaviors like juggling with six empty beer bottles while maintaining equilibrium on a tightrope, or the ability to grind out "golden oldies" on the piano in a hotel lobby while figuring out how to renovate the bathroom at home. Controlled processing, on the other hand, is characteristic in situations that are new or unusual: deciphering

Kanji characters when you are three weeks into a course on reading Japanese, or learning how to set your new high-tech digital watch with its forty-three timing and calendar functions.

Functionally these two processing modes, automatic and controlled, are intimately related. The acquisition of skills, for instance, involves a gradual shift from controlled processing to automatic processing. Novel information is initially processed and stored under conscious control as, what is frequently called, declarative knowledge (Anderson, 1983). Declarative knowledge—*knowing what*—remains consciously accessible and is easily updated in the light of additional information; we can talk about it. With repeated usage knowledge tends to be increasingly transformed into procedural knowledge—a matter of *knowing how*. Procedural knowledge is immediate but almost inaccessible to conscious manipulation and therefore difficult to change deliberately (See Figure 2.1).

This functional interdependency of the two processing modes also works the other way around. The memory blackouts suffered occasionally by performing artists, or that particularly scenic road to Auntie Janet's Highland cottage you knew so well last year but need a map for this time, characteristically trigger a reverse transfer of action control from automatic to controlled processing. What normally comes smoothly and without noticeable effort suddenly requires hard thinking, and even then may proceed only haltingly.

Although functionally there is this intimate relation, theoretically there seems to be a tremendous conceptual gap. For a long time information processing theory has been dominated by two opposing movements; let me call them *direct realism* and *constructivism*. Both fail by wishing to account for the human mind in terms that are essentially applicable to only one mode of processing. This problem, in my view, is similar, in a nontrivial sense, to the wave–particle duality that took physicists such a very long time to accept. Today psychologists do not (yet) recognize the dual nature of their distinction between automatic and controlled processing. If they did, however, they would conceptually come quite close to some recent trends in physics. The automatic-controlled duality seems to correspond, for instance, to the distinction implicate–explicate made by the physicist Bohm; that is, the distinction between a description of the world in terms of potential fields, wave fronts, and energy distribution on the one hand, and discrete (particulate) matter, sharply defined events, and dynamic trajectories on the other. It is, metaphorically, the distinction between the distributed world of the hologram and the focused world of the lens (Bohm, 1980).

In the remainder of this chapter I wish to expound the following two assertions derived from the argument thus far:

- *Timing your mind* is primarily, if not exclusively, a matter of automatic processing of external (perceptual) as well as internal (stored or represented) data; timing your mind enables you to stay in tune with an intrinsically temporal world but, as I shall argue, not necessarily by explicitly representing time as a point or an interval in time, that is, as the variable t in mathematical equations.

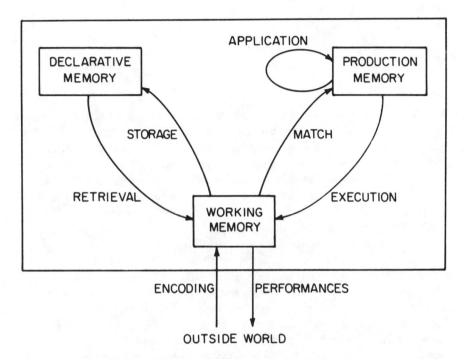

Figure 2.1. Summary diagram of the information processing model of J. R. Anderson. Communication between the actual world and the mind is established through a process known as "working memory." The useful lifetime of information in working memory is of the order of 1 to 30 seconds and may be identified with the specious present or Now. There are two information processing modes—as described in the text. One deals with declarative (fact-oriented) knowledge, the other with procedural (skill-oriented) knowledge. Declarative knowledge is explicitly stored and accessible through consciously controlled retrieval strategies. While new knowledge is initially stored as declarative knowledge, repeated usage in working memory will sooner or later create more condensed procedural rules for applying this knowledge. Such rules, known as *productions*, can be formally characterized in terms of conditional statements: *If* the light is red, *then* stop. Proceduralized knowledge is a matter of tuning (viz. matching with some external event or situation) and automatic execution. (From Anderson, 1983, p. 19. Reproduced by permission of The Harvard University Press, Cambridge, MA).

- *Minding your time*, on the other hand, is primarily, if not exclusively, a consciously controlled way of coping with those aspects of the world to which we cannot directly tune ourselves because we are not geared to those aspects by evolution or learning.

Incidentally, if I call controlled processing *conscious* I do not, in the present context, mean the awareness of personal identity which we also call consciousness or self-awareness.

Timing Your Mind: Tuning to Reality

Tuning

> And what if all of animated nature
> Be but organic harps diversely fram'd
> that tremble into thought?
> COLERIDGE: *THE EOLIAN HARP.*

What kind of tuning forks are we if timing our mind is resonance-driven, as Coleridge suggested over a century and a half ago? Why would the capacity for tuning develop in the course of evolution in the first place? Actually, if you come to think of it, animals have pretty good reasons for behaving like organic harps or resonators. Their major concern is to maintain their internal structure irrespective of highly variable outward conditions and, even more importantly, irrespective of a large variety of goals. To achieve this internal stability they must stay sharply tuned to their environment (Michon, 1985).

The prototypical example of these internalized tuning mechanisms is the circadian rhythm (Moore-Ede, Sulzman, and Fuller, 1983; Aschoff, 1984; Groos and Daan, 1985). But chronobiological research has also brought to light numerous other "clocks" and "timers" from which the organism can almost always select one or more that suit its tuning needs (Richelle and Lejeune, 1980). Especially important are the regulatory processes in the range between one-tenth of a second and ten seconds that govern the tuning to most common behavioral phenomena. Speech rate is a good example: voice recognition and speech comprehension, for instance, depend critically on the temporal characteristics of the speech signal. My favorite illustration of this dependency is an experiment (Dooling, 1974) in which subjects are presented with a series of simple sentences, all with an identical stress pattern, say, a trochaic pattern as in "this is a háppy pérson." After eight such sentences a change in stress pattern is suddenly introduced: the ninth sentence to be presented may be iambic, as for instance in "this is a remóte contról." The comprehension of this last sentence turns out to be dramatically worse than that of the earlier sentence simply as a result of the change in temporal structure from trochaic to iambic. In a similar way, highly automatic motor skills, such as the athletic long jump (Lee, Lishman, and Thomson, 1982) or handwriting (Thomassen and Teulings, 1985) entail a very complicated and highly idiosyncratic internalized temporal organization which is extremely difficult to change or imitate. The relevance of studying the intrinsic temporal organization of such skills is illustrated by a recent investigation ordered by the Dutch Government to establish the authenticity of the diary written by Anne Frank (Nederlands Instituut voor Oorlogsdocumentatie, 1986). It being one of the most important *documents humains* of the Holocaust, its authenticity has over the years been questioned by a number of people, mostly for rather unsavory reasons. The recent investigation, to an important extent based on our latest insights into the temporal organization of handwriting, has finally put the issue to rest. The diary of Anne Frank is authentic, scribble for scribble, letter for letter, and word for word.

Patterning

Resonators, the category of entities to which "organic harps" and tuning forks belong, may be broadly conceived as pattern detectors. As such they pick up (and represent) regularities or recurrences in their environment. Tuning in the human organism may be defined as the matching of patterns of symbolic events in the mind–brain to patterns of events in the external world. In this context a pattern may be understood as a relatively compact, efficient description of the structure of a state of the world, say a series of events. Such pattern descriptions are always in terms of a code; that is, a set of symbols and a set of rules for combining these symbols. When I call a pattern relatively compact and efficient, you will perhaps think of the number π, which seems a most compact and efficient way of writing the digit sequence 3.14159. . . . If that is indeed what you think, however, you are on the wrong track. The symbol π does not qualify as a pattern description because it is not a recipe for generating 3.14159 . . . , unlike, for instance, a description like "*n* squared for increasing $n > 0$" which tells us how to generate the digit sequence 1 4 9 1 6 2 5 3 6. . . .

Pattern descriptions are always in terms of a code, that is, a number of symbols and a set of rules for combining these symbols. In the past fifteen years the art of defining clever codes that allow descriptions of all kinds of perceptually relevant patterns—visual, auditory, linguistic—has made considerable progress (Restle, 1970; Simon, 1972; Leeuwenberg and Buffart, 1979; Jones, 1985), but an important question remains: to what extent are such coding theories psychologically relevant? To what extent do codes which describe sequential or temporal patterns reflect internal tuning processes?

Patterns are what they are by virtue of the context in which they appear. In isolation they can have no meaning and no structural significance. A wedge-shaped symbol V will be different as an element of the set of consonants (B, V, F, S), than when it belongs to the set (¬, V, &, →) of familiar logical symbols (meaning *not*, *or*, *and*, and *if–then*, respectively). An important question that proves very difficult to answer is what, or should we say *who*, determines the context that will specify the meaning of a given pattern or set of patterns. This difficulty is a matter of considerable dispute in contemporary cognitive psychology as well as in the philosophy of mind (Goodman, 1984).

In these discussions it is pointed out that coding theories remain incomplete and arbitrary as long as it is not made clear why some pattern structures appear to invite or to "afford" one particular interpretation rather than another. Some interpretations of a pattern—a melody or a situation—make sense to us, and others simply do not. As the philosopher Nelson Goodman observed, humankind makes versions of the world, and true versions make worlds (Goodman, 1984, p. 34). But how do we know which versions do make true worlds? How does an event sequence evoke in the observer just that special interpretation of context, let us call it *mood*, in which the sequence occurs, so that we can understand and later on recognize or even reproduce it?

Could it be that some patterns carry the key that will unlock their "true codes"? Do these things-in-themselves dictate the way we should perceive them? Several authors have observed that certain strings of events seem to invite us to follow and participate in changing relationships over time, or to derive their appropriate interpretation from the temporal aspects in their structures (Jones, 1985). Attending to various aspects of a series of events is primarily guided by temporal relations (e.g., tempo, rhythm, and meter in music) that are suggested or *afforded* by the structure of the pattern. Temporal structure is thus indicative of what to listen for when a piece of music is heard for the first time. It is also guiding later recollections of that piece (Jones, 1985; Shaffer, 1985).

Unpatterned Patterns

Not all patterns to which humans attend are actually patterns. We cannot help seeing patterns in a completely uniform checkerboard tesselation. More significantly, we cannot resist seeing symmetries in irregular checkerboard tesselations, just as we cannot help seeing faces and animal shapes in clouds, inkblots, or wallpaper. Indeed if we consider the world of *unpatterned patterns* we begin to appreciate how clever evolution has been giving us the broadest possible means of tuning to the world. Although Albert Einstein claimed that the Good Lord does not play at dice, it is clear that Nature herself was not so sure about that: as a precaution she has endowed us with "resonators" that indeed allow us to tune to nonpatterns in our environment. Only quite recently is it becoming clear why this may be so.

One of the most fascinating developments in modern mathematics—already from an esthetic point of view—is the fractal geometry of Benôit Mandelbrot (1983). Fractal geometry deals with the formalization of irregularity, that is, with spatial and temporal patterns whose irregularity (or fragmentedness) appears the same, irrespective of the scale at which they are considered. Imagine, for example, that you are descending over the coast of Norway in a Montgolfière and that you are looking straight down at the shoreline below. You would see fjords, gradually dissolving into smaller and smaller but geometrically similar fjords, until at perhaps a hundred meters altitude or a little less, individual rocks and boulders would begin to dominate (see Figure 2.2).

This self-repeating quality of fractals is called their *scaling property*. It turns out that a good many natural phenomena possess this property, and it seems plausible that evolution has made us particularly sensitive to the way it is revealed in the edges of clouds, in mountain ridges, inkblots, and wallpaper designs.

Apart from producing many extremely attractive spatial configurations

Figure 2.2. A fractal pattern showing the scaling property: the overall characteristic of the pattern remains the same for the three levels of complexity. The pattern in the upper right-hand corner constitutes the limiting condition: further enlarging its scale will no longer retain the characteristic shape. (From Mandelbrot, 1983, p. 53. Reproduced by permission of Freeman & Company, San Francisco, CA.)

(Peitgen and Richter, 1986), fractal geometry has a lot to say as well about temporal unpatterned patterns. Below the lowest level of structural coherence, well below the grammars of counterpoint and harmony, for instance, music may be described in terms of fractal properties. As Mandelbrot (1983) has pointed out: "musical compositions are, as indicated by their name, composed. First they subdivide into movements, characterized by overall tempos and/or levels of loudness. The movements subdivide further in the same fashion. And teachers insist that every piece of music be 'composed to the shortest meaningful subdivisions'" (p. 375).

Barring a few trivialities such as Brahms' command of orchestral instrumentation, the scaling property is what makes a Brahms symphony a Brahms symphony, from the time span of the whole work down to the single bar. Studies by two American audiologists, Voss and Clarke (Voss and Clarke, 1975; Voss, 1978) have shown that pitch, loudness, and timing variations of several musical genres—classic as well as popular—conform indeed with the fractal scaling assumption. They have also shown that sequences of notes that are stochastically tailored to this fractal property sound more like "real" music than do sequences that are generated under other stochastic rules.

Our sensitivity to fractal patterns, wherever they occur in nature, indicates that already at a very deep stochastic level many things in this world are internally coherent: fractals retain their overall character globally as well as locally. And so, coming back to the question of why we pick up some kinds of unpatterned patterns, the answer is that the randomness of a large class of relevant natural phenomena is highly constrained and that the human mind–brain has developed means of tuning to this kind of randomness. The fractal scaling property, it appears, is a very fundamental aspect of whatever is capable of attracting and holding attention. Unpatterned patterns outside this rather limited range of fractal scaling seem to lack internal structure. Such nonpatterns can only be encoded and retained by human beings in a long process of explicit memorization, of the sort required to commit such abominations as the number π to memory (Chase and Ericsson, 1982). Einstein notwithstanding, Nature decided at an early stage in evolution to endow us with a defense against the rock-bottom indeterminism of the world in which we live.

"Affordances"

Although I am dealing here mostly with the temporal aspects of the tuning process, tuning involves a much more general relation to the external world. In particular James J. Gibson (1966, 1979) has repeatedly pointed out that tuning is, in a very general sense, a matter of extracting invariant properties from the environment. In his view, the geometry of our perceptual environment provides what he had called "affordances." Nature "affords" such complex information as the *looming* of a hawk approaching a newly hatched chick, the *sit-onableness* of a slab of marble to a tired visitor of the Forum Romanum, or indeed the *land-onableness* of the landing strip at an airport (see Figure 2.3).

Based on Gibson's ideas an extremely interesting line of research has developed that goes under the name of *kinematic geometry*. An excellent example is the research program of Roger Shepard and his colleagues (Shepard and Metzler, 1971; Shepard and Cooper, 1982; Shepard, 1984). Shepard has shown that people are quite capable of mentally representing the movements of a solid object through three-dimensional space (see Figure 2.4). Among other things he has demonstrated that complicated simultaneous movements of an object and an observer in three-dimensional space are always perceived and represented according to a unique, minimally complex trajectory which preserves the solid character of natural objects. In a similar way, imaginary movement of some object will instantiate "the

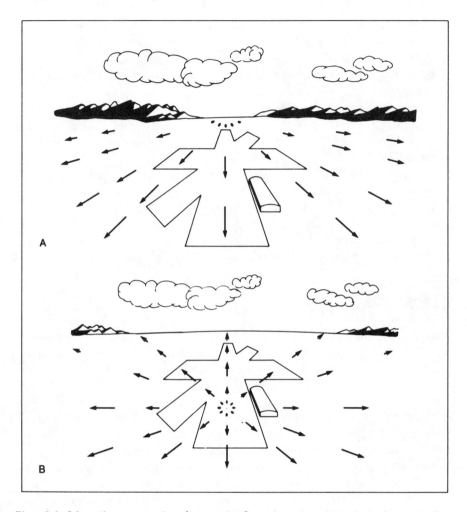

Figure 2.3. Schematic representation of perspective flow when approaching the landing strip of an airfield. The flow pattern affords the "land-onableness" of the strip. (From Reed and Jones, 1982; reproduced by permission of Erlbaum Associates, Hillsdale, NJ.)

continuing existence of the object by means of the unique simplest rigid motion that will carry the one view into the other, and it does so in a way that is compatible with a movement either of the observer or of the object observed" (Shepard, 1984, p. 423).

When we watch and attempt to hold in mind the tortuous trajectory traversed by, say, a falling autumn leaf, we set up a simplistic physics-of-the-falling-leaf mental model which preserves the characteristic rocking movements of such a familiar object. In the most general terms, the perception and mental representation of kinematic information are largely based on the principles of minimal effort, continuity of movement, and object permanence. We retain an idealized trajectory and omit disturbances due to, say, wind gusts or falling rain drops. Special effects in movies require an extraordinary amount of sophistication to fool all the people all the time, because of this sensitivity to "natural" movements.

Other, similar research suggests that people possess a very delicate capability for recognizing the gait and gestures of other people, including their vocal mannerisms. The skill of successful impersonators—and cartoonists—is based on their ability to extract just those high-order invariances that make Margaret Thatcher unmistakably Margaret Thatcher and J. T. Fraser unmistakably J. T. Fraser.

I should add at this point, without further commentary, that such studies all point to the fact that time need not be, and indeed rarely is, encoded directly. Several authors have pointed out that time is not likely to be encoded in the motor command structures controlling complex body or hand movements. Instead, temporal precision seems to be a natural outcome of well-tuned, smoothly performing output systems (Thomassen and Teulings, 1985).

Some Intermediate Conclusions

It appears that tuning to the temporal contingencies of the world is dependent on the availability of a large number of preattunements ("affordances," resonators, internal rhythms), partly learned during the individual's lifetime, but mostly the result of eons of evolutionary development.

If all this worked flawlessly, you would be able to time your mind to perfection. If anything, you would resemble one of the windowless monads envisioned by Leibniz, and you would not need to know the difference between you and the world. In other words, there would be no need for self-awareness. Generally, however, your mind and the world are not quite so perfectly tuned, a fact that will from time to time induce shifts from the automatic to the controlled mode of information processing. Frequently the correlation between you and your world will be so low as to make you painfully aware of this fact. The following peculiar case may help to illustrate this.

Intermezzo: The Discovery of Slowness

Some people appear to suffer from conditions that prevent an easy and successful timing of their minds. They may be dyslexic or dyspraxic and thus have difficulties reading or performing, and there is dysrhythmia, the incompetence to "keep the beat."

Rarely, however, will one find a condition as strange as that which seems to have afflicted Sir John Franklin (1786–1847), British arctic explorer, Commander of the Fleet, and the King's Gouvernor of Tasmania. Very strange indeed, if we are to believe the German novelist Sten Nadolny, author of a somewhat fictional

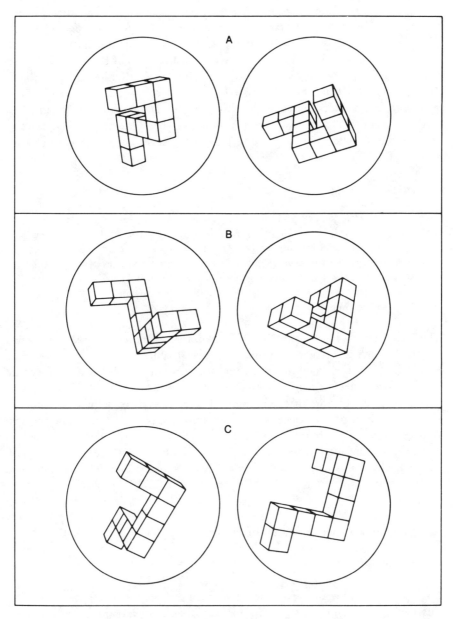

Figure 2.4. In a series of experiments by Roger N. Shepard of Stanford University subjects were shown pairs of pseudo-three-dimensional pictures as in A, B and C. The subjects were asked to decide if the two pictures of a given pair are identical. An answer to that question requires mental rotation of at least one of the objects. It will be seen that the pairs A and B do in fact match, whereas in the case of pair C no such match can be obtained. (From Shepard and Metzler, 1971, p. 701.)

biography of Sir John, *Die Entdeckung der Langsamkeit* (The Discovery of Slowness) (Nadolny, 1983).

    Die Entdeckung der Langsamkeit portrays its protagonist as an extraordinarily clumsy and sluggish boy. His rate of information processing—if you permit this bit of jargon—was so slow that even at the age of ten he could not catch a ball or climb a tree. The ball would be gone long before he realized how it bounced, and when climbing a tree he was far too slow even to reach to a branch if losing his foothold. To cope with his handicap John Franklin decided to learn the world by heart, reviewing and memorizing at night what went too fast for him by daytime. He studied speediness "the way other people study the Bible or the footprints of animals." And John Franklin, having joined the Royal Navy as a midshipman, succeeded.

> Whole fleets of words he had learned by heart, and batteries of answers, to build his defense. He had to be prepared for everything that might be asked, every question, every action. And . . . he managed! A ship, bounded by the sea, could be learned. . . . He paid careful heed to every conceivable route from every place on the ship to every other place, he had even drawn maps, and he had been rehearsing them every night for two full weeks. Now everything went automatically, as long as nothing unexpected happened. Then there was no recourse, and things would go on without fine control: but . . . his excuse formula had been practiced too!

The finite universe that is a ship, could be mastered with everything that happened on it. Although this achievement made life manageable for him, it was only many years later that John Franklin eventually discovered in the Arctic a world where things happen slowly enough for him to feel really at home—and in tune.

    It appears to me that Sir John's handicap—on Nadolny's account, at least—must have been an extremely tardy acquisition of procedural knowledge. In his case the transition from "knowing that" to "knowing how" must have required an unusually long and intense cognitive effort. John Franklin succeeded in *timing his mind* only by laboriously *minding his time*. As an organic harp John Franklin was clearly a misfit!

Minding Your Time: In Search of Useful Metaphors

Conscious or Automatic?

Like John Franklin, however, we too must adopt the controlled mode of information processing in situations for which we have no automatic behavioral procedures. In fact, I am convinced that all conscious time experience is a consequence of controlled processing, and that "temporal information is not processed unless noticed, and not noticed unless meaningful" (Michon and Jackson [1984, p. 305], see also Jackson [1986]). The term *temporal information* implies all relations that specify the order, duration, or position of events in a series, or the apparent rate of temporal flow; in short, all relations that define our conscious experience of time and that have been studied by time psychologists for well over a century with varying degrees of success (see Michon and Jackson [1985], for a recent overview). People can understand, remember, and reproduce temporal relations between objects and events if and only if they succeed in generating some encoding strategy (see in particular Jackson [1986]). People must, in other words, find some kind of language, or semantics, in which they can express what otherwise would be an unmanageable mumbo-jumbo of impressions—unmanageable, because people lack the means for directly tuning in. It seems that there is no natural vocabulary for thinking about, or verbally expressing relations of order, duration, and temporal position. Like wine-talk, *time-talk* essentially relies in a very principled way on the availability of suitable metaphors.

Representations

The claim that *minding your time*, your conscious dealing with the temporal contingencies of a world of change, is dependent on metaphor, is not without support. There are, for instance, those who maintain that "metaphor is pervasive in everyday life, not just in language but in thought and action. Our ordinary conceptual system, in terms of which we both think and act, is fundamentally metaphorical in nature" (Lakoff and Johnson, 1980; p. 3).

More closely connected to the subject matter of this volume, and essentially taking a similar stand, are the contribution of the late Nathaniel Lawrence in *The Study of Time V* (Lawrence, 1986) and my own paper in the same volume (Michon, 1986). Metaphors deeply influence the ways we think. They "tune" our thoughts about an object or an event—our mental representations if you like—to the semantic domain from which the metaphor is borrowed. Thus, the metaphor "Time is Money," thoroughly established in Western society, allows us to think about and act with respect to time as something that is valuable, that can be saved, lost, or wasted. Choosing to speak and think about time in these terms highlights some characteristics, at the cost of others. It suppresses among many other things, the connotations that belong to other temporal metaphors: in the context of "Time is Money," time does *fly* only to the extent that one can conceive of situations in which money flies.

There is ample reason to assume that all metaphors are not created equal. Some are sporadically used or even invented for a special occasion. Other metaphors, however, perhaps between fifty and one hundred of them, occupy a central position in human cognition (Lakoff and Johnson, 1980; Ortony, 1979). Especially powerful among these are the metaphors that refer to semantic domains that can be "physically envisioned" (Carbonell, 1982; Johnson-Laird, 1983; Jackendoff, 1985).

The spatial metaphor is particularly pervasive. Temporal relations are, indeed, most frequently interpreted in spatial terms, which suggests—I am using the words of the psycholinguist H. H. Clark—"the availability of a thoroughly spatial metaphor, a complete cognitive system that space and time expressions have in common" (Clark, 1973, p. 62). I take this to mean that there are aspects of both space and time that are expressible in the abstract spatial terms that are used in measurement theory. This is exactly what I proposed in my contribution to the 1983 conference of our Society (Michon, 1986). In that paper I suggested that the means we have available for representing temporal relations are, foremost, the ordering properties and measurement scales as they can be derived from some of the basic metaphors that serve us to make sense of the world.

But how is this abstract space to be dressed up? Clark's analysis of temporal expressions suggested to him that the representation of time conventionally takes the form of imagining time as a straight arrow passing from back (the past) to front (the future) through our body (the present). But this metaphor is clearly too simple to cover all the subtleties needed for representing temporal relations of order, duration, or position. So, clearly a richer conceptual framework is required.

An important step in the right direction was taken by Miller and Johnson-Laird (1976), who starting, like Clark, from the prevalence of a quasi-spatial linear conceptualization of time, pointed out that ultimately we possess no genuine *sense* of time, and that there can be therefore, no natural correspondence between temporal relations in the world outside and our mind–brain representations of them. While color, size, or tactile pressure directly trigger representations that can spontaneously be given verbal labels—"red," "what a whopper!", or "ouch!"—no such connection exists to help us mind our time, and we are forced to rely on such metaphors as the "arrow through the body." Miller and Johnson-Laird then went on to consider what can be said about the mental representation of temporal relations if we treat them as formal rather than natural, as conceptual rather than as directly perceivable. For this purpose they chose an instant logic as their model frame. In the context of instant logic (Van Benthem, 1983) every elementary temporal proposition about an event is evaluated. It is determined if it was always, sometimes, or never true before an instant t, whether it is true or false at the instant t, and whether it will always, sometimes, or never be true after the instant t. Thus, for every elementary proposition, the person's working memory must carry the weight of $3 \times 2 \times 3 = 18$ truth values, to be evaluated upon input. The temporal meaning of the simple sentence: "The shop is open until seven" is completely determined by specifying that the assertion "The shop is open" is true for all instants $t < t_o$, false for the instant $t = t_o$, and false for all instants $t > t_o$. That this quickly becomes a task of prohibitive complexity is readily seen if you attempt to analyze the following sample sentences each of which contains only a few elementary propositions:

1. With a flawless last set in the final match against Ivan Lendl, Boris Becker proved that his earlier victory at Wimbledon had been no accident.
2. Mary got out some money to buy herself a cup of coffee during the intermission of *Nabucco*.

Think for a moment what it would be like to extract truth-table representations from such statements! Each would impose an inordinate burden on our memory.

Or, even worse, take that exasperating full-page newspaper advertisement by Heineken Breweries, published when The Netherlands went on daylight saving time a year or so ago and shown in Figure 2.5. Those of you who have got a bit rusty on your Dutch will probably need the following translation:

3. In principle this is a very simple matter: the clock is advanced one hour. So it seems one hour later. But it is one hour earlier. That is because one hour is taken away in the evening and therefore it stays light longer. But that time is added in the morning and therefore it stays dark longer . . .
Ah, well, what is time anyway?

This mind-shattering advertisement leaves me urgently in need of a glass of beer every time I see it. (Incidentally: I have it mounted and framed on the wall of my study.) It reveals the tremendous difficulties human beings are facing when two sets of intervals (or temporal scales) do not just entertain a temporal scaling relation, but a change in this relation must also be taken into account.

Something else is required to cope with such complex relations, and that is the insight that when people do indeed use spatial metaphors to encode temporal relations like order, duration, and position, they tend to do so in terms of intervals rather than instants. This insight coincides with some crucial developments in temporal logic: interval logic has come of age in the past decade (Van Benthem, 1983, 1985).

It now seems that minding our time may efficiently (and in a psychologically plausible way) be represented as a knowledge base consisting primarily of relations between intervals. This not only provides a richer set of elementary relations; it can also be given a natural perceptual interpretation. Instead of the three relations in instant logic—before, at, and after—interval logic has exactly thirteen of them. Of two intervals A and B, A may *precede* or *be preceded by, meet* or *met by, overlap* or *be overlapped by, start* or *be started by, contain* or *be contained in, terminate* or *be terminated by* B, and finally A may also (uniquely) *coincide* with B (Allen, 1984; Allen and Kautz, 1985). Here the terms starting and terminating, as well as being started or terminated by, should not be given a causal interpretation.

It turns out that complicated expressions such as 1, 2, and 3 can easily be represented in this formalism. Sentence 1 generates three intervals: *Wimbledon*, the *men's single final*, and the *final set* (see Figure 2.6). The first interval contains the second, which in turn contains the third interval, and the last set of the final terminates simultaneously both the men's single final and Wimbledon. By implication sentence 3 also generates a similar triad for the preceding tournament at Wimbledon. Adding new information, such as

4. Perhaps the brief spell of sunshine during the early part of the game had inspired the players.

Eigenlijk is het heel eenvoudig: de klok
gaat een uur vooruit. En dus lijkt 't
een uur later. Maar 't is een uur vroeger.
Want er gaat 's avonds een uur af
en dus is 't langer licht. Maar dat komt
er dan 's ochtends weer bij en daardoor
blijft 't langer donker.

Ach, wat is tijd.

Figure 2.5. Advertisement confusing a majority of the population when The Netherlands shifted to daylight saving time in the spring of 1986. (By kind permission of Heineken Breweries, Amsterdam, The Netherlands).

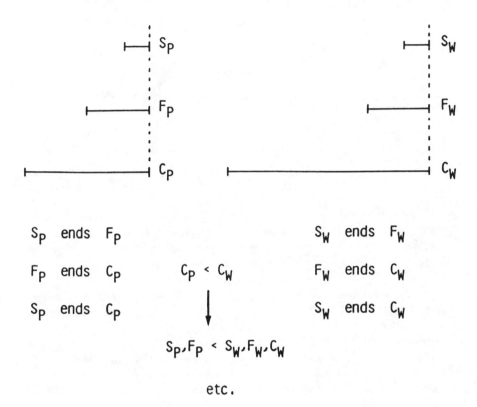

Figure 2.6. Schema of interval relations between elementary propositions contained in sentence 1 in the text.

to the temporal knowledge base already available, is straightforward if the semantics of words such as "during" in sentence 4 are understood. A occurs *during* B if and only if B *contains* A, or B *equals* A, or B *starts* A. The information contained in the facts that there was only a *brief* sunny spell and that it occurred *early* in this year's men's final, imposes certain constraints on the total set of possible temporal relations. Adding further propositions will eventually fix the network of temporal relations that together provide the chronology of "Wimbledon 1986." A similar analysis of statement 2 shows that here too the temporal relations are not quite determined by the information contained in the sentence (see Figure 2.7). No doubt, you will appreciate that I am not going to bring up the Heineken advertisement (3) for further discussion right now, concerned as I am for the reader's mental well-being.

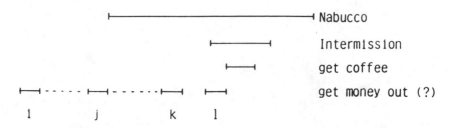

Figure 2.7. Schema of interval relations between elementary propositions contained in sentence 2 in the text. The actual time at which Mary gets her money out is not fully determined; intervals *i*,. . . ,*l* all qualify.

On the basis of a straightforward set of rules for encoding temporal expressions in terms of relations between intervals, it has been possible to construct models for parsing and integrating all such complex temporal relations as you may find in narrative and real life alike. Although their psychological relevance is not entirely clear yet, these models may be considered as important steps toward a formal theory of the way intelligent entities—and that presumably includes reader and author—are minding their time. Such is the case even though the prime motivation for the development of these models lies in a growing interest in automated knowledge systems that will be able to comprehend temporal relations and, as a result, to plan and execute complex sequences of actions (McDermott, 1982, 1985; Allen, 1984; Georgeff and Lansky, 1987). There is considerable practical value in an expert system or a robot that is able to mind its time without our having to time its mind in advance.

Epilogue: Can We Construct a Time-Experiencing Robot?

Having established (1) that the timing of our mind relies on the ability of the human organism to *attune* to highly complex temporal relations in a dynamic environment, and (2) that the minding of our time is a rule-driven, conscious act of intelligence, requiring one or several specific modes of abstract representation, metaphorical and formal, we should finally consider our chances of designing an intelligent system that really understands time. That was, as you will recall, the task I defined following my discussion with David Park in the gardens of the Villa Serbelloni.

In order to keep fantasy within reasonable bounds I will, for the sake of my present argument, restrict myself to the vastly simpler task of building a computer that can really appreciate music. Since music is the ultimate temporal art anyway, I am certain that this simplification will appeal to most people.

Of course, there are already computers that compose some sort of not quite trivial music, and in recent years we have indeed come a long way toward highly intricate forms of synthesized musical performance. The problem, therefore, must be phrased even more specifically: Will a computer ever compose or perform really masterly music; that is, will it ever move us in the way Bach, Brahms, or Bernstein can move us? And what about that twin computer still to be designed, a listening automaton that is really moved as we are when we are listening to great music? Will that ever see the light of day? The answer, in my view, is that both will indeed materialize sooner or later, but that we may never know if and when we have really succeeded (Dennett, 1978; Michon, 1984). The reason is simple enough: some domains of experience are extremely difficult to tackle, though not because we might not be able in principle to simulate in an artificial system the feeling of pain or the joy of listening to a Mozart piano concerto. We could easily let it beep or produce drops of an isotonic saline solution from a pair of tubes on its front panel according to some scale ranging from bliss to distress. But what would be needed to make such a system really feel pain or enjoy music?

Upon further reflection that question turns out to be meaningless. People are quite aware of the fact that they react very differently to pain, as well as to music. Your headache is not my headache, and your appreciation of music need not at all be consistent with mine. In fact, my music may even be your headache! Now, if as human beings we differ already so fundamentally among ourselves, if a single person even can stand some pains and some music at some time that he or she cannot stand at other times, how then could we ever agree on precisely what properties to build into one computer to make it really suffer pain or really love Brahms? Music, along with pain, dreams, love, and some other important domains of experience, is a product of mental activity with such a rich phenomenology that we cannot formulate a consistent set of design requirements for a music-loving computer. If we ultimately accept a computer, or any other nonhuman intelligence, as really understanding music, it must be by act of faith. That will be the case when, and only when, we are prepared to accept an alien intelligence as a person, as one of us.

Some reflection on the troubled communication with autistic people seems relevant here. Music frequently appears to be one of the few gateways to the otherwise inaccessible world of autistic individuals; they may seem to appreciate music a great deal, and they may show emotional reactions to it. But do they really understand music? Are they really moved? The answer is that they do to the extent we believe them to share a musical semantic or meaning with us. And the sad fact is that we may not be unconditionally convinced that such is really the case.

And so, yes, eventually we shall build a computer that really creates or understands time. But we will only know if we have been successful when we are prepared to believe that we have been successful, that is, when we are prepared to accept such a contraption as an equal, as a consciousness, as a person. Unfortunately I need only refer to the very inhumane ways in which human beings may treat each other to know that the probability of this ever being the case is arbitrarily close to zero. But this consideration returns me to my infernal point of departure. And so we have swung full circle, thereby paying the smallest possible tribute to a totally different representation of time, and one that I have altogether excluded from this address: circular time.

References

Allen, J. F. (1984), Towards a general theory of action and time. *Artificial Intelligence*, 23:123–154.
———— Kautz, H. A. (1985) A model of naive temporal reasoning. In: *Formal Theories of the Commonsense World*, eds. J. R. Hobbs & R. C. Moore. Norwood, NJ: Ablex Publishing Corporation, pp. 251–268.

Anderson, J. R. (1983), *The Architecture of Cognition*. Cambridge, MA: Harvard University Press.
———— (1985), *Cognitive Psychology and Its Implications*, 2nd ed. San Francisco: Freeman.

Aschoff, J. (1984), Circadian timing. In: *Timing and Time Perception. Annals of the New York Academy of Sciences*. Vol. 423, eds. J. Gibbon & L. Allan. New York: New York Academy of Sciences, pp. 442–468.

Bohm, D. (1980), *Wholeness and the Implicate Order*. London: Routledge & Kegan Paul.

Carbonell, J. (1982), Metaphor: An inescapable phenomenon in natural language comprehension. In: *Strategies for Natural Language Processing*, eds. W. Lehnert & M. Ringle, Hillsdale, NJ: Lawrence Erlbaum Associates: pp. 415–434.

Chase, W. G., & Ericsson, K. A. (1982), Skill and working memory. In: *The Psychology of Learning and Motivation*, Vol. 16, ed. G. H. Bower. New York: Academic Press.

Clark, H. H. (1973), Space, time, semantics, and the child. In: *Cognitive Development and the Acquisition of Language*, ed. T. E. Moore. New York: Academic Press, pp. 27–63.

Dennett, D. C. (1978), *Brainstorms: Philosophical Essays on Mind and Psychology*. Hassocks, Sussex, U.K.: Harvester Press.

Dooling, D. J. (1974), Rhythm and syntax in sentence perception. *J. Verbal Learn. & Verbal Behav.*, 13: 255–264.

Elkin, S. (1979), *The Living End: A Triptych*. New York: Dutton.

Georgeff, M. P., & Lansky A. L., eds. (1987), *Reasoning About Actions and Plans*. Los Altos, CA: Morgan Kaufmann.

Gibson, J. J. (1966), *The Senses Considered as Perceptual Systems*. Boston: Houghton Mifflin.
———— (1979), *The Ecological Approach to Visual Perception*. Boston: Houghton Mifflin.

Goodman, N. (1984), *Of Mind and Other Matters*. Cambridge, MA: Harvard University Press.

Groos, G., & Daan, S. (1985), The use of biological clocks in time perception. In: *Time, Mind, and Behavior*, eds. J. A. Michon & J. L. Jackson. Berlin: Springer Verlag, pp. 65–74.

Jackendoff, R. S. (1985), *Semantics and Cognition*. Cambridge, MA: MIT Press.

Jackson, J. L. (1986), *The Processing of Temporal Information*. Unpublished dissertation, University of Groningen, The Netherlands.

Johnson-Laird, P. N. (1983), *Mental Models*. Cambridge: Cambridge University Press.

Jones, M. R. (1985), Structural organization of events in time. In: *Time, Mind, and Behavior*, eds. J. A. Michon & J. L. Jackson. Berlin: Springer Verlag, pp. 192–214.

Lakoff, G., & Johnson, M. (1980), *Metaphors We Live By*. Chicago: University of Chicago Press.

Lawrence, N. (1986), The origins of time. In: *Time, Science, and Society in China and the West: The Study of Time V*, eds. J. T. Fraser, N. Lawrence, & F. C. Haber. Amherst, MA: University of Massachusetts Press, pp. 23–38.

Lee, D., Lishman, J., & Thomson, J. (1982), Regulation of gait in long jumping. *J. Experiment. Psychol.: Hum. Percept. & Performance*, 8:449–459.

Leeuwenberg, E. L. L., & Buffart, H. E. J. M., eds. (1979), *Formal Theories of Visual Perception*. New York: John Wiley.

Mandelbrot, B. B. (1983), *The Fractal Geometry of Nature*, 2nd ed. San Francisco: Freeman.

McDermott, D. V. (1982), A temporal logic for reasoning about processes and plans. *Cog. Sci.*, 6: 101–155.

——— (1985), Reasoning about plans. In: *Formal Theories of the Commonsense World*, eds. J. R. Hobbs & R. C. Moore. Norwood, NJ: Ablex, pp. 269–318.

Michon, J. A. (1984), Over de metatheoretische grondslagen van de psychonomie. In: *Metatheoretische Aspecten van de Psychonomie*, eds. J. W. G. Raaijmakers, P. T. W. Hudson & A. H. Wertheim. Deventer: Van Loghum Slaterus, pp. 18–41.

——— (1985), The compleat time experiencer. In: *Time, Mind, and Behavior*, eds. J. A. Michon & J. L. Jackson. Berlin: Springer Verlag, pp. 20–52.

——— (1986), J. T. Fraser's "levels of temporality," as cognitive representations. In: *Time, Science, and Society in China and the West: The Study of Time V*, eds. J. T. Fraser, N. Lawrence, & F. C. Haber. Amherst, MA: University of Massachusetts Press, pp. 114–146.

——— ——— (1984), Attentional effort and cognitive strategies in the processing of temporal information. In: *Timing and Time Perception. Annals of the New York Academy of Sciences*, Vol. 423, eds. J. Gibbon & L. Allan. New York: New York Academy of Sciences, pp. 298–321.

——— ——— (1985), *Time, Mind, and Behavior*. Berlin: Springer Verlag.

Miller, G. A., & Johnson-Laird, P. N. (1976), *Language and Perception*. Cambridge: Cambridge University Press.

Moore-Ede, M. C., Sulzman, F. M., & Fuller, C. A. (1983), *The Clocks that Time Us*. Cambridge, MA: Harvard University Press.

Nadolny, S. (1983), *Die Entdeckung der Langsamkeit*. Munich: Piper Verlag.

Nederlands Instituut voor Oorlogsdocumentatie (1986), *De dagboeken van Anne Frank*. The Hague: Staatsuitgeverij.

Ortony, A., ed. (1979), *Metaphor and Thought*. Cambridge: Cambridge University Press.

Peitgen, H.-O., & Richter, P. H. (1986), *The Beauty of Fractals: Images of Complex Dynamical Systems*. Berlin: Springer Verlag.

Reed, E., & Jones, R., eds. (1982), *Reasons for Realism: Selected Essays of James J. Gibson*. Hillsdale, NJ: Lawrence Erlbaum Associates.

Reed, S. (1982), *Cognition: Theory and Applications*. Monterey, CA: Brooks & Cole.

Restle, F. (1970), Theory of serial pattern learning: Structural trees. *Psycholog. Rev.*, 77:481–495.

Richelle M., & Lejeune, M. (1980), *Time in Animal Behaviour*. London: Pergamon Press.

Shaffer, L. H. (1985), Timing in action. In: *Time, Mind, and Behavior*, eds. J. A. Michon & J. L. Jackson. Berlin: Springer Verlag, pp. 226–241.

Shepard, R. N. (1984), Ecological constraints on internal representation: Resonant kinematics of perceiving, imagining, thinking, and dreaming. *Psycholog. Rev.*, 91:417–447.

——— Cooper, L. A. (1982), *Mental Images and Their Transformations*. Cambridge, MA: The MIT Press.

——— Metzler, J. (1971), Mental rotation of three dimensional objects. *Science*, 171:701–703.

Simon, H. A. (1972), Complexity and the representation of patterned sequences of symbols. *Psycholog. Rev.*, 79:369–382.

Thomassen, A. J. M. W., & Teulings, H.-L. (1985), Time, size and shape in handwriting: Exploring spatio-temporal relationships at different levels. In: *Time, Mind, and Behavior*, eds. J. A. Michon & J. L. Jackson. Berlin: Springer Verlag, pp. 253–263.

Van Benthem, J. F. A. K. (1983), *The Logic of Time*. Dordrecht: Reidel.

——— (1985), Semantics of time. In: *Time, Mind, and Behavior*, eds. J. A. Michon & J. L. Jackson. Berlin: Springer Verlag, pp. 266–278.

Voss, R. F. (1978), 1/f noise in music: Music from 1/f noise. *J. Acoust. Soc. Amer.*, 63: 258–263.

——— Clarke, J. (1975), "1/f noise" in music and speech. *Nature*, 258:317–318.

Perspectives

In his Presidential Address, Professor Michon maintains that there is a duality between time and mind. The two are "complementary but equally important aspects of the structure of reality." He adds that "time is real although it requires a mind to be aware of temporal relations" (p. 18).

One of the tasks of the mind, he reasons, is to help the body "stay in tune with an intrinsically temporal world" in which the passing of time was a reality long before there were minds to recognize the passage and rhythm of the universe. He describes this staying in tune as "timing your mind" and remarks that it involves, primarily, automatic processing. By "minding your time" he means the coping with those temporal processes of the external world to which we cannot automatically tune ourselves because there have been no prior evolutionary conditions that could have selected for appropriate behavioral responses.

3

The Processing of Temporal Information: Do We Indeed Time Our Minds?

Janet L. Jackson

Abstract Ever since psychology developed into an experimental science, time has frequently been used as a dimension within which to measure reaction times or the persistence of certain events. In other words, time has been treated as a dependent variable. Only over the last few years has a change in direction become obvious: time can also be viewed as an independent variable, as information in its own right. This reconsideration of the status of time has led to an increase in empirical research which aims to study time within the framework of traditional cognitive research areas such as memory, attention, or psycholinguistics.

The research to be described in this chapter is part of this movement, and looks at the relationship between time and memory processes. More specifically, it begins to explore the variables that govern our ability, or lack of it, to distinguish by memory the ordering of events in time. Although three fundamental questions relating to the *what, when,* and *how* of temporal information processing are posed, the empirical data presented concentrates on the third issue, the *how*.

This important question asks whether temporal information is processed as an inevitable, automatic by-product of information processing in general, or whether temporal information processing in itself requires specific cognitive effort. Unlike several researchers, such as Hasher and Zacks (1979), who believe that temporal information is automatically encoded, we believe that it requires effort. Using criteria similar to those specified by Hasher and Zacks, we have collected a considerable amount of data which directly challenges their automaticity stand. We believe that we do indeed "mind our time"!

Time is a mystery which has fascinated and engrossed men and women in past centuries, and still continues to do so in the present age. Such a long history of human thought about time has inevitably brought with it a broad spectrum of theories, concepts, and insights. While such developments have undoubtedly led to some progress in our understanding and awareness of time in its many guises, our knowledge remains somewhat obscure, and even after many centuries of study, no definitive answers can as yet be offered to questions such as "Quid enim est tempus?"

The fact that no solutions are readily available should not come as too great a surprise, for, with a subject as elusive as time, firm answers are hard to come by. As a result, scholars of time hold many different views and follow many varied approaches in their search for better understanding. Consensus is absolute, however, with regard to the conceptual status of time. As is evident within the pages of this book, all scholars agree that time is not a simple concept. As with space and causation, which also have very early roots in human thought, time cannot easily be decomposed into simpler concepts.

This complexity becomes particularly evident when attempts are made to catalogue the issues directly related to time and its passing. This form of inventory was compiled in 1978 by J. T. Fraser and included no fewer than 300 problems. Among these could be found all the well-known fundamental philosophical questions about the status of the distinctions before–after and past–present–future, the true nature of time, its origin, its reversability, and its continuity. And yet, as it has been argued elsewhere (Michon and Jackson, 1985), while these problems offer themselves to the philosophical mind, they are not necessarily, or even primarily, philosophical problems. Some questions about time are more likely to be raised and answered by physicists (such as those of "time's arrow"); others clearly belong to the domain of psychology.

Arguing for strong emphases to be placed on psychological approaches is not of course a new point of view. In classical and medieval philosophy we find many references to observation and rational arguments indicating that time may be a psychological process rather than a general property of nature. This view culminated in Kant's proposition that both time and space are necessary ways of viewing things (Anschauungsformen).

The empirical study of psychological time is well over a century old. Up until roughly 1920 it proved to be a prominent research topic, but declined in the following decades. Fortunately, however, it is possible to trace a distinct revival of interest in the psychology of time since around the 1960s. Much of this renewed interest can be traced back to the monograph *Psychologie du Temps* (1957) by the distinguished French scholar Paul Fraisse. This excellent monograph triggered a number of experimental studies in which modern experimental techniques and theoretical views were used to reconsider some of the classical (and often still unanswered) questions. Interest in the topic of time therefore continues to grow, and indeed, particularly within the last few years, an ever-increasing number of studies have appeared in the current experimental psychology literature whose aim has been to study time within the framework of traditional cognitive research areas such as memory, attention, or psycholinguistics. The work carried out at our laboratory in Groningen has been part of this new development. Our specific research topic has involved looking at the relationship between time and memory processes.

Before this increase in interest could evolve, however, a paradigmatic shift had to take place. To a typical experimental psychologist brought up within an information processing approach such as that described by Michon in the preceding chapter, time did not present itself as a new concept. I, as well as many of my colleagues, had frequently used time in our research as a dimension within which to measure reaction times or the persistence of certain events. In other words, time was viewed as a dependent variable, as a characteristic of a subject that can be observed and measured, and its merits as an independent variable, as information in its own right, were seldom if ever considered. It was therefore something of a revelation to encounter the equivalence postulate as it was first formulated by Michon (1972, p. 247). This postulate advances the assumption that temporal relations between events are treated by the human organism as information in the same way as size, intensity, or color. In other words, that time is explicitly represented in the mind and should be studied as a psychological phenomenon in its own right.

Although at first glance this assumption seemed a somewhat unusual one for an experimental psychologist to be postulating, on further study it quickly became evident that, in fact, psychologists have for a long time realized, albeit implicitly, that time is a fundamental concept. Otherwise it would not be used by them so frequently in definitions of many other concepts. It therefore only requires a short step to come to the belief that time must indeed occupy a central role in how we represent reality. Furthermore, since the main topic of study for cognitive psychologists is in fact the structure of mental representations, the point has been reached where we can no longer avoid the issue of time as information and must begin to take seriously the notions of simultaneity, order, and duration.

Time and Memory Processes

The work carried out over the last few years by Professor John Michon and myself has therefore been founded on two basic propositions (for a more comprehensive overview, see Jackson [1986]). The first of these states that time means information to man. As such, it should be viewed as an independent property of the flow of information that we experience as reality and cannot be distinguished from properties or patterns of information such as size, color, or spatial location. The second proposition refers to the relationship between time and memory processes. Over the last few years, experimental studies in the field of memory research have become more focused on the ways in which humans process temporal information. The main aim of our studies has been to further this approach and to begin to explore the variables that govern our ability, or lack of it, to distinguish by memory the ordering of events in time. The specific questions we have been asking include:

What mechanisms and processes underlie the experience of time?
How do we represent, internally, concepts such as before and after?
What aspects of reality are perceived directly and automatically?
What is inferred directly through the cognitive process of construction?

Perhaps not surprisingly, these questions are in fact closely related to the theme and title of the preceding chapter, namely, to "timing your mind and minding your time." Having first described an information processing system (Anderson, 1985) which distinguishes between two functionally different and complementary ways of processing information, namely automatic or controlled processing, John Michon went on to describe timing your mind as being primarily, if not exclusively, a matter of automatic processing of external as well as internal data. Timing your mind enables you to stay in tune with an intrinsically temporal world but not necessarily by means of representing time explicitly. Furthermore, he argues that tuning to the temporal contingencies of the world is dependent on the availability of a number of preattunements or schemata, some of which are learned during a lifetime, but which come about mostly as a result of evolutionary development.

It should be evident, however, that the flow of information need not always contain recurrences that can be dealt with automatically by the organism. When schemata are insufficient, it becomes necessary to employ controlled processing. Minding your time therefore implies that all conscious time experience is a consequence of controlled processing. The view has been summed up on a number of previous occasions with the statement, *"temporal information is not processed unless noticed and not noticed unless meaningful"* (Michon and Jackson, 1984, p. 305; Jackson, 1986, p. 15). Not all psychologists agree with this position, however. In the literature on memory, we find several authors holding opposing views: they claim that all temporal information is encoded automatically. One of the main aims of this chapter is to provide a body of empirical data which I feel must surely undermine this automaticity viewpoint.

The Processing of Temporal Information: Three Fundamental Questions

As I have previously stated, the main thrust lying behind this research endeavor has been an attempt at understanding the variables that govern our ability, or lack of it, to distinguish by memory the ordering of events in time. To guide such research, I have had to pose three important questions which relate to the what, when, and how of temporal information processing. The *what* issue involves asking what in a sequential stimulus configuration actually constitutes the functional stimulus or temporal attribute which serves as the input for temporal judgments. The second question, the *when* issue, asks whether the temporal attribute, once identified, is encoded upon acquisition or, instead, constructed during retrieval. Third, the *how* question asks whether temporal information is processed as an inevitable, automatic by-product of information in general, or whether temporal information processing in itself requires specific cognitive effort.

These three questions are, of course, not independent, but are indeed intricately intertwined. However, given the overwhelming evidence from the cognitive psychology of time that temporal information processing requires cognitive effort and, since I wish to provide evidence here to show that we "mind our time," I will take as our starting point the third issue: *how.*

Before tackling this question, however, I would like to mention one further theoretical issue from cognitive psychology which is necessary and important for the arguments. In cognitive psychology, an important current trend has been to emphasize a framework which distinguishes between *structure* and *process*. Various sets of distinctions have been described, such as strategy and structure; software and hardware; cognitive penetrability and cognitive impenetrability (Pylyshyn, 1980); and performance and competence (Chomsky, 1967). Though these distinctions are not interchangeable, they do resemble each other quite closely in that they all share the view that some aspects of the cognitive system are fixed while others are flexible, dynamic, and variable. Any adequate cognitive theory must therefore distinguish between the fixed capacities of the mind (often referred to as the functional architecture) and the particular representations used in specific tasks.

In the work of our research group we stress the fact that events, which are successive in physical reality are also perceived in their correct order, and that this correspondence should be seen as an impenetrable function, as part of the "hardware"; in other words, that it relates to the structure of the mind. The particular representations and processes used in temporal judgments on the other hand, should be viewed as flexible and variable and are affected by factors such as task demands, instructions, and goals.

The reason for stressing this distinction is that some other researchers, such as Hasher and Zacks (1979), who have argued that temporal information is automatically acquired and stored in memory as a by-product of perceptual information processing, have failed to distinguish between structure and process, between timing your mind, which may be a psychophysical necessity, and minding your time. I believe that this conceptual confusion weakens their automaticity argument.

A Framework for Combining Research on Capacity and Memory

Let us now look more closely at the work of Hasher and Zacks. In a much acclaimed article published in 1979, these authors not only succeeded in provoking a great deal of discussion but also stimulated much research. In the article, the authors consider memory processes as a function of attention and two qualitatively different types of processing. They distinguish between two kinds of mental activity: automatic processing which requires very little or no attentional capacity and effortful processing which requires considerable attentional capacity. They suggest, however, that there is a continuum of attentional requirements among encoding processes and that automatic and effortful processing constitute the end points of such a continuum. Hasher and Zacks then go on to specify several criteria for determining through which information processing mode a certain attribute is actually encoded. They argue that varying instructions, level of practice, state variables, divided attention requirements, and developmental trends ought not to affect task performance if information is processed in the automatic mode.

Having cited the necessary criteria for distinguishing between automatic and effortful processing, Hasher and Zacks then proceed to review the literature seeking either evidence or contradictions to substantiate their hypotheses. Since our area of interest relates to the processing of temporal information, we shall restrict ourselves to data relating to this particular form of processing. Let us consider the evidence collected by Hasher and Zacks, as summarized in Table 3.1. It focuses on five different experimental techniques:

1. Intentional versus incidental learning: In incidental learning tasks subjects are required to carry out tasks such as judging the pleasantness of the stimulus words or counting how often an "a" appears, but they are not instructed to learn the words. Any learning that occurs is therefore not intentional but is a by-product of the task activities they carry out. While subjects in the intentional conditions also carry out similar tasks, they are also given explicit instructions to learn the stimulus words. If the encoding of temporal information is indeed automatic, temporal judgments made under incidental learning conditions should be no different from those made by subjects who are explicitly instructed to pay attention to temporal information.

2. Effects of instruction and practice: If the coding of temporal information is carried out automatically, neither explicit instructions about how to carry out temporal judgment tasks nor practice in making such judgments should increase performance.

3. Task interference: If the processing of temporal information is automatic and requires no effortful processing, it will not interfere with the processing of other more effortful components of memory such as item recall.

4. Depression or high arousal: Under conditions of stress such as depression or high arousal, attentional capacity is assumed to be reduced. If, however, the processing of temporal information requires no attentional capacity, such stress conditions should have no effect on the efficiency of temporal judgments.

5. Developmental trends: If temporal information processing is indeed automatic or genetically endowed, it follows that such processing must be acquired early in life and should show little change with age and no decline with old age.

Examination of Table 3.1 shows the evidence to be far from complete: there are not yet sufficient data to evaluate all the criteria listed by Hasher and Zacks (e.g., no data relating to effects of practice, depression, or aging); only part of the evidence cited actually supports their framework (e.g., Mathews and Fozard's [1970] study of developmental trends in children showed contradictory results); and finally, we have argued elsewhere that part of the evidence proves to be inadequate (in particular, a paper by Zimmerman and Underwood [1968], discussed in Jackson and Michon [1984]). Notwithstanding the paucity of evidence, however, Hasher and Zacks proceeded to reach the firm conclusion that temporal information is among the attributes of information that are indeed encoded automatically; that is, we time our minds.

Table 3.1. Evidence from the Literature Cited by Hasher and Zacks (1979) as Support for Their View That Temporal Information Is Encoded Automatically

	Data Which Support Framework	Data Which Contradict Framework	No Relevant Data
1. Intentional versus incidental learning	Zimmerman & Underwood (1968); Miller, Hicks, & Willette (1978)		
2. Effects of instruction and practice			0
3. Task interference	Zimmerman & Underwood (1968)		
4. Depression or high arousal			0
5. Developmental trends: (a) children	Brown (1973)	Mathews & Fozard (1970)	
(b) elderly			0

Some Experimental Results

Although we are obviously not in agreement with Hasher and Zacks' hypothesis that the recording of temporal information occurs automatically, our group has made use of their explicit set of criteria in our own empirical studies. By using a line of reasoning similar to that used by these authors, attacking them with their own weapons as it were, we aim to rebuff the automaticity viewpoint and show that we mind our time. Let us consider a selection of these experiments which explore performance on order, lag, and position judgment tasks. In experiments which make use of order judgments, subjects are required to judge which of a pair of words appeared earlier in the original series. Lag judgments require subjects to judge how many words appeared between a particular pair in the original series while position judgments require subjects to judge the exact position of items in the original series.

1. If temporal information is processed automatically, similar temporal judgments should be expected for words that have different semantic characteristics. The concrete–abstract distinction was explored in two experiments (Jackson and Michon, 1984) which employed a directed forgetting paradigm (Bjork, 1972). Within this paradigm, subjects are either cued to remember or to forget each presented item. This is done by directly following each individually presented item

by either a remember-cue (R-cue) or a forget-cue (F-cue). In our experiments the cues used were red and green colored slides respectively. According to Bjork, the effect of being cued to forget information has the effect of stopping rehearsal of that item. In other words, these F-cued items receive no effortful processing. Results, summarized in Figure 3.1 show that F-cueing not only prevents rehearsal but is also highly effective in eradicating temporal order information. Results also show that temporal order retention is higher with concrete R-cued than with abstract R-cued lists. Such a difference suggests that something extra, possibly related to selective attention demands or processing strategies, plays an important role. Both of these explanations, however, belong to the domain of controlled processing.

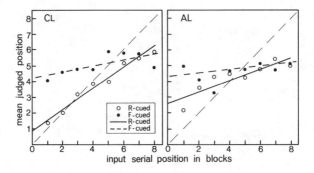

Figure 3.1. Mean judged position for the R-cued and the F-cued words as a function of their actual serial position (in blocks); within the concrete (CL) and the abstract (AL) word lists. (R = to-be-remembered words; F = to-be-forgotten words).

2. Two experiments were carried out to explore the effect of incidental versus intentional acquisition of temporal order information for both concrete (CL) and abstract (AL) word lists (Jackson, 1986). In the incidental condition, subjects were given a recognition instruction (RI). They were told that they would be shown a list of words and would then be asked to complete a recognition test which included the original words as well as several new words. They would also be asked to indicate their confidence that they had already seen the word on a 5-point scale ranging from 1, "very sure not old," to 5, "very sure old." In the intentional condition, the temporal position instruction (TPI) stressed the importance of the recall of serial position. Subjects were told that they would be asked to assign a position judgment to each of the words. The actual test situation varied somewhat from the instructions in that all groups were presented with recognition as well as position judgment tests. The results shown in Figure 3.2 suggest that the type of instruction, that is, recognition (RI) or temporal position (TPI) instructions does appear to affect temporal position recall. This effect is particularly clear when abstract material is used. The conclusion must therefore be that, particularly with complex material, temporal information need not be simply an automatic process but requires a deliberate shift in the priority of attentional processes if temporal judgment tasks are to be performed adequately.

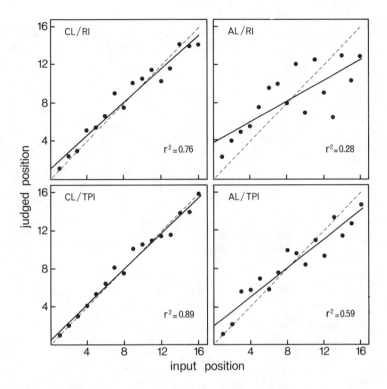

Figure 3.2. Mean judged position as a function of their actual input serial position; within the concrete (CL) and abstract (AL) word lists. (RI = recognition instructions; TPI = temporal position instructions.)

3. In a further experiment (Jackson, Michon, Boonstra, de Jonge, and de Velde Harsenhorst, 1986), a different way of examining the performance of temporal judgment tasks following an incidental learning task was carried out. A level of processing procedure similar to that of Craik and Lockhart (1972) was used. This procedure involves presenting lists of common words and requiring subjects to respond to orienting questions relating either to the word structure (e.g., does a particular letter appear in a word) or to the semantic features of these words (e.g., does the word fit a particular sentence). Half of the orienting questions required a yes response and the other half a no response.

After completing this task, subjects were required to perform various binary decision temporal judgment tasks. Examples of the tasks and types of question asked are shown in Table 3.2. The use of binary questions allowed us to test performance against a random guessing level of performance. The results, presented in Table 3.3, show that subjects who performed the physical structure orienting tasks were very poor indeed in making temporal judgments. In no instance did

Table 3.2. Examples of Orienting and Test Questions

Level of Processing	Orienting Questions	Correct Response	
		Yes	No
(1) Shallow (word structure)	Is there an *a* in the word?	hand	tree
(2) Deep (semantic features)	Would the word fit the sentence: "A — has a tail"?	horse	flag

Type of Judgment Task	Test Questions	Binary Choice
(1) Order judgments	Which of these two words appeared earlier in the original series?	b or a
(2) Lag judgments	How many words appeared between these two in the original series?	8 or 14
(3) Position judgments	What was the exact position of this word in the original series?	11 or 7

their performance exceed a random guessing level. Such guessing behavior was also evident in the lag judgments made by subjects after the semantic orienting task. Performance in the other two judgment tasks following this orienting task was, however, well in excess of a random guessing level for order judgments and was approaching an above-chance level for position judgments.

Table 3.3. Observed Values of *t* Against Chance

Condition	Temporal Judgments		
	Order	Position	Lag
Physical Structure	1.52	1.93	2.21
Semantic Feature	3.05*	2.67	1.07

* Significant at 5% level.

These results again challenge the view expressed, albeit implicitly, by Hasher and Zacks, suggesting that *all* temporal coding takes place automatically. Instead, they support our earlier findings (Jackson and Michon, 1984; Michon and Jackson, 1984) suggesting that relative order judgments may indeed reflect some automatic encoding of intrinsic order, but that such coding is not sufficient to enable subjects to perform more complex temporal judgment tasks adequately. These require more controlled processing.

4. The following set of experiments were carried out to explore the developmental criterion of Hasher and Zacks (1979). If, as these authors suggest, the processing of temporal information is automatic, it should follow that performance on temporal tasks is relatively insensitive to developmental variables. Three experiments were carried out to test this hypothesis: two of these studied the performance of young children (5- and 11-year-olds), and the third compared the performance of two adult groups (24- and 60-year-olds) (Jackson, 1986).

The first experiment with children explored performance on order judgments for pictures presented either in short (7 items) or long series (28 items). Performance on short series was well above chance level in both age groups, but the 11-year-olds performed significantly better than the 5-year-olds. With the long series both age groups were again above chance but the developmental effect disappeared.

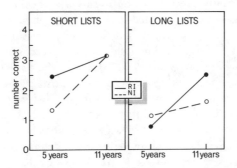

Figure 3.3. Average correct responses as a function of age and instruction. (RI = rehearsal instructions; NI = no rehearsal instructions.)

In a second experiment a position judgment task was used. Results from this task show the older age group to be performing significantly better than the younger group in both the short and long item tasks. Such developmental effects obviously argue against the claim that all temporal information is automatically encoded in memory. The suggestion that the improvement in performance is a result of controlled processing is strengthened when we consider the effects of induced rehearsal: when young children are encouraged to adopt rehearsal strategies with the shorter series, their performance does improve, even though it does not yet reach the level of the older children. With the longer series, however, this improvement disappears (see Figure 3.3). Though no effects are found with the older children given the shorter series, an improvement in performance does occur as a result of rehearsal instructions when the longer series are presented (see Figure 3.3). This result suggests that although eleven-year-olds may spontaneously rehearse, such rehearsal strategies may be far from optimal. By stressing the use of particular rehearsal procedures, the older children may have been encouraged to develop a more efficient, task-related strategy.

The third developmental experiment explores the performance of young (mean age 24 years) and older adults (mean age 60 years) on both order and lag judgment tasks (Jackson, 1986). The results in the order tasks show the performance of both age groups to be well above chance level and, moreover, the difference in the percentage of correct judgments between the young and older group (70 and 62% respectively) was not significant. With lag judgments, however, a different pattern of results emerges with the younger subjects now performing significantly better than the older adults.

Results from these developmental experiments both strengthen and weaken Hasher and Zacks' stance: with some temporal judgment tasks, no developmental effects were observed; with other tasks, however, significant developmental differences were indeed found. Such results are, however, once more in agreement with our earlier finding which suggested that order judgments may reflect some automatic encoding of intrinsic order. Other temporal judgment tasks on the other hand, do require additional controlled processing in order to produce accurate levels of performance. Since it is precisely with this this type of controlled processing that developmental effects occur, we predicted that developmental effects would be found with position as well as lag judgments. Our predictions were met.

5. In the group of experiments that have been discussed up until now, the main emphasis has been on group data. Although the use of this approach has successfully identified many interesting variables, during the course of experiment-ing it became clear to us that it was also tending to obscure the actual processing that was going on in the subjects' efforts to cope with the task. An early exploratory examination of individual results did in fact reveal subjects to be behaving in quite varied, unexpected ways. In a small in-depth study, protocol analyses were used to discover the strategies individuals were actually using when carrying out various temporal judgment tasks. Verbal protocols are obtained by asking subjects to overtly verbalize their thought processes, and to "think aloud" while they are carrying out their task. The recorded verbalizations are then transcribed. The resulting protocols are then used to construct a fairly extensive and comprehensive list of the various strategies which could be adopted (reported in Michon and Jackson, 1984; Jackson, 1985).

In several other experiments in which verbal protocols were obtained, a simplified coding system was adopted. This involved grouping strategies into two main clusters, simple or elaborative rehearsal. Simple rehearsal involves the use of rote rehearsal, the simple repetition of single words or blocks of words. Such rote rehearsal tends to produce poor recall performance. Elaborative rehearsal requires more effort. It involves adding information beyond what is strictly necessary in order to make the material more memorable. Examples are the use of mnemonics

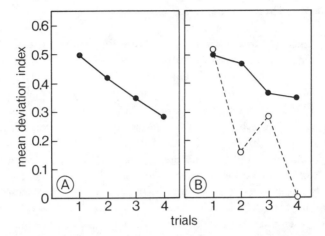

Figure 3.4. (A) shows mean deviation index scores over the four trials. (B) mean deviation scores as a function of trial and strategy. (Solid line represents simple rehearsal strategies; dotted line represents elaborative strategies.)

such as "one is a bun" or a strategy which involves incorporating all the words into one connected story. During the study and test phase of the experiment, subjects in each condition were treated as a uniform group. Prior to statistical analyses, however, depending on their protocols, they were assigned to one of the two strategy groups. An important research question which was explored in this set of experiments asked whether there was a relationship between strategy use and performance on temporal judgment tasks. Results from all of these experiments revealed positive effects, with subjects who used elaborative strategies performing significantly better. (A more comprehensive view of the data can be found in Jackson [1985]). One example of such significant results is shown in Figure 3.4B for the two strategy groups on a position judgment task. (It should be noted that the performance measure used here for temporal judgments is the Deviation Index (D). Its value varies between zero and one, with a score of zero signifying perfect performance. Further discussion of the measure can be found in Jackson [1986]). Performance on temporal judgment tasks is therefore closely related to the strategies individuals use to carry out the tasks. Since rehearsal processes are firmly entrenched within the domain of controlled processing, this result must certainly raise problems for those who view temporal coding as an automatic process.

6. Results from the set of experiments just described therefore show performance on temporal tasks to be closely related to the strategies the subjects used. In addition, however, they also showed performance to be affected by level of practice. In Figure 3.4A, we see an example of this significant "practice effect" over all the subjects; and in Figure 3.4B, for the two strategy groups apart. "Effect of practice" is, however, among the criteria cited by Hasher and Zacks as being indicative of the controlled mode of information processing!

Answers to the Three Fundamental Questions

In an earlier section of this chapter, I raised three fundamental issues related to the what, when, and how of temporal information processing. How far have we reached in our search for adequate answers? Humans live in an ever-changing environment with events occurring in *reality* more or less as and when one observes them occurring. In order to interact successfully with such an environment, man has evolved in such a way that he must be aware of, or be using, the relations of simultaneity, order, temporal locus, and duration.

The development of the conditions which make the formulation of such variables possible was explored in detail in the writings of Fraser (1978, 1982, 1987) and is summed up in his chapter in the present volume (chapter 1).

Assuming that the order of events can be specified, our task as psychologists becomes one of establishing how this order is coded and represented. Our view is that intrinsic order constitutes the functional stimulus which serves as the input for temporal judgments. Although it has not been possible to present the relevant data here, this belief is supported by results from several of our experiments. Moreover, these results also answer the second fundamental question, namely, the when issue. Our claim is that the functional stimulus is intrinsic order and that this attribute is encoded upon acquisition. The third issue relating to the how question is not so straightforward.

I have challenged the position adopted by Hasher and Zacks which implies that the recording of temporal information is a genetically endowed automatic process. I have argued that this claim stems, at least in part, from a conceptual confusion: psychophysical necessity, or timing your mind, should not be confused with automatic processing! Instead, a more appropriate limited definition should be adopted: automaticity involves those processing activities that do not require attentional resources and that, consequently, are not subject to interference from other concurrent tasks.

Also, using their own criteria, our research group have collected a considerable amount of data which directly challenges Hasher and Zacks' (1979) automaticity stance. (Interestingly enough, since our initial studies, Zacks, Hasher, Alba, Sanft, and Rose [1985] have also reported data which challenge two of their original automaticity stances. They too are beginning to accept that we "mind our time"!). The evidence we have collected, however, is still not completely satisfactory. Take for example, the developmental studies where performance varied depending on the type of task carried out. These and other experimental results have led us to suggest that encoding intrinsic order relationships is a necessary but not a sufficient condition to produce adequate temporal retention in all tasks. Instead we suggest that a hierarchy exists such that different temporal judgment tasks demand different levels of processing: simply being available in working memory for further processing is a necessary condition to lay down old–new relationships, and these in turn are in the main sufficient to produce above chance levels of performance on order judgments. In contrast, both position and lag judgments require further deliberate processing of these old–new relationships in order to produce high levels of performance.

The position adopted assumes that the temporal information which is coded relates to sequential information, and that other temporal information, such as interval information, is derived from this coded information. Unless attended to and processed further, however, such information loses validity. While a loss of validity affects position and lag judgments, order judgments can still be made fairly adequately..

References

Anderson, J. R. (1985),. *Cognitive Psychology and Its Implications*, 2nd ed. San Francisco: Freeman.

Bjork, R. A. (1972), Theoretical implications of directed forgetting. In: *Coding Processes in Human Memory*, eds. A. W. Melton & E. Martin. Washington, DC: Winston, pp. 217–235.

Chomsky, N. (1967), The general properties of language. In: *Brain Mechanisms Underlying Speech and Language*, eds. C. H. Millikan & F. L. Darley. New York: Grune & Stratton, pp. 73–88.

Craik, F. I. M., & Lockhart, R. S. (1972), Levels of processing: A framework for memory research. *J. Verbal Learn. & Verbal Behav.*, 6:49–54.

Fraisse, P. (1957), *Psychologie du temps*. Paris: Presses Universitaires de France.

Fraser, J. T. (1978), *Time as a Conflict: A Scientific and Humanistic Study*. Basel, Switzerland: Birkhaeuser.

———— (1982), *The Genesis and Evolution of Time: A Critique of Interpretation in Physics*. Amherst, MA: University of Massachusetts Press.

———— (1987), *Time, the Familiar Stranger*. Amherst, MA: University of Massachusetts Press.

Hasher, L., & Zacks, R. T. (1979), Automatic and effortful processes in memory. *J. Experiment. Psychol.: Gen.*, 108:356–388.

Jackson, J. L. (1985), Is the processing of temporal information automatic or controlled? In: *Time, Mind, and Behavior*, eds. J. A. Michon & J. L. Jackson. Heidelberg: Springer Verlag, pp. 179–190.

———— (1986), *The Processing of Temporal Information*. Unpublished doctoral dissertation. University of Groningen, The Netherlands.

———— Michon, J.A., (1984), Effects of item concreteness on temporal coding. *Acta Psycholog.*, 57:83–95.

———— ———— Boonstra, H., de Jonge, D., & de Velde Harsenhorst, J. (1986), The effects of depth of processing on temporal judgment tasks. *Acta Psycholog.*, 62:199–210.

Mathews, M. E., & Fozard, J. L. (1970), Age differences in judgments of recency for short sequences of pictures. *Development. Psychol.*, 3:208–217.

Michon, J. A. (1972), Processing of temporal information and cognitive theory of time experience. In: *The Study of Time*, eds. J. T. Fraser, F. C. Haber & G. H. Muller. Heidelberg: Springer Verlag, pp. 242–258.

———— Jackson, J. L. (1984), Attentional effort and cognitive strategies in the processing of temporal information. In: *Timing and Time Perception*, eds. J. Gibbon & L. Allan. *Ann. NY Acad. Sci.*, 423:298–321.

———— ———— (1985), The psychology of time. In: *Time, Mind, and Behavior*, eds. J. A. Michon & J. L. Jackson. Heidelberg: Springer Verlag.

Miller, G. W., Hicks, R. E., & Willette, M. (1978), Effects of concurrent rehearsal and temporal set upon judgments of temporal duration. *Acta Physiolog.*, 12:173–179.

Pylyshyn, Z. W. (1980), Computation and cognition: Issues in the foundations of cognitive science. *Behav. & Brain Sci.*, 3:111–169.

Zacks, R. T., Hasher, L., Alba, J. W., Sanft, H., & Rose, K. C. (1985), Is temporal order encoded automatically? *Memory & Cognition*, 12:387–394.

Zimmerman, J., & Underwood, B. J. (1968), Ordinal position knowledge within and across lists as a function of instructions in free-recall learning. *J. Gen. Psychol.*, 79:301–307.

Perspectives

Dr. Jackson presents and analyzes laboratory experiments, designed to fine-tune Dr. Michon's concept of "timing our minds." She demonstrates that the processing of temporal information requires specific cognitive efforts and hence even in the domain of "timing our minds" there is a contribution from "minding our time"; there is an effort of deliberate processing of temporal information. If certain examples of temporal retention, demonstrated in experimental tasks, are to be explained, future work will have to identify the mechanics and levels of that deliberate processing.

As to the division of intellectual labor in the study of time, Dr. Jackson maintains that while experimental psychology can contribute its share to an understanding of time and mind, certain questions, such as those concerning time's arrow (the one-directional passing of time), "are more likely to be raised and answered by physicists" (p. 44).

4

A Contextualistic View of Time and Mind

Richard A. Block

Abstract A contextualistic model for experiments involving psychological time suggests new ways of viewing theoretical and research problems pertaining to time and mind. In this model, temporal experiences are understood to involve a changing cognitive construction based on the interactions of four major contextual factors: the characteristics of an experiencer, the contents of a time period, the activities of the experiencer during that time period, and time-related behaviors and judgments. The model reveals some of the limitations of the mechanistic views that characterize biological, behavioral, and early cognitive models. It also illuminates the varying ways in which psychological time is constructed. It does so by emphasizing how the activities of a person, such as his or her strategies of information processing, and the relation between these activities and the contents of the time period interact with other contextual factors. The findings of an experimental study of the "watched-pot" phenomenon also support a contextualistic model of temporal experience. Given our present understanding of time and mind, a contextualistic model will probably continue to be a useful one for psychological research on temporal experience.

Introduction

Cognitive psychological research suggests that people construct and represent time by relying on various kinds of changes.[1] These changes form the ongoing context which underlies time-related behaviors and thoughts. As environmental demands and personal characteristics change, so also do the salient aspects of these changes which a person uses to construct and to represent time. I will explore here the ways in which these salient changes in contextual factors affect the construction and representation of psychological time.

[1]It has been argued that time is nothing more than changes. For example, Guyau (1890) concluded that time is simply an organization of mental representations to describe change in the universe, rather than something which exists independently in the universe. This contention is essentially irrelevant for present purposes, and it will not be developed here.

Before reviewing some recent experiments and theories on time and change, consider a Chinese document dating to the century before Confucius, *The I Ching, or Book of Changes*. It distinguishes among different kinds of change (*I Ching*, pp. 280–281). What is called *nonchange* is the frame of reference, or background, to which any change is referred. *Cyclic change* is recurrent variation in the physical universe and the organic world. Biological rhythms and the alteration of the seasons are examples of cyclic change; they influence mind and behavior in various ways, usually as a result of the operation of automatic, mostly nonconscious, processes. *Sequential change* [2] is a progressive, nonrecurrent variation of events. Progression occurs as events influence one another. The human cognitive system usually handles sequential change in a controlled, or conscious, way; and so sequential change forms the primary basis for the construction and representation of time in the mind (see chapter 2 for a discussion of the distinction between automatic and controlled processes). For this reason, sequential change is the major focus of this chapter.

When we discuss these kinds of change, we are considering the underpinning of psychological time, a concept which is as multifaceted as the concept of change. Research on time within even a single discipline displays much complexity and diversity. In psychology, for example, there are studies on biological rhythms, duration experiences, and cultural tempos. Approaches to the subject may be biopsychological, behavioral, cognitive, developmental, psychoanalytic, or social–psychological. Researchers currently study humans, rats, pigeons, and a few other species. Investigations also vary in other dimensions.

It is helpful and undoubtedly necessary to adopt a multidimensional perspective on a multifaceted concept like that of time. But as Kaye (1977) reminded us: "Although it would seem that a multidimensional perspective should dictate families of holistic unities, in my vision of reality things are nested within things, relate as things to things . . . defy total absorption, and moreover, exist in several contexts simultaneously" (p. 346). This is probably why most theorizing on the psychology of time is limited in scope. It is difficult to find any "families of holistic unities," even within a single topic area in a single discipline. Attempts to broaden the scope usually result in a classification of different phenomena, with little attempt to interrelate the different categories in any pragmatic way.

Cognitive psychological research is emphasized here, using examples mostly from studies of the human experience of duration. Duration experience is a major result of sequential change. Although this chapter draws heavily on my own work, it also mentions the work of others and contrasts my theoretical approach with theirs.

---

[2]C. F. Baynes (*I Ching*) translated this term as *sequent change;* however, I am using the more familiar term, *sequential*. Note that the word *sequential* is used here in a special sense, to imply nonrecurrence of events.

Pepper's *World Hypotheses* and Time

There is now renewed interest in Stephen Pepper's work (Efron, 1982; Block, 1985a; Michon, 1986). Pepper (1942) proposed four root metaphors as vehicles to represent four world hypotheses or, as I prefer to call them, world models. They are formism, mechanism, organicism, and contextualism. Only a contextualistic root metaphor explicitly suggests a multifaceted view of time. In this chapter I will demonstrate why contextualism is the world model of choice for understanding and explaining time in the human mind. First, though, let us consider the useful roles of the other three.

Formism

The root metaphor of formism is similarity, or the common-sense perception of patterns of relationships among different particular objects. Formists analyze the universe by classifying objects; they do this by organizing particulars into categories according to their various properties. One valuable use of a formistic approach in the psychology of time is the classification of different types of temporal experience, such as simultaneity, successiveness, rhythm, duration, and temporal perspective (Ornstein, 1969; Block, 1979). In a more extensive classification, Fraser (1975, 1982, 1987) proposed that there are five hierarchically nested levels of temporality.

Mechanism

The root metaphor of mechanism is a machine. A mechanistic analysis attempts to explain the universe in terms of relationships among its various parts. In psychology, information-processing models rely heavily on a mechanistic root metaphor, in that they compare humans to the system embodied in the modern digital computer and its associated programs: that is, general purpose symbol manipulators. These models are useful because they explicitly detail sequences of cognitive processes involved in the performance of any task.

Organicism

The root metaphor of organicism is the organic process. The notions of adaptation, resolution of contradictions or conflicts, and internal drives toward integration are central to organicism. In direct contrast to contextualism, organicism holds that time and change are not real, but derivative: Just as a tree develops from a seed, each phenomenon ends in a form which is implicit in its earlier forms. Organicism requires progressive categories, such as time and change, to give it scope; but according to organicism, these categories do not exist. It is particularly relevant here to note Pepper's (1942) claim that organicism "convicts itself of inadequacy" because it "takes time lightly or disparagingly; [however,] contextualism takes it seriously" (pp. 281, 314).

Contextualism

The root metaphor of contextualism is the historic event, not as some past occurrence, but rather as a "dynamic dramatic active event," which is "intrinsically complex, composed of interconnected activities with continuously changing patterns" (Pepper, 1942, pp. 232–233). The term *context* comes from a Latin verb meaning "to interweave." The image of interweaving is particularly appropriate, because it involves complex, interconnected, and continuously changing patterns. Contextualism, then, focuses on sequential change—events unfolding over time. Each event contains dynamic, interpenetrating features that change, giving rise to novelty. An event has a certain quality—roughly, its "total character"—and a certain texture—"details and relations which make up that character" (Pepper, 1942, p. 238).

Thus, contextualists divide the world into two basic ontological categories—events and changes. Change and novelty are inherent in observer–environment interactions, and every event has a unique quality and texture. Contextualism rejects the notion of permanent structures; instead, it emphasizes the "salient or important aspects of events" that depend upon "the observer's particular purposes" (Hoffman and Nead, 1983, p. 519). Because time and change are basic ideas underlying contextualism, it is ideally suited for clarifying the nature of psychological time.

Contextualism has been rejected or ignored during most of the history of psychology, especially by behaviorists. Psychologists are only recently reexploring the implications of contextualism and its metaphorical orientation, which is a kind of realist interactionism (Rosnow and Georgoudi, 1986). Jenkins (1974), a contextualist who recently discussed memory, said: "What is remembered in a given situation depends on the physical and psychological context in which the event was experienced, the knowledge and skills that the subject brings to the context, the situation in which we ask for evidence for remembering, and the relation of what the subject remembers to what the experimenter demands" (p. 793).

Pepper (1942) surmised that "whatever system there is in the world is of the mechanistic type, and whatever dynamic vitality, of the contextualistic sort" (p. 148). My own theorizing about temporal experience is a somewhat eclectic mixture of more traditional mechanistic thinking and less traditional contextualistic thinking.

A Descriptive Model of Temporal Experience

Recently, I proposed a tetrahedral model which represents four general factors that influence temporal experiences (see Figure 4.1).[3] Each of the four vertices of the

[3]This is an adaptation of a model proposed by Jenkins (1979), which is suggested by his statement on factors that influence remembering. The adaptation to temporal experience is in Block (1985b).

tetrahedron represents one of the four factors; that is, a cluster of related variables that influence temporal experiences. An understanding of the complexities of any time-related experience or behavior is possible only if all four of these general factors are viewed as interacting. Each of the six edges of the tetrahedron represents two-way interactions of factors, and each of the four planes represents three-way interactions. Finally, the whole tetrahedron depicts the complex, four-way inter-actions.

The tetrahedral model is a useful visual aid for appreciating the contextualistic approach. In the experimental psychology of time, ordinarily only one or two of these factors are studied in any experiment, and the model shows clearly what is needed in any more complete account of temporal experiences. Let us now consider these factors.

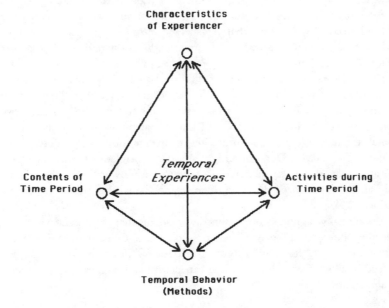

Figure 4.1. A general contextualistic model showing the four factors that interact to influence temporal experiences.

The factor at the top of the figure is the *characteristics of the experiencer,* including such variables as species, sex, personality, interests, and previous experiences. It also includes a person's temporal perspective, or temporal orientation; that is, his or her characteristic ways of viewing and relating to the psychological concepts of past, present, and future. We may regard these characteristics as forming a person's history; however, it is important to realize that this factor is operating dynamically in the present. Previous experiences influence a person's current temporal experiences and judgments. For example, some studies show that prior experience in a particular situation reduces the remembered duration of a subsequent time period spent in the same situation (Block, 1982).

The factor at the left is the *contents of the time period* which a person is experiencing and, perhaps, evaluating and judging. The specific contents of a time period include various psychologically relevant attributes of events, such as their number, complexity, modality, duration, and so on. In one experiment, I found that if the complexity of a sequence of events increases, a person remembers the duration of that sequence as being relatively longer (Block, 1978). Usually, a person focuses mainly on external events; however, in activities such as daydreaming, the psychologically important events occupying a time period are mainly internal, since there is a reduction in task-relevant information processing.

The factor at the right is *activities during a time period.* These include relatively passive nonattending to external events, such as in daydreaming, as well as various kinds of more actively controlled processes, such as strategies in which a person engages in the process of acquiring information. Cognitive psychology is increasingly focusing on controlled strategies of information processing. Several years ago Block and Reed (1978) found that if a person changes strategies during a time period, rather than maintaining a single strategy, he or she remembers the duration as being relatively longer.

The final factor, at the bottom, is the kind of *temporal behavior* under consideration; this is ordinarily assessed in experiments by using different methods of temporal judgment, or estimation—simultaneity, rhythm, order, spacing, duration, and so on. In several studies I found that duration judgment and other temporal judgments (e.g., serial-order judgment) are influenced differently by the other contextual factors. Duration judgments also depend on whether they are made in a prospective or in a retrospective situation; in other words, whether the person is judging the experienced duration or the remembered duration of a time period (see Block [1979]).

A potential weakness of the tetrahedral model is that the precise ways in which the factors interact is not immediately obvious. Contextualistic models are sometimes criticized for their imprecise accounts of processes, or dynamics. The next section shows how contextualism can clarify and suggest process models of time and mind.

Process Models of Temporal Experience and Behavior

According to the tetrahedral model, the contexture of psychological time is a complex, multifaceted pattern, a result of dynamically interacting contextual factors. The experience we call *time* is a phenomenon that emerges from interactions of these four kinds of changes—changes in characteristics of an experiencer, changes in contents of a time period, changes in activities of the person, and changes in time-related behaviors and judgments. Any complete account of time and mind must consider all of these changes. When any one of these factors changes, the interactions of the others also change.

An examination of the more limited models of other psychological approaches shows clearly how intrinsically incomplete they are. The following critique and comparison will elucidate the major findings and limitations of these other approaches.

Biological Psychology

Consider first a biological approach. Chronobiologists have discovered that endogenous biological rhythms control some time-related behaviors, such as those seen in circadian ("about a day") cycles of activity level.[4] Research involving such species as ground squirrels and honeybees suggests a prototypical model, which is summarized in Figure 4.2. (see Aschoff [1984]; Groos and Daan [1985]). In this model, biological rhythms, which are genetically programmed characteristics of a species, control behavioral rhythms. Neural pacemakers, such as the one apparently located in the suprachiasmatic nucleus of rodents, generate the biological rhythms. These pacemakers are entrained (synchronized) to external cues called *zeitgebers* (literally, "time-givers"). The onset of light is an example of an external cue.

This general biological model seems both necessary and relatively sufficient to explain how cyclical behaviors are regulated. If chronobiologists also were to consider strategies of the organism—such as a person choosing when to sleep and when not to sleep following time-zone shifts that result in jet lag experiences—the model might become completely sufficient as an explanation for circadian and other observed periodicities in behavior.

Some early chronopsychologists tried to extend this model beyond its domain of validity. For instance, in the early part of this century, internal clock theories became influential. One example is Hoagland's (1933) attempt to explain duration experiences solely in terms of biochemical reactions. It is now clear that many time-related experiences and behaviors involve more than the relatively simple processes proposed in the biological models.

Behavioral Psychology

Another limited model is the behavioral one. Behavioral psychologists, working mainly with animals such as pigeons and rats, study the effects on overt behavioral responding of the contents of relatively short time periods, such as those measured in second and minutes (see Roitblat [1987]). Figure 4.3 illustrates a general behavioral model for their research. Investigations into schedules of reinforcement find that animals are sensitive to different interval schedules. On these schedules, the presentation of a reinforcer, or "reward," such as food is contingent upon the organism emitting a specific response, but only after a certain interval has elapsed since the delivery of the previous reinforcer.

A basic question arises: In addition to using any available changes in external stimuli to discriminate intervals, do animals also use an event-independent timer,

---

[4]Chronobiologists use the term *endogenous* to refer to processes within an organism, which I am calling *characteristics of the experiencer*. They use the term *exogenous* to refer to factors outside of an organism, which I am calling *contents of the time period*.

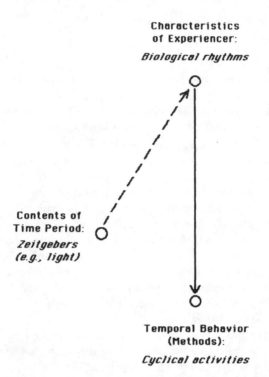

Characteristics
of Experiencer:

Biological rhythms

Contents of
Time Period:

*Zeitgebers
(e.g., light)*

Temporal Behavior
(Methods):

Cyclical activities

Figure 4.2. A general biological model representing the ways in which biological rhythms, entrained by zeitgebers, control cyclical activities.

an internal clock? The answer seems to be *yes*. One specific version of this general model assumes that there is an internal clock consisting of a pacemaker, a switch, and an accumulator (Church, 1984). The pacemaker produces pulses at more or less regularly spaced intervals. One implication of this is that a relatively linear relationship exists between subjective duration and actual duration; this is, in fact, reliably observed. At the start of an external timing signal, the switch engages, allowing pulses to be counted in the accumulator. The switch is needed in order to account for the finding that changes in stimuli (e.g., an interrupted timing signal) may stop the clock (i.e., the accumulation of pulses from the pacemaker). In other words, the internal clock operates like a stopwatch. Associated with the accumulator is a working memory which can briefly maintain a total pulse count. A reference memory stores a record of the approximate number of pulses that elapsed prior to some past reinforcement. On interval schedules of reinforcement, responding increases in probability as a comparison (by a comparator mechanism) of working memory and reference memory reveals a similar number of pulse counts.

This behavioral model can handle the findings of a number of different experiments. The proposed timing system can time various kinds of signals, and so it is quite flexible. However, the general contextualistic model, shown in Figure

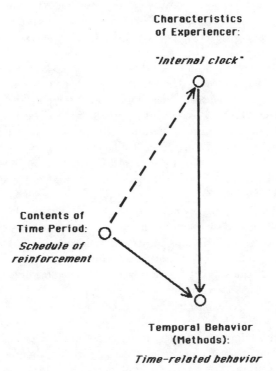

Figure 4.3. A general behavioral model showing the ways in which time-related behavior may be controlled by an "internal clock" in addition to external cues, such as the schedule of reinforcement.

4.1, suggests that this behavioral model is limited because it does not consider other potentially important factors. It fails to include the ways in which activities of the organism during an interval may also influence time-related behaviors. For example, some animals may use an "external clock" by engaging in various progressive or repetitive movements that consume an appropriate amount of time. More fundamentally, whether this animal model can be generalized to studies of time in the human mind seems doubtful. For similar models of human timing, see, for example, Treisman (1963) and Thomas and Weaver (1975).

Early Cognitive Psychology

In the early days of psychology, James (1890) espoused a pragmatic, functionalistic approach to the psychology of time which relied on a decidedly contextualistic world model. Guyau (1890) proposed a more explicit cognitive theory in which several factors influence time judgments (see Michon and Jackson [1984]). Another early example of a nonmechanistic approach is Janet's (1928) discussion of duration as the underpinning of adaptive actions oriented toward irreversible changes. More recently, Fraisse's (1963) influential book, *The Psychology of Time,* contained a mixture of contextualistic and organismic root metaphors. He said, for example, that direct time judgments are "founded immediately on the changes we experience and later on the changes we remember" (p. 234). He also discussed various organic adaptations to change.

Much cognitive research on time, though, relies too heavily on single-factor investigations and explanations. The typical experiment varies the contents of a time period and observes the effect on a single kind of temporal judgment, such as duration judgment. I characterize this approach as *stimulus-based* rather than *context-based,* because the nature of external stimuli occurring during the time period is regarded as the only important factor influencing temporal experiences (Block, 1985b). Ornstein (1969), for example, rejected internal-clock theories of duration experience on the grounds that they could not account for the results of his studies on information processing—specifically, on the complexity of coding of information during a time period. Figure 4.4 illustrates the main process characteristics of Ornstein's hypothesis. Among the contents Ornstein found to be critical were the number of stimulus events and their complexity. He also assumed that people with different prior experiences might encode the same stimuli differently, and his data support the notion that this assumed coding-complexity process influences remembered duration.

Ornstein's theory relies on a mechanistic, computer metaphor—what he called *storage size* in memory. He referred to the storage size taken up by encoded and retrievable stimulus information as determining the remembered duration of a time period, and assumed that if more stimuli occur during a time period, or if the person codes the stimuli in a more complex way, the experience of duration lengthens.

This work was done during a period when cognitive psychology was still firmly in the grips of a mechanistic metaphor—the mind as a digital computer. Thus, although Ornstein's storage-size metaphor displays a few of the characteristics of contextualistic models, it relies on a misleading memory metaphor and fails to handle a more dynamic, contextualistic view of psychological time, such as is suggested by results of subsequent experiments.

Recent Cognitive Psychology

Beginning in the 1970s and early 1980s, other cognitive research emphasizes strategies of information processing. As shown in Figure 4.5, the type and the rate of information dictate a range of strategies for effective information processing. It is then an important step to realize that a person chooses an information-processing strategy or strategies after assessing the contents of the time period. The process picture is now more complete. Among theorists commenting on the psychology of time, Michon and Jackson (1984; Jackson, 1985, 1986; chapters 2 and 3, this volume) have most convincingly made the important point that individual strategies are intimately involved in temporal information processing. In addition to information-processing strategies, time-related strategies might be adopted in special situations. These range from relatively simple ones, such as counting in

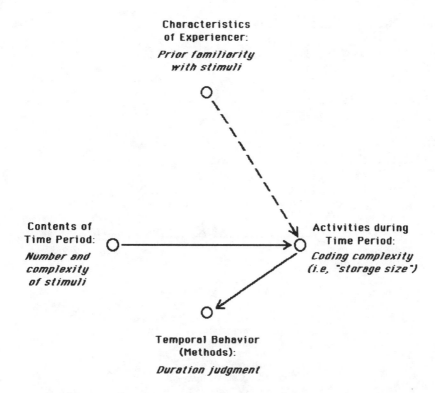

Figure 4.4. Ornstein's storage-size model showing that duration judgment is affected by coding complexity, which is mainly influenced by the number of stimuli and their complexity.

order to try to time an interval, to relatively complex ones, such as constructing a stable temporal perspective.

The information-processing view provides considerable evidence supporting the notion of a continuum ranging from more automatic to more controlled processes. Strategies are prime examples of controlled processes. In terms of the general contextualistic model illustrated in Figure 4.1, interactions of factors shown toward the left half of the figure are those that are relatively automatic—in Michon's terms, they are involved with "timing your mind"—whereas interactions of factors shown toward the right half of the figure are those that are relatively controlled—they are involved with "minding your time" (see chapter 2).

Evidence Supporting a Contextualistic Model

Earlier, I briefly mentioned some of my research. I will now summarize some of my findings on duration experience and show why the findings forced me to adopt a contextualistic model of time and mind. My earliest studies led me to reject

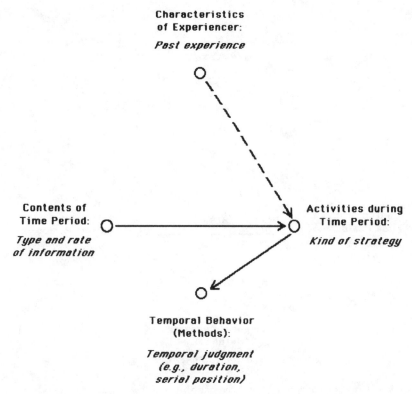

Figure 4.5. A model showing that the kind of information-processing strategy, chosen by a person upon assessing the type and rate of information, influences various temporal judgments.

stimulus-based hypotheses like Ornstein's storage-size hypothesis, which emphasizes the stimulus contents of the time period. It was not until several years later, though, that I began to see the necessity for a context-based approach. Shortly thereafter, other researchers also began to obtain similar evidence favoring a context-based approach. Space does not permit a review of these other studies, but see, for example, Poynter and Homa (1983).

Changes in Context

Block and Reed (1978) found that the remembered duration of a time period lengthens if there are changes in the activities, or strategies, that a person uses to encode the contents of the time period. This finding led us to propose a *contextual-change* hypothesis. This says that remembered duration is a construction based on memory for the overall amount of change in cognitive context during a time period. The quality of the mental events that occur during the time period apparently change memory in a fairly direct way, perhaps as a by-product of particular kinds of information processing. One's subjective reaction to the qualities of the situation is critically important. A person apparently relies on these qualities—what we called the *amount of contextual change*—in order to judge the duration of a time period in retrospect. Although admittedly there is a danger of circularity, if our speculation turns out to be valid, judgment of duration may play a central role in any contextualistic account of memory: "Retrospective judgment of duration may serve . . . as an index of the overall amount of change in cognitive context" during a time period (Block and Reed, 1978, p. 665).

Some recent experiments investigate environmental context as another potential source of contextual change. A major finding is that previous experience in a particular environment—a room containing various objects, an experimenter, and so on—shortens the remembered duration of a time period spent in that environment (Block, 1982). The apparent reason is that there is less psychological change near the beginning of the time period if the person is in familiar surroundings. The previous experience changes the person, which then influences his or her temporal experience.

Interactions

These studies are basically one-factor experiments like those I criticized earlier. But other research also shows that these contextual variables interact to influence remembered duration. Figure 4.6 shows one such interaction between changes in cognitive activities, or strategies, and familiarity with (i.e., changes in) environmental context, one characteristic of the experiencer. The combined interactions of different contextual factors influence time-related judgments. Other findings suggest that certain factors may at times be more salient than others. Which contextual changes are most salient depends on the total quality of the situation.

Other experiments use a different kind of preceding activity and a different kind of task during the time period (Block, 1986). The results show a similar interaction, which suggests that this kind of interaction is found reliably. In addition, though, these experiments enable us to distinguish between two versions of a contextual-change hypothesis. One version involves a rather mechanistic explanation: It says that the number, or variability, of contextual associations is critical. This explanation, which resembles Ornstein's storage-size hypothesis, cannot explain certain findings. Another version, which is admittedly somewhat less specific, says that an overall change in context from the preceding period to the judged duration, operating during the judged duration, produces the interaction. In other words, process explanations of temporal experiences must refer to interactions of the complete constellation of all of the factors I have described. To my knowledge, though, no one has yet thoroughly and systematically explored the complex, four-way interactions predicted by the contextualistic model.

Watched-Pot Phenomenon

Block, George, and Reed (1980) did, however, conduct several experiments in which they varied four factors, as shown in Figure 4.7. In these experiments on the

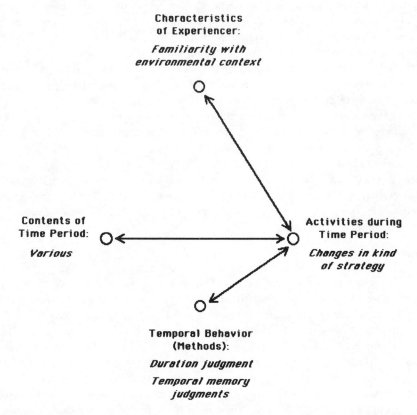

Figure 4.6. A model showing that familiarity with an environmental context and changes in kind of strategy, which operates on presented information, interact also with temporal judgments.

"watched-pot" phenomenon ("a watched pot never boils"), we asked people simply to observe a beaker of water on an electric burner. We told some of them that they would later be asked to judge duration; this is a *prospective* outlook. Others received no such forewarning; this is a *retrospective* outlook. This factor varied the characteristics of the experiencer. For some of the observers, the water boiled; whereas for the others, it did nothing at all. Thus, some of the people experienced changes in the focal contents of the duration. While the observers watched the beaker, we distracted some of them with questions unrelated to the task. So some of the people experienced a change in their activity during the duration. These three factors produced a three-way interaction, the nature of which depended on whether the duration-judgment task involved reproduction or verbal estimation of the duration.

The interactions were too complex to describe fully here, but we did arrive at a better understanding of the watched-pot phenomenon. Consider several possible explanations for the phenomenon. Theories have been expressed in terms like

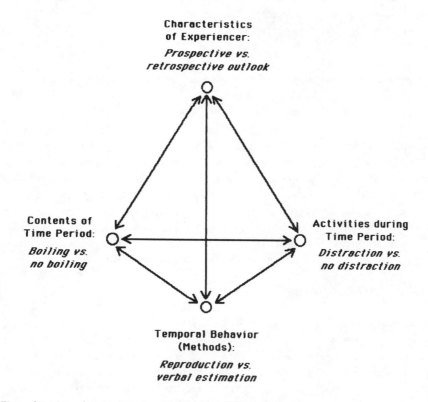

Characteristics
of Experiencer:

*Prospective vs.
retrospective outlook*

Contents of
Time Period:

*Boiling vs.
no boiling*

Activities during
Time Period:

*Distraction vs.
no distraction*

Temporal Behavior
(Methods):

*Reproduction vs.
verbal estimation*

Figure 4.7. A model showing that all four kinds of factors in the general contextualistic model interacted in a series of experiments on the "watched-pot" phenomenon.

attention to the passage of time, waiting, vigilance, and *selectivity of attention.* One factor confirmed by this study as being critical is the degree to which a person attends to the passage of time. Observers in the prospective condition, who we can assume were highly aware of the duration while it was in progress, reproduced it as being longer than did observers in the retrospective condition. This explanation is also supported by the finding that when there were no changes in the focal contents of the duration (i.e., no boiling), observers in the prospective condition reproduced it as being longer if they were not distracted than if they were distracted.

What does it mean, then, to be "attending to the passage of time"? The answer may be that it involves a recurrent awareness of changes in contextual factors during the duration. This awareness seems to be characteristic of a person adopting a prospective outlook on the ongoing situation. Circumstances which are thought to produce the watched-pot phenomenon did not influence reproductions in the expected way for observers in the retrospective condition. The remembered duration of the time period lengthened if there were either changes in the focal contents of the time period (i.e., boiling), changes in the activities of the observer (i.e., a distraction), or both. These findings support, instead, a contextual-change hypothesis on remembered duration like the one I described earlier.

Time-Order Effect

Another major, reliable finding of research using retrospective duration judgment is what is called a *positive time-order effect* (Block, 1985b). With all other factors equal or counterbalanced, the first of two equally long time periods is remembered as being longer in duration than the second time period. This effect plays an important role in the present contextualistic view, as well as in the exploration of the influence of various contextual factors. The positive time-order effect is eliminated if the environmental context prevailing during the second of two durations is changed (Block, 1982). It is also eliminated if changes in emotional context that would ordinarily occur during the first duration occur instead during an experimental task that precedes the first duration (Block, 1978). Thus, the usual finding of a positive time-order effect can be attributed to the greater contextual changes that ordinarily occur during the first of two durations.

Beliefs About Time and Temporal Experiences

My colleagues and I recently designed and conducted a reasonably comprehensive survey of nonscientists' beliefs about time and temporal experiences. We gave our questionnaire to college students in the United States, Malawi, and Japan (Block, Saggau, and Nickol, 1983–1984; Block, Buggie, and Saggau, in preparation). Respondents from all those countries agreed that many different kinds of variables influence duration experiences. In other words, people tend to be "naive contextualists" in the sense that they apparently believe that a wide variety of variables influence the quality of human temporal experiences. If individuals from these different countries develop these similar beliefs as a result of their shared personal awareness of contextual influences on psychological time, we are then left with the suggestion that people become naive contextualists as a result of experiencing certain common phenomena of psychological time, such as the lengthening of experienced duration when one is waiting for something to happen.

This personal awareness of contextual influences on duration experiences is somewhat limited, however. When we asked respondents about how various factors, such as strong emotion, might influence the rate at which time seems to pass, their reported beliefs usually were in accord with evidence from studies using prospective duration judgments. But when we asked respondents how the same factors might influence remembering whether a time period seemed relatively short or long, their reported beliefs frequently were not in accord with evidence obtained in studies using retrospective duration judgments. In general, reported beliefs did not reflect the typical experimental finding that a time period which seems to pass slowly (for whatever reason) is later remembered as being relatively short, rather than relatively long. Thus, the naive contextualism displayed by our respondents may differ considerably from the scientific contextualism revealed by empirical studies of temporal experiences.

Timelessness in Altered States of Consciousness

Now one must ask, what happens if there is little or no change in any of the four contextual factors? In altered states of consciousness, such as meditative and mystical states, some people have what are sometimes called *experiences of timelessness* (Block, 1979). Such an experience is usually ineffable—it is virtually impossible to describe—but one characteristic of it is an altered mode of temporal perspective in which "divisions of time, including divisions into past, present, and future, are [experienced as] . . . illusions. Events do not 'happen' or 'occur,' they 'are'" (LeShan, 1976, p. 92).

A possible explanation of this phenomenon may be that there is a temporary diminution or absence of processes that ordinarily contextualize events and interpretations of events. In other words, we experience timelessness if the momentary environmental and psychological conditions lead us to stop constructing a context for our experiences. We cease to maintain our usual assumptions about time and reality, do not attend much to external events, passively attend to "pure awareness" itself, and only with great difficulty are able to judge the duration of such a time period. Experiences of timelessness may provide an interesting and valuable limiting case for a contextualistic model of time and mind.

Conclusion

The general contextualistic model explored here is a useful tool for viewing both experimental findings and other theoretical models. Biological and behavioral models—those emphasizing biological rhythms and a hypothetical internal clock—are found to be somewhat lacking in generality because of their failure to consider strategies of the time experiencer. Similarly, early cognitive models, such as the storage-size model, fail to detail the numerous interactions of contextual factors which are found in studies of duration experience. Recent cognitive models, which emphasize a person's information-processing strategies, are more complete. The contextualistic model has additional value, however, because it forces us to consider and to appreciate the complex interactions of contextual factors involved as people construct and represent time.

Beyond this heuristic value, we seem to need a contextualistic model in order to understand certain recent findings of experimental psychology. For instance, many experiments (only a few of which were mentioned here) show that changes in context from a preceding activity to a new one during a time period, as well as changes in context during the time period itself, lengthen a person's remembered duration of the time period. Previously proposed models cannot accommodate these findings. They also cannot explain the finding of a reliable positive time-order effect which is influenced by contextual factors. Only a contextualistic framework can accommodate these and other kinds of findings. Beliefs about time which have been reported by nonscientists, as well as experiences of timelessness which have been reported by various people, are also consistent with a contextualistic account.

We should continually question our assumptions about time, as well as the models we implicitly or explicitly adopt. Given our present understanding of time and mind, a contextualistic model will probably continue to be a fruitful one.

References

Aschoff, J. (1984), Circadian timing. In: *Timing and Time Perception,* eds. J. Gibbon & L. Allan. New York: New York Academy of Sciences, pp. 442–468.

Block, R. A. (1978), Remembered duration: Effects of event and sequence complexity. *Memory & Cog.,* 6:320–326.

——— (1979), Time and consciousness. In: *Aspects of Consciousness,* Vol. 1, eds. G. Underwood & R. Stevens. London: Academic Press, pp. 179–217.

——— (1982), Temporal judgments and contextual change. *J. Experiment. Psychol.: Learn., Mem., & Cog.,* 8:530–544.

——— (1985a), World models for the psychology of time. *Teorie & Modelli,* 2, Suppl. 1:89–111.

——— (1985b), Contextual coding in memory: Studies of remembered duration. In: *Time, Mind, and Behavior,* eds. J. A. Michon & J. L. Jackson. Heidelberg: Springer Verlag, pp. 169–178.

——— (1986), Remembered duration: Imagery processes and contextual encoding. *Acta Psycholog.,* 62:103–122.

——— Buggie, S. E., & Saggau, J. L. (in preparation), Beliefs about time in Japan, Malawi, and the United States.

——— George, E. J., & Reed, M. A. (1980), A watched pot sometimes boils: A study of duration experience. *Acta Psycholog.,* 46:81–94.

——— Reed, M. A. (1978), Remembered duration: Effects of event and sequence complexity. *Mem. & Cog.,* 4:656–665.

——— Saggau, J. L., & Nickol, L. H. (1983–1984), Temporary inventory on meaning and experience: A structure of time. *Imagin., Cog., & Personal.,* 3:203–225.

Church, R. M. (1984), Properties of the internal clock. In: *Timing and Time Perception,* eds. J. Gibbon & L. Allan. New York: New York Academy of Sciences, pp. 566–582.

Efron, A., ed. (1982), The Pepper papers: A symposium on the metaphilosophy of Stephen C. Pepper: Root metaphor theory. *J. Mind & Behav.,* Special issue, 3.

Fraisse, P. (1963), *The Psychology of Time.* New York: Harper & Row.

Fraser, J. T. (1975), *Of Time, Passion, and Knowledge: Reflections on the Strategy of Existence.* New York: Braziller.

——— (1982), *The Genesis and Evolution of Time: A Critique of Interpretation in Physics.* Amherst: University of Massachusetts Press.

——— (1987), *Time, the Familiar Stranger.* Amherst: University of Massachusetts Press.

Gibbon, J., & Allan, L., eds. (1984), *Timing and Time Perception.* New York: New York Academy of Sciences.

Groos, G., & Daan, S. (1985), The use of the biological clocks in time perception. In: *Time, Mind, and Behavior,* eds. J. A. Michon & J. L. Jackson. Heidelberg: Springer Verlag, pp. 65–74.

Guyau, J.-M. (1890), *La Genèse de l'Idée de Temps.* Paris: Alcan.

Hoagland, H. (1933), The physiologic control of judgments of duration: Evidence for a chemical clock *J. Gen. Psychol.,* 9:267–287.

Hoffman, R. R., & Nead, J. M. (1983), General contextualism, ecological science and cognitive research. *J. Mind & Behav.,* 4:507–560.

I Ching, or Book of Changes, The, trans. R. Wilhelm & C. F. Baynes. Princeton, NJ: Princeton University Press, 1967.

Jackson, J. L. (1985), Is the processing of temporal information automatic or controlled? In: *Time, Mind, and Behavior,* eds. J. A. Michon & J. L. Jackson. Heidelberg: Springer Verlag, pp. 179–190.

———— (1986), *The Processing of Temporal Information.* Unpublished doctoral dissertation. University of Groningen, The Netherlands.

James, W. (1890), *The Principles of Psychology,* Vol. 1. New York: Henry Holt.

Janet, P. (1928), *L'évolution de la Mémoire et de la Notion de Temps.* Paris: Chahine.

Jenkins, J. J. (1974), Remember that old theory of memory? Well, forget it! *Amer. Psycholog.,* 19:785–795.

———— (1979), Four points to remember: A tetrahedral model of memory experiments. In: *Levels of Processing in Human Memory,* eds. L. S. Cermak & F. I. M. Craik. Hillsdale, NJ: Lawrence Erlbaum, pp. 429–446.

Kaye, H. (1977), Early experience as the basis for unity and cooperation of "differences." In: *Life-Span Developmental Psychology: Dialectical Perspectives on Experimental Research,* eds. N. Datan & H. W. Reese. New York: Academic Press, pp. 343–364.

LeShan, L. (1976), *Alternate Realities.* New York: Evans.

Michon, J. A. (1986), J. T. Fraser's "Levels of Temporality" as cognitive representations. In: *Time, Science, and Society in China and the West, The Study of Time V,* eds. J. T. Fraser, F. C. Haber, & N. Lawrence. Amherst: University of Massachusetts Press, pp. 114–146.

———— Jackson, J. L. (1984), Attentional effort and cognitive strategies in the processing of temporal information. In: *Timing and Time Perception,* eds. J. Gibbon & L. Allan. New York: New York Academy of Sciences, pp. 298–321.

Ornstein, R. E. (1969), *On the Experience of Time.* Harmondsworth, U.K.: Penguin.

Pepper, S. C. (1942), *World Hypotheses: A Study in Evidence.* Berkeley, CA: University of California Press.

Poynter, W. D., & Homa, D. (1983), Duration judgment and the experience of change. *Percept. & Psychophysics,* 33:548–560.

Roitblat, H. L. (1987), *Introduction to Comparative Cognition.* New York: Freeman.

Rosnow, R. L., & Georgoudi, M. (1986), *Contextualism and Understanding in Behavioral Science: Implications for Research and Theory.* New York: Praeger.

Thomas, A. C., & Weaver, W. B. (1975), Cognitive processing and time perception. *Percept. & Psychophysics,* 17:363–367.

Treisman, M. (1963), Temporal Discrimination and the Indifference Interval: Implications for a Model of the "Internal Clock." *Psychological Monographs,* Vol. 79, Issue 576.

Perspectives

Cognition is the act or process of knowing; cognitive psychology is concerned with whatever enables us to know; that is, to learn and to retain what has been learned. The construction of the temporal frame of experience is regarded as an active process, made possible by various cognitive abilities of the mind. When such a construction refers to short-term intervals—the present, the immediate future, and past—human time perception resembles time perception observed in many other species. In contrast, long-term perspectives demand an advanced skill in which the members of our species excel: that of forming symbolic transformations of experience.

Professor Block extends the purview of our concerns beyond the biological, behavioral, and early cognitive models of time perception, which are all of somewhat limited scope. He does so by drawing attention to the significance, for the useful interpretation of any experimental results obtained, of the context in which the experiments were carried out.

In the first three chapters we have been concerned primarily with the thoughts and judgments of experimental subjects. Though Professor Block does not mention it, cognitive psychology has also begun to deal with emotions, but thus far, no compelling analysis of emotions has been developed that employs the information processing paradigm of cognitive science.

Therefore, to join emotion with cognition, we now leave the model of humans as cognitive clocks and enter the rich fray of life lived, with its emotions felt and its passing experienced.

II

Clinical and Depth Psychology

5

Time as Emotion

Jacob A. Arlow, M.D.

Abstract From the beginning of life, duration and sequence of events, the basic elements of time sense, are associated with the affectively dominated experiences of need and gratification. Concepts of reality, causality, and selfhood emerge in the context of mingled time-emotion. Originally the self is the constant element against which change and time are understood. Only later in mental development is this notion superseded by more objective and socially affirmed scientific concepts of time. Although the idea that the flow of time is independent of human experience is discovered, guided, and unified in juxtaposition to the development of selfhood, this notion is repetitively disrupted and time sense distorted because of the close connection in subjective experience between time and emotion. In figures of speech and in fantasy formations, time becomes reified and anthropomorphized to the end that the subjective experience of time may be transformed in keeping with the individual's various conscious and unconscious psychological needs.

Time is a feeling before it is an abstraction. From the very inception of mental life, time and emotion are closely intermingled. According to many current psychoanalytic observers (Zilboorg, 1933; Rangell, 1955, 1967; Zetzel, 1960; Schafer, 1964; Brenner, 1974a,b), the many and varied complex feeling states later recognizable as discrete emotions develop out of fundamental aspects of pleasure or unpleasure. These are inherited biological predispositions, products of the evolution of the human species. It seems clear that affects must have had survival value in the course of evolution. For the most part, what was noxious created unpleasant sensations and was to be avoided. Conversely, pleasurable sensations must have been connected with safe, nurturing experiences worthy of repetition. Freud's two principles of mental functioning (1911) were clearly based on biological assumptions. The earliest drives, he said (1905), were anaclitic; that is, they depended upon the nurturing biological aspect of the pleasure-giving activity.

This primordial linkage between nurturance and affect is inextricably related to the emergence of the sense of time. There are two fundamental components of the sense of time: one is the awareness of duration, the other the awareness of the succession of events. Most observers agree that the beginning of time sense is intermingled with the impression of physiological time duration experienced in the intervals between need and its gratification. At the beginning of life, pleasurable feelings lead to states of quiescence, while unpleasant feelings cause tension, which in turn initiates signals of distress. The beginning of time sense is associated with the awareness of enduring unpleasant, distressing sensations of ungratified needs. Thus, duration is originally experienced as part of a cycle in which need tension is followed by pleasurable relief. Accompanying this relief is the appearance of a set of sensory perceptions later to be identified as the need-satisfying object (i.e., the mother or the primary caretaker). Thus, if feelings of frustration in the interval between need and satisfaction give rise to the sense of duration, it is the ultimate pleasurable experience of gratification that dramatizes the significance of the sequence of events. Accordingly, one can see that, from the very outset of mental life, the two basic components of time sense, duration and succession, and the basic affects of pleasure and unpleasure, are inextricably intermingled.

Out of these elemental feelings, through a process of development and maturation, emerge the more complex and sophisticated affect states we designate as emotions. What is experienced as an emotion consists of three components: a feeling tone, which may be pleasurable or unpleasant; a set of physiological concomitants; and a specific ideational content. Usually the individual is aware of the nature of the mental content of his emotion, but this is not always the case. In fact, evidence from psychoanalytic investigation indicates that very frequently affective states have an important element representing the influence of unconscious mental activity (Arlow, 1977). The beginning of time experience, thus, is linked to affect, and the connection between the two is never really severed.

The implications of this correlation of time and affects are far-reaching indeed. Out of repeated experiences of need, accompanied by unpleasure, followed by gratification, accompanied by pleasure, events begin to fall into a pattern of need, distress, signal, and gratification. The result is an ordering of happenings into a sequence that comes to have meaning. Furthermore, as a result of the ability to interpret each element of the linear sequence as one of a series of signals leading to gratification and pleasure, a more distant signal, for example, the appearance of the mother's face, may serve as a reassuring, temporary substitute for the actual experience of gratification. The child thus has begun to anticipate. Under these circumstances, duration becomes tinged with pleasure, a reassuring calmness pervades the present, with the promise of pleasure in the immediate future. Here is the dawning of the concept of the future. (For children whose early experience has been fraught with prolonged tension and disappointment, the future does not seem quite as promising. They do not console easily.)

In this way, time becomes an important ingredient in the composition of the concept of causality and reality and in the evolution of the concepts of self and object. Piaget (1937) observed that the realization by the infant that his activity (e.g., crying when hungry) is effective in getting him what he wants creates in the infant a feeling of efficacy, generating along with it the consciousness of activity itself as a means of establishing a causative link between his desires and their fulfillment. Out of repeated experiences of need, accompanied by unpleasure, and gratification, accompanied by pleasure, events begin to fall into a pattern of sign and satisfaction, to an ordering of events into a sequence that comes to have meaning. Appreciating the significance of the contiguity of elements in time, of the ordering of sequences, becomes the basic underpinning of primitive concepts of causality. This may be one of the reasons why in later life it is so hard to shed the notion of post hoc, ergo propter hoc.

Calmly anticipating impending gratification is one of the first steps in the development of object constancy (Kris, 1950). The ability of the child to anticipate quietly that the mother will return to relieve his discomfort indicates that she exists as a separate entity, independent of his immediate feelings of distress. The development of object constancy points to the evolution of an organized concept of an "other," functioning independently in time and space. It also marks the beginning delineation of the self.

The evolution of the self and the construction of reality depend upon a number of maneuvers and manipulations correlated with changes in time. Since the processes involved have been studied extensively, only brief reference will be given to some of the elements that pertain to our present subject. Through his activity, the child begins to be able to interpret sequences of events, ultimately leading to the ability to distinguish between what is internal and what is external, between image and percept; that is, between real and unreal. What happens to an image when the eyes are closed or open, or how the image shifts or changes relative to the child's motion, or the difference in sensations between parts of the body coming in touch with each other, as distinguished from sensations experienced when only part of the body is in contact with an object—in each of these instances, the change in sensation is related to an anticipation of the immediate future. To be convincing, the reappearance of the object in consciousness with a change of muscular activity has to be immediate. Its reality is confirmed when it becomes part of a consistently predictable immediate future (Freud, 1915).

The ability to correctly anticipate the immediate future seems to have a reassuring quality for infants. This is a tendency that persists in one way or another in the human individual for the rest of his life. In adult life, when something happens in which the sequence of events fails to conform to the familiar and the immediately predictable, a sense of unease is generated in the observer. Sometimes this gives rise to a feeling of "uncanniness." A reliable anticipation of the sequence of events in the future underlies the stability of the sense of reality. For the child, when a sequence of events does not conform to the established (i.e., familiar), patterns of experience, the inability to predict the immediate future may be felt as unsettling, perplexing, and even frightening. Both his image of a stable, predictable world and of himself in relationship to it are challenged.

Children differ in their capacity to become acclimated to things that are new, unfamiliar, and alien. The classic "stranger anxiety" described by Spritz (1957, 1972) may be the most familiar and striking example of this reaction, which to some extent, enters into the psychology of all individuals. Ostow (1982) has suggested that this inherent tendency toward xenophobia may be one of the root causes of the persistence of prejudice. There exists a wide range of emotions of unpleasant feeling tone connected with confrontation with what is strange and unpredictable. In confronting unaccustomed places and societies, individual reactions may vary all the way from "culture shock" to feelings of strangeness and unreality. Even the coherence of the self may come into question, since many individuals have reported feelings of depersonalization under such circumstances (Arlow, 1966). Whatever fails to conform to the causal ordering of events that man projects onto the external world as its necessary lawfulness, is often experienced as unnatural or supernatural. These are often described as miracles. In literary works and religious chronicles, the reaction of the populace to miracles is expressed in terms of awe and dread.

In evaluating the present against the background of the past and in anticipation of the future, the element of preparation plays an important role. Children react unfavorably to surprises and so do most adults. Preparation for a new and strange experience, however, makes possible anticipatory assimilation of new impressions against a background of what is known, what is familiar, and what has been mastered in the past (Fenichel, 1945). Thus, a child may tolerate or even enjoy frightening stories when, as a result of repeated retelling of the story, he may safely anticipate the successful resolution of even the most unpleasant of situations. Only after the child has established a relatively firm hold on the concepts of cause and effect is he able to be amused by magic tricks, secure in the knowledge that what he is observing is an illusion. At an earlier stage, a child, observing a motion picture run in reverse, finds such an experience perplexing and even frightening. Even adults, who promptly understand that the motion picture is being shown in reverse, will find the experience amusing only in the short run. After a while, a reverse showing becomes boring and irritating. Similar considerations apply to dreams. The total disregard of the accustomed order of events in time is one of the elements that serves to bring about the feeling of unreality and absurdity that we attach to dreams. Time should behave itself and make sense. Thus we can see that, from its inception, the mind processes the data of perception according to the criteria of familiar or unfamiliar, pleasurable or unpleasurable (Freud, 1925; Arlow, 1980).

Turning now from issues of futurity to another dimension of time, one can see how categorizing mental representations according to the criterion of familiarity introduces some precursor of the notion of the past and of memory. A meaningful concept of the past is achieved later in the course of development than the concept of the future. "For memory to acquire the quality of 'pastness,' it is necessary to perceive the fact that the recalled experience can no longer be altered, either by the subject's own action or passively by some intervention from the outside" (Hartocollis, 1983, p. 39). Also, since no new experience can, in fact, ever achieve a complete perceptual identity with a memory of previous experience, it may be assumed that the grouping of mental representations according to pleasure and familiarity involves a set of approximations rather than identity. Accordingly, various memory systems may be established, in which experiences are associatively linked according to criterion of similarity. From early on, then, there is a very human tendency to assimilate experiences metaphorically, a tendency that paves the way for the mental mechanisms of substitution, displacement, allusion, and symbolism. The record of associative linkage, as established in the course of psychoanalytic therapy, furnishes convincing evidence of how concepts and memories are related according to the principle of similarity (Arlow, 1979). Thus, the integration and correlation of the individual's memories of the past tend to be along lines of emotional significance.

There are no receptive sensory structures for perceiving time. "Our direct experience is always in the present and our idea of time comes from reflecting on that experience" (Whitrow, 1980, p. 61). Fraser (1975) pointed out that time is a construct that refers to the perception or imputation of change against some background that is taken to be relatively permanent. The relatively permanent background against which change is perceived is, from its very inception, the self. It is the self of which we are conscious. It is the self which is enduring and yet continuously changing. The self has a history, and it is the self that has a past, present, and future.

The self concept is a difficult one. It is a unique and curious symbol. There is nothing in the external world which corresponds to it. It represents an object, the "I," which is assumed to function in the external world as do all other objects; yet it cannot ever be totally apprehended by our senses, as one can do in the case of other objects, to some of whom we impute selves as well. We think of our selves as residing in our bodies and, to a considerable extent, we incorporate the body image into our concept of our selves. As in the case of other objects, we do not always understand it nor do we always like it, but we feel secure in the knowledge of its history, which we can conjure up in the form of representations, which constitute the memory of an organized past, of a continuity of identity.

The self is a time-bound concept. The sense of continuity and permanence of the self concept is stoutly maintained. Upon recovering from lapses of consciousness, that is to say, a discontinuity of self-awareness, the individual experiences anxiety or confusion. He will most assuredly attempt to reorient himself in time and space, as he reflects on the loss of the sense of self and time. There is an inwardly acknowledged conviction of self-identity, of continuity that parallels but remains forever stronger than the sense of continuity and permanence pertaining to an object. Identity implies that a self or an object is the same entity at different points in time, no matter what changes or transformations may have taken place in the intervening years. Earlier representations of the self may have been repudiated or disavowed, but the sense of connection is hardly ever sundered in an absolute way except for psychotic states. Since no sense of time would be possible without the consciousness of self, it is not surprising that disturbances of the sense of self invariably are accompanied by distortions in the sense of time.

As a consequence of empathic or intuitive processes, a sense of self is projected onto or recognized in others. A sense of selfhood may even be projected onto institutions or nations, endowing them with a sense of continuing collective identity with the illusion of permanence. But all illusions of permanence and grandeur, whether of the self, of others, or institutions, fade as the individual becomes aware of the reality of death. We live in time, and death means the extinction of the self, of consciousness, and, accordingly, of time. By way of compensation and illusory wish fulfillment, the shattered sense of a persistent, unchanging self is projected outward onto objects we hope or assume will persist forever. Thus, the poet endows nature with a consciousness so that it may serve as permanent witness to his passing life and love, the astrophysicist imagines an enduring consciousness observing the cosmic changes, and the religionist posits an all-knowing eternal deity with a self-consciousness not very different from that of His own creations. Nothingness is as inconceivable as death is unacceptable.

As mentioned earlier, our direct experience is always of the present. Far from being a simple matter of direct sensation, even our psychological present must be regarded as the product of an elaborate construction. It is intimately related to our past, since it depends upon our immediate memory, but it also determines our attitude to the immediate future and, in turn, is determined by that attitude. More than that, persistent elements in the mind, sometimes originating as far back as early childhood, exert a dynamic effect upon how sensations are perceived, interpreted, and responded to. These forces take the shape of unconscious fantasies that articulate an unstable compromise of passion, reason, and guilt. Not only do they create the mental set against which the data of perception are apprehended; they also play a significant role in furnishing the ideational content which endows the emotions with their specific character. It will be recalled, as stated earlier, that the emotions are essentially experiences of pleasure or pain of varying intensities, with an ideational content that determines their specific quality. Accordingly, the manner in which time is subjectively experienced is deeply influenced by these various factors.

I should like to illustrate this thesis with several examples, beginning first with two instances of a sense of abnormally extended duration of time. The first patient was a young woman who had entered treatment because of depression. Although she did not know it at the time, the depression was related to her guilt for having been partly responsible for her father's death. As a young adolescent, while visiting wealthy relatives, because she felt humiliated on account of her family's inferior station, she willfully insisted that the weekend visit be terminated and the family return home despite a heavy snowstorm. On the way home, there was an accident, in which her father sustained injuries that ultimately led to his death.

On the Monday following Father's Day, the patient entered and said, "I feel like I haven't been here for a hundred years. I must have been asleep. So much has happened." Since it seemed to me unlikely that anyone would know what it was like to be asleep for one hundred years, I directed her attention to how she had characterized her time experience. In her responses, the patient associated to a fantasy of being Sleeping Beauty, awakened after one hundred years by a prince. Her thoughts turned to Father's Day, the missing father, and to the pleasurable reassurance of coming to the treatment. (In this and the other illustrations to be cited, it is impossible for reasons of space to include a detailed exposition of the rich material and the elaboration of the themes.) What pertains to our purpose here is the fact that the feeling that she had been wakened from a sleep of one hundred years' duration was the conscious fragment of an unconscious fantasy of being Sleeping Beauty, a fantasy which served to change death into sleep, to suspend time, to reverse the roles of the quick and the dead, and at the same time to make possible reunion with the father, who had in reality been removed for all time. The sense of extended duration represented a wishful intrusion into the experience of time of a latent, unconscious thought.

In another instance, misjudgment of time duration was connected to a magical wish to extend time. This patient, a physician, had harbored hostile wishes toward his mother and his younger sister. When he was a year old, his mother left him in the grandmother's charge in order to complete her professional training. When he was four years old, a younger sister was born. She was sickly and required constant care. The patient felt abandoned by his mother and ousted by his rival sibling. When his mother entered menopause, the patient administered hormone injections to alleviate some unpleasant symptoms. Subsequently, she developed cancer of the breast, for which the patient blamed himself. When the mother was in the terminal stages of the illness, the patient had the following experience. He fell asleep wondering if he would receive a call during the night that his mother had passed away. Toward morning, he awoke with a start, feeling that he had long overslept his customary time for rising. He looked at the clock and saw that it was only ten minutes past five. He fell asleep again for what seemed to be a long time and awoke once again with a start. He was sure that he had overslept. Actually, only two minutes had elapsed. He was surprised by his misjudgment of time and fell asleep again. Once again, he awoke with the same anxiety, looked at the clock and again discovered that only a few minutes had elapsed. Each time he reflected, "There's still plenty of time left." In repeating this experience during the session, he thought of the limitations of his mother's time, and realized that this misperception of duration was part of his feeling of guilt and contained the wish that he could grant his mother lots more time and therefore not have to bear the blame for her death. He was also expressing the hope that his own time would be extended and not shortened in retaliation for what was happening to his mother.

The same considerations pertain to the experience of timelessness. In a recent publication, I was able to demonstrate from clinical data how experiences of timelessness in two patients could be viewed as special forms of affective or emotional experience, the specific quality of the experience being determined by the nature of the underlying conscious and unconscious ideational content. In both instances, the sense of timelessness was determined by a wish to extend time indefinitely. Momentarily the wish was experienced as if fulfilled, and this element determined the form in which time was sensed. One patient, for example, experienced timelessness while in a state of exultation over a success which she felt she owed her father. He was ill and she wished to be able to endow him with health and life so the two of them could live happily *ever* after. Another patient, whose fear of retaliation over competitive wishes was experienced in terms of fear of death, never wanted to grow older. When he found himself in positions that evoked in him fear of punishment by mutilation or death, he would defensively experience a sense of timelessness as a form of victory over death (Arlow, 1984). It should be noted in passing that, in both instances, feelings of timelessness were associated with some alteration of the sense of self.

Because of its unchanging character, the past in many ways continues to haunt the individual throughout his life. The past is something which cannot be altered except in fantasy. This realization serves as a serious blow to the infantile sense of grandiosity. It undermines the sense of omnipotence and leads in time to feelings of lowered self-esteem. Not only is it impossible to re-create the pleasures and triumphs of the past; it is also impossible to undo the hurt and the humiliations that have been experienced. Such considerations seem to be central in the psychology of depressed patients. They dwell on a past that they can neither alter nor forget, and they cannot free themselves of that dilemma (Arlow, 1986). It is out of such considerations that modern psychoanalytic theorists (Zetzel, 1960; Brenner, 1974a,b) have conceptualized the major affective components of psychopathology in terms of the time dimension. Depressive affect is related to the past, to the conflicts growing out of the catastrophes of childhood, to the awareness that something bad has happened which cannot be undone. Anxiety, on the other hand, is a dimension that pertains to the future. It is a response to a catastrophe that threatens, a danger that is about to materialize. It involves an estimate on the part of the individual of his capacity to master the impending danger.

Whatever unpleasant changes come *with* time may, by a process of displacement and anthropomorphization, be leveled *against* time. Time then gets to be treated as an agent. It is said to give and to take away. It may heal or destroy. It may flow or stand still. In these images, time is both reified and anthropomorphized. The metaphors employed regarding time represent modes of organizing and conceptualizing experience and fantasy wishes regarding time (Arlow, 1984). Metaphors frequently are outcroppings of unconscious fantasies (Arlow, 1979). There is a rich and voluminous literature representing the metaphoric revolt against the tyranny of time. Time becomes identified with the frustrations imposed by reality, by authority figures and by caretakers. The hostile emotions generated by the conflict with time have been described in many contributions to the psychoanalytic literature (Yates, 1935; Gifford, 1960; Loewald, 1962; Orgel, 1965; Hartocollis, 1972; Kafka, 1977; Jaques, 1982). For all the varied forms this rebellion takes, in the end it expresses a response to the essential impotence of the individual in the face of frustration, in the face of a necessity. Time, thus, becomes one of the chief instrumentalities whereby reality subdues pleasure and on that account, to a certain degree, it is forever after resented.

Out of a sense of despair, frustration, vulnerability, and impotence emerge grandiose, magical fantasies of mastering time. This tendency may take many forms depending upon the emotional disposition of the individual. In fantasy, time may be reversed, slowed down, speeded up, made to stand still, or eliminated altogether, as in apocalyptic visions. The psychological context in which such fantasies appear is rich and varied.

The ones most commonly encountered in literature and in therapeutic work derive from the inevitable defeat of oedipal wishes and the inevitability of death. In the iconography of Western civilization, as well as in our patients' associations, time is most often identified with the father, the unyielding, omnipotent power interposed between forbidden wishes and their realization. Time prevents the young child from ever catching up and being of the same age and marrying the parent who is loved. This unyielding barrier of time becomes one of the sources of romantic love, of the unending quest for the unattainable object. A method for overcoming this barrier is expressed in fantasies of time warp, fantasies of the time experience that make possible the loving union of two people from different generations, temporarily becoming roughly the same age in a world of suspended time. Ultimately, whatever magic spell brings about the warp in time or the standing still of time is broken. The magic world vanishes and the world of time, of reality, and of death is inexorably reestablished. Accordingly, capturing a moment of joyous self-awareness and giving it concrete, if inanimate, timeless form, is how the poet and the artist defy time and try to actualize the illusion of immortality (Arlow, 1984). Even in some of the most objectively founded scientific concepts, it is possible to detect a projection into the far distant future of an unconscious aspiration to continue at least some derivative expression of one's self and of one's mental experience. The appeal of space travel, science fiction, and extraterrestrial communication is part and parcel of this process (Arlow, 1982).

The most definitive retreat from the unpleasant feelings occasioned by the awareness of time takes the form of lapsing into states of timelessness, of attaining a feeling of eternity. The most popular avenue of entry to that domain of bliss appears to be by way of drugs or meditation. Discussions of timelessness usually convey a sense of mystical transcendence. Timelessness has been identified with the so-called "oceanic" feeling, with a sense of merging with the universe that is supposed to characterize certain experiences of religious ecstasy. Most psychoanalysts, following Freud's lead (1930), regard the attainment of a sense of timelessness as a regressive recapitulation of the experience of blissful satiety which the infant enjoyed while falling asleep in his mother's arms. This is a difficult proposition to substantiate. Convincing clinical evidence to support this hypothesis has not been forthcoming.

In my own investigations (Arlow, 1959, 1966, 1982, 1984, 1986), I have come to interpret experiences of timelessness as representing the inclusion into conscious mental life of derivatives of unconscious conflicts. For a variety of motives, the wish for endless duration, for nothing ever to change, is experienced consciously as already fulfilled, much as occurs in the manifest content of a dream. When Freud spoke of the timelessness of the unconscious, what he wished to emphasize was that the wishes of childhood remain persistently active in the mind. They do not change with time (Loewenstein, 1958). These wishes become part of the persistent unconscious fantasies that continue to exert their influence on mental activity. Such unconscious fantasies create the mental set against which the data of sensation are selectively perceived, registered, interpreted, and responded to (Arlow, 1969a,b). According to Bartlett (1932), memory is not a set of static, but, rather, dynamic engrams which is continuously influenced by the changing framework of associations determined by the evolution of our interests and our powers of reason and imagination. In other words, recall is a constructive process and never literally repeats our past experience or activity. Memory, in particular, is affected by the persistent influence on the present of the dynamic unconscious fantasies of the past.

These considerations lead directly to the all-important question of the flux of time. Jaques (1982) raised this issue as his point of departure in considering the question of time. "All the difficulties of understanding the meaning of time are contained in the riddle of the past, present and future. Are they coterminous? Does one flow into the other? Does the future become the present and then the past?" (p. 4). The response to these questions is beautifully expressed by Whitehead (1920): "What we perceive as the present is the vivid fringe of memory tinged with anticipation" (pp. 72–73). All the dimensions of time are represented in the immediate experience. The flux of time is precisely the concern of psychoanalysis. Our direct experience is always of the present. More than any other discipline, psychoanalysis sheds light on the coexistence of past, present, and future. It is the affective component of time, its relationship to the underlying ideational content, that determines which dimension of time will predominate, but all modes are represented.

Loewald (1962) points out that psychic structures must be regarded as temporal in nature. They exist in time and they develop in time. The time concept involved is psychological time, which implies an active relationship between the temporal modes past, present, and future. From the point of view of objective time, what we call the past, as in transference, is not *in* the past, but in the present. It is active in the now. Furthermore, as I have indicated, there is a reciprocal interplay between unconscious fantasy and external stimuli. Current events activate the appearance of derivatives of unconscious fantasies and unconscious fantasy wishes influence how the present experience is apprehended. Thus, in the transference during treatment, the experience and fantasy wishes of the past are foisted upon subjects in the present and are felt as anticipations of gratification in the future. In a clinical study of the phenomenon of premonition, for example, Stein (1953) was able to demonstrate how a repudiated (death) wish of the past, dynamically active in the present, was experienced as an inevitable, dreaded anticipation of the future. In an analysis of experiences of the déjà vu phenomenon, it was possible to demonstrate how a perception of the present, which portended danger in the future, was reassuringly endowed with the quality of an experience in the past, an experience of danger that had been successfully mastered (Arlow, 1959). In this way, psychoanalytic investigations serve to dispel some of the dilemmas associated with the flux of time by demonstrating the influence of all the dimensions of time upon the present moment.

Ontogenetically viewed, the concept that time "flows," independent of human will and experience, is a relatively late development in the psychology of the individual. While the contemplation of time may be fascinating and intriguing, it is also sobering and humbling. The conceptualization of time, as described above, follows upon the conceptualization of our selfhood. In the beginning, our understanding of time is guided and unified in relation to the awareness of one's selfness. Soon enough, however, the grandiose, infantile, emotionally suffused appreciation of the self is subject to disappointment and disillusionment. The ultimate disappointment comes with our appreciation of the finite nature of our relationship to time. With such painful awareness, the tendency to regress to a more personal, subjective experience of time, one that can be altered by wish-fulfilling fantasy, seems irresistible.

References

Arlow, J. A. (1959), The structure of the déjà vu experience. *J. Amer. Psychoanal. Assn.*, 7:611–631.
——— (1966), Depersonalization and derealization. In: *Psychoanalysis: A General Psychology. Essays in Honor of Heinz Hartmann*, ed. R. M. Loewenstein, L. Newman, M. Schur, & A. Solnit. New York: International Universities Press, pp. 456–478.
——— (1969a), Fantasy, memory and reality testing. *Psychoanal. Quart.*, 38:28–51.
——— (1969b), Unconscious fantasy and disturbances of conscious experience. *Psychoanal. Quart.*, 38:1–27.
——— (1977), Affects and the psychoanalytic situation. *Internat. J. Psycho-Anal.*, 58:158–170.
——— (1979), Metaphor and the psychoanalytic situation. *Psychoanal. Quart.*, 48:363–385.
——— (1980), Object concept and object choice. *Psychoanal. Quart.*, 49:109–133.
——— (1982), Scientific cosmogony, mythology and immortality. *Psychoanal. Quart.*, 51:177–195.
——— (1984), Disturbances of the sense of time. With special reference to the experience of timelessness. *Psychoanal. Quart.*, 53:13–37.
——— (1986), Psychoanalysis and time. *J. Amer. Psychoanal. Assn.*, 34:507–528.
Bartlett, F. C. (1932), *Remembering*. Cambridge: Cambridge University Press.
Brenner, C. (1974a), Depression, anxiety and affect theory. *Internat. J. Psycho-Anal.*, 55:25–32.
——— (1974b), On the nature and development of affects: a unified theory. *Psychoanal. Quart.*, 43:532–556.
Fenichel, O. (1945), *The Psychoanalytic Theory of Neuroses*. New York: W. W. Norton.
Fraser, J. T. (1975), *Of Time, Passion and Knowledge*: *Reflections on the Strategy of Existence*. New York: George Braziller.
Freud, S. (1905), Three essays on the theory of sexuality. *Standard Edition*, 7:125–245. London: Hogarth Press, 1953.
——— (1911), Formulations of the two principles of mental functioning. *Standard Edition*, 12:218–226. London: Hogarth Press, 1934.
——— (1915), Instincts and their vicissitudes. *Standard Edition*, 14:109–140. London: Hogarth Press, 1934.
——— (1925), On negation. *Standard Edition*, 19:235–239. London: Hogarth Press, 1950.
——— (1930), Civilization and its discontents. *Standard Edition*, 21: 64–143. London: Hogarth Press, 1961.
Gifford, S. (1960), Sleep, time and the early ego. Comments on the development of the 24-hour sleep–wakefulness pattern as a precursor of ego function. *J. Amer. Psychoanal. Assn.*, 8:5–42.
Hartocollis, P. (1972), Time as a dimension of affects. *J. Amer. Psychoanal. Assn.*, 20:92–108.
——— (1983), *Time and Timelessness*. New York: International Universities Press.
Jaques, E. (1982), *The Form of Time*. New York: Crane Russak.
Kafka, J. (1977), On reality. An examination of object constancy, ambiguity, paradox and time. In: *Psychiatry and the Humanities*, Vol. 2. New Haven, CT: Yale University Press, pp. 133–158.
Kris, E. (1950), Notes on the development and on some current problems of psychoanalytic child psychology. *The Psychoanalytic Study of the Child*, 5:24–46. New York: International Universities Press.
Loewald, H. (1962), Superego and time. *Internat. J. Psycho-Anal.*, 43:264–268.

Loewenstein, R. M. (1958), Panel on psychoanalytic theory of thinking, reported by J. A. Arlow. *J. Amer. Psychoanal. Assn.*, 6:143–153.

Orgel, S. (1965), Of time and timelessness. *J. Amer. Psychoanal. Assn.*, 13:102–121.

Ostow, M., ed. (1982), *Psychoanalysis and Judaism*. New York: KTAV Publishing House.

Piaget, J. (1937), *The Child's Construction of Reality*, trans. M. Cook. London: Routledge & Kegan Paul, 1955.

Rangell, L. (1955), On the psychoanalytic theory of anxiety. A statement of the unitary theory. *J. Amer. Psychoanal. Assn.*, 3:369–414.

———— (1967), Psychoanalysis, affects and the "human core": On the relationship of psychoanalysis to the behavioral sciences. *Psychoanal. Quart.*, 36:172–202.

Schafer, R. (1964), The clinical analysis of affects. *J. Amer. Psychoanal. Assn.*, 12:275–299.

Spitz, R. A. (1957), *No and Yes and the Genesis of Human Communication*. New York: International Universities Press.

———— (1972), Bridges. On anticipation, duration and meaning. *J. Amer. Psychoanal. Assn.*, 20:721–735.

Stein, M. (1953), Premonition as a defense. *Psychoanal. Quart.*, 22:69–74.

Whitehead, A. N. (1920), *The Concept of Nature*. Cambridge : Cambridge University Press.

Whitrow, G. J. (1980), *The Natural Philosophy of Time*. Oxford: Oxford University Press.

Yates, S. (1935), Some aspects of time difficulties and their relation to music. *Internat. J. Psycho-Anal.*, 16:341–354.

Zetzel, E. R. (1960), Symposium on depressive illness. I. Introductions. *Internat. J. Psycho-Anal.*, 41:476–480.

Zilboorg, G. (1933), Anxiety without affect. *Psychoanal. Quart.*, 2:48–67.

Perspectives

Dr. Arlow takes the time-and-mind bull by its emotional horns. He gives reasons, grounded in clinical and theoretical work, why he believes that the human experience of time is not merely influenced by emotions but more fundamentally, arises out of the emotional needs of the individual.

To state his conclusions in Beckett's words, in all our lives we are "waiting for Godot." Early in life, the repeated experiences of waiting and gratification give rise to notions of continuity, temporal ordering, and causation. The idea that time "flows," that it has an "arrow," is a late developmental step in the growth of the individual, being coemergent with the conceptualization of selfhood. Mature experiences then modulate and enrich the constellation of ideas that relate to time, and the individual finds himself carrying the burden imposed and the hope granted by the knowledge of time.

We learned from Dr. Arlow that the early acquisition of the idea that causation is a necessary aspect of reality may be one of the reasons why, in adult life, "it is so hard to shed the notion of post hoc, ergo propter hoc" (p.87).

Dr. Arlow does not speculate on the ontological status of time, or why our notions of time are so stunningly appropriate for the description of natural process. He assumes the existence of an objective temporal matrix, a cosmic phenomenon of some kind in which physical, biological, and psychological processes take place. Human emotions may then be seen as the psychic forces that push us toward the discovery of a man-independent flow whose ultimate nature, perhaps as Kant would have it, must remain forever unknowable.

6

Disorders of Time and the Brain in Severe Mental Illness

Frederick T. Melges, M.D.

Abstract Distortions of time—of sequence, rate, and temporal perspective—are common in psychiatric disorders, and they also can serve to differentiate the major clinical syndromes in psychiatry. Problems with sequence characterize organic brain disease and schizophrenia; rate problems are prominent in manic-depressive illness; and misconstrued temporal perspectives are associated with neurotic-personality disorders. In severe mental illness, distortions of time alter consciousness and impair reality testing.

Distortions of time during acute psychosis appear to be related to underlying derangements of subcortical regions of the brain. In acute schizophrenic psychosis and psychotomimetic drug intoxication, uncanny time experiences, such as déjà vu, are frequent and reflect a confusion of past, present, and future. This telescoping of temporal sequences appears to be related to a dysfunction of limbic-frontal connections mainly in the left cerebral hemisphere. This subcortical dysfunction impairs immediate memory, the coordination of sequences, and goal-directed thinking. Thus, temporal distortions not only appear to be manifestations of psychosis, but also point to basic disturbances of the brain–mind.

The purpose of this chapter is to present an overview of the role of time distortions in psychiatric disorders.

Time distortions may be a manifestation of, or a mechanism for, mental illness. That is, the experience of time distortion may be a manifestation of an underlying disease, an epiphenomenon of a psychodynamic process, or a basic mechanism that is a substantive contributory cause of the nature of the mental illness. For severe mental illness, I favor the latter position because, as detailed previously (Melges, 1982),[1] the experience of time distortion usually precedes the signs and symptoms

---

[1]In *Time and the Inner Future* (1982), research methods and findings about temporal derangements in psychiatric disorders are presented in detail. The concepts and findings summarized here, particularly the first half, are elaborated further in the book.

of these severe psychiatric illnesses. Moreover, manipulation experiments that induce temporal distortions in normal subjects give rise to psychiatric symptoms that closely mimic those found in severe mental illness. Furthermore, the intensity of the time distortions and the psychiatric symptoms have been found to wax and wane concomitantly. Although in the behavioral sciences it is difficult to be sure of causal relationships, the finding that time distortions precede many severe psychiatric symptoms and thereafter show concomitant variation is strongly suggestive of a reciprocal, if not causal, interaction.

Even though a time distortion may be "caused" by an underlying brain aberration, such as an epileptic discharge, or by a social factor, such as sensory deprivation, once it occurs at the psychological level of organization, whatever its originating cause, it alters the form of consciousness. Among animals, an advanced and extensive sense of time, timing, and temporal perspective appears to be unique to human consciousness. Psychological time is more than a perception. It is an important component of self-awareness and plays a key coordinating role for other mental functions. Distortions of perceptual senses, such as vision and hearing, although upsetting, do not wreak as great a psychological havoc as that induced by time distortions. This will become clearer in the sections that follow. Thus, at least for heuristic purposes, I will argue and maintain as my central thesis that the occurrence of time distortions at the psychological level, whatever the underlying cause, alters consciousness and the capacity for testing reality.

Reality testing, as understood in psychiatry, refers to the ability to distinguish fact from fantasy and external events from internal events. Distinguishing fact from fantasy often involves the testing of hunches or predictions by systematic subsequent observations: the present and past are confirmed or disconfirmed by the future. Distinguishing external events from internal events also involves a time process because if the inward registration of external events is temporally disordered, it would be difficult to compare and test memories and expectations with the order and continuity of outside perceptions. Inner events would not reflect the order of external reality.

Defective reality testing is central to the diagnosis of psychosis. Although the *sense* of reality can be altered by unconscious psychodynamic wish-fulfillment factors in normal and neurotic persons (Freud, 1915; Arlow, 1959), I will deal largely with the process or occurrence of defective reality *testing* as seen in psychosis. The central thesis will be explored in terms of (1) how greater degrees of time distortions are associated with greater difficulties with reality testing, and appear to differentiate more severe forms of psychiatric illness from the less severe forms of illness, and (2) by reviewing studies of the relationship of specific kinds of time distortions to psychiatric symptoms that indicate defective reality testing. Subsequently, with regard to severe mental illness, I will conclude with some relevant hypotheses and studies about derangements of temporal information processing in the brain.

Time Problems in Psychiatric Disorders: An Overview

Most of the major psychiatric disorders can be classified as disorders of sequence, rate, or temporal perspective. These temporal factors of psychological time are interrelated with each other, and their relationship influences the perception of clock time. Sequences (successive events perceived by the mind) are related to the rate of mental time. The latter influences the perception of clock time. Although contextual factors and anticipation also determine the perceived rate of mental time, in general it can be said that the shorter the intervals between successive mental events, the faster is the rate of mental time; clock time, then, seems to be passing by slowly. By contrast, the longer the intervals between successive events, the slower is the rate of mental time, and clock time is perceived to be passing by quickly. Temporal perspective refers to the larger sequences of past, present, and future—to the awareness of broad temporal horizons.

Table 6.1 outlines a hierarchy of time problems associated with the major psychiatric disorders. Sequence difficulties are the most disruptive of mental functioning because the order of successive perceptions and thoughts is disrupted. Sequence problems commonly give rise to disturbances of rate and temporal perspective. Although rate variances do not usually alter the order of successive events, rate problems can induce temporal perspective problems by influencing the span of attention given to the past, present, or future. These problems with temporal perspective can occur alone, without sequence or rate distortions.

Table 6.1. Hierarchy of Time Problems and Psychiatric Disorders

Time Problem	Psychiatric Disorder
Sequence	Organic Brain Disease
	Schizophrenia
Rate	Manic-Depressive Illness
Temporal Perspective	Neurotic-Personality Disorders

Degrees in the severity of defective reality testing in mental illness correspond to this hierarchy of time problems; that is, sequence problems occur in the most severe forms of mental illness, such as organic brain disease and schizophrenia, in which reality testing is often impaired. Rate problems are common in manic-depressive illness in which reality testing is defective mainly during extreme alterations of rate. Temporal perspective problems are associated with neurotic and personality disorders in which there is no pervasive loss of contact with reality. Thus, the defective reality testing of psychosis occurs predominantly with the sequence problems of organic brain disease and schizophrenia, occasionally during extreme alterations of rate in manic-depressive illness, and rarely with the temporal perspective problems of neurotic-personality disorders.

The nature of these disorders and the corresponding time problems will become clearer in the sections that follow. Psychiatrists are familiar with the time disorientation of organic brain disease, such as is seen in delirium or dementia, where the person has difficulty orienting himself to clock and calendar time. In organic brain disease, these severe problems with sequence stem from impairment of short-term and long-term memory such that the recall of simple sequences often is out of order; for example, ABCD may be recalled as BDCA or merely AD. Such pervasive problems with sequence produce secondary problems with rate and temporal perspective. When the brain is impaired by diffuse chemical or neuronal imbalances, all components of time sense—sequence, rate, and temporal perspective—go awry. This indicates that an intact brain is necessary for the temporal organization of thinking and behavior. Patients with global disease of the brain lose their moorings in time. Whereas this is common knowledge in psychiatry, the role of time distortions in other forms of mental illness described below presents a new frontier of inquiry.

Sequence Problems in Schizophrenia

Whereas organic brain disease is characterized by pervasive problems with ordering events, a prominent feature of schizophrenia is *intermittent* difficulty with keeping track of goal-relevant sequences. In organic brain disease the sequences of external reality may not be remembered or are recalled out of order; in schizophrenia the order of the events is usually recalled correctly, without marked disorientation to calendar time, but they are poorly reorganized and timed in relation to reaching a goal or making a plan. Unlike the problems with short-term and long-term memory in organic brain disease, the schizophrenic patient's difficulty is largely with immediate memory functions related to keeping track of sequences relevant to a goal. These symptoms appear off and on, intermittently, as the patient gets worse or better.

As I shall propose later, tracking difficulties probably underlie most of the core signs and symptoms of schizophrenia, ranging from confused thinking to paranoid reactions and hallucinations. Although there are different types and degrees of schizophrenia, the actively psychotic, acute schizophrenic patient has marked difficulties with sequencing, often accompanied by uncanny and mystifying experiences of timelessness, making the person feel as if he were in a waking dream.

Much of my own research has focused on the relationship between different degrees of tracking problems and the various signs and symptoms of psychosis seen in schizophrenia. The research called for the study of covarying changes of time distortions and psychotic symptoms. Patients and experimental subjects were followed longitudinally. Measurements involved systematic inventories and cognitive tests. When substantial and significant change correlations were found in clinical patients, we tested the relationships by inducing time distortions in normal subjects through the use of tetrahydrocannabinol (THC), an active ingredient in marijuana and hashish. Tetrahydrocannabinol is a potent distorter of time sense, and at high doses, in the range that is found in hashish, it induces marked tracking difficulties. The induction of tracking difficulties in normal subjects allowed us to test whether the time distortions were fundamentally involved in the precipitation of psychiatric symptoms. In these manipulation experiments, we found that the tracking difficulties slightly preceded the emergence of schizophreniclike symptoms. Thereafter there was a substantial covariation of the intensity of the tracking difficulties and the symptom under study, often yielding change correlations greater than 0.70. Although in some instances I will present a blend of research findings and clinical experience, most of what is presented below not only reflects our systematic studies of psychiatric patients but also has been confirmed by the manipulation experiments that enabled us to make stronger inferences about the fundamental relationship between time distortions and psychotic symptoms.

In clinical practice, classical schizophrenia is diagnosed by Bleuler's (1911) four A's (loosening of *a*ssociation, incongruity of *a*ffect, *a*mbivalence, and *a*utism) in conjunction with Schneider's (1959) first-rank symptoms of schizophrenia, such as *h*allucinations, *i*deas of influence, and *t*hought broadcasting (mnemonic: HIT). If a person has the four A's as well as HIT, psychiatrists would diagnose him as schizophrenic.

Of the Bleulerian four A's, loosening of association means that the schizophrenic patient's speech wanders off the point with irrelevant non sequiturs. In Bleuler's description, "associations lose their continuity" and the "most important determinant of the associations is lacking—the concept of purpose" (1911, pp. 14–15). This lack of goal-directedness with irrelevant words and phrases is the crux of the schizophrenic thought disorder. Simply stated, the schizophrenic patient does not make sense. Loosening of associations in speech has been found to be related to deficiencies in keeping track of goal-relevant sequences (Melges, Tinklenberg, Hollister, and Gillespie, 1970a). Cognitively, there is an inability to coordinate sequences toward a goal. The information is available but it is mistimed. Words and phrases are not brought in at the right time in order to make a point; as a result, sentences are derailed from the topic at hand. The narrative sequences of schizophrenic speech lack coherence and hierarchical organization (Hoffman, Stopek, and Andreasen, 1986). Subjectively, difficulties with tracking sequences are often reported by schizophrenic patients as follows: "I frequently lose my train of thought"; "thoughts slip out of my head before I can quite grasp them"; and, "I forget the first part of a sentence by the time I get to the last part." If a person cannot remember what he just said or what he intends to say, his thoughts are apt to wander haphazardly off the point, giving rise to loosening of associations in his speech. Because of his tracking difficulties, the schizophrenic patient often withdraws into himself because of his problems with conversing with other people (Chapman, 1966).

Difficulties with tracking sequences over time have been found to be related to problems with immediate or "working" memory. This is not merely an immediate memory dysfunction since the sequences are capable of being recalled; what happens is that they are not temporally integrated with a goal at the right time. Rather than just a lapse of memory it is the mistiming of sequences. The schizophrenic patient's immediate memory appears to be vulnerable to distraction (Lang and Buss, 1965; McGhie, Chapman, and Lawson, 1965; Braff, Callaway, and Naylor, 1977; Saccuzzo and Braff, 1981). Vulnerability to distraction appears related to the schizophrenic's inability to maintain an anticipatory set (Shakow, 1963) or incapacity to shift sets with changing circumstances such that he perseverates on previous material after the subject has changed (Weinberger, Berman, and Zec, 1986). As outlined later, these tracking difficulties appear to stem from deficient information processing in the left cerebral hemisphere of the brain (Wexler, 1980; Braff, 1986; Weinberger et al., 1986). A cardinal manifestation of tracking difficulties is blocking in which there is an absence of all thought for 10 to 120 seconds. Blocking may be related to a minor seizure in the left cerebral hemisphere.

Incongruity of affect, which is the second key Bleulerian diagnostic sign, means that the schizophrenic patient's emotional expressions are often at odds with the temporal context of the situation. For example, the patient may giggle while talking about depressing or frightening events. Tracking difficulties may account for these incongruities of affect since the patient is responding to thoughts and feelings that are not relevant to the temporal context of the interpersonal situation (Hamilton, 1974).

Schneider's (1959) first-rank (HIT) symptoms of schizophrenia are conspicuous signs of psychosis; most people would associate them with being "crazy." They would recognize auditory hallucinations (hearing voices speaking when no one is around), feelings of being influenced by alien unseen forces (e.g., being physically touched or moved), and thought-broadcasting (transmitting one's thoughts to others without speaking, or having thoughts inserted into one's mind by outside forces), as experiences indicating loss of contact with reality. Although these experiences may occur occasionally in milder form in other types of mental illness, they are more frequent and severe in acute schizophrenia. These first-rank symptoms represent a confusion of inner and outer events. Research has shown that these symptoms of inner–outer confusion are correlated, and that they wax and wane, with temporal disorganization (Melges and Freeman, 1977). The covarying changes are particularly robust for difficulties with tracking sequences. One explanation for the uncanny experiences is that a confusion and telescoping of the larger sequences of past, present, and future gives rise to inner–outer confusion. What is inside the person (past memories and future expectations) becomes confused with what is outside the person (the effects of present perceptions). Events diffused in time become dislocated in space.

The progression of stages of psychosis is related to temporal disorganization. As the patient experiences increasingly severe psychotic symptoms, there are greater degrees of the temporal disintegration of sequences (Table 6.2; Melges, 1982, p. 135).

Table 6.2. Stages of Acute Schizophrenic Psychosis

Degree of Sequence Problems	Associated Psychotic Symptoms
Mild	Psychedelic Experiences
Moderate	Loosening of Associations
Severe	Depersonalization
Extreme	Delusional Ideation
	Paranoid Connectivity
	Inner–outer Confusion

Early and mild degrees of sequential problems appear to highlight and prolong the sense of the present since the present becomes somewhat disconnected from the past and future. This heightened and prolonged present appears to give rise to psychedelic experiences in which thoughts and perceptions seem to loom in the mind with an unusual vividness and freshness, as though never experienced before (Melges, Tinklenberg, Hollister, and Gillespie, 1971). As further difficulties develop with tracking sequences, loosening of associations emerges in the person's speech. As the sequences of the past, present, and future become disconnected and discontinuous, depersonalization emerges. That is, as the person loses the time line of past, present, and future through which he has become familiar with his self, he experiences the self as strange, unfamiliar, and depersonalized (Melges, Tinklenberg, Hollister, and Gillespie, 1970a). Finally, when past, present, and future become indistinguishable, florid psychotic symptoms appear, such as delusional ideation, paranoid connectivity, and inner–outer confusion (Melges and Freeman, 1977).

Delusions, characterized by the conviction that there is a conspiracy directed against one's self, are common in paranoid schizophrenia. These patients experience a vast array of events as connected to them personally. This paranoid connectivity has been found to be related to the patient's inability to distinguish past, present, and future (Melges and Freeman, 1975). Sequences coalesce to become experienced as uncanny coincidences, with these coincidences then forming the nidus around which paranoid ideas grow (Melges, Tinklenberg, Deardorff, Davies, Anderson, and Owen, 1974; Melges, 1976). The imputation of a plot or masterminded scheme centering on the self comes from the experience of many events, ordinarily separated by clock time, coming together in a timeless *now* into which past and future have telescoped.

The underlying causes of the schizophrenic patient's problems with tracking sequences and related temporal aberrations are not precisely known. But recent studies of the biochemical and brain physiology of schizophrenia are beginning to unravel this problem. Some of these findings will be summarized in a later section on possible brain mechanisms. It is of interest that the phenothiazine drugs, which are useful in treating schizophrenia, improve the tracking difficulties and the temporal span of comprehension (Braff and Saccuzzo, 1982; Braff, 1986).

Rate Problems in Manic-Depressive Illness

Patients with manic-depressive illness have periodic one- to nine-month episodes of actually either going too fast or too slow. Compared to their normal states, their speech and locomotor activity is either much faster or much slower. In the manic phase, thoughts and actions are speeded up and the emotions are usually euphoric, with unbridled optimism about the future. By contrast, in the depressed phase, thoughts and movements are slowed down, the emotions are morose and sad, and the future is viewed as hopeless. Severe hopelessness commonly begets thoughts and plans of suicide. Compared to judgments of clock time during normal periods, time perception tests have shown that in mania, a fast internal clock ticks away, whereas in depression a slow internal clock moves sluggishly along. In mania, because of the accelerated internal rate, future time perspective is overly extended and the patient is bursting with diverse plans and images. In depression, because of the slow rate, future time perspective is often foreshortened and the patient feels devoid of options and plans.

Although manic patients may have a "flight of ideas" in which they jump discursively from topic to topic, their speech has greater temporal coherence of hierarchically organized sequences than that of classical schizophrenic patients (Hoffman et al., 1986).

Extreme acceleration of mental rate as seen in acute mania is accompanied by defective reality testing. The reason may be that a greater number of internal events become associated with one another and remain unchecked by external events than would occur at a normal rate of mental events. Conversely, in severe depression, extreme slowing of mental events may have the opposite effect: there is a paucity of internal events relative to the registration of external events. This predominance of external events may give rise to defective reality testing because external circumstances, compared to normal periods, seem to control the patient.

Manic-depressive illness is thought to be an inherited disorder of biological rhythms (Wehr and Goodwin, 1983, p. 3). The drug lithium carbonate, which is highly useful in treating mania, has been found to slow biological clocks in plants and humans. By contrast, the tricyclic antidepressant drugs, useful in treating depression, have been found to accelerate internal rate.

Temporal Perspective Problems in Neurotic-Personality Disorders

Temporal perspective problems refer to an overfocusing on the past, present, or future and are common in neurotic and personality disorders. The hallmark of neurosis is anxiety, or anxiety tinged with guilt or sadness. Patients with personality disorders exhibit ingrained patterns of interacting with other people such that they frequently get in their own way, or obstruct the social discourse of others. Neurotic-personality disorders do not have marked problems with sequence or rate and rarely show marked defective reality testing. However, as we shall see, they tend to frame one's temporal perspective in peculiar ways.

In anxiety neurosis, the patient commonly overfocuses on past experiences of being rejected or controlled; he also tends to avoid or even dread the future for fear that his past experiences will recur. In obsessive-compulsive neurosis, the patient is consumed with fears that something catastrophic will happen in the future, such as being humiliated for being found less than perfect. He often performs magical rituals, such as hand-washing, in order to ward off such future threats. He is overfocused on the future and is not comforted by present events that disconfirm his dire predictions. The antisocial personality, seen in devil-may-care or criminal individuals, is overly focused on the present and disregards future consequences to himself or to others. He seizes the moment for impulsive acts and takes risks that by normal people are deemed heedless of the past or future.

The "splitting" (rapid switches between love and hate) in borderline personality disorders may also be related to difficulties with integrating the continuum of past, present, and future (Hartocollis, 1978). That is, depending on whether other people are perceived as nurturant or nongratifying, the borderline patient becomes consumed by his present emotional state without integrating other past or anticipated interactions with significant other persons.

For the most part, neurotic-personality disorders are treated with various types of psychotherapy. Psychodynamic and family psychotherapy can be conceptualized as a relearning process that corrects hidden connections between interpersonal sequences of the present and those of the past or anticipated future. Present sequences lasting minutes to hours are connected with longer sequences of days, weeks, months, years, or decades (Breunlin and Schwartz, 1986). Through a circular interactive process with the therapist, the patient's schemas of temporal perspective and the ways in which he misconstrues events are gradually revised. The patient and therapist create a dialectic narrative of new connections, assigning different meanings to the patient's life story (McHugh and Slavney, 1986, p. 126).

The Brain and Disorders of Time

We will now turn to an exploration of possible brain factors that may underlie these temporal distortions, particularly those seen in psychotic illnesses.

Through an appeal to phylogenetic evolution, MacLean (1973) shows that the human brain contains three brains: reptilian (such as that of a snake alive today), paleomammalian (such as that of a dog), and neomammalian (such as that of a primate). Parallel to this evolutionary development there have also been progressive increments in the capacity to extend sequences into the past and future, thus advancing powers of anticipation that culminate in the human brain. Although the human brain works as a whole through the interplay of its diverse parts, each of its evolutionary brains appears to subserve different temporal functions as related to certain psychiatric disorders. This general proposal may be elucidated with the help of Figure 6.1.

In terms of this interpretation of brain structure, the rate and rhythm problems of manic-depressive illness may reside largely in the reptilian brain, which contains the pacesetting arousal functions of the reticular activating system, as well as the regulators of biological rhythms, such as the hypothalamus and suprachiasmic nucleus. The sequence problems of schizophrenia may correspond to dysfunctions of the paleomammalian (dog) brain, which includes the limbic-prefrontal lobe functions that subserve emotions, immediate memory, and moti-vational states related to sex and aggression. The temporal perspective problems of neurotic-personality disorders can probably be related to difficulties with the neomammalian brain, which contains the human higher cortical functions of the cerebral hemispheres and the frontal cortex. That is, temporal perspective is probably constructed from the interplay of left (dominant) hemisphere powers of language, right (nondominant) hemisphere visual–spatial patterns, and frontal lobe goal-corrected feedback processes (Luria, 1980).

Although these correspondences of problems with rate, sequence, and temporal perspective are roughly in accord with neuropsychological brain research as reviewed by Mesulam (1985), the temporal integration of these various components of the brain involves a much more complex process. The uncanny time distortions of severe mental illness likely occur when the brain's component functions become desynchronized with one another.

Before addressing the issue of some of these perturbations, it should be emphasized that the brain functions as a whole. It does so in ways that are difficult to envision by traditional analogies with telephone switchboards or the serial operations of the digital computer. Modern integrative models of the brain emphasize parallel and simultaneous temporal processes. For example, it appears that sensory input is widely distributed throughout the brain in the form of temporal frequencies and rhythmic patterns of electrical waves that, after reinforce-ment and the learning of appropriate responses, become diffusely reactivated in later similar situations with specialized brain areas taking the lead (John, 1976; Olds, Mink, and Best, 1969). The temporal frequencies may be encoded as memories in the form of holographic patterns throughout the brain (Pribram, 1977). These patterns or images may generate expectancies that constitute tests for feedback and correction of plans of action (Miller, Galanter, and Pribram, 1960; Powers, 1973; Young, 1978; Grossberg, 1980). Although certain areas of the brain are key way stations for the processing of certain kinds of information, such as the occipital cortex for vision, the brain has considerable plasticity and redundancy (e.g., visual information is widely distributed, even to the frontal cortex). Moreover, there is no

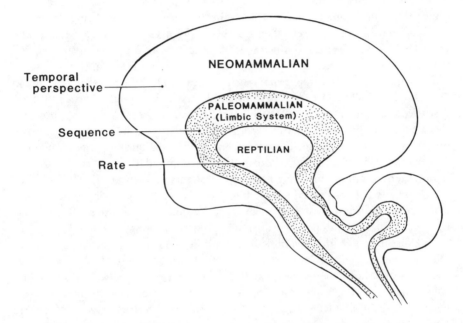

Figure 6.1. Diagram of organization of three evolutionary brain types which have become part of the human brain (taken with permission from MacLean [1973, p. 9]). Slightly modified to include proposal about different time functions of rate, sequence, and temporal perspective subserved by each of these evolutionary brains.

one "timing center" in the brain, and the brain as a whole can be considered, to use J. T. Fraser's (1975, pp. 235ff) phrase, the "organ of time sense."

Nevertheless, neuropsychological studies indicate that certain parts of the brain appear to make different predominant contributions to the temporal harmony of the mind (for review, see Melges [1982, pp. 11–12, pp. 24ff]). At this point, I will briefly highlight some of these relationships (see Figure 6.2).

The hippocampal formations (part of the subcortical limbic system) play a key role in immediate memory and the tracking of goal-relevant sequences. It is likely that the so-called "mental present" and "stream of consciousness" are related to hippocampal functions, although Flor-Henry (1976) marshals evidence that the "seat of consciousness" extends from the hippocampus and related limbic structures to the left prefrontal cortex. In this regard, there is much research that points to the hippocampal-limbic-prefrontal cortex of the left hemisphere as being primarily involved in schizophrenia (Flor-Henry, 1969, 1976; Gur, 1979; Wexler, 1980; Gruzelier, 1983; Bogerts and Meertz, 1985; Braff, 1986). Seizures in this region, which can be considered as the left paleomammalian (limbic) brain, give rise to acute symptoms of schizophrenia, such as tracking difficulties and auditory hallucinations (Bear and Fedio, 1977; Trimble and Perez, 1982; Sherwin, 1982). A particularly elegant study by Weinberger, Berman, and Zec (1986) indicates that this area (especially the left dorsolateral prefrontal cortex) in schizophrenic patients did not show the normal increase in cerebral blood flow during periods when the patients were challenged to perform tasks that required them to track and sort information according to changing categorical sets. Moreover, the left limbic-prefrontal area has been found to have higher levels of turnover of dopamine, which is an activating neurotransmitter involved in the impaired attention and information processing of schizophrenia (Reynolds, 1983; Matthysse, 1978).

Thus, it appears that the difficulties with keeping track of sequences in acute schizophrenia are related to dysfunction of the left hippocampal-limbic-prefrontal area. Yet this should not imply that this is the only area involved. The detailed studies of Luria (1980, pp. 246–259) of patients with damage to more anterior portions of the frontal lobe suggest striking similarities to characteristics of chronic schizophrenia, such as irrelevant associations when carrying out a serial narrative plan, perseveration, loss of drive and initiative, and flattening of affect (emotions). From a temporal standpoint, it is of interest that the frontal lobes, which are distinctly more highly developed in man compared to other primates, appear to be involved in the suppression of the interference of previous actions on a current task, the comparison of the effects of action with an intended plan of action, and choice among several reasonable possibilities (Milner and Teuber, 1968; Hecaen and Albert, 1975; Luria, 1980). In particular, the frontal lobes are involved in freeing the person from immediate control of stimulus-response from environmental input for delay of actions and comparison of possibilities (Lhermitte, 1986; Milner and Petrides, 1984; Mesulam, 1986). These future-oriented frontal lobe feedback processes related to intentionality are important for the temporal organization of plans of action, which often are impaired in schizophrenia, perhaps as secondary

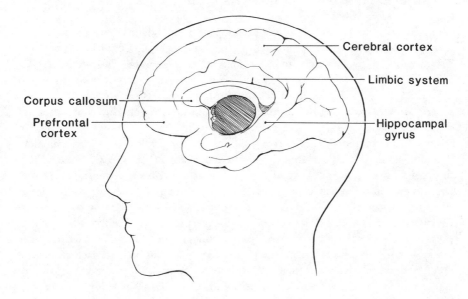

Figure 6.2. Diagram of some key areas of temporal integration in the human brain.

manifestations of the subcortical limbic-prefrontal disturbances (Melges, 1982, pp. 146–147).

Moreover, schizophrenia appears to affect the language functions of the left cerebral hemisphere, which is dominant for speech in right-handed individuals. Schizophrenic speech is characterized by frequent derailments, loosening of associations that are irrelevant to an ongoing narrative, and poor editing of malapropisms that normal persons correct before continuing with further speech (Hoffman et al., 1986). It is probably no accident that the most common type of hallucinations in schizophrenia are of the auditory type (Asaad and Shapiro, 1986). The interpretation of auditory signals, unlike visual and proprioceptive inputs, requires higher powers of the temporal analysis of frequencies that must be collated through time. Efron (1963a) proposed that language depends on the capacity of the left cerebral hemisphere for the discrimination of temporal signals. This is particularly true for the temporal ordering of sequential consonants while the right cerebral hemisphere is providing background connecting links in the form of vowels (Luria, 1980, p. 380).

Although there are overlapping functions and redundancies, the left and right hemispheres appear to have different temporal modes of cognition (Levy and Trevarthen, 1976; Ben-Dov and Carmon, 1976; Gazzaniga and Volpe, 1981; Sperry, 1982). The left cerebral hemisphere is primarily involved with linear and sequential analysis of functional relationships, whereas the right cerebral hemisphere appears to process information simultaneously for the comparison of visual–spatial patterns (Levy and Trevarthen, 1976; Luria, 1980, pp. 374–884). In terms of the temporal perspective functions proposed for the neomammalian (human) brain, the left cerebral hemisphere appears to order past, present, and future in linear sequences, typified by linguistic analysis. The right cerebral hemisphere, on the other hand, "sees" elements of the past, present, and future as superimposed whole patterns. If this is a correct description, it implies that the construction of temporal order beyond the mental present (Jackson, 1986; Michon, chapter 2, this volume) is primarily a left hemisphere function, whereas the visual–spatial images of the right hemisphere are more immediate, lack sequential order, and are relatively timeless. With this background, we are now prepared to explore further possible neurological mechanisms for some uncanny time experiences associated with psychotic symptoms and abnormal alterations of consciousness.

Déjà Vu, Depersonalization, and Dissociation

Déjà vu, depersonalization, and dissociative states commonly are associated with uncanny disruptions of the normal flow of experiential time and feelings of unreality. Although these experiences can occur in normal and neurotic individuals as the result of unconscious wishes to alter time (Arlow, 1959, 1966), this discussion will explore possible brain mechanisms for their occurrence in more severe forms of neuropsychiatric illness.

Déjà vu (from the French, "already seen") refers to the experience of current external perceptions as having occurred before in exactly the same way. Although this occasional reduplicative experience is normal, particularly during adolescence and young adulthood, its frequent occurrence is commonly seen in acute schizophrenia and temporal-lobe epilepsy. Efron (1963b) has explained déjà vu on the basis of dysynchrony between the normal exchange of information transmitted rapidly via the corpus callosum between the right and left cerebral hemispheres. His basic proposal is that the left (dominant) hemisphere, which has greater powers of temporal discrimination compared to the right, receives the same information twice. Normally, input from the right hemisphere is not noticeably delayed in crossing over to the left hemisphere, but in déjà vu it is delayed by a minor seizure in the lower brain near the corpus callosum, usually in the right hemisphere. The delayed information coming from the right hemisphere is relatively unlocalized in time and is experienced as happening somewhere before at an unspecified time. In support of this proposal is the finding that déjà vu and illusions of familiarity are predominantly produced by the electrical induction of seizures in the right, rather than the left, cerebral hemisphere (Mullan and Penfield, 1959). Also, in patients with temporal-lobe epilepsy who report déjà vu, the right hemisphere usually has the predominant epileptic focus.

Depersonalization refers to feelings of strangeness about the self and, in acute mental illness and psychotomimetic drug intoxication, to the fragmentation of identity. Depersonalization has been found to covary substantially with discontinuity of the past, present, and future (Melges, Tinklenberg, Hollister, and Gillespie, 1970b; Melges, Tinklenberg, Deardorff, Davies, Anderson, and Owen, 1974; Freeman and Melges, 1977). That is, as the person loses the time line of past, present, and future through which he has become familiar with the self, his sense of identity becomes vague and unfamiliar. This lack of holistic grasp of temporal continuity may stem from dysfunction of the right hemisphere, which commonly is associated with feelings of self-alienation (Schenk and Bear, 1981). Moreover, a lack of synchrony between the two hemispheres may exist so that temporal perspective is poorly constructed. This dysynchrony may relate to the common depersonalized experience of a "participating self" being watched by an "observing self"; that is, as a form of split-brain consciousness, the desynchronized cerebral hemispheres may be watching one another (Schenk and Bear, 1981; Mesulam, 1981).

Dissociative states, such as fugues, psychological amnesias, and multiple personalities, are puzzling psychiatric disorders in which an alternate mode of consciousness takes control over the individual. These patients commonly report long "time gaps" in their awareness. One explanation is that interhemispheric dysynchrony is induced in these patients by spontaneous or neurochemical hypnotic mechanisms thought to be related mostly to the right (nondominant) hemisphere. In this regard, Mesulam (1981) has found that dissociative states and multiple personalities more often develop in patients whose predominant brainwave abnormality is in the nondominant temporal lobe; sometimes the change in personality is accompanied by a change in handedness (Schenk and Bear, 1981).

Time Telescoping and Inner–Outer Confusion in Acute Psychosis

Time telescoping refers to the indistinction between past, present, and future. As discussed, it is common during the acute stages of psychosis and psychotomimetic drug experiences, and is substantially correlated with symptoms of inner–outer confusion such as thought-broadcasting and hallucinations (Melges and Freeman, 1977). That is, when past, present, and future are indistinguishable, events inside the person (memories and expectations) become confused with outer events (present-time perceptions).

What might be happening in the brain to cause this time telescoping? How does the brain distinguish the *now* from the *then*? This question, as Lord Brain (1963) emphasized, is fundamental to the brain–mind problem: How are simultaneous "brain states" of memories, perceptions, and expectations discriminated in the mind as past, present, and future? While it is difficult to offer any definitive answer to this enigma, some plausible leads may be suggested by exploring time telescoping in terms of research on brain dysfunctions in acute schizophrenia.

William James (1890) described the mental present as the "saddle back" between the fading past and the emerging future. Bergson (1922) pointed out how the simultaneous perception of successive events in terms of the future becoming present then past is necessary for the apprehension of the mental present. Brain (1963) suggested that immediate memory may provide the mechanism for the linking of the transient now with the fading past. These relationships provide clues for how time telescoping might take place in the brain. It is likely that a dysfunctional immediate or "working" memory will disrupt the ongoing synthesis of the flow of successive past, present, and future events, thus giving rise to a fragmented or dimly perceived mental present. Once the mental present is misperceived or fragmented, the brain no longer has the index of the present for distinguishing and ordering longer term memories and expectations. As a result, the now could not be discriminated from the then; memories and expectations would commingle and become confused with present perceptions.

We have already reviewed how acute schizophrenia is characterized by deficiencies in immediate memory and by difficulties with keeping track of goal-relevant sequences. Sophisticated studies have shown that, compared to other psychiatric patients, the schizophrenic deficiency in immediate memory occurs at an early stage (within 120–300 milliseconds) after the initial registration of input (Saccuzzo and Braff, 1981; Braff, 1986). Moreover, similar findings have been found for THC intoxication (Braff, Silverton, Saccuzzo, and Janowsky, 1981). The disruption of the microstructure of one second is likely to interfere with normal time-dependent processes such as conditioned reflexes and the perception of causality (Michotte, 1958; Fraisse, 1963).

As already reviewed, the schizophrenic dysfunctional immediate memory appears to be localized primarily in the hippocampal–limbic prefrontal region of the left (dominant) hemisphere. If this region can be conceived as the temporal "seat of consciousness," as Flor-Henry (1976) argues, then its impairment in schizophrenia might make it vulnerable to an influx of information from other parts of the brain, whether subcortical or cortical. Thus, there would be a lack of retroactive and proactive inhibition of other memories and expectations because of the immediate memory deficiency in this region. The normal "filtering" of irrelevant information would break down (Yates, 1966). The then would invade the now.

Moreover, the impairment of the left prefrontal cortex in schizophrenia (Weinberger et al., 1986) suggests malfunction of anticipatory sets that normally may determine the serial order of immediate stimuli (Lashley, 1951). As a result, the usual stream of consciousness might no longer be apprehended as a temporal series of the emergent future becoming present then fading into the past.

Such a time telescoping process in the left limbic-prefrontal region might help explain hallucinations. Prior subcortical perceptual events, similar to vivid dreams, might invade consciousness as though they were happening in the present (Penfield and Perot, 1963; Asaad and Shapiro, 1986). Alternatively, without the index of the mental present in the left hemisphere, nonlinear images from the right hemisphere might invade consciousness and be experienced as timeless perceptions without temporal reference (Horowitz, 1975; Bazhin, Wasserman, and Tonkonogii, 1975; MacKay, Golden, and Scott, 1981). In this way, hallucinations may be similar to a prolonged déjà vu experience. Thus, dysfunction of the limbic–prefrontal region, which is known to play a key role in the integration and gating of perceptions and memories (Mesulam, 1985), may give rise to hallucinations.

In summary, time telescoping in acute schizophrenia may occur when the mental present becomes deranged by immediate memory dysfunctions of the hippocampal–limbic–prefrontal area of the left (dominant) cerebral hemisphere. As a result, the now cannot be distinguished from the then, and the then invades the mental present. Reality testing becomes chaotic because the brain–mind, without the index of the present for differentiating past and future, cannot tell whether a memory, expectation, or fantasy is a present perception. Inside events (memories, expectations, and fantasies) become confused with outside events (present perceptions).

These proposals about time telescoping and temporal disorganization resonate with longstanding clinical observations. Bleuler (1911) described schizophrenia as a "disharmony of the mind." Minkowski (1927) emphasized the loss of the present "I-here-now" position in schizophrenia. It may well be that this loss of the I-here-now present position engenders disharmony of the mind in schizophrenia. Without the indexing function of the mental present, past and future telescope into the present.

Conclusions

We have reviewed how problems with sequence, rate, and temporal perspective differentiate the major psychiatric disorders. Pervasive problems with sequence characterize organic brain disease, and intermittent problems with keeping track of goal-relevant sequences appear to underlie the common symptoms and signs of acute schizophrenia. In manic-depressive illness, rate is accelerated in mania and slowed down in depression. In neurotic-personality disorders, temporal perspective problems predominate with overfocusing on the past, present, or future. The sequential difficulties of organic brain disease and schizophrenia and, when extreme, the rate problems of manic-depressive illness, are associated with marked alterations in consciousness and defective reality testing, whereas the misconstructions of temporal perspective in neurotic-personality disorders do not significantly alter consciousness or reality testing.

At the psychological level of discourse, the studies suggest that different types of time distortions play a fundamental role in disrupting normal consciousness and impairing reality testing in severe mental illness such as organic brain disease, schizophrenia, and manic-depressive illness. This does not mean that the time distortions are the sole causes of psychotic symptoms. For example, there may be biological or social factors that give rise to the time distortions at the psychological level. Or, within the psychological realm, a paranoid delusional patient may attribute unusual meanings to time and thereby distort it. In my experience, for severe mental illness, the time distortion appears to be fundamental and not secondary to other psychological factors, although once a time distortion gives rise to psychiatric symptoms the process may become reciprocal with the time distortion aggravating the psychological derangements and vice versa. However, for the milder forms of mental illness as seen in neurotic-personality disorders, the distortion of temporal perspective probably is secondary to other psychological aberrations such as developmental learning factors and emotional difficulties. In psychiatry the question of which factor is primary or secondary is often not as important as the discovery of interacting variables that generate a vicious cycle or spiral. In this regard, time distortions can be thought of as key intervening variables that distort consciousness and engender psychopathological spirals associated with defective reality testing. Thus, to reiterate the central thesis, once a time distortion occurs at the psychological level of organization, whatever its originating cause, it alters consciousness and impairs the capacity to test reality.

As a concluding statement, I would like to extend Pieron's (1923) metaphor of the present as being the hollow of one's hand, through which flows the stream of consciousness, like a waterfall or river. Normally, the stream of consciousness is momentarily contained in the hand (the present) as the stream flows through it. In organic brain disease, the hand is like a sieve. In schizophrenia, the hand intermittently opens or closes such that it is difficult for the individual to get a consistent grasp of the present or tell what is upstream or downstream. In manic-depressive illness, the hollow of the hand (the present) is essentially normal, yet the rate of flow of the stream is speeded up in mania and slowed down in depression. In neurotic and personality disorders, the hand (the present) and the rate of the stream are normal, but the person's focus on the stream may be an abnormal overfocus on the past, present, or future. In different ways, then, these problems with sequence, rate, and temporal perspective distort the comprehension and testing of ongoing reality.

References

Arlow, J. A. (1959), The structure of the *déjà vu* experience. *J. Amer. Psychoanal. Assn.*, 7:611–631.
———— (1966), Depersonalization and derealization. In: *Psychoanalysis—A General Psychology: Essays in Honor of Heinz Hartmann*, eds. R. M. Loewenstein, L. M. Newman, M. Schor, & A. J. Solnit. New York: International Universities Press, pp. 456–478.
Asaad, G., & Shapiro, B. (1986), Hallucinations: Theoretical and clinical overview. *Amer. J. Psychiat.*, 143:1088–1097.
Bazhin, E. F., Wasserman, L. I., & Tonkonogii, I. M. (1975), Auditory hallucinations and left temporal lobe pathology. *Neuropsychol.*, 13:481–487.
Bear, D. M., & Fedio, P. (1977), Quantitative analysis of interictal behavior in temporal lobe epilepsy. *Arch. Neurol.*, 34:454–476.
Ben-Dov, G., & Carmon, A. (1976), On time, space, and the cerebral hemispheres: A theoretical note. *Internat. J. Neurosci.*, 7:29–33.
Bergson, H. (1922), *Durée et simultanéité*. Paris: Alcan.
Bleuler, E. (1911), *Dementia Praecox or the Group of Schizophrenias*, trans. J. Zinkin. New York: International Universities Press, 1950, pp. 14–15.
Bogerts, B., & Meertz, E. (1985), Basal ganglia and limbic system pathology in schizophrenia. *Arch. Gen. Psychiat.*, 42:784–791.
Braff, D. L. (1986), Attention, habituation and information processing in psychiatric disorders. In: *Psychiatry*, Vol. 3, eds. R. R. Michaels, J. O. Cavenar & J. L. Houpt. New York: Basic Books, pp. 1–15.
———— Callaway, E., & Naylor, H. (1977), Very short-term memory dysfunction in schizophrenia. *Arch. Gen. Psychiat.*, 34:25–30.
———— Saccuzzo, D. P. (1981), Information processing dysfunction in paranoid schizophrenia: A two factor deficit. *Amer. J. Psychiat.*, 138:1051–1056.
———— (1982), Effect of antipsychotic medication on speed of information processing in schizophrenic patients. *Amer. J. Psychiat.*, 139:1127–1130.
———— Silverton, L., Saccuzzo, D. P., & Janowsky, D. S. (1981), Impaired speed of visual information processing in marihuana intoxication. *Amer. J. Psychiat.*, 138:613–617.
Brain, W. R. (Lord) (1963), Some reflections on brain and mind. *Brain*, 86:381–402.
Breunlin, D. C., & Schwartz, R. C. (1986), Sequences: Toward a common denominator of family therapy. *Fam. Proc.*, 25:67–88.
Chapman, J. (1966), The early symptoms of schizophrenia. *Brit. J. Psychiat.*, 112:225–251.
Efron, R. (1963a), The effect of handedness on the perception of simultaneity and temporal order. *Brain*, 86:261–284.
———— (1963b), Temporal perception, aphasia, and déjà vu. *Brain*, 86:403–424.
Flor-Henry, P. (1969), Psychosis and temporal lobe epilepsy: A controlled investigation. *Epilepsia*, 10:363–395.
———— (1976), Lateralized temporal-limbic dysfunction and psychopathology. *Ann. NY Acad. Sci.*, 280:777–797.
Fraisse, P. (1963), *The Psychology of Time*. New York: Harper & Row.
Fraser, J. T. (1975), *Of Time, Passion, and Knowledge: Reflections on the Strategy of Existence*. New York: George Braziller.
Freeman, A. M., & Melges, F. T. (1977), Depersonalization and temporal disintegration in acute mental illness. *Amer. J. Psychiat.*, 134:679–681.
Freud, S. (1915), The unconscious. *Standard Edition*, 14:159–215. London: Hogarth Press, 1964.
Gazzaniga, M. S., & Volpe, B. T. (1981), Split-brain studies: Implications for psychiatry. In: *American Handbook of Psychiatry*, 2nd ed., rev., Vol. 7, eds. S. Arieti & H. K. H. Brodie. New York: Basic Books, pp. 25–45.
Grossberg, S. (1980), How does a brain build a cognitive code? *Psycholog. Rev.*, 87:1–51.
Gruzelier, J. H. (1983), A critical assessment and integration of lateral asymmetries in schizophrenia.

In: *Hemisyndromes: Psychobiology, Neurology, Psychiatry,* ed. M. S. Myslobodsky. New York: Academic Press, pp. 265–326.

Gur, R. (1979), Cognitive concomitants of hemispheric dysfunction in schizophrenia. *Arch. Gen. Psychiat.,* 36:269–274.

Hamilton, M., ed. (1974), *Fish's Clinical Psychopathology: Signs and Symptoms in Psychiatry.* Bristol, U. K.: John Wright & Sons, Stonebridge Press, p. 74.

Hartocollis, P. (1978), Time and affects in borderline disorders. *Internat. J. Psychoanal.,* 59:157–163.

Hecaen, H., & Albert, M. L. (1975), Disorders of mental functioning related to frontal lobe pathology. In: *Psychiatric Aspects of Neurological Disease,* eds. D. F. Benson & D. Blumer. New York: Grune & Stratton, pp. 137–149.

Hoffman, R. E., Stopek, S., & Andreasen, N. C. (1986), A comparative study of manic vs schizophrenic speech disorganization. *Arch. Gen. Psychiat.,* 43:831–838.

Horowitz, M. J. (1975), A cognitive model of hallucinations. *Amer. J. Psychiat.,* 132:789–795.

Jackson, J. L. (1986), *The Processing of Temporal Information.* Unpublished doctoral dissertation. University of Groningen, The Netherlands.

James, W. (1890), The perception of time. In: *The Principles of Psychology,* Vol. 1. New York: Holt & Co.

John, E. R. (1976), A model of consciousness. In: *Consciousness and Self-Regulation,* eds. G. E. Swartz & D. Shapiro. New York: Plenum Press, pp. 1–50.

Lang, P. J., & Buss, A. H. (1965), Psychological deficit in schizophrenia. II: Interference and activation. *J. Abnorm. Psychol.,* 70:77–106.

Lashley, K. S. (1951), The problem of serial order in behavior. In: *Cerebral Mechanisms in Behavior,* ed. L. A. Jeffress. New York: John Wiley, pp. 112–136.

Levy, J., & Trevarthen, C. B. (1976), Meta-control of hemispheric function in human split-brain patients. *J. Experiment. Psychol.: Hum. Percept. Perf.,* 2:299–312.

Lhermitte, F. (1986), Human autonomy and the frontal lobes. II. Patient behavior in complex and social situations. The "environmental dependency syndrome." *Ann. Neurol.,* 19:335–343.

Luria, A. R. (1980), *Higher Cortical Functions in Man,* 2nd ed., rev. New York: Basic Books.

MacKay, S. E., Golden, C. J., & Scott, M. (1981), Neurophysiological correlates of auditory and visual hallucinations. *Internat. J. Neurosci.,* 15:87–94.

MacLean, P. D. (1973), *A Triune Concept of the Brain and Behavior,* eds. T. G. Boag & D. C. Campbell. Toronto: University of Toronto Press.

Matthysse, S. (1978), A theory of the relation between dopamine and attention. *J. Psychiat. Res.,* 14:241–248.

McGhie, A., Chapman, J., & Lawson, J. S. (1965), Effect of distraction on schizophrenic performance: I. Perception and immediate memory. *Brit. J. Psychiat.,* 3:383–390.

McHugh, P. R., & Slavney, P. R. (1986), *The Perspectives of Psychiatry.* Baltimore: Johns Hopkins University Press.

Melges, F. T. (1976), Tracking difficulties and paranoid ideation during hashish and alcohol intoxication. *Amer. J. Psychiat.,* 133:1024–1028.

——— (1982), *Time and the Inner Future: A Temporal Approach to Psychiatric Disorders.* New York: John Wiley.

——— Freeman, A. M. (1975), Persecutory delusions: A cybernetic model. *Amer. J. Psychiat.,* 132:1038–1044.

——— ——— (1977), Temporal disorganization and inner–outer confusion in acute mental illness. *Amer. J. Psychiat.,* 134:874–877.

———Tinklenberg, J. R., Hollister, L. E., & Gillespie, H. K. (1970a), Marihuana and temporal disintegration. *Science,* 168:1118–1120.

——— ——— ——— ——— (1970b), Temporal disintegration and depersonalization during marihuana intoxication. *Arch. Gen. Psychiat.,* 23:204–210.

——— ——— ——— ——— (1971), Marihuana and the temporal span of awareness. *Arch. Gen. Psychiat.,* 14:564–567.

——— ——— Deardorff, C. M., Davies, N. H., Anderson, R. E., & Owen, C. A. (1974), Temporal disorganization and delusional-like ideation: Processes induced by hashish and alcohol. *Arch. Gen. Psychiat.*, 30:855–861.

Mesulam, M. M. (1981), Dissociative states with abnormal temporal lobe EEG: Multiple personality and the illusion of possession. *Arch. Neurol.*, 38:176–181.

———— (1985), *Principles of Behavioral Neurology*. Philadelphia: F. A. Davis.

———— (1986), Frontal cortex and behavior. *Ann. Neurol.*, 19:320–324.

Michotte, A. (1958), Causality and activity. In: *Readings in Perception*, ed. D. C. Beardsley & M. Wertheimer. Princeton, NJ: Van Nostrand, pp. 382–389.

Miller, G. A., Galanter, E., & Pribram, K. H. (1960), *Plans and the Structure of Behavior*. New York: Holt, Rinehart & Winston.

Milner, B., & Petrides, M. (1984), Behavioral effects of frontal-lobe lesions in man. *Trends in Neurosci.*, November:403–407.

———— Teuber, H. L. (1968), Alteration of perception and memory in man. In: *Analysis of Behavioral Change*, ed. L. Weiskrantz. New York: Harper & Row.

Minkowski, E. (1927), *La Schizophrénie: Psychopathologie des Schizoïdes et des Schizophrènes*. Paris: Desclée de Brouwer, 1953.

Mullan, S., & Penfield, W. (1959), Illusions of comparative interpretation and emotion. *Arch. Neurol. & Psychiat.*, 81:269–284.

Olds, J., Mink, W. D., & Best, P. J. (1969), Single unit patterns during anticipatory behavior. *Electroencephalogr. & Clin. Neurophysiol.*, 26:144–158.

Penfield, W., & Perot, P. (1963), The brain's record of auditory and visual experience. *Brain*, 86:596–696.

Pieron, H. (1923), Les problèmes psychophysiologiques de la perception due temps. *Année Psychol.*, 24:1–25.

Powers, W. T. (1973), *Behavior: The Control of Perception*. Chicago: Aldine.

Pribram, K. H. (1977), Holonomy and structure in the organization of perception. In: *Images, Perception, and Knowledge*, ed. J. M. Nicholas. Dordrecht: Reidel.

Reynolds, G. P. (1983), Increased concentrations and lateral asymmetry of amygdala dopamine in schizophrenia. *Nature*, 305:527–529.

Saccuzzo, D. P., & Braff, D. L. (1981), Early information processing deficit in schizophrenia. *Arch. Gen. Psychiat.*, 38:175–182.

Schenk, L., & Bear, D. (1981), Multiple personality and related dissociative phenomena in patients with temporal lobe epilepsy. *Amer. J. Psychiat.*, 138:1311–1316.

Schneider, K. (1959), *Clinical Psychopathology*, trans. M. W. Hamilton. New York: Grune & Stratton.

Shakow, D. (1963), Psychological deficit in schizophrenia. *Behav. Sci.*, 8:275–305.

Sherwin, I. (1982), The effect of the location of an epileptogenic lesion on the occurrence of psychosis in epilepsy. In: *Temporal Lobe Epilepsy, Mania, and Schizophrenia and the Limbic System*, eds. W. P. Koella & M. R. Trimble. Basel: Kargar, pp. 81–97.

Sperry, R. W. (1982), Some effects of disconnecting the cerebral hemispheres. *Science*, 217:1223–1226.

Trimble, M. R., & Perez, M. M. (1982), The phenomenology of the chronic psychoses in epilepsy. In: *Temporal Lobe Epilepsy, Mania, and Schizophrenia in the Limbic System*, eds. W. P. Koella & M. R. Trimble. Basel: Kargar, pp. 98–105.

Wehr, T. A., & Goodwin, F. K. (1983), *Circadian Rhythms in Psychiatry*. Pacific Grove, CA: Boxwood.

Weinberger, D. R., Berman, K. F., & Zec, R. F. (1986), Physiological dysfunction of the dorsolateral prefrontal cortex in schizophrenia. I. Regional cerebral blood flow evidence. II. Role of neuroleptic treatment, attention, and mental effort. *Arch. Gen. Psychiat.*, 43:114–135.

Wexler, B. E. (1980), Cerebral laterality in psychiatry: A review of the literature. *Amer. J. Psychiat.*, 137:279–291.

Yates, A. J. (1966), Psychological deficit. In: *Annual Review of Psychology*, Vol. 17, eds. P. R. Farnsworth, O. McNemar, Q. McNemar. Palo Alto, CA: Annual Reviews, pp. 111–144.

Young, J. Z. (1978), *Programs of the Brain*. Oxford: Oxford University Press.

Perspectives

It is very difficult to specify what comprises the right and correct rate at which time flows. Curly Maclain's song, "I have a beautiful feeling / Everything's going my way," in Rogers and Hammerstein's musical Oklahoma! *speaks of something unusual, and not of something usual. It suggests the ecstasy of timelessness; it is not a laboratory report stating that "time at the moment is passing at the correct average rate."*

But it is very easy to recognize when time does not flow at the right rate, when something is wrong with our experience of time. This is not unlike the fact that one does not feel one's teeth until they start hurting. The mind is sensitive to all disturbances that upset its perceptive and cognitive balance. It signals perceived irregularities in the causal order attributed to the universe; it reports if the affective coloring of events is strikingly different from what was expected; and it registers all things unusual in the distribution of labor, as it were, among the categories of future, past, and present.

From the large store of reports about there being something wrong with the flow of time, Dr. Melges has selected a number of samples. He classed them under three categories of time distortion: those of temporal sequence, in the rate at which events happen, and of temporal perspectives.

The norms, with respect to which these deviations are recognized as distortions, are those of collectively learned notions about the nature of time. The "collective" in this case is primarily the society to which a person belongs, but it is also our species, and even the evolutionary journey of life itself. Time distortion is experienced whenever the rhythms and rites of time's passage differ from what society has taught us is normal, what personal memory recognizes as appropriate, and what our genetic endowment expects in the life process.

This whole virtuoso performance may be credited to the coordinating and creative labor of a molecular instrument, the human brain. It is a fifty-millionth generation computer that weighs between 43.5 and 49.5 ounces. Its structural design, its synaptic organization is rather complex; its power of integration rather great. From among its myriad functions Dr. Melges identified a number of brain disorders that appear to be regularly associated with experiences of certain time distortions. His topological survey is a necessary first step toward an eventual understanding of how the brain distinguishes among the categories of future, past, and present.

III

Physical Science

7

Should Physicists Say That the Past Really Happened?

David Park

Abstract This chapter is concerned with the dogma that just as we cannot know the future, so we cannot change the past. But what is the past? Quantum physicists tend to treat both past and future more as mental constructions than as facts, but there is no special reason to do so unless it leads to some novel but verifiable conclusion regarding past events. An example would be the existence of a situation in which an action taken now affects the course of events that have already happened. John Wheeler has pointed out some quantum phenomena in which with a reasonable use of language this could be said to occur, and has suggested by analogy that since the laws of nature cannot have existed before the beginning of the universe they must have arisen then or later, and that they may have been shaped in some way by later events. There is evidence that supports this extraordinary claim. This chapter gives the arguments as I understand them. At the end will be some critical remarks.

Introduction

Several times, in papers read before the International Society for the Study of Time and elsewhere, people have spoken of the radical difference between the concept of time as used in physical science and in the description and analysis of the ordinary experiences of life. We live our lives in a moment we call now. This is the moment when we experience the world and think our thoughts. Past and future are quite different from now. We can think about them and produce bits of evidence pertaining to them, but since nothing we may say about them is now accessible to direct confirmation or refutation by observation, we should be prepared to treat both past and future as intellectual constructions. For most purposes this should be

I thank Professor Wheeler for discussions on these and other matters at the Bellagio workshop in 1981, and Professors Albert Shalom and William Wootters for critical comments on this paper.

taken as an unimportant remark. It is also true that the center of the sun is not accessible to observation, and yet astrophysicists talk of it without embarrassment. The difficulty arises out of the fact that the incomplete science of physics has two epistemologies, which must be carefully distinguished.

On the one hand we have the epistemology of classical physics, which encourages whatever tendency we may have to think positivistically. The center of the sun is objectively characterized by pressure, temperature, and constituent particles. The positions and momenta of moving bodies are given by numbers which correspond to the results of possible observations. There are no failures in the scheme and one tends to state as an objective fact, "This body is here, and is moving with a definite momentum. A moment ago, with equal certainty, it was in this place and a moment hence it will be in that one." This is the vision expressed by Laplace (1843–1847) in his myth of the calculating demon, and in it past, present, and future share the same kind of reality.

On the other hand, in quantum physics, there are no numbers to describe events in terms of objective properties like position and momentum; instead, the numbers of the theory ultimately refer to the way in which a macroscopic observer interacts with the quantum world. Here the calculations are probabilistic, but more important, one cannot, except in a very schematic way, describe the thing one is talking about, abstracted from the experiment, in the objective language of classical physics. The paradoxes of quantum theory arise when a quantum phenomenon manifests itself on the macroscopic scale; then one does not know what language to use in order to explain what is going on. Because the language of classical physics is unambiguous, and because it describes all the pieces of apparatus we see and touch in the attempt to acquire knowledge, one tends in these cases to try to describe not only the phenomenon but also the underlying noumenon in classical language, but in doing so, as we shall see in a moment, we are led to make strange assertions. Or we can play safe and phrase every proposition in experiential terms as the logical positivists do: "If you do this to the apparatus you will read that number on the meter." There is an immediate consequence: every experiment is performed now; we cannot experiment yesterday or tomorrow, and this is why a quantum physicist, faithfully following the line of thought the theory requires, is sometimes obliged to say that past and future are intellectual constructions.

According to conventional wisdom, the realms of past and future separated by the present instant can be distinguished in this way: We can know the past but cannot act so as to affect it; we can act so as to affect the future but we cannot know it. If physical theory is not to conflict with experience it must explain how, if one chooses an arbitrary instant on the scale of time, one's ability to know and to act in the intervals earlier and later than this instant is subject to those limitations. There is an immense literature on the subject; the arguments generally refer to the second law of thermodynamics and are easy to accept if one believes the law, but the law is derived from more basic principles, and the questions of how it is derived and under precisely what conditions it is valid are still not settled. These matters have been discussed in previous volumes of papers deriving from meetings of the

International Society for the Study of Time, and I predict (though I cannot know) that they will be discussed in the future; they are not our concern at the moment.

To show that future events are not always determined by present circumstances, and therefore cannot always be known in advance, it would suffice to show that living creatures are endowed with free will, but even if freedom turns out to be an illusion it has long been evident that on the quantum scale the laws of physics do not allow exact predictions to be made: there are limits to the precision with which we can know the present, and these impose larger and larger uncertainties as we try to project further and further into the future. The situation becomes more complicated if we want to argue from present knowledge to reconstruct the past.

The fundamental laws of physics are (with one small and, for our purposes, unimportant exception) symmetric with respect to past and future. One might at first think that the task of assigning probabilities to the possible past causes of some present event would be completely symmetric to finding the probabilities, given the present event, of various future events; actually it is not. Effects always follow causes; the situation is not symmetric, and one cannot reconstruct the past from present data without assigning a priori probabilities, perhaps quite arbitrarily, to the possibilities one wishes to consider. (The statistical theory used here goes back to Thomas Bayes in the eighteenth century and is found in any text on statistics.) Nevertheless experiments are not made and interpreted instantaneously, and the act of measurement has no meaning unless we can argue from an experimental result obtained now to the earlier moment at which the measurement was actually performed, and so we must always try to use theory to reconstruct the past. We find ourselves in a rather tangled intellectual situation, and if we want to look for paradoxes they can easily be found. The question is: Do these paradoxes merely point up the weakness of our formulations, or do they go deeper and point out unexpected features of the world? That the latter is the case has been eloquently urged by John Wheeler, formerly of Princeton University. I shall explain what I understand to be his arguments, review the evidence, and finally say what I think.

Reconstructing the Event from the Experience

The task of pure science is to explain what we see of the world. The main intellectual tool of physical theory is mathematics, but when we look out of the window we do not see any mathematics. Physical science undertakes to create mathematical structures which are in some sense isomorphic to what we experience of the universe, but almost nobody feels that mathematical structures by themselves are fully explanatory. Theory should explain what we observe in terms of other things we observe, or can observe, and the terms of explanation should not be jargon or mathematical symbols but the kind of plain talk we use every day.

Mathematical content should be translated into the language of ordinary experience. It is in the realm of the quantum that the translation is especially difficult, and it is here that, as we shall see, if we talk plainly we must use language that cannot and must not be taken literally. As Heisenberg has remarked, "Quantum theory . . . provides us with a striking illustration of the fact that we can fully understand a connection though we can only speak of it in images and parables" (1971, p. 210).

In cosmogony the problem of explanation is somewhat different. Here we create a model that represents the early universe as governed by certain physical laws which we do not invent ad hoc but assume are the same as those we use to explain what we observe in the universe today. (This last assumption, which perhaps seems very bold, is supported by several astronomical and geological observations which show that during at least the last few of the seventeen or so billion years that the universe has existed, the changes, if any, have been exceedingly small [Park, 1981].) A model cosmology is considered to be a good one if it yields numbers pertaining to the present universe which agree with what is observed. But of course nobody is interested in models as such. The model is interesting only if we think that, taken more or less literally, it tells us something about what really happened at the beginning of time. But how can we talk of taking such a picture literally if the laws of quantum physics forbid it? I have mentioned that astrophysicists are accustomed to talk objectively about the insides of stars without worrying about the limitations imposed by quantum phenomena. One might hope that an account of the beginning of something as large as the universe would be similarly immune from the difficulties that arise in describing nature on the quantum scale. But cosmologists are now talking about processes that occurred when the space now occupied by the entire known universe was only a few centimeters across and its entire mass was not more than a few grams, and they tend to assume that the universe originated in a quantum process. It is therefore possible that we can get into trouble if we objectively represent the distant past. Having stated the situation in general terms, let me show how trying to reconstruct the past of a quantum process can lead us away from common-sense conclusions.

Figure 7.1a shows an observation of a bright star a hundred light years away. In front of a photographic film we put a screen with a small hole in it and then expose the film for a short time. When the film is developed we may find it blank. Very well, we try again, and presently we find a film that has a single darkened grain. We now reconstruct the events as follows: A century ago the star was shining brightly, emitting photons in all directions. They travel through space along lines that are straight or very nearly so; one of them happened to pass through the hole while the film was in place and so its arrival was recorded on the film and became visible when it was developed.

Let us repeat the experiment, exposing the film for quite a long time. This time (Figure 7.1b) a number of dots appear, somewhat spread out in space. The spreading can easily be understood if photons are assumed to obey Heisenberg's

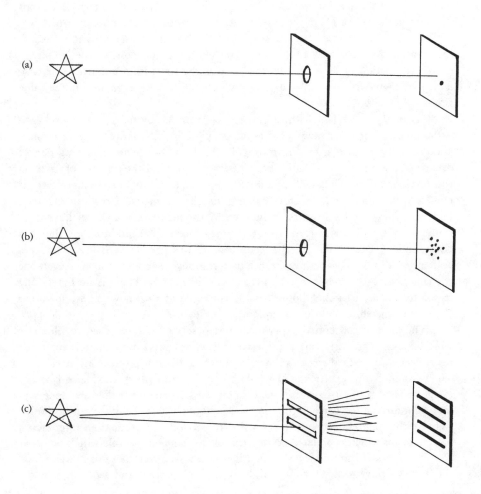

Figure 7.1. Varying exposures of light from a bright star.

principle of indeterminacy: the hole localizes the photon in the plane of the screen so that it acquires a corresponding uncertainty in its transverse momentum. [1]

Finally, let the light press through a screen with two apertures, but in order to make the experimental result easier to talk about let the apertures be not holes but a pair of parallel slits, close together. Figure 7.1c shows the result of a long exposure. The developed film shows a regular alternation of exposed and unexposed regions, known as an interference pattern. Since the separation of these regions depends on the separation of the slits, it seems that the path of a photon, whichever slit it goes through, is affected by the other slit. In some sense, hard to visualize, the photon goes through both slits. The effect cannot possibly be due to a cooperative action of different photons because the light from a distant star is so faint that there will probably never be two photons in the apparatus at the same time.

Let us try to see which slit a photon goes through by installing behind each slit a counter to register the photon as it goes past. If the slits are of the same size, photons will pass through them in roughly equal numbers, and, assuming perfect counting, the total number of counts registered will equal the number of spots on the developed film. Thus each photon triggers one and only one counter; there is now no question of one photon going through both slits. How can we then understand how its path can be influenced by the presence of a slit it did not go through? We look more carefully at the developed film produced in the new arrangement. The action of the counters on the photons passing them has obliterated all traces of the interference pattern; they disappear as soon as even one efficient photon-counter is installed (Park, 1988, note J). There is no longer any reason to suppose that the photon passing through one slit knows where the other slit is, and therefore nothing to explain.

The kind of conceptual experiment just described is often used to illustrate what has been carelessly called the wave–particle duality, even though there has never been a theoretical structure more perfectly unified than quantum mechanics. The version of the experiment in which counters are in place is explained by the image or parable of a particle: if one counter registers the other does not, one says that light arrives as a particle that goes through one slit or the other but not both. Remove the counters and present two slits to the light source and an interference pattern forms which is understood in terms of the image or parable which says that the photon passes through the slits as if it were a wave, even though it registers on the film as a single dot. Of course, light is not both particle and wave; in fact, the

---

[1] If the diameter of the hole is d, a photon passing through it has a position in the plane of the screen that is uncertain by an amount of the order of d. According to Heisenberg's relation, the photon will gain a corresponding uncertainty in its lateral momentum given by $\hbar/d$, where $\hbar$ is Planck's constant divided by 2π. If its forward momentum is p, the angular spread of the beam after it passes the hole is the ratio of these momenta, $\hbar/pd$. Since by de Broglie's relation $\hbar/p$ is the photon's reduced wavelength λ, the angular spread can also be written as λ/d, a result derived from the theory of waves long before the invention of quantum theory. The phenomenon is easily observed.

question should not be pursued. Experiment does not tell what anything is; it merely tells what happens. As Niels Bohr repeatedly emphasized, one is only allowed to speak of wave phenomena or particle phenomena if one includes in the word *phenomenon* not just the appearance that is observed but the context in which it is observed—in the experiments just described terms such as *wave phenomenon* must be applied not to the observed pattern of dots but to the whole experiment (Petersen, 1968). Again in Bohr's terminology (this will be important in what follows) the phenomenon is brought to a close by the act of detection in which it is observed—here, by the exposure and development of the photographic film. At that point the film can be inspected by one and all; we know from experience (and not from any a priori argument) that everyone will agree as to whether or not there is a spot on it and if so, where it is located. "Les jeux sont faits. Rien ne va plus." In Wheeler's pregnant words, "No phenomenon is a phenomenon until it is a registered phenomenon" (Wheeler, 1980, p. 358). Then the quantum game is over.

I must emphasize that the result of the conceptual experiments just described are fully and clearly explained by the mathematical apparatus of the quantum theory (Park, 1988). From the mathematical point of view there is no mystery. But we are here talking about the kind of explanation which perhaps ought to be primary, a mental and verbal reconstruction of events leading up to what is observed, and the terms of such a reconstruction, ought, as far as possible, to relate to ordinary experience. In the present instance we need to consider three kinds of trajectory for the photon: one which goes through the upper slit and not the lower one, one which goes through the lower one but not the upper, and one which in some way manages to go through both. The three trajectories can be clearly distinguished accordingly as they fire one counter or the other, producing no interference pattern on the film, or, in the absence of counters, produce an interference pattern. The problem of explanation is this: The light left the star a hundred years ago. How did it know, at the moment it left, that there was going to be a pair of slits at this point and whether or not there were going to be counters in place? It would seem that as we install or remove counters the photon must make a midcourse correction so as to go through one slit or both.

I don't think that solution of the problem is very reasonable, especially since we have a simple mathematical explanation of the whole effect which, though not translatable into ordinary language, dispenses with extravagant hypotheses. But suppose I insist on an explanation in ordinary language. Then it seems I am obliged to say that my decision to install or remove the counters produced an effect a century earlier, before I was born, on the trajectory of photons that happened to be heading in my direction. Experiments of this kind, in which the experimenter chooses a procedure after the particle has already left its source, are called delayed-choice experiments. Wheeler calls the process by which the observer is said to influence the prior event observer-participancy, and concerning it he writes: "In the delayed-choice experiment we, by a decision in the here and now, have an irretrievable influence on what we will want to say about the past—a strange inversion of the normal order of time" (Wheeler, 1980, p. 356). Note that in the phrase "what we will want to say" Wheeler makes it clear that he is far from talking about ontology, a little closer to epistemology perhaps, but scientific discourse has a way of establishing its own categories, and the giving of a coherent verbal explanation of things is not really a matter of epistemology either. In any case, I must emphasize that although observer-participancy can be described in plain language, as I have tried to do, the nature of the interactive process by which present decisions are said to influence past events is entirely unspecified. It is also unspecified in the mathematical theory. All one can say is that it is required by the theory's general mode of description.

The Genesis of Law

Let us try to apply these ideas in studying the beginning of the universe. As to how it began, we have models that explain the basic properties of the universe as we know it, but since we do not know for sure what fields and forces were involved, or even how many dimensions to assign to space–time in the first moments, there is no standard model. In some models it is impossible even in principle to talk about any time before the beginning. Stephen Hawking, in a popular article (1984), compares the situation to trying to talk about a place one kilometer to the north of the North Pole: even though there are no barriers or discontinuities it follows from the nature of the earth and the definition of north that no such place can be found. Let us assume for a moment, with Plato and St. Augustine and many others, that there was no time before Creation.

Given a model of the early universe, how does it develop after the initial instant? At present the answer to such a question is a little awkward. One has to assume several things. First, matter must come into being which, after various transformations, will become the kinds of matter we know. Second, there must be laws of motion that govern the system's development from the initial instant. And third, since laws of motion tell only how things change, there must be an account of the initial condition of the entire system. Appropriate assumptions can be made, and though no present theory is either complete or entirely convincing, one can see how a theory *might* be formulated that fits with what we know about the present constituents of the universe, its general morphological characteristics, and the laws according to which physical processes take place now. The more successful such a theory may be, the more urgent becomes a simple question: What is the status of the physical laws governing the universe if there is no universe? Can laws exist independently of the universe that embodies them? (Note that I do not speak of conditions before there was space–time, for that may not make any sense.) Physical law is expressed in terms of the variables that describe space–time, and this is because all our knowledge comes from experiments performed in the space–time in which we live and breathe. At the initial instant there are no space–time variables. Everything is in a knot, a singularity as it is called, a condition in which functional relationships cannot be defined. (The necessity of such a singularity follows from very general assumptions [Hawking and Ellis, 1973]). If there is no space–time there cannot be any way of expressing laws in space–time. Can we then say that there is no law?

We do not know whether the universe will expand forever or whether it will finally collapse under the pull of its own gravitation; if the latter, then will law cease to exist along with matter, as suddenly as it began?

It is a strange thing to think of the laws of nature passing discontinuously into and out of existence. Here is what Wheeler says:

> How can one possibly believe that the laws of physics were chisled on a rock for all eternity if the universe itself does not endure from everlasting to everlasting? If law, field, and substance come into being at the big bang and fade out of existence in the final stages of collapse, how can a change so all-encompassing take place except through a process, the elementary nature of which has already made itself known? In what other way does an elementary quantum phenomenon become a phenomenon except through an elementary act of observer-participancy? To what other foundation can the universe itself owe its existence except billions upon billions of such acts of registration? [Wheeler, 1980, p. 362].

(Occasionally, as in the above passage, Wheeler seems to forget his caution that he is talking about modes of explanation. The point is, however, made clearly in a more recent article [1986].)

Wheeler is assuming that the universe originated in a quantum process. His word *registration* reminds us of the dictum "No elementary phenomenon is a phenomenon until it is a registered phenomenon." Registered, that is, in a device that responds to and retains it: a photographic film or a punched tape or a human or animal memory. Though he does not say it, Wheeler seems to have in mind that the phenomena will be closed by the perceptions of sentient beings, and it is the organizing power of consciousness, even at a primitive level, that must react back to help organize the universe. The universe, as we perceive and understand it, must therefore have originated so as to allow sentient beings to develop.

Well, that is not much of a conclusion. For all our faults we are sentient beings and here we are and obviously the world has allowed us to develop, whether or not we try to make anything of it by propounding theories.[2] There must be a little more to the argument than that, and we can begin to see what it is if we look at the arrangements that the universe has made to accommodate us.

---

[2]That the universe must (obviously) be such as to have permitted human beings to evolve in it leads to some definite restrictions on its nature and history. This was apparently first pointed out by Whitrow (1955) (see also Dicke [1961]). This remark, so obvious on the surface and so rich in implications, has been named the Anthropic Principle. It has given rise to a large literature, summarized ably if a little tendentiously by Barrow and Tipler (1986) and commented upon by Professor Shalom in chapter 9 of this volume.

Remarkably Good Luck

The examples that follow are adapted from the account given in chapter 18 of Park (1988), where more footnotes will be found.

As we look around us we realize that we are in an environment that is well adapted for us to live in. And of course, we are well adapted to live in it. That's not really the point. There are nine planets in the solar system. Ours is obviously favorable to the development of life—see how many different species there are, and it is hard to think why there would not be other planetary systems in which conditions exist that are equally favorable to some forms of life. The more interesting questions relate to the universe itself. I will mention two of them: What conditions must exist in the universe in order that it can bring forth sentient beings of any kind, and are these conditions met in a wide variety of universes that we can imagine, or are they restrictive? The answers we can give are at best plausible; at worst they only show how little we know and how little imagination we have. If there are immense thinking organizations of cosmic material like Fred Hoyle's Black Cloud (1957) or beings made entirely of neutrons who live at the rate of many lifetimes per second on the periphery of a neutron star, I have little to say about their probable likes and dislikes, but for creatures like ourselves who build their bodies out of carbon compounds, not any old universe will do.

First, what properties must the universe have if it is to produce and maintain reasonably complex living creatures? I will suppose that their tissues involve fairly large molecules made of a number of different chemical constituents. I will also suppose that however life may start, complex forms that can think and speak and make music develop by an evolutionary process that takes billions of years. Third, I suppose that an environment is most favorable for the development of life if it does not change very much. If the Earth's average temperature were occasionally to go above the boiling point or below the freezing point of water, few of our present species could exist. Finally, I suppose there must be some place for a creature to sit down. (Admittedly whales do not sit down, but neither, it seems, do they think conceptually. Perhaps there is some relation between sitting and thinking.) To meet these needs a number of special requirements must be met.

1. It seems that the most likely home for life is a planet circling a star whose output of light is roughly constant over billions of years. Such stars tend to be small like the sun and there are lots of them; what fraction of them have planets around them is anybody's guess.

2. The universe must evolve so that there are not too many stars close to a solar system, since if a star wanders past it is likely to change the orbit of a life-bearing planet, subjecting it to alternations of heat and cold if it does not fling it out of the system altogether. Luckily for us, stars throughout the galactic disc are spread quite uniformly a few light years apart so that intrusions are unlikely, but if they were much closer we might very well not be here.

3. Stars are made mostly of primeval hydrogen and helium with a few heavier elements mixed in, while planets are made largely of heavier elements. Stars burn slowly and evenly; let us think about the conditions necessary for that. Stars

produce their energy by a variety of nuclear reactions, but in smaller stars like the sun, the hydrogen reaction controls the others. In this reaction two protons come together and one turns into a neutron. It does this by emitting a neutrino and a positron. Then the neutron and proton stick together to from a particle called a deuteron, while the energy released in the process is carried off by the two emitted particles and some of it ultimately heats the star. In a simple notation,

$$p + p \rightarrow \bar{e} + \nu_e + \boxed{(np)}$$

where $\bar{e}$ is the positron and ν_e is the neutrino. In stars like the sun this reaction goes on slowly for billions of years until the hydrogen is used up; then the star undergoes dramatic changes in size and temperature and new reactions begin. The proton-proton process is slow because it involves what is called a weak interaction—all processes involving neutrinos are weak. Basically, it is very difficult for a proton to turn into a neutron in the very short instant while the other proton is near, and there must be many trials before this finally happens. A typical proton in the burning region of a star has to wait about 10^{10} years.

   Protons and neutrons have very similar interactions. Why don't two protons stick together as two neutrons do? Because their electric charges repel each other, and the attractive nuclear force which binds a deuteron together is not quite strong enough to overcome the repulsion. This is a lucky thing, since if the nuclear force were only a few percent stronger it would produce a bound pp particle and the reaction would go this way:

$$p + p \rightarrow \gamma + \boxed{(pp)}$$

where γ represents a gamma ray, an energetic photon (Dyson, 1971). This reaction involves no neutrino and its speed would be much greater. How much greater would depend on how firmly the pp was bound, but a factor of something like 10^{13} is reasonable. Forming out of gravitational contraction in a cloud of hydrogen, stars would explode as soon as they were hot enough and dense enough for the reaction to begin.

   4. On the other hand, if the nuclear interaction were only a few percent weaker there would be no deuterons and then again we would be in trouble, for the process of forming the heavy elements of which we and our earth are composed begins with the formation of deuterons.

   5. Given the deuterons, how were the heavier elements formed? When two deuterons come together inside a star they easily combine to form an alpha particle, ^{4}He, consisting of two neutrons and two protons. Then if two alphas collide they form ^{8}Be, an isotope of beryllium. But this isotope is unstable and immediately breaks up into two alphas again unless another alpha arrives and sticks to it to form ^{12}C, a stable isotope of carbon, before it has time to break up. The third alpha has only an instant to do this, and the event would rarely occur except that by a very happy coincidence the interactions that determine the structure of ^{12}C happen to produce what is called a resonance in the nucleus at just the energy that most of the

alphas have when they arrive. This resonance makes the capture process enormously more probable than it would otherwise be, and the carbon produced in this way is an essential step in the formation of the elements that compose us and our Earth.

6. The elements heavier than the primordial hydrogen and helium are cooked up in stars which live their lives and then explode. Our planet is formed out of the debris of such a burned-out star. The universe must exist long enough for stars to form plus the entire life span of at least one star plus (judging from our own history) 4 or 5 billion years for intelligent life to evolve on a planet formed from the cosmic wreckage. This is why a universe that supports the kind of life I am talking about must be well over 10 billion years old, as ours seems to be. Listening to astronomers and physicists rattle on about millions and billions, members of the audience have been known to wonder audibly if the whole arrangement is not a bit excessive, if a smaller universe might not have done just as well. But here again the universe seems to be playing our game. We do not know whether it is finite or infinite, but if it is finite it must not be too small. According to the equations of cosmology, the lifetime of a finite universe is proportional to its size at maximum extent. It is just as well that there was a little extravagance at the Creation.

These are a few examples of what appear to be lucky coincidences, both in the laws of nature and in the structure of the universe we live in, that allow us to live and think. A single lucky coincidence would be worth mentioning but it would hardly be enough to suggest any portentous questions. In order to illustrate Wheeler's arguments and those of Professor Shalom in this volume, I have mentioned six, and there are many others.

Ever since these coincidences began to be recognized, people have sought to dismiss or explain them. To dismiss them, the principal line of argument is to say that since we are here, the universe necessarily has the properties that enable us to be here and we have no business guessing about other possibilities. Besides, who is to say whether a given value for a certain number is probable or improbable a priori? The whole argument, skeptics maintain, is so fuzzy and conjectural that it is hardly worth refuting.

To this it can be answered that all arguments about the universe depend on our present state of knowledge. We find that only models using a very special combination of laws and numerical values are capable of explaining how we can be here. At present these values seem like coincidences. But even if they are not, if there is a still unknown master law that establishes all the laws and numbers (and we hope to find one), how did the master law get that way?

Is Law Contingent?

What are laws, anyhow? They are man-made generalizations based on our experience of nature through our five senses. Laws are not deduced from experience; rather, as Einstein often said, they are free creations of the human mind. Consider, for example, the highly successful theories of gravity given us by Newton and Einstein. Newton's theory assumes that space is Euclidean and uses the idea of force. Einstein's theory assumes noneuclidean space (and space–time) and does not speak of force. Both theories fit the facts excellently well, Einstein's a little better than Newton's. In thinking about the laws of nature we must remember that they are man-made, not uniquely determined by the facts, and that any theory of cosmogony based on them has the same quality. We may yearn for an account of beginnings in ontological terms: "This is the way it really was," but in dealing with quantum processes science must avoid a simple ontology. If we go to scientists to learn what the universe is and how it happens that we are in it, we must be content with a scientific answer, and if such an answer has its roots in the quantum epistemology, its language must be carefully scrutinized.

When we look at the development of scientific ideas it is clear that the structure of physical law is contingent on a society's interests and suppositions as well as on the nature of its scientific knowledge and perhaps on accidents of history. The question is, is it contingent on anything else? The obvious answer to this question is that it is contingent on the way the world is, but that is not Wheeler's answer. His answer is that law has been built by the action of sentient beings, that "law, 'reality,' and substance . . . in some way, yet to be discovered, they must all be built upon the statistics of billions upon billions of such acts of observer-participancy" (Wheeler, 1980, p. 359). "Yet to be discovered": this means that though Wheeler senses an analogy with the way in which an insistence on clear pictorial formulations seems to force us to say that the choice of a procedure for observing a beam of photons (or other particles) that has long been in transit acts to alter the conditions that existed at the moment the particles started out, he has no way of explaining in words how such quantum influences are exerted. The conceptual experiment with light encourages us to explain the undoubted facts it exhibits by *saying* that in such a situation an observer can act in defiance of the normal order of cause and effect to change a cause. Wheeler claims that the same must be true of the universe as a whole: that our *description* of the quantum process that began its development, and therefore the laws we deduce from this account, must similarly violate the natural sequence so that the observing creatures the universe ultimately produces *may be said* to have had a hand in forming the conditions that allow them to exist.

But, we ask in frustration, this argument relates entirely to rhetoric, to things we say about the world. What about what really happened? Does Wheeler claim we *really* act so as to affect what happened at the beginning? If he believes the world began in a quantum process, I do not see how he can make such a claim.

That's the end of it, as far as I can see: the puzzle is to explain how the universe and the laws governing its development can have come into existence at one instant of time; the solution Wheeler offers is that the course of its development was established by the participation of many conscious beings, however primitive, and the evidence offered is the apparent cosmic coincidences that permit us to live and think. Perhaps the laws develop higgledy-piggledy, as Wheeler says, but always so as to allow conscious beings to evolve, however restrictive the requirements for that may be. And if one believes that the cosmic coincidences are strange enough to require explanation but does not believe Wheeler, one needs to find some other explanation. Arguments as unspecific as Wheeler's are hard to refute and I shall not try, but I can at least add some considerations that point the other way.

Few theoretical physicists believe any more that it is possible to express the fundamental laws of physics in a space–time of four dimensions. At present the favored number is ten, but that has changed and will doubtless keep changing. The idea is that at some moment in very early history all the dimensions but four rolled up into a multidimensional ball of very small diameter whose existence is detected only by its indirect effects. If by any chance this is so, the universe may have existed in a strange but lawful form before the three spatial dimensions began the sudden expansion known as the big bang. Law need not have been born at that moment.

Finally, I question the assumption that every physical explanation, in order to be a proper explanation, must ultimately be expressed in plain language. It would be a very good thing if this were true, since there would then be some hope of interesting the public in the great changes in physical theory that are now taking place, but if the effect of the assumption is to encourage people to take the verbalizations more literally than they should and support them by extravagant arguments, I think the cure may be worse than the disease. Perhaps we will finally have to accommodate ourselves to fundamental theories whose content cannot be expressed in words.

To return to the question that is the title of this chapter, I think we can conclude that following general usage, and using language in the way that is most clearly understood, physicists, like everybody else, ought to speak as if the past really happened, but they should remember that this is a manner of speaking rather than a demonstrable truth. Further, following this precept literally can cause them to say things, such as that effect can come before cause, which defy experience and common sense. At that point discretion might suggest it is better to retreat to the old formula "it can be shown," but if so, one had better be sure that it *can* be shown. That, I think, is the problem that arises when one tries to interpret the cosmic coincidences in the light of quantum theory.

References

Barrow, J. D., & Tipler, F. J. (1986), *The Anthropic Cosmological Principle*. Oxford, U.K.: Clarendon Press.
Dicke, R. H. (1961), Dirac's principle and Mach's cosmology. *Nature*, 440–441.
Dyson, F. J. (1971), Energy in the universe. *Sci. Amer.*, September, 225:50–59.
Hawking, S. W. (1984), The edge of spacetime. *Amer. Sci.*, 72:355–359.
——— Ellis, G. F. R., *The Large Scale Structure of Space-time*. Cambridge: Cambridge University Press.
Heisenberg, W. (1971), *Physics and Beyond*. New York: Harper & Row.
Hoyle, F. (1957), *The Black Cloud*. London: Heinemann.
Laplace, P. S. de (1843–1847), *Oeuvres*, Vol. 7. Paris: Imprimerie Royale, p. vi.
McCrea, W. H., & Reese, M. J., eds. (1983), *The Constants of Physics*. London: Royal Society.
Park, D. (1981), The beginning and end of time in physical cosmology. In: *The Study of Time IV*, eds. J. T. Fraser, N. Lawrence, & D. Park. New York: Springer-Verlag.
——— (1988), *The How and the Why*. Princeton, NJ: Princeton University Press.
Petersen, A. (1968), *Quantum Physics and the Philosophical Tradition*. Cambridge, MA: MIT Press.

Wheeler, J. (1980), Beyond the black hole. In: *Some Strangeness in the Proportion.*, ed. H. Woolf. Reading, MA: Addison-Wesley.

———— (1986), Hermann Weyl and the unity of knowledge. *Amer. Sci.*, 74:366–375.

Whitrow, G. J. (1955), Why physical space has three dimensions. *Brit. J. Philos. Sci.*, 6:13–31.

Woolf, H., ed. (1980), *Some Strangeness in the Proportion.* Reading, MA: Addison-Wesley.

Perspectives

Early in his chapter Professor Park notes that "the fundamental laws of physics are (with one small and, for our purposes, unimportant exception) symmetric with respect to past and future" (p.127). In other words, the equations of physics (classical, relativistic and quantum physics) are appropriate to a world in which, although not everything happens at once, time cannot be said to have a direction, time does not "flow." The temporalities of the physical world are thus more primitive—less articulate, as it were—than those of life and of the human mind. But the relative paucities are only some of the time-related peculiarities of the physical world.

Another group of peculiarities is that elementary objects—the objects of interest to quantum physics—have both a particle and a wave nature. If you ask an elementary object whether it has a particle nature, using an experiment designed to show it to have a particle nature, the object will answer, "Yes, I do." If you ask an elementary object whether it has a wave nature, through an experiment designed to show it to have a wave nature, the object will answer, "Yes, I do."

An elementary object behaves as does a structure in space, such as a pumpkin; it also behaves like a beat, a wave, such as the rhythm of a waltz. Yet, the denizens of the quantum world should not be thought of as waltzing pumpkins but rather as pumpkins that are also waltzes.

The question, "Are you a wave?" or "Are you a particle?" may be addressed to an elementary object, such as a photon, millennia after it began its journey from a distant star to earth. The answer, appropriate to the experiment, will always be "Yes, I am." According to an interpretation of this outcome, proposed by Professor Wheeler and discussed in detail by Professor Park, our free and unpredictable choice of the experiment will have made the photon, retroactively, a particle or a wave.

On this interpretation, the idea that the past cannot be changed is, indeed, a "dogma" (p.125); that is, a belief without adequate grounds. It would then further follow that the continuous change of an undetermined future into a determined past may be all in the mind as it were, and hence the responsibility for identifying the sources of the flow of time must revert back to psychology. Such a conclusion challenges the validity of the assumptions of the five preceding chapters on psychology, namely, that the passing of time is independent of the mind of man and is, both in an evolutionary and ontological sense, prior to it.

In the macroscopic world of our senses space and time are sharply distinguished: we can have no experiences of pumpkins that are also waltzes. The great qualitative difference between our experiential world of space and time and the quantum world with its hazy distinctions between space and time is, I believe, the main reason why quantum theory can only be handled through mathematics, the most abstract of all languages. In natural languages we do not even have words to describe pumpkins that are also tunes, which is why I have been speaking, faute de mieux, *of elementary objects.*

141

8

Physical Time and Mental Time

K. G. Denbigh

Abstract No conflict need be involved in the use, in different contexts, of physical time and mental time, the former being such that the reference moment is some chosen physical event whereas in the latter it is the transient *now*. But physical time, taken on its own, needs the auxiliary assumption of causal interaction between mind and body since otherwise it cannot explain why there is interpersonal agreement on the content of *now*.

Russell and the A- and B- Theories

Concerning time, C. D. Broad wrote: "I have altered my mind too often on this most perplexing subject to feel any confidence that my present opinions are either correct or well-founded" (p. 84). I must confess to similar vicissitudes and to me the issue creating greatest perplexity is the ontological status of *now* (or *the present*), together with the associated issue about becoming. Is the moment we pick out as *now* a fully objective feature of the world-at-large, or is it a psychological phenomenon, a peculiarity of consciousness? Both views can be, and have been, strongly defended.

The issue came to the fore with the advent of special relativity in 1905. Einstein's theory made it clear that two events which are simultaneous for one observer may not be simultaneous for another observer who is in rapid relative motion. As a consequence, the notion of a *world-wide now* does not correspond to physical reality. Yet this conclusion does not invalidate the view that at each location in space there can be a *now*, or a *present*, conceived as the moment when events at that location allegedly happen or take place.

From 1905 onwards a group of philosophers which included Russell (1915), McTaggart (1927), and Broad (1927) began to give much thought to this issue. Russell in particular gave clear formulations to the concepts of physical time and mental time. Roughly speaking these terms correspond respectively to the two distinct ways of knowing about temporal succession—namely from external events,

143

on the one hand, and from inner experience on the other. More importantly these two times differ from each other in regard to the choice of a *reference moment*.[1] Physical time uses some chosen physical event, such as the birth of Jesus, which thus becomes the zero point for a system of timing and dating. Mental time, in contrast, uses as its reference point the privately experienced and transient *now*.

In short, physical time uses the notions earlier than, simultaneous with, and later than relative to a fixed zero point. This provides a system of dating in which all events can be referred to *tenselessly*. Mental time uses the notions of various degrees of pastness and futurity relative to a *changing* zero point which is the *now* or *present*, and statements made in terms of mental time are necessarily *tensed*.

Physical time thus offers the advantage that a given pair of events are related to each other *permanently* in the same way. For example Queen Anne's death (1714) is *always earlier* than Queen Victoria's (1901). Physical time provides "eternal truths" such as was expressed by McTaggart in a beautiful paraphrase: "Before the stars saw one another plain, the event in question was the death of a queen." And of course statements with unchanging truth values cannot be achieved with mental time. For instance it is now the case that the end of my talk is future, but that statement will not remain true. Eventually—thank goodness, you may say!—that ending will be briefly present and then it will be past.

The big difference between these alternative bases for the theory of time therefore lies in the ontological status of *now*. If this moment, along with past and future, were taken to be fully objective, then it might appear that *now* could be interpreted as a moment when being is precipitated out of nonbeing. This is the notion of becoming, the subject of much ardent debate (but not my present concern). On the other hand, if nowness or presentness were nothing more than an aspect of consciousness, a psychological state, then becoming too would not be objective—or at least not in the full sense as meaning independent of man's presence in the world. In that case it would appear improper to apply the notion of presentness to any geological period prior to man's existence. That indeed was Russell's view, for he wrote: "In a world in which there was no experience there would be no past, present or future, ..." (1915, p. 212).

It will be seen that Russell's physical time and mental time correspond respectively to a basing of the time concept on McTaggart's B-series and A-series. The former is the series generated by the terms *earlier than* and *simultaneous with*, whereas the latter is the series generated by events having different degrees of pastness or futurity relative to the transient *now*. Gale (1968) aptly coined the terms *A-theory* and *B-theory*. For present purposes these terms will be taken as referring respectively to the viewpoints that *now* is a fully objective feature of the world, and to the denial of that viewpoint, that is, to the Russellian position that *now* is mind-dependent.[2]

---

[1] I have departed a little from Russell's method of presentation in order to show the relationship with McTaggart's A- and B-series.

[2] At first sight it might appear that the B-theory implies determinism. That this is not the

In my 1981 book I listed what I believed to be the relative merits of the A- and B-theories and came to the conclusion that no empirical (scientific) findings could give any guidance as to which of them should be preferred. At about the same date Schlesinger (1980) published an excellent analysis, but likewise came to no decision. More recently Hamlyn (1984) has indicated some preference for the A-theory whereas Mellor (1981) has argued very cogently for his version of the B-theory. Apart from these books there have been some recent papers which have contributed valuably to the debate (Sosa, 1979; Butterfield, 1984, 1985; Plumer, 1984).

Although the issue remains an open one, my own opinion (stable since 1981!) is that it is mistaken to suppose that the status of *now*, within the larger concept of time, need be a genuine ontological problem. What we call time *is not an existent;* one of the necessary conditions for anything to be said to exist is that it continues in time and it would surely be vacuous to claim that time continues in time! Thus time is not *a something* which has determinate properties or attributes, fixed by nature. This is not to say, of course, that the *temporal relations* between events are in any sense unreal. Far from it. The concept of the *linear temporal order,* to which a consideration of these relations leads, is much more closely defined than is the imprecise notion of time.

Indeed it has perhaps been taken for granted too much that time is the sort of notion for which there is any *single* meaning. It would be in no way contradictory to say that there is a physical time *and* a mental time satisfying different constraints; the former is sufficient for all purposes of physical science whereas mental time is made to satisfy certain *additional* requirements which arise in human affairs. Physical time and mental time are alike in providing what is required (i.e., properties of asymmetry, transitivity, and connectivity) for achieving a serial ordering of events, the temporal order, but mental time is the *richer* of the two in that it includes the *now* of human awareness.

From this point of view (as developed in Denbigh [1981, p. 168]) mental time can be thought of as being the more comprehensive of the two concepts, physical time being derived from it by the discarding of *now*, and other forms of tense, which are superfluous to the needs of physical science. But, equally well, physical time could be taken as the more basic and objective, mental time being obtained from it by a process of enrichment.

My Now and Your Now

A number of readers may prefer a concept of time more closely delimited than has been advocated above and they may opt for physical time as "the only time." If so I want to point out that they need to make use of an additional assumption such as

case was argued very clearly by Smart (1963), who pointed out that successive time slices, as he called them, may not be related to each other in an entirely law-bound manner.

it adopted in interactionist treatments of the mind–body problem. Its necessity may be seen by posing these questions:

If the awareness of *now* is a purely mental affair and is private to each person, as is claimed by the Russellians, why do the members of a group of people seem to share *the same now*? In particular why are they able to agree that they are in a room together, that they are looking at the same clock and obtain the same reading of that clock?

It may seem that this is a peculiar question to raise since we tend to take it for granted that there is nothing problematic about sharing the same *now*. Nevertheless it seems to me an important and genuine problem for those who regard time as being physical time, *tout court,* since this offers no physical correlate of *now.* Certainly it would not be a sufficient answer to say that we share the same *now* because this sharing is essential to our social existence. And neither can it be said that the sharing is entailed by the virtually equal speeds of impulses arriving at different people's brains. For it is not the brain events but rather the conscious awarenesses of them which is the matter at issue and it remains to be argued below that a brain event is followed *at once* by the awareness of it.

Consider first of all what it is to be aware of *now*, of *the present.* Normally, I think, we have no such awareness! When we are attending to our affairs, just living, we are not aware of time passing (to use a deceptive phrase!), or even of a present moment. It is only when we *self-consciously* examine our states of mind that we seem able to pick out such a moment. As Grünbaum (1969) put it, the nowness of an event to a person is the experiencing of that event *together with* the self-awareness that he *is* experiencing it. If so it seems unlikely that nowness exists as clearly for other animals as it does for man. No doubt they all pass, during the wakeful parts of their lives, through a sequence of *states of attention;* that is to say, states in which the animal prepares to take action in the face of impending danger, or of the arrival of food, and so on. But the sense of nowness is something more than that for it depends on the human ability for attention to include the awareness of self (Oakley, 1985).

Notice that our awareness of time differs from our awareness of space in this important respect: that in *any one* state of attention we can be conscious of things or events as being at different places but not as being at different moments. The awareness of time is thus *punctiform* (or nearly so, for there seems to be a small spread, the so-called *specious present*), and this approximately punctiform character is surely due to the fact that the state of attention *is itself an event* and, as such, it has the characteristics of events in general. In particular it has a position within the temporal order.

Pursuing this line of thought let us adopt the familiar representation of time as if it were the straight line in space:

$$\begin{array}{cccc} & \text{E} & & \text{E}' \end{array}$$

| 10.15 | 10.16 | 10.17 | 10.18 |

Such a representation is quite appropriate to the Russellian (i.e., B-theory) viewpoint since this regards all instants as being equally real, just as are the points on a line. None are privileged as a *now* or as a *here.*

Notice that the so-called happening or taking place of an event E is not a *further* event over and above E itself. (For if it were we could go on to speak about the "happening of the happening," and so on in infinite regress.) The putative happening or taking place is nothing more, on the Russellian view, than an artifact of language, and means no more than that the event E has some particular location along the *t*-line or coordinate. Furthermore it would be incorrect to say that the event E ever changes its position on the coordinate. A given event retains the same dating always; as Goodman (1966) put it: "no time is at another time, . . ." (p. 375). But of course if E is a change, or part of a change, in some physical object, that object may undergo a further change, E', located at a different point.

Notice too, and for the same reasons, that a clock on its own does not pick out and identify some particular instant as being the present instant. The hands of the clock move *continuously* round the dial and each one of their coincidences with a number on the dial *is equally real* according to the Russellian view. (To be *real* may be taken as being capable of acting as a cause.) Thus if I look at the clock and report, say, that "The time is now 10.17" it is my consciousness, with its awareness of a present, which picks out, from the continuous sequence, some particular reading as being *the present reading*. In short, the judgment that a certain reading *is now*, rather than that it appertains to past or future, is made within ourselves. Quite literally we *tell* the time!

How then do we manage to agree about the present (i.e., as between different people), as if the present were fully objective and impressed upon us from the outside, a matter denied by the Russellians? To answer this question account must be taken of the physical and causal conditions which underlie the process of perception and which *are* fully objective. Obviously enough I can't *now* perceive anything whatsoever that I might wish—say a woodland scene—nor can I perceive the clock readings in some arbitrary sequence of my choice, say, 10.45, 6.50, 9.41. What can be experienced at each one of my moments of attention is determined by a causal chain extending from the external world into my brain and finally into the seat of my consciousness. Thus it is not a matter of my own choosing.

Consider the situation in more detail. The clock is in front of me. Photons are reflected from its surface and form an image of the hands and dial on my retinas. There follows a further causal process of transmission along my optic nerve right up to my cortex. Then there is a most mysterious "jump" into my consciousness; I became *aware* of particular clock readings and each of them can be experienced as one of my successive *nows*.

The same is true of anyone who is with me in front of the clock. At the instant when the clock hands are at 10.17 on the dial the image of that state of affairs occurs on that person's retinas simultaneously with occurring on mine, and the reception of the message "10.17" is present at that person's cortex almost simultaneously with its being present at mine. This much is guaranteed by the reliability of the causal processes which are involved in the physical mechanism.

But what about that final jump into consciousness, yours and mine? This is something with which physics and neurology cannot deal—not yet at least. In order to explain why we do in fact agree on the clock reading—or indeed any other event—we must make the assumption that there exists a reliable and almost instantaneous process of transmission from cortex into consciousness, a process which would be called causal if it were physical. It follows from this supposition that when the clock hands are at 10:17 we can all have the same *mental* experience that the hands are indeed at 10:17. Those of us who, at that moment, happen also *to be aware* of having that mental experience satisfy the conditions, as outlined earlier, which allow them to say "*Now* it is 10:17."

The occurrence of causal interaction between brain and mind has, of course, been taken for granted by most students of the mind–body problem since Descartes. Nevertheless the mechanism of the supposed interaction has never been made at all intelligible in the context of dualist theories. We normally regard causality as acting between *physical* things, usually with transfer of energy, and no doubt this was one of the difficulties which led to the rejection of brain–mind interaction by the epiphenomenalists, such as T. H. Huxley. Of course this particular difficulty does not arise in physicalist theories of the mind (such as the Identity Theory), or at least not with the same force.

However, it was far from my intention to say anything about the mind–body problem. Let me briefly summarize the second half of this chapter which is about a certain difficulty faced by the theory of physical time (B-theory) although little commented on in the literature. If *nows* have no reality in the external world, as the theory supposes, how does it come about that the perceptual contents of *nows* are the same for different people? To answer this question the B-theory must assume that there is a causal relationship between brain and mind—and of course just such an assumption is commonly adopted although not always made explicit.

References

Broad, C. D. (1927), *Scientific Thought*. London; Kegan Paul.
——— (1938), *Examination of McTaggart's Philosophy*. Cambridge: Cambridge University Press.
Butterfield, J. (1984), Seeing the present. *Mind*, 93:161–176
——— (1985), Indexicals and tense. In: *Exercises in Analysis*, ed. I. Hacking. Cambridge: Cambridge University Press.
Denbigh, K. G. (1981), *Three Concepts of Time*. Heidelberg: Springer Verlag.
Gale, R. M. (1968), *The Language of Time*. London: Routledge & Kegan Paul.
Goodman, N. (1966), *The Structure of Appearance*, 2nd ed. Indianapolis, IN: Bobbs-Merrill.
Grünbaum, A. (1969), The meaning of time. In: *Essays in Honor of Carl G. Hempel*, ed. N. Rescher. Dordrecht: Reidel.
Hamlyn, D. W. (1984), *Metaphysics*. Cambridge: Cambridge University Press.
McTaggart, J. M. E. (1927), *The Nature of Existence*. Cambridge : Cambridge University Press.
Mellor D. H. (1981), *Real Time*. Cambridge: Cambridge University Press.
Oakley, D. A., ed. (1985), *Brain and Mind*. London: Methuen.
Plumer, G. (1984), Why time is extensive. *Mind*, 93:265–270.
Russell, B. (1915), On the experience of time. *Monist*, 25:212–232.
Schlesinger, G. (1980), *Aspects of Time*. Indianapolis, IN: Hackett.
Smart, J. J. C. (1963), *Philosophy and Scientific Realism*. London: Routledge & Kegan Paul.
Sosa, E. (1979), The status of becoming. *J. Philosophy*, 76:26–42.

Perspectives

Professor Denbigh distinguishes between physical and mental time. They are, he writes, "alike in providing what is required . . . for achieving a serial ordering of events, the temporal order, but mental time is the richer of the two in that it includes the now of human awareness" (p.145). Thus, it is the mind that introduces the present into the presentless world of physics.

As I stressed earlier, it is not possible to speak of the flow of time except in the context of future and past, and future and past must always have a referent: the now. If it is the mind that creates the now, then the flow of time is not a cosmic phenomenon, evolutionarily and ontologically prior to mind (as assumed by the psychological papers), neither is it born with life (as maintained by Fraser).

Dr. Denbigh observes that—unless, I would assume, they are quite distant from each other—there is an interpersonal agreement among people on the existence of a common now. People believe that they share the same present moment, from moment to moment. The effectiveness of social behavior based on this belief suggests its reasonableness. In order to account for the interpersonal agreement on a common now, we must assume, Dr. Denbigh maintains, the existence of an "almost instantaneous process of transmission from cortex into consciousness, a process which would be called causal if it were physical" (p. 148). He thus joins the problems of time and mind to those of the brain and mental experience.

The broad critical issue that forms the background to Dr. Denbigh's reasoning is, as I see it, the question of how timing and minding fit in the scheme of the universe.

9

Time and Mind in the Constitution of the Universe: A Critique of the Participatory Anthropic Principle*

Albert Shalom

Abstract The anthropic principle has been arousing increased interest among philosophically minded scientists. J. A. Wheeler's "participatory anthropic principle" is perhaps the most systematic form of the argument. The purpose of this chapter is to clarify the nature of the argument and to question its validity. The central point of the analysis is the attempt to demonstrate that this metascientific argument is very basically self-contradictory. The implication is that metascience, as a discipline directly derived from the physical sciences considered as ultimate basis, is not a viable substitute for metaphysics.

Situating the Problem

Theories concerning the ultimate nature of the universe have been formulated in a number of different ways. The earliest mode of approach was through religious mythologies, such as those of ancient Egypt or early Greece. A second mode is illustrated by the cosmological mechanisms of the Presocratic forerunners of science. The approach underlying their speculations is close to that of science, from the seventeenth century on. The atomism of Democritus is one instance. Another is the similarity between the universe of Empedocles, oscillating through the opposition of forces he calls "love" and "hate," and the contemporary physicist's universe, oscillating between big bang and big crunch. A third mode conceives of the universe as formed and fashioned, directly or indirectly, by a demiurge or god identified with mind or thought; this is the approach of the metaphysical

*I would like to express my appreciation to Dr. Kenneth Denbigh F.R.S., and to Dr. David Park, of the Thompson Physical Laboratory, Williams College. They have enabled me to avoid some errors. Those which remain are mine alone.

151

cosmologies of Plato and Aristotle. And yet a fourth mode of approach is based on the Judeo-Christian conception of an absolute Creator God, bringing the universe into existence *ex nihilo*, from nothing. This mode implies a metaphysical ontology quite different from that of the Greeks.

What is being called the anthropic principle, represents the realization by a number of philosophically minded scientists that their disciplines can no longer remain immune to a generalized theory of cosmology involving quasi-metaphysical considerations. But the formulators of this principle wish to present it as a scientific principle. In order to do this, they exclude religious and metaphysical consider-ations as extraneous, and endeavor to find an immanent principle relating the initial conditions of the physical universe to its latest evolutionary manifestation, man himself. In its most abstract form, the anthropic principle can perhaps be characterized as an attempt to find the sense and meaning of the physical universe in the fact of the appearance of man: it being clearly understood that this has no religious connotation, that man is purely a product of the physical universe as understood by the physical sciences per se.

We can approach the problem more systematically. Since the rise of Christianity in the first century, and the development of the sciences from the sixteenth, cosmological theorizings in philosophy have been in terms of a relationship between the physical universe and a Creator God. The fundamental Judeo-Christian concept of a God creating the universe out of nothing has meant that from the first, the most basic form of these cosmological theorizings had to do with the existential status of the universe relative to that of God. The assertion of the existential primacy of God had reached its high point in the thirteenth century, in the work of Thomas Aquinas. Basing himself on a physics which is no longer valid, Aquinas starts his five proofs of the existence of God by stating that since motion requires a mover, and since the universe is in motion, it follows that there must be a prime mover. Having thus asserted the need to recognize an absolute God as the source of motion, Aquinas goes on to generalize this position by holding that the very existence of the universe would not be possible without presupposing a God, because the universe does not possess its own reason for being, whereas God must be conceived as existence itself. It is only subsequent to these existential considerations that Aquinas raises the question of the structure or design of the universe.

It is important to bear this sequence in mind when considering the general thesis of the anthropic principle. For this principle implicitly presupposes the very contrary position, namely that the universe is meaningfully self-sufficient. That is why it is no accident that in their massive work on *The Anthropic Cosmological Principle* (1986), Barrow and Tipler devote an exceedingly long chapter (pp. 27–122) not to the problem of the existence of the universe but to the problem known as the design argument for the existence of God, considering it as a speculative precursor of a scientific cosmology. The essential point of this scientific cosmology is that the fundamental factors in the design of the universe are a set of highly improbable conditions which have had the extraordinary result of bringing into existence man, capable of understanding that very universe. It will be noticed that the primacy given to design results in the primacy given to science. We have gone from an existential foundation to be sought for in a God conceived as ultimate existent and ultimate raison d'être of human existence, to a formal foundation, the raison d'être of which is scientific knowledge.

Leaving the problem of existence aside, we can now examine more closely this scientific modification of the traditional theistic argument from design. One of the historically better-known instances of this argument is that of the English theologian William Paley. The subtitle of Paley's last significant work, *Natural Theology* (1802), reads as follows: "Evidences of the existence and attributes of the Deity collected from the appearances of Nature." The essential theme is that adaptive mechanisms in, for instance, living creatures must be regarded as evidence of an intelligent Creator, just as we naturally assume that there can be no watch without an intelligent watchmaker. This eighteenth-century imagery is not very far from the thinking of John A. Wheeler, the main proponent of the anthropic principle with which we shall shortly be concerned. But what we should also notice is that the design argument brackets out the problem of the existence of the universe, which is taken for granted. To be more precise, a theist like Paley would simply assume that the design argument somehow entails an answer to the ontological problem of the universe: that it exists because God created it.

But the philosopher David Hume, a far more powerful thinker than Paley, had already anticipated the weakness in Paley's mode of argumentation: it does not prove, but presupposes, the existence of a Creator God. In the *Dialogues Concerning Natural Religion* (1777), published a year after Hume's death, the argument from design is shown to be based on an unwarranted presupposition. What we take to be evidence of an intelligent Creator—adaptive mechanisms and, by extension, the intelligent organization of the universe—is simply a fact of experience and does not authorize the conceptual leap to an absolute Creator. It is of some importance to grasp as clearly as possible what is happening here. In the Judeo-Christian Western world God is quite naturally assumed to be an absolute Creator. Therefore any theistic design argument is simply taken to *mean* reference to a Creator God. But there is, in fact, no such inherent necessity in the argument itself. Plato's forming and fashioning demiurge is not a Creator God in the Judeo-Christian sense, but he quite specifically is the object of an argument from design.

What this means is that the design argument can only function as a confirmation move for presuppositions which are already held. If I already believe in a Creator God, then the intelligent design of the universe is a confirmation of this belief. By itself, the design argument is not powerful enough to be convincing. It is this weakness in the argument which Hume so clearly saw. For if we consider the order of the universe without having any belief in demiurge or Creator, that order or design does not necessarily entail the need to believe in any sort of god. Since Newton had just demonstrated that there were universal physical laws inherent in the functioning of the physical world, a demonstration far more powerful than Descartes' analogous attempt, it clearly followed that there was no need to go any further and look for Creator or demiurge. This is the fundamental point of Hume's rejection of the argument from design.

It is now necessary to situate the anthropic principle within the context of these theological considerations. An initial point which can be immediately made is that insofar as the Hume-Paley debate is concerned with the existence or the nonexistence of a Creator God or of a Platonic demiurge, the adherents of the anthropic principle are not on Paley's, but on Hume's side. They are certainly not arguing for the existence of a God, nor are they reviving the notion of a demiurge. But on the other hand, they are not simply saying what the common-sense realist might say: that the perceived order of the universe is a fact which must simply be taken for granted, as a fundamental background for scientific activity. It is precisely their rejection of this which has made for the interest of their work among scientists. The point is that the attitude of presupposing a stable world and its processes, which can be assumed for much of eighteenth- and nineteenth-century science, no longer seems possible. Since the advent of relativity in the first quarter of the twentieth century, and since the development of quantum theory during the second quarter, science can no longer consider the subject as no more than a presupposed observer.

In any event, a first point is clear: the adherents of the anthropic principle are not arguing for the existence of any god. And yet they are fundamentally concerned with design, as Barrow and Tipler make clear. But since the importance they give to design arguments is not in order to confirm the existence of God, what is it for? Its basic aim, as a first move, is to emphasize the negligibly small degree of probability for such a structure as this Earth and its inhabitants to have occurred at all. This is how Wheeler expresses it: "Not only is man adapted to the universe, the universe is adapted to man. Imagine a universe in which one or another of the fundamental dimensionless constants of physics differs from this world's values by a few percent one way or the other. The consequences for the physics of the stars so multiply themselves up that man could never have come into being in such a universe" (1986, p. 372).[1] Philosophically, one might be inclined to say that if true, the assertion is certainly striking, but that it does not seem to prove anything. According to our diverse presuppositions, we could take the alleged fact as support for the theory of a Creator God, as support for the theory of an indefinite number of possible worlds, or simply as evidence of a quite remarkable accident.

The important point is that what matters from the standpoint of science is what actually, what concretely, happens. What Wheeler holds is that the conditions for the appearance of this world were remotely improbable, and yet not only did this world appear, but it gave rise to man who is capable of knowing the world. The principle is called "anthropic" because the center of attention has moved from the assertion of a design meant to prove the existence of God to the assertion of a design which has, in fact, given rise to man—against all odds. In other words, the formation of planet Earth and the consequent evolution of man was statistically so improbable that it is leading some scientists to wonder whether their own existence as scientific observers might not constitute the finality of the design itself.

We can perhaps now begin to situate the problem more clearly. It has to do

---

[1] I am indebted to Dr. Park for reference to this paper.

with the question of how it is that the universe is adapted to man. Philosophically, we know that idealism has proposed an answer to this problem: the universe is adapted to man because it is fashioned in terms of the categories of an absolute mind or spirit, in which man participates directly. And we will shortly see that there are definite analogies between philosophical idealism and the anthropic principle. But there is also a fundamental difference: the formulators of the anthropic principle have as sole framework the evolution of the physical universe per se, without reference to any absolute mind or spirit.

We are thus faced with the strange problem of a physical universe existing billions of years before man appeared on the scene, and yet apparently "adapted to man" in the sense that from the start, the universe manifests remotely improbable conditions resulting in the appearance of man—and all this without any allowable reference to a God, for which science can offer no evidence. Some initial expressions of this adaptability of the universe to man will lead us to what Barrow and Tipler call "the weak anthropic principle" (WAP). In 1955 G. J. Whitrow suggested that space has three dimensions because of the "anthropic self-selection idea" (quoted in Barrow and Tipler, 1986, p. 12). In the article referred to, "Why physical space has three dimensions," Whitrow writes as follows: "I suggest that a possible clue to the elucidation of this problem is provided by the fact that physical conditions on the Earth have been such that the evolution of man has been possible" (Whitrow, 1955, p. 29). In 1957, the astronomer R. H. Dicke, referring to the "large cosmic numbers," wrote that those numbers were "not random but conditioned by biological factors" (quoted in Barrow and Tipler, 1986, p. 16). In his brief letter to the editor of *Nature*, Dicke's specific reference is to a range of numerical values which must be "limited by the biological requirements to be met during the epoch of man" (Dicke, 1961, p. 440). And in 1961 Brandon Carter expressed the anthropic principle thus: "our location in the universe is accessorily privileged to the extent of being compatible with our existence as observers" (Carter, 1974, p. 291).

As a prelude to the analysis of Wheeler's "participatory anthropic principle," let us look a little more closely at the implications of this weaker form of the anthropic principle, symbolized as WAP. The very fact that it is called "weak" indicates that the principle, though in some sense a truism, might nevertheless imply more than might at first appear. This is Barrow and Tipler's formulation of it: "The observed values of all physical and cosmological quantities are not equally probable but they take on values restricted by the requirement that there exist sites where carbon-based life can evolve and by the requirement that the universe be old enough for it to have already done so" (1986, p. 16). For our purposes, the key phrase in this definition is the twice-repeated expression "restricted by the requirement that." Though the authors immediately refer to the mathematics of probability (1986, pp. 17–19), probability is not, itself, an explanatory principle but a tool of calculation. However many the number of "possible worlds," each actualization of such a world will need its own specific principles of explanation. Hence the ambiguity of the quoted expression. As regards this actual world, what the expression means is that from the very beginning of time, from the start of the big bang, the values of "all physical and cosmological quantities" are "restricted by the requirement that" man, the eventual scientific observer, should appear on this planet (Barrow and Tipler, 1986, p. 16).

But two quite different senses can be given to this restricting clause. It can either mean the truism that since man *has* appeared on this planet, then quite obviously the conditions of his appearance must be presupposed. This may well be what is intended by WAP, but the vocabulary is not entirely consistent with such neutrality. What creates the problem is the very notion of a restricting requirement at the start of the universe. Such an assertion distinguishes the adherent of the anthropic principle from the vast majority of his scientific colleagues, for it eliminates the category of "accident," which means "no known explanation," which is usually used in the description of inorganic and organic evolution.

Such a category is there to indicate that it is only by virtue of the contingency and fortuitousness of physicochemical interactions that the evolutionary process occurred at all. Thus, for instance, in the three hundred pages Ernst Mayr devotes to evolution in his *Growth of Biological Thought* (1982, pp. 301–627), there is no indication that the selection process is a matter of any cosmological requirement. And again, when the chemist Harold Blum (1968) referred to evolution, he quite naturally used the concept of "spontaneous generation" (p. 166). Even when the chemist takes a great step forward in the elucidation of the processes of the emergence of living matter, as did M. Eigen with his analysis of systems in disequilibrium (Eigen and Schuster, 1977, 1978), the very fact that such systems occurred at all is still regarded as basically a matter of accident, mutation, or selection. Thus, writes Eigen, "The hypercycle must have a precursor, present in high natural abundance, from which it originates gradually by a mechanism of mutation and selection" (Eigen and Schuster, 1978, p. 354).

Philosophically, this is of course unsatisfactory because the question of whether life, and in particular man, exist accidentally or by virtue of some transcendent or immanent purpose is among the most basic of metaphysical and religious problems. But it is usually taken for granted that such problems cannot be solved by the use of scientific methods because these require a vocabulary of experimental verification incompatible with the assertion of cosmic purposes or requirements. It is just here that the adherents of the anthropic principle separate themselves from the majority of scientists. And this brings us to the second of the two possible meanings which can be given to the clause "restricted by the requirement that." This second meaning is the explicit transposition of the language of "requirement" into the language of "purpose." This transposition can be observed, for instance, in the language frequently used by neurologists when they write of nerves "wanting" or "intending" to grow in this or that direction.

But nerve cells do not, themselves, *want* or *intend* in the sense in which we ordinarily use these words. Or if the neurologist really means what he is saying, then he is subscribing to some form of primitive animism and not to science. Within the framework of science, the language of purpose can only be metaphorical. And this immediately raises the question of whether the restrictive "requirement" of the anthropic principle does or does not imply "purpose." That is to say, the supposition that the highly improbable set of factors which conditioned the appearance of planet Earth and its subsequent evolution occurred *in order that* man, the scientific observer of the universe, should appear on the scene. We will see, shortly, that Wheeler does, in fact, make this suggestion.

This interpretation is analogous to certain religious themes concerning the appearance of this world, but with a very basic difference as regards the question of origins and of the consequent finality involved. The religious theme holds that man is, in some sense, a specific entity which must find both its source and its finality in God. But for the adherent of the anthropic principle, the origin and the finality of man are to be found, respectively, in the physical universe as understood by science, and in the scientist's ability to understand that universe. It would therefore be more accurate to describe the anthropic principle as the doctrine according to which the physical universe itself achieves a form of self-knowledge through and by means of man. Wheeler even has a diagram expressing this thesis. Therefore to say, as do Barrow and Tipler in their definition of WAP, that the original parameters of the big bang are "restricted by the requirement that there exist sites where carbon-based life can evolve" is to say a good deal more than the truism that since man already exists, the conditions of his appearance must have been present from the start.

This latter statement can be taken as the tacit presupposition of all those scientists who have endeavored to work out just how that evolution can have occurred, and who have alluded to its various phases as accidents or mutations required by selection. Conversely, the adherents of the anthropic principle are projecting backwards into the long-distant cosmological beginnings of a universe which produced them only after several billion years, an intention on the part of those physical cosmological beginnings themselves. They are saying that the appearance of a creature able to grasp the nature of the evolution of the universe is the very purpose and meaning of the existence of that physical universe. The concept of an anthropic principle implies a development of that principle itself from an initial, exploratory, formulation called the "weak anthropic principle," to its fully developed or explicated form. It is at the fully explicated stage that a fundamental choice must be made: either to go to the logical conclusion, as does Wheeler, or to reintroduce the traditional, religious theme.

The "strong anthropic principle," or SAP, states that "The universe must have those properties which allow life to develop within it at some stage in its history" (Barrow and Tipler, 1986, p. 12). The essential step here is the move from a "restrictive requirement" to the assertion of a "must." We are here left in no doubt that the universe exists in order that man, the observer and knower of the universe, shall have come into existence. This strong anthropic principle means no more than that the scientist himself is beginning to realize the inherent implications of his own general concept of an "anthropic principle." He is showing in act, so to speak, that there is such a thing as a conceptual logic which is determined by the nature of those key concepts which he has chosen as the basis of his theory.

Formulating the general idea of an anthropic principle is, in effect, holding the conception that the universe exists in order to produce man. The realization of the full force of this assertion must have led to a certain amount of self-questioning on the part of some of the adherents of this "principle." For what, after all, does it really mean to say that the physical universe exists for the appearance of man? Does it imply what the Hebrew text has been asserting for four thousand years and Christianity for two: that it is a God who inscribed the finality of man in the initial cosmological explosion, there called "creation"? Or does it imply that the initial cosmological explosion simply happened to have, or itself decided to have, inscribed within it the finality of man? Would this be the language of "accident," of "possible worlds," or would we be saying that the initial nuclear explosion itself determined itself toward that finality? Barrow and Tipler are perhaps referring to the consequences of this ambiguity when they state that a number of men of science hold to the strong version of the anthropic principle but interpret the position as "religious in nature" and as not amenable "to proof or to disproof" if left in that form (1986, p. 22).

With the above points in mind, we can now turn to the last task of this first section: a brief situating of the anthropic principle. As we know, the principle is meant to be a scientific principle. But science is a latecomer in history, and though it has now acquired the power to annihilate us, it is not at all certain that it possesses the ability to explain our existence. It would therefore be an appropriate preliminary step to situate the nature of this latecomer in history.

From the earliest times the endless process of birth and dying, coupled with the instinct for survival, must have led to endless tales of life after death. And it must have taken a very long time indeed before these stories could be put to the test of rational thinking. In Greece, putting mythologies to the test of rational explanation meant the emergence of the mode of thinking which characterizes the Presocratics, a combination of quasi-scientific thinking with relicts of religious mythology. The implicit questions were: "what is everything made of?"; "how does the world function?"; "where are the gods to be situated?" In its turn, this early questioning gave rise to a more systematic mode of thinking which attempted to integrate cosmological speculations into a general metaphysics. The only point of significance for us here is that in all these modes of thinking the eternity of physical existence was taken for granted.

For the more radical questioning of physical existence itself, it is necessary to go from Greece to Judea. Whatever the cause, it is in Hebrew religious thinking that there eventually arose, for the first time, the dual and reciprocal concept of a radically absolute being called "God," and a radically contingent physical universe. This conceptual framework of a full being on one side and a fundamentally dependent or radically contingent being on the other, was a very different framework from the essentially Greek conception of a "hierarchy of being." However close Plato's *Symposium* may be to Christianity in other respects, it does not and cannot manifest the fundamental ontological thesis of Judeo-Christianity: the Hebrew concept of "creation out of nothing." We shall see that Wheeler accepts the same thesis, but without the notion of a Creator God.

Despite the inadequate brevity of this sketch, it can be used to formulate the following three successive questions as a background summary of the anthropic principle. The questions themselves represent mere fragments of a complex situation:

1. The Presocratic question of what the physical universe is made of and how it functions;

2. The Platonic and Aristotelian question of how mind or the divine are related to the physical universe;

3. The implicit Hebrew question of how we are to understand the radical contingency of the universe and its creation by an absolute God.

In a very rough manner, one can perhaps consider that long period collectively called "the Middle Ages" as something like an extended attempt to clarify the third of these questions by using the tools of the second, the concepts of Greek philosophy. It is for that reason that it has for so long a period been taken for granted that first beginnings meant a creation "from nothing" by an absolute God: that is, the assertion of the ontological primacy of a Creator God considered as absolute being, and the radical ontological contingency of a created physical existence. It is for the same reason that any proof of the existence of God was spontaneously predicated of the absolute God of the Hebrews, and not of the forming and fashioning demiurge of Plato's *Timaeus*.

The retreat from this position might have started in the fourteenth century with Ockham's nominalism, or even earlier with St. Anselm's misnamed "ontological proof." The attempt to demonstrate the existence of God by defining God as "that concerning which nothing greater can be thought" shifts the focus of attention from the status of the universe relative to the status of a Creator God, to the problem of the status of mind or thinking relative to God. The significance of this for us here is that Anselm constitutes a first step away from a natural realism which takes for granted the existence of the perceived physical universe and which is the natural basis for the question of the ontological status of this universe.

What is of particular concern to us here is that by the time we reach Descartes' seventeenth-century elaboration of the metaphysical implications of the rise of mechanism, we discover that Anselm's proto-idealistic orientation through ideas or "contents of mind," is now combined with a new scientism. This new orientation no longer emphasizes the contingent existence of the physical universe as a basis for asserting the existence of God. It emphasizes Anselm's incipient idealism and analogously aims at proving the existence of God by means of ideas, of the "content of mind," more specifically the idea of Perfection. It therefore also constitutes a partial return to Platonism, though we can here clearly see the effects of the long medieval process of establishing the Judeo-Christian concept of an absolute Creator God. Though Descartes attempts to prove the existence of God through the idea of Perfection, the God he spontaneously has in mind is not the demiurge or fashioning god of Plato's philosophy, but the absolute Creator of Judeo-Christianity—in spite of the fact that the concept of Perfection does not imply the notion of a Creator God. It is just because Descartes' God is, in fact, the God of Judeo-Christianity that he can attribute to this God the "continuous creativity" needed to explain the continued existence of the physical universe, a problem which does not exist for Plato's cosmology.

It is important to clarify some of the implications of Cartesianism in order to situate the anthropic principle. The fundamental point we have to bear in mind concerning Descartes' physics, most clearly formulated in *Le Monde* (Descartes, 1979, pp. 48–78), is its definition of matter as "extended substance." This was perhaps the clearest expression of early mechanism's rejection of the Aristotelian conception of an original matter which is to be conceived as pure potentiality. But the consequence of this redefinition of matter was to exclude from physical reality all potentiality for motion, change, or development. The simple idea of a solid block of indefinitely extended matter excludes the idea that this extended matter can contain within itself the powers of motion, of chemical interaction, of growth and decay, of biological evolution. The motions of the physical universe have to be explained in terms of a cause outside itself. Hence the Cartesian and Newtonian conception of a God who sets the physical world in motion, like a clockmaker setting the mechanism of a clock in motion.

It needs to be underlined that this conception is by no means an obvious truth: Descartes is not describing the physical universe as we know it. He is proposing a *theory* about physical reality. The universe we experience and know is a universe in which motion, change, growth, decay, and death already exist. In order to explain these processes purely in terms of matter in motion, it was necessary for Descartes to posit a God setting that matter in motion, and it was necessary for him to attempt to explain chemical change and biological growth and decay in terms of the differing patterns of matter in motion. But it is also of fundamental importance for us to realize that the deity responsible for these diverse motions of matter need not be a Creator God: a Platonic demiurge would do just as well. It was as a believing Catholic that Descartes wrote, and that is why he so easily uses the concept of "creation." But the concept of a physical reality as being fundamentally an extension of pure matter does not, per se, imply a Creator God because that extended matter could, itself, be eternal. The retreat from the concept of a Creator God was by no means stopped by the birth of science, and we shall see that the anthropic principle carries that retreat to its logical end.

But a second, equally fundamental, consequence of Descartes' metaphysical interpretation of the implications of mechanism is the radical separation he is obliged to assert between matter and mind. Matter as pure physical extension cannot accommodate mind, so that mind must be allocated a separate, substantial existence. This, again, is a return to the early Plato and an explicit rejection of the Aristotelian attempt to combine the physical and the mental in terms of potentiality and actualization (see Shalom [1984] for a more detailed analysis). But this time, the mathematical analysis of matter and its motions will lead to an extraordinary development in the physical sciences. Mind, however, thus detached from matter and transformed into an inexplicable pure observer of the processes of matter, will constitute a realm of experiences and ideas from which must be derived the philosophical themes of God and subjectivity which cannot be derived from the descriptions of the motions of matter. It is here, of course, in the realm of ideas, that Descartes will situate his theory of a "thinking substance" and find the source of his proofs of the existence of God.

What does all this have to do with the anthropic principle? The Cartesian revolution in philosophy is the expression of a split in human knowledge, a split between scientific methodology applied to the physical world and a philosophical reorientation toward the inner world of mind. This split, indispensable for the early development of mechanism, was made at the expense of the Aristotelian attempt at a unified conception of the universe. It was also made at the expense of the non-Aristotelian concept of an absolute God and of the thesis of the radical contingency of the physical universe. In terms of metaphysics, the ontologically absolute God, radically differentiated from his radically contingent creation, will become, through Spinoza, then Kant and Hegel, a radically immanent process of Absolute Spirit, itself encompassing the laws of science and the events of history. The physical universe thereby becomes locatable as a moment in the process of Absolute Spirit. We can therefore now add a fourth question to the previous three:

4. It is the Idealist question of how the physical universe can be encompassed and subordinated to the process of an Absolute Idea.

When Descartes defined matter as radically other than mind, he in effect set up a specific domain as the proper object of future scientific activity. Correlatively, the assertion of a pure thinking substance meant the transformation of the living human subject into a pure "observer" who could apply mathematical thinking to the spatial essence of matter in motion. On the one hand, then, an isolated domain of matter in motion; on the other, a correlatively separate domain of experience and thinking grounded in a "thinking substance." With some minor exceptions, this observer–observed conceptual scheme has been the natural framework of science from the seventeenth century to the first quarter of the twentieth century.

At the same time, the progressive transformation of the concept of a radically transcendent Creator God into a radically immanent Mind or Absolute Spirit implied that the observer–observed framework was, in fact, a provisional construction resulting from the inner laws of a more fundamental reality. The existential reality and opacity of the physical world was no longer to be interpreted in terms of a transcendent Creator God whose ultimate laws are beyond the range of our concepts. On the contrary, the physical world was to be interpreted in terms of the processes of an immanent Mind which itself was responsible for positing the observer–observed dichotomy. The fundamental Judeo-Christian distinction between Creator and created becomes the metaphysician of mind's distinction between a subject and object self-posited as a basic move in the autobiography of Absolute Spirit.

From this standpoint the observer–observed distinction, which Descartes believed to be irreducible, was to be understood as the dual manifestation of the new absolute, a metaphysical and transpersonal immanent Mind. And of course, only those metaphysicians able to perform "transcendental" or "phenomenological" analyses could claim to reveal the ultimate reality of nature and of history. Philosophy as the metaphysics of mind posited itself as the high point of understanding. Unfortunately for itself, it did so at a time when real understanding of the physical universe was being daily achieved by the great developments in the physical sciences, and this inevitably led to a gradual and fundamental change in outlook in Western philosophy. Within less than a century, for instance, the "phenomenology of mind" was transformed into the current problem of how neurochemical brain processes can give rise to subjective experience at all. The conversion of absolute idealism into unitary materialism is the background to the anthropic principle. And this naturally leads us to the formulation of a fifth question:

5. It is the scientistic question of how life and mind can be reduced and subordinated to the processes of the physical universe.

The conceptual framework of absolute idealism is a mythological "absolute mind." The conceptual framework of the physical sciences is a very real physical world, to which must be added a methodology which has not ceased to manifest its effectiveness. The question to be raised concerns the range of this methodology. If it is unquestioned when dealing with certain kinds of physical problems, does it follow that it is able to deal with every kind of problem raised by the existence of the physical universe? It is understandable that some scientists should believe this to be the case. Thus, for instance, Steven Weinberg informs philosophers that they are "out of their jurisdiction" when they "speculate" on such subjects as "space, time, causality, ultimate particles" (Weinberg, 1977b, p. 175). And Professor P. C. W. Davies informs his readers that "It is a striking thought that ten years of radio astronomy have taught humanity more about the creation and organization of the universe than thousands of years of religion and philosophy" (Davies, 1977, p. 211).

The analysis of the anthropic principle, in particular Wheeler's version of it, will illustrate the kind of teachings science can lead to when it oversteps the limits of its proper domain. But more generally, how are we philosophers to respond to these claims of the scientist? The brain surgeon, R. Sperry, has made the same generalized claim about "the number one proven method" which he also believes can solve "the age-old problems" of philosophy (1965). And yet it is the very weakness of Sperry's proposed solution to the body–mind problem which shows the limits of science. The neurologist's universe of discourse is necessarily in terms of the vocabulary of his discipline. Therefore unless he can actually show how the language of subjectivity can be in fact *derived* from the language of neurology, all he can actually do is indicate the neurological correlates *of* subjective experience. And that is not a solution to the body–mind problem.

The same can be said for Weinberg and Davies. The fundamental problems of metaphysics are the existential groundings of the physical universe, and the source of animal and human subjectivity. Is the idea of a "big bang" an existential grounding of the physical universe? Weinberg himself has answered that question by reflecting, at the end of his *First Three Minutes,* that the more comprehensible the universe seems, the more meaningless it appears to him to be (Weinberg, 1977a, p. 154). And to suppose that "space, time, causality" and the metaphysical equivalent of "ultimate particles," which is the sense to be given to the existence of the physical, are concepts which are limited to the calculations of science is as parochial as the idealist's attempt to legislate for the activities of science.

But it is now time to turn to the scientist's attempt to make his own discipline the basis for metaphysical assertions. The attempt to treat science as the ultimate basis for philosophical assertions is what I call "metascience." Professor Wheeler is convinced that his formulation of the anthropic principle is a matter of science, and that it will eventually be scientifically demonstrable. In the meantime, this volume on time and mind gives at least one philosopher the opportunity to examine the conceptual presuppositions with which Wheeler has been working. I can therefore appropriately end this section by formulating a sixth and last question which it is the object of the rest of this chapter to analyze:

6. It is the anthropic principle's question of whether the past-oriented observations of the present astronomer–physicist prove that in coming into existence, the future-oriented "big bang" intended the occurrence of such observations.

Metaphysics and Metascience

The purpose of this section is to illustrate, by reference to Barrow and Tipler, the essential difference between a metaphysical and a metascientific approach to the problem of time and mind in the universe. At the start of their chapter on design arguments, Barrow and Tipler characterize the anthropic principle as "just the latest manifestation" of an argument which can be traced back, they say, to the "metaphysics" (which they put in quotes) of the period "when philosophy and science were conjoined" (Barrow and Tipler, 1986, pp. 27–28). They add that one of the apparent characteristics of the disjoining of these disciplines is that "scientists rarely take philosophers seriously." Let us take their own assertions seriously and see where they lead.

The traditional arguments from design were meant to prove the existence of a God, whether interpreted in terms of absolute existence or in terms of absolute mind. We may therefore infer that after the emergence of science from philosophy, the scientific interest of the argument from design does not have anything to do with proving the existence of a God. If we ask what it is that a William Paley or a David Hume has in mind when he is discussing design arguments, it will be clear that the nature of the argument is as follows: whether the fact of design is, or is not, a sufficient basis for inferring a God. When a scientist is considering design, it is not in order to refer to something transcending the design: it is in order to analyze the design itself, as well as its possible implications. Since the anthropic cosmological argument is based on the improbability of the occurrence of the universe and of man, the metascientific problem is that of analyzing this fact in order to discern some revealing patterns or relationships in the design itself.

It is at this point that we are faced with the first really fundamental difference between metaphysics and metascience: the problem of ontology. Is the existence of the universe to be taken for granted or does its very presence need justification? But what would it mean, to justify the presence or the existence of the universe except to raise the problem of the existence of a God? And since we know that this question is merely the nonscientific precursor to the anthropic principle, we also know that the question of the existence of the universe cannot be a real question for the adherents of the anthropic principle. Since the frame of reference for scientific research is the presupposition of the existence of the physical universe, what could it possibly mean for a scientist to put into question the very framework of his own activity? He would in effect be turning from science to philosophy or religion, and would thereby be abandoning the very basis of metascience. Without needing to go into any detail here, we can see that it is this which explains, for instance, the misleading section on the argument from contingency at the end of Barrow and Tipler's chapter on design arguments. Since the authors define existence in terms of empirical observation—"an entity x is said to exist, if it is possible, at least in principle, to observe it, or to infer it from the observation of other entities" (Barrow and Tipler, 1986, p. 108)—how could there be any question regarding the existence of the universe?

To summarize the point briefly, what appears to characterize the philosophical approach to the problem of the existence of the physical universe, is the search for a source in something other than the physical universe per se. The metaphysician will look for an answer in God, in a transcendental mind or ego, or in an absolute spirit constituting the sense and meaning of the physical universe. If he abandons all such answers, he will also abandon metaphysics, which a number of philosophers have done in the modern period. The metascientific approach, on the other hand, is to ignore or dismiss any problem of contingency, and to consider all problems related to the universe as problems immanent to the physical activity of the universe itself. If a scientist has any religious belief, and many scientists clearly do, it is unlikely that this belief will have been derived from his work as a scientist. It will have been presupposed, and science will then tend to confirm belief or disbelief.

Thus the first basic difference between metaphysics and metascience is that the problem of the contingency of the universe itself is basic for metaphysics but irrelevant for metascience. And this now leads us to the second difference between these two approaches. This second difference has to do with the human or "anthropic" subject himself. For metaphysics, the problem of the subject is a function of the problem of the status of the physical itself. Thus, for instance, Descartes' assertion that the physical is essentially material extension carries with it the consequence that the subject can only be conceived as "pure thinking substance." And this means that Descartes' statement *about* the physical is itself a metaphysical statement and not a statement *of* physics. But for metascience there is no such conception as the metaphysical status of the physical: the physical is what the physicist says it is, and Descartes was simply wrong. One can understand Weinberg's easy dismissal of philosophy!

But the dismissal is a little too easy. The anthropic principle is an attempt on the part of some men of science to situate man within the physical universe. The metaphysical approach to the problem is to situate the activity of mind relative to that of body. A more useful formulation of the problem would perhaps be to say that since man appears to have emerged from the processes of the physical universe, what are the conditions required for that emergence? Thus, the metaphysical problem of man becomes the problem of considering the specific characteristics of a physical reality which can explain the emergence of the subjective or the mental. This is not the approach of metascience. For the adherents of the anthropic principle, the appearance of man is simply to be taken as a fact, a fact which is explainable in terms of chemistry and of biological evolution. For the metascientist, there is no characteristic of subjective experience which is not in principle explainable by one or other of the physical sciences.

No scientist has, in fact, been able to reduce even the simplest of sensations to neurological processes. But this does not worry the adherent of the anthropic principle since his unquestioned presupposition is that science must be able to solve this problem. And hence the consequence of this presupposition is that the anthropic theorist shifts the problem elsewhere. Taking the existence of man for granted, he proposes to use that fact as the fundamental factor which is to make sense of the emergence of the universe. Relative to metaphysics, metascience operates here an inversion: instead of asking what kind of conditions must be attributed to a physical reality which can give rise to an experiencing entity like man, metascience uses the existence of man as the essential factor which makes sense of the emergence of the universe. And this is not to be understood in the religious or metaphysical sense of referring to a God or to an Absolute Mind, but in the sense that the physical universe itself has man inscribed within it as its intended finality. Such a conception supposes that this finality is inscribed in nuclear radiation and in elementary particles per se; it supposes that space, time, and causality are in themselves intentional; and it supposes that the future determines the past, a conception supposedly verified by the delayed choice experiment. These assertions are not being made by wild, woolly, and irresponsible metaphysicians going beyond what Weinberg imagines to be their "jurisdiction": they are being made by well-known men of science who believe that the astrophysics of cosmological evolution implies the metascience of the anthropic principle.

But this time it is we, the metaphysicians, who must ask for evidence and for convincing analyses. Unfortunately, such evidence and analyses are not easy to come by. In fact, when we consider the language used by Barrow and Tipler, we are faced with a vocabulary of metaphors which immediately raises the question of whether metascience is conceptually equipped to deal with these problems. For instance, when discussing Absolute Idealism, which the authors rightly feel has clear affinities with the anthropic principle, they proceed as follows. Stating first that "Mind is in some way essential to the cosmos" (Barrow and Tipler, 1986, p. 125), they indicate that Hegel's notion of the "Absolute Idea" is a good prescientific approximation to a view which they hold to be scientifically acceptable. What they mean by this is the need to transform the Hegelian "Absolute Idea" into the concept of a "Universal Programme" (pp. 154–155). In other words, the first sentence of a metascientific genesis should read "In the beginning there was a Universal Programme and the observing scientist is its finality." Are we really to take such a "scientific" inference seriously?

Again, a little later in the text, when the authors are considering Wheeler's combination of quantum theory with anthropic principle, Barrow and Tipler write that if Wheeler is correct, there "is no reason why we should not regard *all* electron properties as contingent in principle on some sort of observation. . . . Perhaps *all* properties—and hence the entire Universe is brought into existence by observations made at some point in time by conscious beings . . ." (p. 470). If we raise the question of just who these "conscious beings" might be, the authors concede that since "we ourselves can bring into existence only very small-scale properties like the spin of the electron," then it must "require intelligent beings 'more conscious' than ourselves, to bring into existence the electrons and other particles . . ." (p. 470). Leaving aside the theological undertones of this remarkable text, it will be noticed that the mode of argumentation is, first, the projection on a cosmological scale of the scientist's activity, and second, the reification of the result of this projection as "intelligent beings 'more conscious' than ourselves." Are these "beings" angels or Platonic gods functioning as superscientists? In point of fact, the only observers the authors can really refer to are what Wheeler calls those "solid outposts of observation" who are the physicists themselves. But short of supposing that we are indebted for our present existence to the observations of twentieth-century physicists, we must conclude that Barrow and Tipler are referring to the exceedingly vague idea of an "observing" somehow giving rise to a "universal programme" inherent in the initial "big bang." As a sample of that mode of thinking which P. C. W. Davies has described as far surpassing "thousands of years of religion and philosophy" (1977, p. 211), this is not very promising. To project backward the notion of information processing whilst attributing it to some kind of mysterious "being," which is nowhere seriously analyzed, this is not a mode of argumentation which, at least philosophically, can carry us very far.

In point of fact, the weakness of metascience is directly derivable from its basic presupposition: that a satisfactory explanation for the existence of human beings can be directly derived from the physical sciences. What such a conception fails to realize is that what has made for the strength of scientific method in its proper domain, also makes for its weakness when it attempts to go beyond that domain. The human being as pure observer has been the strength of science. When we have to consider the human being as existential participant rather than simple observer, then the vocabulary of science is just not equipped to deal with the problem. That vocabulary simply has no provision for explaining the emergence of subjective experience.

An analysis of the texts of Barrow and Tipler shows that science is not equipped to deal with this problem. To refer briefly to evolution and selection might refer to some of the necessary conditions for the emergence of subjectivity, but it says nothing about the actual fact of the emergence of subjectivity itself. There is no scientific analysis of how chemical interaction can give rise to the fact of experiencing. Simply to presuppose the presence of man, as do the anthropic theorists, is to evade the problem. No observer, in any sense in which we can understand the term, could possibly exist in the "cosmic soup" of the initial big bang. Quite independently of the theory of an initial big bang, it remains necessary to understand what basic conditions would be required to account for the emergence of conscious subjects or observers from that initial explosion of energy. It is this basic problem which is ignored by metascience. And yet the entire conception of the anthropic principle is based on the ontological and even cosmological priority given to the observer, his measurements, and his calculations. To assert the priority of this emergent entity whilst avoiding any serious analysis of that emergence itself is, philosophically speaking, a vicious circle.

That the observing scientist is not a pure observer considering things *sub specie aeternitatis* was first made clear to the scientist by the theory of relativity: the spatiotemporal location of observed astronomical events depends on the diverse movements involved in the observer's astronomical position. The subsequent problem of quantum theory, Heisenberg's uncertainty principle, could only reenforce this transformation of a pure observer into an observer who is also a participant, and who has a role to play in bringing about something of the nature of what he observes. When, a few years later, cosmological coincidences on the large scale led to the formulation of the anthropic principle, it was quite impossible to suppose that this principle had nothing to do with the consequences of both relativity theory and quantum theory. It would, in fact, seem more likely that the anthropic principle is what some scientists see as the logical conclusion of both previous theories. At any rate, it can hardly be an accident that the most powerful and systematic attempt at a justificatory analysis of this principle comes from a physicist who explicitly combines it with quantum theory.

It is important to note that Wheeler symbolizes the universe as a serpent-shaped large U, with a thin tail at one end, symbolizing the start of the universe, and a serpent head with large eyes looking at its own tail at the other end, symbolizing humanity, and more particularly the observing scientist. It is an excellent illustration of metascience as distinct from metaphysics. It pictorially summarizes the course of events as a quite general actualization of what was potentially present from the start. But it presupposes the existence of the serpent itself, and the existence of its eventual observing capacities. It is just these issues which are the problems of metaphysics.

A Metaphysical Analysis of Wheeler's Metascientific Position

J. A. Wheeler's participatory anthropic principle is, so far as I know, the most systematic and powerful attempt to argue for this position. The first point Wheeler makes in *Frontiers of Time* (1979) is that the laws of physics must, themselves, have come into being, and that they cannot have come into being by way of any other laws (see also Wheeler [1980, p. 366, note 8]). He refers to this situation as "law without law." There is nothing extraordinary about the idea that the laws of physics are not "eternal and immutable" (1979, p. 1), not "chiseled on a rock for all eternity" (1980, p. 342), that they "must have come into being" (1980, p. 352). But as soon as one perceives the presupposition with which Wheeler is working, then the full force of just how extraordinary this conception really is becomes apparent (Wheeler, 1979, p. 5). For not only is he saying that the laws of physics have "come into being," he is also saying that the physical universe itself, along with the laws of its behavior, has come into being "without anything to guide it into being" (1980, p. 5). And he expands this statement by asserting that "The Universe had to have a way to come into being out of nothingness, with no prior laws, no Swiss watchworks, no nucleus of crystallisation to help it" (1979, p. 7). And right at the end of *Frontiers of Time* he says it again: "Everything came from 'nothing'" (1979, p. 85).

The use of quotation marks in this last text pinpoints the word *nothing*. The intention is indicated by the following quotation which shows that Wheeler means it in a fundamental ontological sense: "'Nothing' is not the vacuum of physics, loaded with geometry and field fluctuations; it is the zeroness of existence" (1979, p. 21). We can immediately see why Wheeler's is the most powerful formulation of the anthropic principle. Without any posturing about philosophical absurdity or "deconstruction," Wheeler is himself positing the source of this posturing. He is agreeing with the Judeo-Christian conception of a physical universe appearing from "nothing," and he is rejecting the Judeo-Christian conception that an appearance "from nothing" can only make sense by presupposing a Creator God. His fundamental ontological statement is that the physical universe emerged from "the zeroness of existence."

We are here at the most basic point of traditional ontology and metaphysics, and Wheeler is making an assertion which goes counter to the fundamental metaphysical discovery concerning the basic condition and structure of rational thinking: that understanding depends on reasons and causes. He is not saying, with the Greeks, that since the universe is there it must have existed from all eternity. He is saying that it is meaningful to assert that something can be derived from nothing. It is therefore imperative to clarify this basic thesis of Wheeler's metascience.

The idea of a creation from nothing only came into being as a consequence of the Hebrew conception of an absolute and all-creating God. The Presocratic "physicists," who were responsible for the gradual breaking up of the mythologies of the all-too-human Homeric and Hesiodic gods, never developed the concept of a creation "from nothing." Insofar as they applied rational thinking to the processes of nature, their basic presupposition was that of an eternally existing physical universe. One can therefore begin to measure just how remarkable is this starting point of Wheeler's metascience. In his most recent paper, "Hermann Weyl and the Unity of Knowledge," Wheeler has more to say about existence than in his other papers: "Existence, the preposterous miracle of existence! To whom has the world of opening day never come as an unbelievable sight?" (1986, p. 371). In the desert of modern philosophy how paradoxical, and how heart-warming to read once more, and from a physicist, the accent of authentic philosophical wonder—the source, as the medievals tell us, of all truly philosophical thinking! But this accent of ontological wonder is no medieval reference to the wonder of God's creation: it is a reference to the wonder of quantum metascience. "Any view of existence which does not reckon with quantum theory and the elementary quantum phenomenon is medieval" (p. 370), writes Wheeler, adding that "Machinery of existence for us means laws of physics under the overarching governance of the quantum principle; in brief, laws and the quantum" (1986, p. 372). And both, let us bear in mind, emerging "from nothing." This is the ontology of the anthropic principle.

It is this which leads straight to the picture of a "self-exciting circuit," which Wheeler summarily expresses in the following sentence: "The Universe viewed as a self-exciting circuit grows and in time gives rise to observer-participancy which in turn gives tangible reality to the Universe" (1979, p. 11). It is very dangerous to play with the basic logic of the world and of man's thinking about the world. It is not an accident that the source of science itself is to be found in a people among whom was formulated the basic principle both of reality and of human thinking about reality: the Aristotelian principle of noncontradiction. Wheeler's metascience is founded on the rejection of that principle: a "self-excited circuit" which excites itself into existence "from nothing" is a magical concept, and not a concept of scientific rationality. If taken seriously, it will bring us straight back to barbarism.

Wheeler's implicit rejection of the principle of noncontradiction does not derive from the difficulties of the experimental situation: it derives from his interpretation of how reality is to be conceived, given the difficulties of the experimental situation and the decision that the experimental situation is ontologically primary. The first step in Wheeler's eventual rejection of this principle occurs in his manner of formulating the uncertainty principle: "Momentum . . . or position . . . of the electron waiting to be found as we start to probe the atom? Pure fantasy!" (1979, pp. 4–5). And again, more explicitly: "physics once thought that the position and momentum of the electron existed 'out there', independent of any act of observation" (1979, p. 4). And the question is: just how far is Wheeler going in the rejection of "out there"? What is happening is that quantum observations are leading Wheeler to substitute the discipline of quantum physics for the recognition of ontological reality, of physical existence per se; and the reason is that in the quantum situation there does not seem to be a "physical existence *per se.*"

But the expression Wheeler uses is hyperbolic and tends to imply a generalized rejection of "out there." This does not mean that he is advocating solipsism: his concern is not with subjective experience as such, but with the results of recording instruments, the existence of which he presupposes. It is the indeterminism intrinsic in the formulation of quantum theory which Wheeler applies to the origin of the universe itself. And this means that he is conflating two senses of objectivity: *that* there is something which can give rise to recordings, and *what* it is that is in fact recorded. Wheeler is in effect trying to interpret the former in terms of the latter. This gives rise to an ambiguous situation which eventually results in assertions which are nothing short of self-contradictory. It must be noted, however, that he is himself aware of the ambiguity of his position and that he creates his own literary foil in an attempt to raise and to answer the difficulties of his position. But as I shall try to show, I do not think that he succeeds in extricating himself from his initial misguided starting point.

"Surely the Universe existed long before any acts of observation were going on." Thus begins the literary foil. And he goes on: "Doesn't that mean that the Universe cannot possibly owe either its structure or its existence to those elementary acts [i.e., of observer-participancy] however numerous they are in the more recent history of the Universe?" (1979, pp. 10–11). In other words, Wheeler is saying that he quite recognizes the common-sense view in terms of which the Universe clearly existed "out there" long before there were any observers. For after all, "the big bang occurred some 10.10^9 [years ago]" (1979, p. 11). But for Wheeler the common-sense view represents ordinary or naïve realism, and he clearly finds it as difficult to conciliate ordinary realism with quantum observation as Hume found it difficult to conciliate ordinary realism with the primacy he gave to sense impressions.

Therefore Wheeler's next tactical move is to lead his reader to the problem of the constructing process which he holds to underlie ordinary realism. He starts this move by asking the natural question regarding the initial big bang: "how do we get that information?", to which the initial, neutral, reply is: from radiation, "and by way of photons from far away stars" (1979, p. 11). He is now in a position to examine the conditions of observation which have allowed for the construction of the "out there" of ordinary realism.

The fundamental rule of procedure in quantum physics, writes Wheeler referring to Niels Bohr, is that "no photon is counted as a photon until it is an observed photon" (1979, p. 11), or, as he later reformulates it in order to eliminate any suspicion of subjectivism, "no elementary phenomenon is a phenomenon until it is a recorded phenomenon" (1980, pp. 354–356). We are now at the heart of the dilemma because, philosophically, we need to know which, if either, is more fundamental in Wheeler's metascience: physical existence as a reality which is presupposed by any form of recording, or recordings as such (whatever that means) which constitute the basis for inferential statements about a constructed reality. And Wheeler at this point leaves us in no doubt that he is not on the side of realism: "the information about the electron is brought into being, step by step, by the experiments that the observer chooses to make" (Wheeler, 1979, p. 4). Since indeterminism reigns, this means that the "information brought into being step by step" would necessarily vary according to the variations of the experiments themselves, which hardly accords with realism.

So we are now led to the literary foil's crucial question, and to the quantum theorist's crucial answer to the question: "But what about the unbelievably more numerous relict photons that escape our telescope? Surely you do not deny them 'reality'?" (1979, p. 12). The reply here is of the utmost importance: "Of course not: but their 'reality' is of a paler and more theoretic hue. The vision of the Universe that is so vivid in our minds is framed by a few iron posts of true observation—themselves resting on theory for their meaning—but most of the walls and the towers in the vision are of papier-maché" (1979, p. 12), a much repeated thesis and the key to Wheeler's position. It constitutes a vivid picture of what Wheeler means by the "participatory anthropic principle": a givenness of observed photons, without any real justification to refer to the great mass of unobserved "relict photons," which therefore become of "a paler hue"; and the consequent contingent constructions dependent on the sorts of observations actually made. How could this quasi-Humean position result in anything else but "walls and towers" made of "papier-mâché"?

But if we now leave aside poetic and metaphorical expressions and go to the logic of the argument, I think we will find that Wheeler is in a contradictory position. He is saying, in one and the same breath, that the physical universe came into being as a nuclear explosion several millions of years ago, *and* that the unobserved "relict photons" of this same nuclear explosion are of "a theoretic hue." These two assertions are mutually incompatible because they constitute the self-contradictory statement that the overwhelming majority of photons, the "relict photons," both exist and do not exist. On such a basis, whatever the experimental results, there would be no physical universe to which physical science could be applied. What allows Wheeler to get away with this contradiction is not only his capacity for poetic formulation, but mainly the fact that he transmutes the contradiction into an ambiguous play on the relationship between existence and experience. But even here, it is not difficult to bring out his essentially contradictory position: the assertion that the existence of the physical universe precedes observation, but that since this very assertion is dependent on observation, then existence does not precede observation.

If one were to object that an assertion about past existence is not of the same order as the recording of a present observation, Wheeler would perhaps point to one of the delayed choice experiments to prove that there does seem to be a relationship between past existence and present observation, and that the latter does in fact seem to affect the former.[1] If the experimenter's present choice in the manipulation of a recording apparatus seems to affect what has been the behavior of a photon which started on its journey eons ago, does not this mean that in one sense physical reality does precede observation, and that in another sense it does not? But when a situation reaches this kind of incipient self-contradiction it generally means that the problem itself is being misconceived. In principle, this would lead us to questioning the experimental set-up, or the human observer as well as his recording apparatus. After all, Wheeler has himself designated one of the ambiguities in that framework, an ambiguity quite specifically connected with time: "how are we to understand that puzzling conservation of 'I' from decade to decade?" (Wheeler, 1986, p. 374). However much he might wish to eliminate the subject, or to reinterpret him in terms of information theory,[2] Wheeler cannot and does not avoid

[1] The epistemological problems of the uncertainty principle are abundantly described by Bohr (1959, Vol. 1, pp. 201–241). The delayed choice experiment is described by Wheeler (1979, pp. 21–26).

[2] There is no "cellular" account of consciousness which does not already presuppose consciousness. Wheeler's reference (1979, p. 10) is to modes of thinking which establish correlations; nor is there an elimination of the "barrier" between awareness and the computer (1979, p. 9); and the brain as "servomechanism" (1979, pp. 73–74) refers to the means whereby an unexplained "I" can consciously distinguish between "past" and "present." The "machinery of memory" is not the same thing as the act of "remembering." Nor does the "now" I actually experience have anything to do with the anticipations N. Wiener built into cybernetic machines.

the fact that the subject is necessarily part of the experimental set-up, even if it is only in terms of interpretation.

The real problem is that of the actual explosion which is said to have occurred in the past, and where primordial radiation and billions of photons, most of them "relict," were actually doing the job. That explosion actually occurred or it did not, quite independently of the present scientist and his observations. Those myriads of relict photons either existed or they did not. If they did not exist, then Wheeler is forced into a solipsism which he nowhere advocates. If they did exist, then that is the clear statement that billions of electrons and photons existed "out there," constituting physical reality quite independently of the observer. We ourselves, together with our observations, are very recent products of cosmological evolution, as Wheeler's serpent indicates. To suppose that this recent product can "now" determine, by dint of an obscure conceptual device which Wheeler calls "observer-participancy," something of the nature of behavior of what *has been* cosmological evolution at the start, is nothing but a consequence of having identified physical existence itself with the practice of quantum physics.

This fallacy manifests itself in the question which Wheeler raises: "Is the machinery of the universe so set up, and from the very beginning, that it is guaranteed to produce intelligent life at some long-distant point in its history-to-be?" (1986, p. 372). Within Wheeler's framework of a physical universe emerging from "the zeroness of existence," such a question has some quite remarkable implications. There is nothing or nobody to "set up the machinery of the universe": it has to be conceived as a self-setting up. As we have already seen, that is a first difficulty; a second one immediately follows. If the universe autonomously sets itself up "to produce intelligent life," this vocabulary means that having magically conjured itself up out of nothing, it has done so with a purpose or an intention, which is itself a manifestation of "intelligent life." But where are we to situate this intention or intelligent life? In the nuclear explosion? In the temperature? In the photons and electrons? If I may borrow an expression from Wheeler himself: Pure fantasy!

But if we simply project the ambiguous observations of quantum experimentation on the long-distant past of cosmological evolution and conclude that "now" has an effect on "has been," then can we not conclude that the locus of intelligent life was (or is?) the scientist-to-be? That is surely more in line with what Wheeler intends. This, then, brings us to the last theme which must be considered in the present analysis: the processes of a universe emerging from nothing and having man as its future finality. The emergence from nothing need concern us no longer, and the analysis of the proximate conditions for the emergence of subjectivity is not Wheeler's concern. But the analysis of how to conceive of *physics*, if physics is to allow for such an emergence, that does concern Wheeler. Therefore the problem is to try to understand something of what Wheeler calls "the plan of physics," his interpretation of how physics is to be understood if the anthropic principle is to be validly asserted.

The first point concerns the laws of physics. These must be recognized as uniformly statistical in nature. The reason for this will be clear shortly. Here is how

Wheeler expresses the point: "when we view each of the laws of physics—and no laws are more magnificent in scope or better tested—as at bottom statistical in character, then we are at last able to forego the idea of a law that endures from everlasting to everlasting. Individual events. Events beyond law. Events so numerous and so unco-ordinated that, flaunting their freedom from formulae, they yet fabricate firm form" (1979, pp. 5–6). On the one hand, then, events free from the constraints of formula, of any outside imposition; on the other, the same events giving rise to statistical laws. Using language which is meant to remind us of "the laws of physics" emerging "unguided" from "nothing," Wheeler underlines the fact that "It is not new for a regularity to develop unguided. Thermodynamics, we know, rests upon the random motion of billions upon billions of molecules. Ask any molecule what it thinks about the second law of thermodynamics and it will laugh at the question. All the same the molecules, collectively, uphold the second law" (1980, p. 352).

It is no doubt entirely true that from the standpoint of physics, all this is perfectly orthodox, except that Wheeler has an obvious penchant and talent for metaphorical formulae. But having already had occasion to note that metaphysically Wheeler is anything but orthodox, the question can be raised: what is the reason for this metaphorical use of language? Events "flaunt" their freedom from constraint, individual molecules "laugh" at a law of physics. What does such language intend except to persuade that the ultimate basis of physical reality is to be thought of as autonomous events or particles? And he who says autonomy and freedom says something very like the possibility of intention or finality. Situating this metaphorical language within the context of Wheeler's basic aim, the implication becomes clearer. This aim is to formulate a "plan of physics" which will justify the anthropic principle, the idea that the elementary particles of the initial explosion direct themselves toward the finality of man, the future scientific observer. To characterize the individual events of the initial explosion as "free" yet able to converge to statistical laws, is to support Wheeler's own unexamined metaphysical presuppositions. The result is not very far from a contemporary form of primitive animism.

To underline this incipient concept of the "freedom" of basic events, Wheeler describes the fundamental "quantum of action" in appropriate terms. In a 1958 essay, Niels Bohr has defined the quantum thus: "the *elementary quantum of action*, which revealed a factor of *wholeness* inherent in atomic processes, going far beyond the ancient idea of the limited divisibility of matter" (p. 2). As it stands, the definition is ambiguous and Wheeler will develop it in his own way. He will eliminate *all* physical constants other than "the quantum" itself. Thus, at the quantum level "Space–time is a classical and approximate concept that utterly contradicts the uncertainty principle" (1979, pp. 15, 37). To be more exact: "'Space–time' is the history of space geometry changing with time. 'World–line' is the history of particle position changing with time" (1979, p. 16). Now since space–time depends on world–line, and since world–line ascribes a spatial coordinate and a momentum to a particle, space–time cannot be applicable to the quantum level. Wheeler quite explicitly writes that "Quantum mechanics allows us to know a coordinate or a momentum, but not both" (1979, p. 2). It therefore follows, according to Wheeler, that space–time and world–line must be "ruled out" as "incompatible with the uncertainty relation." It also follows that "In giving up 'space–time' as a basic idea in the description of Nature, we have to give up 'time' too . . . " (1979, pp. 16–17).

So "Time cannot be an ultimate category in the description of Nature" (1979, p. 20), and there is therefore no meaning to "before the big bang" and "after the big crunch." Nor is there meaning to these concepts "at the scale of the Planck distance." In a word, "before" and "after," concludes Wheeler, "cannot legalistically rule anywhere" (1979, p. 20). The big bang, the big crunch, and the black hole are "frontiers of time" or "gates of time." The same elimination process is applicable to causality: causality is not an ultimate category at the quantum level (1979, pp. 51–53). And therefore the following inference concerning the universe in general can now be made: "There never was a law of physics that did not require space and time for its statement. With collapse the framework falls down for everything one ever called a law" (1979, p. 20). We can here begin to discern something of the implication of Wheeler's basic presupposition: what we are ultimately left with is "the zeroness of existence" from which "the quantum" somehow posits itself; and with its appearance came "the machinery of existence" which Wheeler has already defined as "laws and the quantum." In this theology of the quantum it is not impossible to see how the physicist who wishes to try to transform his discipline into metascience can conjure up a *picture* of how the quantum universe can per se intend man.

But it is also at this point that we must bring in another language used by Wheeler which brings out his essentially contradictory position. For a word he also uses on occasion is the word *chance*, a word appropriate to traditional evolutionary theory, but scarcely appropriate to the finality attributed to the anthropic principle. Thus: "The fantastically elaborate organizations of plants and animals is of nothing but higgledy-piggledy origin. The laws of physics themselves coming into being and fading out of existence: in what else can they have their root but billions upon billions of acts of chance" (Wheeler, 1979, p. 1; 1980, p. 352). Of themselves, these billions of acts of chance start building statistical laws. And the more they build, the more do these statistical laws look like deterministic laws. This is the result of a winnowing process which Wheeler describes by saying that every particle "history" which does not end, as it began, "with prescribed conditions," has gradually been "thrown out as impossible" (1979, pp. 66–68). He calls this the "bias" or "the providence factor": "A factor is at work that pushes the probabilities ever more strongly toward the predetermined end . . . ." (1979, p. 67); or again, a "bias" of "unknown origin" sees to it "that the predetermined end is brought about" (1979, p. 67).

It must of course be understood that Wheeler's "providence factor" is no more theological than his earlier concept of the universe appearing "from nothing." The factor in question is a reference to what Wheeler regards as the *real* underlying "machinery" of physics: "what course offers itself except to try 'acts of observer-participancy' as the underlying 'machinery' and see if out of them one can derive the laws of physics" (1979, p. 36). The concept designated by the expression "observer-participancy" is a creation of Wheeler's, and it is the key to his participatory anthropic principle. It denotes what he defines as the "direct involvement of observation in genesis" (1977, p. 26, quoted in Wheeler [1980, p. 365, n. 8]). The biblical language is not accidental. It is a reminder of the thesis that the universe which is "so vivid in our minds" is that "vision" of "papier-maché" which has been "framed by a few iron posts of true observation"—that is to say the construction made by the human observer, in particular the physicist.

But it seems to me that, metaphysically speaking, Wheeler is now in real trouble. Leaving aside the magical beginnings of a universe which excites itself into existence, he starts off with "billions upon billions" of quanta which he refers to as "acts of chance." As a result of observations which do not yet exist, "future" observations, these "acts of chance" find themselves converging toward collective regularities or statistical laws, which are the basis for cosmological evolution in general. This is what Wheeler refers to as a "bias" of "unknown origin" which "pushes the probabilities" toward a "predetermined end." There is, indeed, as he himself remarks, "something missing!"

The word *participancy* in the expression "observer-participancy" is there to suggest that present observations of the photons from the remote past actually affected the behavior of these photons in what is normally called "the past." This again is a reference to the experimental set-up of the delayed choice experiments. But the consequences here are, in fact, quite impossible. He himself raises the basic question: "How can the quantum ever be understood as powered by meaning?" (1979, p. 36). How indeed, particularly since this "meaning" is also defined as "acts of chance." The basic presupposition of the anthropic principle has led Wheeler to assert that the initial quanta are to be seen as "acts of chance" which must nevertheless be "powered" by "meaning." This is already one contradictory position. Even more significant is that the "meaning" which should be "powering" these elementary particles is something which does not yet exist: intelligent life as the finality of these "acts of chance." The situation requires a link between the actual photons of the initial state of the universe and the observer who will appear only several millions of years "later." Since there is no relationship conceivable at the start of the universe, and since the quantum framework seems to imply a relationship from the standpoint of the present observer, Wheeler deals with the problem by simply adding a supplement, so to speak, to the known problem of quantum observation. That is, he adds the idea of a retroactive participation from the present to the many-million-year past. That appears to be the source of the expression "observer-participancy." Since it is an arbitrary construction designed to save a theory which itself leads to the inherently contradictory notion of meaningful acts of chance, I think we can conclude that the position cannot be seriously upheld.

The subject of this volume is time and mind, and it is clear from the above that both time and mind are the fundamental issues of the anthropic principle. If the critical arguments formulated above have any validity, then this present work has given us an opportunity to show that this particular use of these two concepts has led to an entirely insufficient theory.

References

Barrow, J. D., & Tipler, F. J. (1986), *The Anthropic Cosmological Principle*. Oxford, U.K.: Oxford University Press.

Blum, H. F. (1968), *Time's Arrow and Evolution*. Princeton, NJ: Princeton University Press.

Bohr, N. (1958), Quantum physics and philosophy. *Essays 1958–1962 on Atomic Physics and Human Knowledge*. New York: Vintage, 1966.

——— (1959), *Albert Einstein: Philosopher-Scientist,* Vol. 1, ed. P. A. Schilpp. New York: Harper Torchbook.

Carter, B. (1974), *Confrontation of Cosmological Theories with Observation*, ed. M. S. Longair. Dordrecht: Reidel.

Davies, P. C. W. (1977), *Space and Time in the Modern Universe*. Cambridge: Cambridge University Press.

Descartes, R. (1979), *Le Monde ou Traité de la Lumière*, text & transl. M. S. Mahoney. New York: Abaris Books.

Dicke, R. H. (1961), Letter to the Editor. *Nature*, 192:440–441.

Eigen, M., & Schuster, P. (1977), The hypercycle. *Die Naturwissenschaften*, 541–565.

——— ——— (1978), The hypercycle. *Die Naturwissenschaften*, 7–41, 341–369.

Hume, D. (1777), *Dialogues Concerning Natural Religion*, ed. R. Popkin. Indianapolis, IN: Hackett Publishing Co., 1980.

Mayr, E. (1982), *The Growth of Biological Thought*. Cambridge, MA: Harvard University Press.

McMullin, E. (1981), Is philosophy relevant to cosmology? *Amer. Philos. Quart.*, p. 177.

Paley, W. (1802), *Natural Theology*, ed. F. Young. London: Ward, Lock & Co., n.d.

Shalom, A. (1984), Subjectivity. *Rev. Metaphysics.*, 38:227–273.

——— (1985), *The Body/Mind Conceptual Framework and the Problem of Personal Identity*. Atlantic Highlands, NJ: Humanities Press International.

Sperry, R. W. (1965), Mind, brain and humanist values. In: *New Views of the Nature of Man*, ed. J. R. Platt. Chicago: University of Chicago Press.

Weinberg, S. (1977a), *The First Three Minutes*. New York: Basic Books.

——— (1977b), The forces of nature. *Amer. Scientist*, 65:175.

Wheeler, J. A. (1977), Genesis and observership. In: *Foundational Problems in the Special Sciences*, eds. R. E. Butts & K. J. Hintikka. Dordrecht: Reidel.

——— (1979), *Frontiers of Time*. North Holland: Societá Italiana Fisica.

——— (1980), Beyond the black hole. In: *Some Strangeness in the Proportion*, ed. A. Woolf. London: Addison-Wesley.

——— (1986), Hermann Weyl and the unity of knowledge. *Amer. Sci.*, 74:372.

Whitrow, G. J. (1955), Why physical space has three dimensions. *Br. J. Philos. Sci.*, 6:13–31.

Perspectives

We learn from Professor Shalom's chapter that the anthropic principle, in its so-called strong form, postulates that "The universe must have those properties which allow life to develop within it at some stage of its history" (p. 157). If not a truism, then the postulate is an example of the difficulty of shedding the notion of post hoc ergo propter hoc, perhaps for the reasons set forth earlier by Dr. Arlow. The emergence of life, on this view, must have been among the plans of the Designer.

Our minds continuously seek unchanging regularities—laws, causal relationships— beneath the onrush of apparently chaotic sense impressions. The mind continuously formulates what appears to it as permanent rules that govern the world, and uses them to limit, as much as it can, the domain of the unpredictable. Thus, we seek permanent design patterns in our own behavior, in our fate, and in the fate of the universe.

The identification of stable, universal programs and purposes has been the classic function of all philosophies and religions. A well-known form of identifying purpose in nature is the teleology in the Biblical account of Creation. Its peculiar Christian form is salvation history. This is an interpretation of history that sees the purpose of cosmic time as giving man an opportunity to redeem himself at the end of time from the Fall he has freely taken at the beginning of time. Throughout the history of Christendom salvation history served as a sufficient, or almost sufficient, reason for our travail and for the continued existence of the cosmos.

Today the traditional theologies of the West have lost much of their power to account for the miracles of matter, life, and man, in terms convincing to the intellectual preparedness, and satisfying to the spiritual needs of the pragmatic, critical, and science-oriented men and women of our age. But the human desire to find reason and purpose in existence did not diminish; in reaction to the overwhelming flow of undigested data, irrelevant to our daily purpose, it might even have increased. It is thus that into the spiritual vacuum created by the retreat of mature religions, the teachings on cosmic order and purpose by fundamentalist and quasi-religious movements began to flow. A group of such quasi-religious principles, known as the anthropic principles, appeals to physics for support.

Some of the anthropic principles deal with the scales of nature, some with the position of life and intelligence in the universe, some with the relations among physical constants of nature, some with the relationships among cosmologically important numbers. They are all characterized by tentativeness; they all display elements of faith into which physical data and proven laws on nature have been inserted. B. J. Carr and M. J. Rees, writing about "The anthropic principle and the structure of the physical world" (Nature, 278: April 12, 1979), did not hesitate to acknowledge the metaphysical character of their reasoning, maintaining only the hope that "One day we may have a more physical explanation for some of the relationships [among scales of physical effects] that now seem genuine coincidences" (p. 612).

Many, probably most, great scientific ideas began from observations about unexplained coincidences; many were inspired by tenets of religions and philosophies. It is not surprising, therefore, that those familiar with the history of ideas will recognize the reputable, but

177

usually unacknowledged ancestry of the various anthropic principles in thought that harks back to Greek Antiquity, to the Middle Ages, or to the Renaissance. We encounter modern forms of the Great Chain of Being, the teleological, cosmological, and ontological proofs of the existence of God, and a good helping of number magic.

Of central interest to Professor Shalom is the participatory anthropic principle. He demonstrates that this form of the anthropic principle is basically self-contradictory and hence untenable. Its insufficiency derives from a category mistake: whereas all science derives from, and is based on, certain (unprovable) metaphysical principles, it is not possible to derive metaphysics from the principles of science.

But he also stresses what, in my view, is the great merit of the anthropic principles. Namely, through the endorsement given to them by physicists highly regarded by the physics community, they have authorized the appearance of "the accent of authentic philosophical wonder—the source, as the medievals tell us, of all truly philosophical thinking" (p. 168).

In our interdisciplinary exercise thus far the ball of responsibility has been traveling back and forth between the courts of physics and psychology. But all forms of human knowledge are collective in their nature; science most obviously so. It is necessary, therefore, to consider next some views on time and mind as seen by the social sciences.

IV

Social Science

10

Time Scales and Social Thought

Robert J. Thornton

Abstract Descriptions of social life are often ambivalent with respect to time, or ignore it entirely, while causal explanations have so schematized time that they have little descriptive validity. This chapter argues that social life and social meanings may be conceptualized as implicit comparisons of temporal (and spatial) scales because all acts of observations are implicitly acts of measurement involving complex transformations between different and incommensurable scales of time. This fact suggests a new definition of contexts as levels in a hierarchy of scales that delimit and frame, and thus determine the kinds of knowledge we have about social life. The notion of contexts is used to develop the idea of temporal neighborhoods of collective behavior, to assist us in understanding the relationships between different kinds of behavior such as language, material culture, institutions, economy, and history. The approach to social thought I am suggesting implies that social reality is stratified, in that certain kinds of contexts may be causally isolated from each other by virtue of their scalar incommensurabilities.

Time and Representations of Social Realities

Unlike physicists, social scientists at least know which direction time is going. For them, time's arrow flies only one way. Social scientists, however, have two goals. One is to describe the objects of their science as accurately as possible; the other one is to place those descriptions in a general explanatory framework. The status of time is ambiguous with respect to the first goal. The very existence of a separate discipline of history is witness to this. The second goal depends on the idea of causation, and almost everyone would accept that a theory of causation entails a theory of time. Even so, I argue here, the epistemology of time in contemporary social science does not permit a true representation of social reality.

In practice, social description demands that a situation, history, event, or social structure be represented in a way that preserves its uniqueness, but permits it to be related to a set of other situations, histories, events, or social structures. Specifying those relationships implies specifying some mechanism or structured image; that is, specifying a cause, or at most a finite set of causes, which can explain the particular configuration that was described.

Although it is clear that anthropologists have made a great deal of progress in the techniques of description since the beginning of this century, the major systems of causal explanation that were first put forward in the nineteenth century, well before most of these descriptive techniques were available, are still the dominant modes of thinking in most social sciences. It seems to me, then, that the major problem facing social scientists is the development of new concepts of cause and explanation that are consistent with what we are able to describe, yet which take seriously the limits of description.

Since any observer of social life is also part of social life, the limits of what we can describe probably also limit what we can explain. In particular, there are limits on what we can describe that are imposed by our (the observers') living life at the same time, "tempo," or "rate," as that which we describe. Since these limits are not taken into account in theory, the various marxisms, structuralisms, functionalisms, and other theories of society and culture have failed to explain adequately or to predict consistently many aspects of real life. As I shall argue here, the reason they have failed is that they have neglected fundamental aspects of human life-in-the-world. In particular, they have neglected time, or have so theorized and reduced the concept that it has ceased to have any descriptive validity.

Particularly telling in this regard is the often-remarked fact that the more detailed and "lifelike" social description is, the more difficult it is to fit any convincing theoretical "explanation" to it. This problem is often represented by means of the metaphor of "distance." The "closer" we are to some aspect of social life, it is said, the more difficult it is to obtain the "necessary distance" to see it clearly. Conversely, maintaining a "proper" observational distance is said to allow us to explain social life more convincingly.

There seems to be a paradox here: get "close" to describe it, but keep your "distance" if you want to explain it. The paradox is not genuine, however, since it is built on the false analogy of stepping away from a painting to see the whole picture, not just the brush strokes, or of seeing the village from the mountain top, not just the particular neighborhood of one's daily life. Society is never observable in the way a painting or village is: we are always "in" it. At the root of this apparent paradox lies a failure to recognize different domains of causality in social phenomena. In order to resolve the paradox we need to examine the relationship between causality and contexts, and to develop a more rigorous concept of contexts based on differing time scales and temporal rhythms of the mind, of the body, and of social life. In order to define contexts in this way, however, we must examine more closely the idea of time scales and the ways they are related to each other.

Scale, Time Scales, and Human Scales

To measure time, Fraser (1982, p. 14) tells us, three conditions must be fulfilled: (1) that there be (at least) two continuous processes, each of which has identifiable states that are countable as instants; (2) that it is possible to recognize two nonsimultaneous events which consist of a pair of two simultaneous instants from each process; and (3) that we are able to define a rule of transformation between the instants of one process and those of another. Implicit in this set of conditions is the further condition that there must be an observer who records the states of these processes. One or both of those processes, of course, may be those of the observer himself. If we add the necessity of an observer, a condition that is clearly implicit in Fraser's treatment of time measurement, then we may begin to ask some questions about the meaning of time, where Fraser has been concerned chiefly with the measurement of time and the quality of different "temporalities."

As far as measurement is concerned, the "rules of transformation," of which Fraser speaks, are in fact "the laws of nature"—those invariable regularities that make the physical sciences so different from the social. The rules are necessary because no rhythmical or cyclical process that we are able to observe is exactly equivalent to any other: they are all more or less incommensurable. The rules tell us how one process can be correlated with another by applying operations of division, comparison, and intercalation. Clocks, timetables, diaries, calendars, log books, and any other registers of process are implementations of these rules for practical purposes.

Michon's discussion of Fraser's rules of time measurement makes it clear that the condition for the possibility of measurement is a context, namely, the context of measurement (Michon, 1985). Minimally, the context of measurement must include two measurable processes, a rule of transformation, and an observer to compare the processes and apply the rule. Once these conditions are met, the measurement of time may become meaningful. In the case of rituals of transition, *rites de passage,* all calendrical rituals, games, quasi-ritual and legal transformations of social status, and many other social activities and behaviors, this activity of measurement is tantamount to the creation of meaning itself. Time-keepers keep time for a reason, and those reasons are distinctly human. Though Fraser recognizes that his third rule of time-keeping—that there be a rule of transformation between different time scales—means, in effect, that a knowledge of the orderliness of nature is also necessary, this principle may be further generalized: a rule of transformation which specifies a relationship between at least two otherwise incommensurable scales constitutes a necessary condition for the emergence of meaning.

All animals, man included, live in a world that is marked by "characteristic rhythms"—the range of frequencies of daily habits and activities that are appropriate to those activities and characteristic of the species or the individual. What is distinctly human, and which defines mankind with less ambiguity than any other criterion, including language or fire, is the ability, indeed the compulsion, to link levels and processes by more-or-less regular rules of correspondence. Transformational rules of this sort are implicit in, and necessary preconditions for, tool use, language, and ritual. They are also essential for other nonlinguistic faculties of interpretation brought to bear in looking at a picture, a diagram, a building, or a map, and in interpreting indexes of all kinds. Each context of measurement, however, demands a different set of transformational rules.

Moreover, different kinds of measurements require different kinds of context, and conversely, different contexts generate different measurements. What is important is that the definition of a context of measurement depends on the kinds and magnitudes of temporal and spatial scales that are characteristic of, and appropriate to, the processes being compared.

Let us examine some of the characteristic rhythms which may define specific human contexts.[1]

The first level that need concern us here is the temporal context of the sentence. Modern linguistics since Chomsky takes the whole sentence, or utterance, as the primary datum of linguistic competence. In analytic terms, this means that the sentence, rather than the so-called "parts of speech" or the letters or sounds of language, is treated as the fundamental unit of language. The smaller units of which the sentence is composed are then considered to be realizations in observable verbal behavior—or "performance," as it is called—of the cognitive unity of the sentence. There is a great deal of persuasive evidence to support this view,[2] but, it is also clear that the composition, performance, and interpretation of a sentence takes a certain amount of time. Naturally, longer sentences take longer to compose, perform, and interpret, but factors such as depth of nesting of clauses, negativity, passivization, emotional content, and so on, also affect the duration of the linguistic processes (Osgood, 1980, pp. 225–239). The time taken either to produce or to interpret a sentence varies over a fairly wide range. This empirical variation suggests that several different cognitive and physiological modes of linguistic processing are involved, and that different processes are mobilized in order to translate internal representations to external performances (Osgood, 1980). The production of a meaningful sentence, then, occurs in a context. There is a range of processing times which can be said to span all the timed durations required to process all sentences that the subject is competent to produce and interpret. This seems to constitute, moreover, one kind of range of fundamental or characteristic rhythms or cycles. In other words, the production or interpretation of a sentence requires what we might call a "temporal neighborhood," and the set of variations of durations of these temporal neighborhoods could be described as a kind of behavioral "frequency band." The linguistic context, then, can be said to have a characteristic behavioral frequency band which sets it apart and defines it.

The next characteristic temporal context of human activity belongs to the

---

[1]The rhythms which I discuss here exclude, for heuristic purposes the circadian rhythms of sleep, wakefulness, appetite, and so on, because these have been dealt with elsewhere, and because they are not active in the conscious generation of social meanings. Similarly, the astronomical cycles, though attributed meaning by humans in various contexts, are not generated by human activity itself.

[2]J. Lyons (1968, pp. 172–173; pp. 1977,467–469ff) discusses the idea of the sentence as the fundamental unit of transformational grammars. The neural basis for the unity of the sentence is probably the process of automatization which renders behavior that is initially conscious and intention-driven, unconscious and automatic (Lieberman, 1984, pp. 57–58).

hand. The rhythms of the hand overlap those of linguistic performance—interpretation times. In fact, systems of manual sign language, such as American Sign Language (Ameslan) used by many deaf Americans, suggests that "temporal band-width" of some forms of speech and manual activity may be identical. More generally, in cultural terms, this overlap allows the rhythmic motions of the hand to act in concert with those of speech and song. The characteristic rhythms range from the practiced dexterity of a pianist in the midst of a rapid arpeggio to the rhythms of knapping a flint arrowhead, planing a board, combing the hair, clapping in time to a song. The periodicities or frequencies of these acts range from 10 cycles per second to perhaps 10 seconds per cycle. When the hands are employed in active manipulation of the material environment, these rhythms furthermore define a *context* of work, and a *rate* of work; that is, they define a periodicity or rhythm of manual manufacture and thus a characteristic temporality for material culture for mankind from the beginning of culture up to the Industrial Age.

There are few ethnographies of the context of the hand, but David Sudnow (1978) has written one such description of the temporalities and spacing-behavior of the hand—his hand— learning to play jazz. Nick Toth (1983, 1986; Toth and Schick, 1986) has pioneered the study of the archaeology of the hand by experimentally investigating how hand-held stone tools might actually have functioned, and the implications of a hand-held lithic technology for patterns of time and space in the earliest human communities. Both writers show that the hand in action exhibits specific rhythms and capabilities which have implications for the organization of larger social situations, whether these are the rhythmic structure of improvized jazz or the rhythms of hunting and meat-eating.

A third temporal context of activity is that of the human body itself (Giddens, 1984, p. 34; Bourdieu, 1977, p. 163). Its characteristic rhythms are observed in formal rituals of religion and politics, in dance, sport, and hunting. The rhythms of the body interact with the rhythms of speech at the level of conversation, oratory, and discourse. The periodicity of this activity is on the order of a few minutes to several hours.

Bourdieu, for instance, discusses the timing of women going to the well in Algerian Bedouin communities. The "submission to collective rhythms" is one way of achieving and enforcing the separation of male and female worlds (1977, p. 163). Bourdieu notes that the disruption of these rhythms by the measures imposed by the French Army during the war of liberation in that country deprived women of the "autonomy they derived from access to a separate time and place," and resulted in enforced cloistering and wearing of the veil (Bourdieu, 1977, p. 232, n. 6).

A fourth temporal context is that of social interactions involving goods. At this level, the temporalities of language, tactile manipulation, and bodily disposition interact with the temporalities of other things outside of the body. Comparisons between scales of time and differing temporalities are implicit in almost all social activities of this level, and are partly responsible for generating the special kind of meaning called "value." All reciprocal exchanges of goods depend on the temporality of the goods themselves, as well as on the temporality of the transaction. Goods such as gold and diamonds, glass beads, and stone axes, which do not decay or change within the life span of individuals, or indeed within the life span of traditions or cultures, are attributed value according to the epoch they measure with their existence. By contrast, the exchange of food or of words marks out different temporalities and acquires different values. Economic transactions also have a periodicity, or recognized rhythm of reciprocity. A "borrowing" becomes a theft when this rhythm is violated, and a gift becomes a sale if another item of similar value is returned too soon (Sahlins, 1974, pp. 192–196). The characteristic periodicities range from days to years.

Each of these "contexts" has a specific range of rhythms, a specific time signature. These rhythms are specific in that they both define the context of action and set limits to the patterns and information that they generate, and limit the kinds and extent of knowledge that we, as observers, may have about them. The rhythm of the hand is experienced in a qualitatively different way from that of the ritual, or of the lives of individuals. This knowledge is conditioned by the specific rhythms of observation itself.

Any concept of a social whole must be based on a specific comparison of scales of time; that is, it must involve a time measurement of the sort that Fraser (1982) has outlined for the more limited context of physical and biological clocks. The measure of social time, however, itself takes time, and is frequently comparable to the epoch being measured since the instrument of measurement is the human observer whose rhythms of observation correspond closely to the rhythms of what is observed.

In this more general sense, social observation, as well as social action is always also a measurement of time. One of the two processes of the context of measurement is, implicitly, some characteristic rhythm of the observer.

Consider the measurements and scale transformations in divination and myth. The diviner observes the patterns that falling stones generate within the tactile space–time of his divinatory act and maps these onto the span of mythical time. Interpretative meanings are generated by acts which bridge between scales or that make explicit the previously implicit relationships between events and rhythms of two different scales. All instances of modeling are examples of this sort of scale-bridging exercise. The orrery as a model of the solar system acquires its significance and its meaning by making explicit in one scale—the tactile scale, or the scale of the near visual field—what is implicit in the partially observed motions of the planets around the sun. The Bushman's drawings on the cave wall make explicit in the scale of social space, what was implicit, for him, in the order of his natural universe. Their meaning emerges from the measure of space and time that they demonstrate. These implicit measures of space and time, then, are what we might call contexts.

Contexts

Until now, the word *context* has not been defined. Given the idea of characteristic temporal scales and cognitive rules of transformation that bring these scales into relation with one another, then, contexts can be conceptualized as levels in hierarchies of temporal scales which limit and frame some part(s) of cognition, behavior and social life. The temporal limits of the process of knowing these contexts limits the scope of causality, and thus, limits the scope of any theory of how social life works. Accordingly, contexts defined in this way are something like "temporal modules" which define the scope or range of social causes. They may, in fact, be sometimes causally isolated from one another. These temporal modules can be defined relative to a set of rhythms or time-scales (behavioral frequency bands) characteristic of human life.

Anthropologists have excelled in descriptions of small-scale societies, and concepts like microcosm, village, local-level politics, kinships, and so on (as opposed to macrocosm, state, national politics, nation), constitute a vocabulary with which we may describe limited social situations in rich detail. Theoretically, these situations are conceptualized as structures, either graphically in the form of maps or kinship diagrams, or more abstractly as "communities" or social structures and formations. In most contemporary sociology, "context" is roughly synonymous with "background"; it has no theoretical content. It is certainly not conceptualized as a temporal domain with definable temporal limits. Although anthropology has been called "The study of man in context," there is little that could be called a theory of context.

The intuitiveness of our concept of context, however, is itself responsible for a number of conceptual errors. For example, we speak of small-scale societies as "closely integrated," while we deplore the loose integration characteristic of modern large-scale societies. The contrast, however, between the integration of kinship, local-level politics, and so on, in the "small-scale" societies, and that of large-scale societies, is only apparent, and depends on the incommensurability of the entities compared. They are incommensurate in the literal sense that the appropriate scales of space, time, and causality are different. In so-called small-scale societies, integration occurs at the level of each individual or group of similar-minded individuals. The small scale of such social interactions means that "integration" can be achieved cognitively; that is, the degree of social order that exists can be comprehended by (potentially) any *one* individual. In larger scale societies, integration depends on patterns of text, space, and time and is never fully comprehended at the scale of the individual. It is a mistake, then, to ignore the different scales of these social phenomena because it makes it appear, wrongly, that it is "society" that is integrated in small-scale societies, rather than individuals who, because of the small scale of their experience, are able to conceive of their social universe in cognitively well-integrated ways, and to act effectively on the basis of these conceptions. The intellectual "scaling-up" of small-scale conceptual integration to the scale characteristic of modern states is partly responsible for the illusion that there is some stable entity called "society" that possesses the quality of being integrated or not, rather than *contexts* which display various degrees of integration within an appropriate scope and scale.

Thus, "The West" or even "American society" cannot legitimately be compared with "Samoa" or "Bushman society," as is so often done. However, contexts, when appropriately defined, can be legitimately compared. Or, to put it another way, levels of cognitive and social organization that are alike in their scope and scale of integration may be understood better in relation with one another.

There are other, similar problems which arise from a lack of sensitivity to scale in either time or space. "Institutions" or "traditions," for instance, are characterized as social patterns which exist *through* time. They are said to endure, or to have duration. This implies that they exist at all times during which they are said to endure. But institutions and traditions are only mobilized from time to time by individuals. Their material and architectural environments (secret men's houses, temples, banks) exist independently of any single enactment of the behaviors which are said to constitute the institution. Paradoxically, then, institutions such as patrilineal clans, religious cults, or banking are discrete, momentary events with their own characteristic rhythms that occur *within* environments that exist in different scales of time. While the behaviors that constitute generational descent, prayer, or banking endure conceptually, over a period of time, they are enacted within a discontinuous temporal structure of moments whose durations can only be described with respect to a different scale of time appropriate to the context of social action, but not to the institution itself. Each behavior takes place and acquires its specific meaning, however, within an architectural or environmental context that must exist, or endure, on a different time-scale. The significance of these acts depends upon our bringing into contact two different scales of time. "Traditions" such as these "measure time" by comparing the fundamental rhythms of human bodily and cognitive acts with the rhythms of physical decay and construction of an architectural environment.

Social facts like those discussed in the previous paragraph, then, must be conceptualized in terms of several overlapping scales of time: the time of enactment, of cognition, of environment, and so on. All such acts imply mensurations of time, from which their meaning emerges.

If this view of temporality were accepted, what then would constitute a social fact? For certain social scientists (demographers, economists, social survey analysts), one test of whether or not something is a social fact would appear to be whether it can be counted. Careful examination of this assumption reveals, however, that the enumerability of most kinds of social facts depends on the choice of an appropriate time-scale, and the acceptance of a convenient fiction of simultaneity or "timelessness."[3]

Words of a language, or persons, seem to be strong candidates for countability. Reflection, however, will reveal that these things are only figments of an imagined simultaneity if time is taken into account. We can count dictionary entries, for example, but these are not all words, nor are they all in use by the time

[3]Counting, or cardinality, is appropriate to a "prototemporal umwelt" in Fraser's terminology (Fraser, 1982, p. 158; Michon, 1984); social facts in a prototemporal world of statistics can be enumerated but not arranged in a determinate order (ordinality). Counting as a guarantee of factuality treats social objects as physical ones, that is, as entities with an inappropriate temporality—and this cannot be descriptively valid.

a dictionary is printed. If we assume that we can distinguish "words" from other kinds of entries, or other sounds that may be uttered, then do we count "exchange" once or twice (the noun and the verb), and do we count "safari" or "etc."? Can we be sure that no new words will have been invented while we were counting? To count words at all, we must adopt the fiction of an "instant" during which all words exist or not. Alternatively, we must rely on the physical representation of these "words" in a physical book. Both alternatives, however, contradict our experience that words take time to say, exist in time, and have histories, and that languages evolve and change.

People present a different set of problems. Large populations of them are never counted, of course, but only estimated by statistical means since there is not time enough to count everyone, and censustakers can never be certain of the truth or the completeness of the data they collect. If we assume for a moment that absolute certainty and completeness of information can be achieved (i.e., that the members of the population in question never lie), it is clear that during the time it would take to collect the information people will have been born or have died. Even if we assume the possibility of an absolutely accurate and instantaneous census, then what of those on the brink of death, at the mouth of the womb, just conceived, not to mention the famous twinkle in a father's eye? Uncertainty in this case is a necessary condition of existence, an inescapable temporal limit on social knowledge.

The time it takes to collect statistics about a population guarantees that we can never observe it entirely. "Society" is always of a scale that is larger than the individual; its implicit "timelessness" depends on the comparison between the time scales of local action, and the time scales of their products and their consequences. These limits force us to the conclusion that the countability of any social fact depends on its temporal scale relative to the temporal scales of the person doing the counting.

But let us imagine that we are not interested in counting, but only in the intensive investigation of a single subject. Again, our mutual existence in time makes this impossible. Let us assume that, given an appropriate time scale, we can fix the moment of occurrence of an individual's birth, the life span, or the moment of the fall of the Mayan civilization, or the rise of a state or culture. It is clear, of course, that the definition of that moment makes sense only within certain scales of time. We can specify the fall of the Mayan civilization in centuries, the Aztecs in years, the birth of an individual in days or even minutes, but not in seconds. But the problem of the time scales of births or becomings, whether of individuals or civilizations, is more deeply perplexing than the choosing of an appropriate scale in which to represent the process might lead us to believe. Consider the person: the human being is relatively discrete with respect to time and space (relative to an appropriate scale, and excluding the time it takes to be born or to die, or matter and energy constantly being exchanged with the physical environment). But, are we to include a person's behavior and mental states in our delimitation of the "person"? To do otherwise would be sociological nonsense, but if we do, the individual's apparent discreteness disappears. Behavior, for instance, is either the consequence of the past, or the result of a concept of the future. Another person's past and future, however, are not directly experienceable, so behavior must be constructed on the basis of memories and concepts. But let us assume, again, that the past and future of some subject can be known and that this knowledge can be used to explain the subject's behavior. How much of the past or future, then, are we entitled to take into account? Moreover, how is the causality to be construed? Behaviorism, for instance, proposes that behavior is the product of its consequences (i.e., its rewards and punishments), while intentionalist theories assert that behavior is the consequence of its mental antecedents. If we choose either account (or, pluralistically, choose both accounts) of behavior, how large are we entitled to make this "neighborhood of simultaneity" in which the stimulus–response–stimulus or intention–action causal chains are supposed to operate?

There is yet another problem with respect to time and certainty. In the investigation of culture, or indeed of any human phenomenon, *the time scale of observation is the same as that of the observed.* This becomes a problem if we take the subject's life span as the significant unit of understanding, assuming that for all practical purposes, birth and death are discrete boundaries of the individual in time. Although there are reasons why we might not wish to accept the life span as the fundamental time boundaries of the person, it seems to be the best candidate for a natural unit. Even so, it is fundamentally unobservable. This is because the observer's time is lived or experienced at the same "rate" as that of his subject. The observer also dies, or is born, and so cannot account for any complete life span, not even his own. He must always rely on constructions, expectations, lies, documents, artifacts, and memories. Phenomena which exist within time scales very much larger or very much smaller than the human scale can be observed or conceptualized as units. Generations, centuries, epochs are examples of social time that can be measured in multiples of life spans, while an election, the sale of a pig, or a circumcision ritual occupy a small fraction of a life span. A process of a thousand years, or of a year's span is far more comprehensible to us, it seems, because of the radical lack of fit between the time scales of our experiences, our umwelts,[4] which requires, again, an implicit act of measurement and comparison between scales. The life of a volcano, or of a mosquito requires unambiguous condensation or magnification to enable humans to comprehend their existence in time. To try to escape this necessary uncertainty, then, we call things like institutions or traditions "timeless" when in fact they are essentially structures of measured time, that come into being only through time, and allocate meaning to the epochs they create.

Any attempt to understand a psychological, cultural, or social "whole" must rest on abstractions and constructions, and it cannot be claimed that it is a representation of social reality as this is experienced by social actors. The uncertainty of any social boundaries must be accepted. The same strictures of uncertainty apply to our knowledge of contexts, but in contrast to the holistic

[4]"Umwelt," "the circumscribed portion of the environment which is meaningful and effective for a given animal species," is used here in the generalized sense, worked out and employed in the writings of J. T. Fraser (1982, p. 21), following the earlier work of J. von Uexkull.

abstractions that have been considered, the context is observable, and constitutes a unity whose existence can be *described* and not merely asserted.

If we accept that contexts may be the object of all social sciences, several problems emerge quite clearly. How long does a context last? What are its boundaries? How does it interact with other contexts?

How long is a context? A question like this sounds as if it could only elicit answers similar to the question "How long is a rope?" The answer, "Long enough to reach from one end to another," is mere word-play, but it does suggest a mode of approach. With the rope, the important thing is that there is a rope. A real rope may be shorter or longer, but it cannot be reduced to an infinitely small rope with no length between its ends without ceasing to be a rope altogether. This is because a rope has an appropriate scale of existence, relative to human contexts of rope use. Beyond this restriction a rope may be a clothesline or the main docking hawser of the *U.S.S. Nimitz.* It may be too short to tie up a parcel, or long enough to reach the deepest seabed. Similarly, a context has an associated appropriate scale which can only be defined relative to other contexts and which can never be precisely delimited or bounded.

In contrast to the continuum of time and space in the physicists' concept of the world, social contexts have specific scales of time, which cannot be violated, and which impose limits on causality. Contexts which exist at one scalar level interact with other scalar levels only in limited and discrete ways. Thus the general question about the size of the context might include questions such as "How long is a motive?" In other words, do the forces which shape human behavior last a moment, for example, an impulse, or do they last an age, for example, a culture?

Conclusion

Many current conceptions of social life are inadequate because they are not adequate accounts of time. In order to have an adequate account of time, we need an adequate account of what I have called *contexts.* In the way I have used the term, contexts are taken to be events that "take place" as well as spatial configurations of people and things that "take time." The importance of this conception is that it gives us a way to think about the temporal neighborhood of behavior, including mental behavior. Most explanations of behavior make sense only when we think of them in a temporal neighborhood.

The transformational–generative grammars, for example, though "timeless" in theory, make sense in practice only if we can think of performance as occurring within a context conceived as a "temporal module" during which a whole sentence is either formulated or interpreted. Even if we take the view that the sentence is somehow formed in a timeless moment, or scaleless point of time, it must take time to perform or to hear, so that at the behavioral level, there is a temporal neighborhood in which the whole sentence somehow comes to make sense.

Another example is the distinction between behaviorist and psychoanalytic psychologies. The difference between them can be conceived as a disagreement over the temporal neighborhood of the behavior in question. The psychoanalytic account is framed in terms of its antecedents. The temporal neighborhood extends back in time to the behavior's putative roots in an earlier psychological trauma. In this sense, Jung's psychology was similar to Freud's in its mode of explanation, except that the scale of time, and the temporal neighborhood of the behavior, was not limited by the lifetime of the single individual, but included the species-history of mankind. Behaviorism, by contrast, accounts for behavior in terms of its consequences, and postulates a relatively short neighborhood of time in which the stimulus–response–stimulus feedback loop is supposed to operate.

By thinking in terms of a theory of context (rather than a theory of "society"), and in terms of "temporal neighborhoods" of behavior, the relationships between the different disciplines of the social sciences can be considered in a new light. Each discipline could be seen as an orientation to different contexts in which the scale of time differs, rather than as studies of entities which differ ontologically such as "mind," "society," or "history." Thus, behavioral and cognitive psychology are concerned with short-term human contexts in which the scale of time is relatively short. Its interest in immediate cognition, language, motor activity, memory, learning, and so on, is a concern not so much with the mind of the individual as opposed to social behavior, but rather with contexts and events that can be measured in seconds, perhaps minutes or hours, but rarely years, and never decades. Sociology, similarly, is not concerned with "society" as opposed to "mind," but rather with intermediate contexts in which the scale of time is never measurable in seconds, but sometimes in minutes, and most often in hours, days, or years. Anthropology and history, finally, are concerned with the long-term temporality of tradition, social change, and human evolution.

One advantage of such a reconceptualization of mental and social reality may be that it allows us to partition this reality in a different way, and so to ask new and different questions about it. If, for instance, these concepts allow us to dissolve the age-old dichotomies between mind and society, or mind and behavior, then the necessity, and thus the sense of dialectical reasoning might also disappear. Though much respected, such methods of reasoning have always seemed to me more mystical than enlightening.

The differences between the disciplines, also, no longer appear to be those of content or method, but rather a difference of particular, appropriate scales of time in which human behavior is situated and explained. Human behavior may be thought of as existing in a set of interacting contexts which differ in the overall magnitude of appropriate temporal scales. These scales can be defined in terms of cognitive, manipulative (tactile), social, and environmental rhythms, and these are measurable because they are comparable in terms of rules of transformation between scales. These differing scales of time, generated by different contexts of human activity, may be causally isolated from each other, however, and interact only in specific ways. The patterns generated through these interactions create history.

References

Bourdieu, P. (1977), *Outline of a Theory of Practice*. Cambridge: Cambridge University Press.

Fraser, J. T. (1982), *The Genesis and Evolution of Time*. Brighton, U.K.: Harvester Press.

Giddens, A. (1984), *The Constitution of Society: Outline of the Theory of Structuration*. Cambridge, U.K.: The Polity Press.

Lieberman, P. (1984), *The Biology and Evolution of Language*. Cambridge: Harvard University Press.

Lyons, J. (1968), *Introduction to Theoretical Linguistics*. Cambridge: Cambridge University Press.

———— (1977), *Semantics*, 2 vols. Cambridge: Cambridge University Press.

Michon, J. A. (1985), Temporality and metaphor. In: *Time, Mind and Behavior*, eds. J.A. Michon & J. Jackson. Berlin: Springer-Verlag, pp. 288–296.

Osgood, C. E. (1980), *Lectures on Language Performance*. New York: Springer-Verlag.

Sahlins, M. (1974), *Stone Age Economics*. London: Tavistock.

Sudnow, D. (1978), *Ways of the Hand: The Organization of Improvised Conduct*. Cambridge, MA.: Harvard University Press.

Toth, N. (1983), The cutting edge: An elephant butchery with stone tools. *Interim Evidence: Foundation for Research into the Origins of Man*, 5:810.

———— (1986), Archaeological evidence for preferential right-handedness in the lower and middle Pleistocene, and its possible implications. *J. Hum. Evol.*, 14/6:607–613.

———— Schick K. D. (1986), The first million years: The archaeology of proto-human culture. In: *Advances in Archaeological Method and Theory*, ed. M.B. Schiffer. New York: Academic Press.

Perspectives

The individual's views on the nature of time and mind are guided by socially acceptable judgments on the nature of reality and on the position of man in the universe. The individual's control of his behavior is guided by socially approved values.

In the words of Professor Thornton, "Social values, goals and patterns, therefore, are not just background scenery while people make discoveries about time in the foreground, but are part of the context in which discoveries are made" (Personal communication).

No scientific law—be it in the exact sciences, in psychology, or in social sciences—is exempt in its principles and form from the influences of social values current at the age and place when and where it is formulated.

This dependence of knowledge on social context is most keenly recognized in the social sciences themselves. To get an intellectual handle on it, to assist in asking questions about time and mind without losing sight of society's influence upon them, Professor Thornton suggests a reconceptualization of social thought itself, by means of an epistemology of time scales.

He notes that different aspects of social behavior may be classed by the ranges of their spatial and temporal domains which "can be defined in terms of cognitive, manipulative (tactile), social and environmental rhythms" (p. 192). When so classed, it is then possible to identify "temporal neighborhoods" that are quasi-independent because their functions involve grossly different scales of time. The epistemology he suggests permits comparisons among temporal neighborhoods in a way that is isomorphic with time measurement. Therefore, he directs our attention to the basic principle of time measurement as formulated by Fraser (chapter 1, p. 10) and notes that it is from the rules of transformations that join distinct temporal neighborhoods that social meanings emerge.

What may be said about the social meaning of time and mind in our epoch of profound social changes?

11

Mind, Technologies, and Collective Time Consciousness: From the Future to the Extended Present

Helga Nowotny

Abstract My observations have focused on the interaction between time embedded in artifacts, especially the time dimensions of technologies, and the symbolic processes of time structuring which lead to the establishment of specific temporal norms.

The new information-intensive technologies have approached the limits of speed that can still be exploited through the old means of organizing social time. By decoupling previously existing temporal constraints they generate a new temporal norm, that of flexibility. The time discipline thus produced differs significantly from that which controlled the age of industrial production.

Two basic features of this time discipline are discerned. One is that of the pressure and the necessity of coping in a more predictable and controlled way with the processes of innovation, repetition, and obsolescence that appear to be wasteful under the new time discipline. The other feature relates to the abolition of the category of the long-term future and its replacement by the idea of a manageable and controllable extended present.

Embedded and Symbolic Time

The ways in which societies conceptualize their experience of time are neither immutable nor universally valid. This holds especially for the familiar notions of past, future, and present, categories separated by shifting boundaries, and by different meanings attributed to the guiding orientations they entail. They are not arbitrary constructs, however, since they reflect society's deeply structured experience of time and the collective time consciousness which is echoed in the mind of an individual living in a given historical period and a concrete societal umwelt. What brings about the social construction of time and its expression in concepts, behavior, in institutional arrangements? What allows the rich and complex patterns of integration and coordination that characterize a society's temporal existence? They are symbolic processes of time structuring, intersubjective and constituted through social interaction both on the behavioral and the symbolic level (Nowotny, 1975).

Institutional mechanisms are usually devised to reinforce these symbolic processes and help them work their way through conflicts between different sets of temporal priorities and the temporal grids criss-crossing societies. But the powerful capacity of the human mind to form abstractions and concepts of synthesis out of social experience, to reach beyond immediacy and be able to "time" by establishing relationships between two or more moving continua of social interaction, is itself restrained (Elias, 1984; Nowotny, unpublished). Time is not only a symbolic construct, it is also, as Torsten Hägerstrand (1985) has reminded us, "embedded" in the spatial configurations of dead and living matter. Embedded time exists in the unmeasurable succession of more and more complex configurations of matter, in the way things appear, transform, change their distribution, and disappear. Even our corporality is to be viewed as a part of nature and, therefore, is a carrier of embedded time.

Time is embedded not only in nature, however, but also in artifacts, those purposeful and instrumental devices that men and women have invented, from early cooking utensils and hunting devices to the vast sociotechnological complexes and megasystems of our technological umwelt. It is embedded in the sense that all these artifacts, especially technologies are neither time-neutral nor time-independent. Rather, as I will show in greater detail, technologies constitute an important determining factor of the ways in which the symbolic processes of time structuring unfold. The construction of our social time, itself fascinating because of the inventiveness of the human mind and the powerful play of symbolic interactions is constrained and directed in specific ways by the embedded time in the artifacts which are increasingly transforming the natural umwelt of our past.

A main purpose of this chapter will be to explore the interaction between constraints exerted upon, and derived from, the time dimensions of technologies on the one hand, and the symbolic processes of time structuring that lead to specific modes of time consciousness, on the other hand. My approach is not to be interpreted, however, as one of technological determinism. *Technologies*, in the broad sense in which I will use the term, are an efficient way of using technical means and procedures to alter both the natural and social umwelt to bring about deliberate change, and achieve present goals. As Marx observed long ago, technologies, in accomplishing this function, alter not only the relationship between humans and the environment, but also the relationship between humans and artifacts. These changes include the way in which artifacts and other human beings are perceived and experienced, as well as the extent to which they shape interaction and attitudes. But artifacts are made by humans: they evolve through specific configurations of skills, knowledge, societal values, and economic preconditions; that is, they depend on the social and economic forces which engender "innovativeness" (Nelson and Winter, 1977; Dosi, 1982).

Control Through Artefacts: The Example of Clock Time

Technological artefacts or the "fabricated populations of material artefacts," as Torsten Hägerstrand calls them, have been a highly efficient and ever-evolving means for extending the range of means through which humans could escape the restrictions of distances and times. They helped expand the effective spatial range by means of transportation and communication; they also complemented and superseded practically all other limitations of our earlier natural habitus and habitat. They hold the promise of delaying death, the inevitable end to our individual existence. Yet in their real accomplishments as well as in the utopian imagination of their liberating tendencies they have also continued to exert new forms of control. These controls are experienced as constraints of the impersonal clock time which still is the underlying regulator of daily life in industrialized societies. These artifacts, by their oppressive use, especially during that intense period of industrial upheaval we call the industrial revolution, have radically transformed the face and fate of our planet. Nowhere has this been better recorded than in accounts of the relentless rationalization of time with which industrial capitalism entered the stage of world history.

The impact of industrialization as a new form of control has been identified with the history of time measurement and with what Lewis Mumford described as "the key machine of the modern industrial age," the clock. It brought about a regimentation which, as Mumford pointed out, was not only essential to the rise of capitalism but also may be considered its product. (Mumford, 1934, p. 42).

I will not dwell on the splendid and well-known accounts of the history of Western civilization under the regime of precision time keeping, provided by such authors as Mumford, Cipolla, David Landes, and E. P. Thompson or extended for purposes of comparison in the work of Joseph Needham. I simply want to emphasize the fact that relationships to artifacts contain important temporal dimensions and produce many and different temporal norms that regulate and control behavior. The clock, the symbol for the underlying profound transformations which industrial capitalism brought about through the clock's continued rationalization, was equated with these processes to such an extent that social time itself became reified in it. Hated, endured, monopolized, and manipulated by different social groups, an instrument of power and at the same time an expression of social integration, time has often been interpreted in accordance with the logic that may be imputed to a reified construct. Social time has been analyzed as something secondary to physical time, as the constant process of adaptation of social institutions to an external, objective, and presupposed reference scale, or as an instrument of oppression. Thus the critics of the corporate technostructure have retained holding the clock as the central instrument of domination, especially in working life. While it is certainly true that there exists a policy of time, the clock, like any other instrument, is neither a neutral time-keeping device, nor a deterministic force in historical development. Clocks are neither liberators nor oppressors. The function they serve in our societies is similar to that of masks in some tribal societies: everyone knows that these masks are produced by humans, yet in the rituals in which they appear, they become representatives of a supranatural entity. Clocks as artifacts embody time and show time which is embedded in them as artifacts. In addition, they symbolize the constraints emanating from the production technologies for whose social regulation they have mainly been used.

But how can we unmask the masks and understand the ritual of which we ourselves form an integral part?

Past, Future, and Present

Time conceptions, as was stated in the beginning, vary from one society to another. This is true not merely because of different cultural and cosmological traditions, but because of differences in the diffusion rate of technologies, the degree and distribution of societal penetration, the cultural usage and functions these technologies have assumed in altering and mediating the temporal relationships that govern the interaction between artifacts and humans.

This brings me to the second major theme of this chapter: namely, the shifting boundaries of past, future, and present, mainly the latter two. Since the onset of industrialization, the great divide in the mode of time-structuring which separated industrialized from nonindustrialized countries, such shifts can be traced back to the different forms of time discipline and temporal norms which time technologies impose upon the social experience of time. Past or future are no longer united in elaborate myths of creation and cosmological accounts but are contained and shaped to a remarkable degree through the processes of interaction between time embedded in technological artifacts and symbolic time constructions as intersubjective structuration.

Thus, it is quite remarkable to observe how the nineteenth century, which bore the brunt of industrialization, was haunted by struggles of coming to terms with both the past and the future. In the realm of science, it provided the first firm basis for establishing the facts of nature's very own past: in 1800, scientists knew well that the earth was ancient, but they had no frame for ordering events into an actual history, the sequence of unique events forming the complex history of life as recorded by fossils, had not yet been developed. By 1850, history had been ordered in a consistent, worldwide sequence of recognizable and unrepeated events, defined by the ever-changing history of life and recorded by a set of names accepted and used in the same way throughout the scientific world (Gould, 1986a). The second half of the century witnessed the triumph of Darwin's "long argument" in which the past (i.e., history), stood as the coordinating reason for relationships among organisms, as a guide to action in research, and the first workable program ever presented for evolution (Gould, 1986b). It was only by bringing nature's own history into science and by firmly establishing the evolutionary order of the past, that the door was opened wide for a future recognized also as evolutionary, and, as such, open to workable programs of scientific and technological intervention as well. But in the same period, all those individuals who found themselves in the upheaval of the industrial revolution recognized their prior knowledge of the past as thoroughly shattered. It had to be rebuilt under scientific guidance in accordance with the new norms that came to dominate the modern world views. Their views of the future, as Marshall Berman has shown in a moving account of the cultural tensions induced by *the tourbillon social,* the social whirlwind, were tinged by the experience of a relentless destruction of the past. Yet, even in the midst of a wretched present, they could imagine an open future (Berman, 1982). The experience forced them to give up a past—the innumerable little worlds of the small hamlets and towns that had survived in an agricultural economy—and to exchange it for a violently uncertain future which they invested with their hopes and fears, their passionate desires, and their will to succeed. For the vast majority of those who were torn out of their normal lives, the present was reduced to the most shaky of experiences, while the past—not of the peasant but of the entire earth—came to be reconstructed by geological science. In turn, this scientifically secured and validated past was used for building a future envisaged as the never ending road toward technological and social progress.

What I find equally remarkable is the fact that the implementation of the future dreamed of in the past, has radically devalued what our own life once held in promises and attractions. Somehow, with many of the technological utopias realized and the miracles in place, the category of the future has also been flattened and exhausted.

The belligerent and overly self-confident claim "we have seen the future and it works" has turned out to be a very shallow claim indeed (Nowotny, 1984). The present predicaments and threat of nuclear annihilation or environmental collapse, of time running out in the wake of technological interventions based on ignorance or willful defiance, have converted the future into a precarious category, experienced for the first time in truly global dimensions. Like similar ventures before, the colonization of the future, so confidently initiated by science and technology, has become recalcitrant, turning against its alleged masters, while we are about to abandon the notion of the future in the sense in which it has been conceived until now. As I will argue in greater detail, it is the discovery and experience of the extended present which opens new visions at a turning point in our collective time consciousness.

Time Technologies and Temporal Norms

In the remaining part of the chapter I wish to distinguish three types of time technologies. They do not appear in an evolutionary sequence. Rather, although major advancements in each of them are concentrated in certain periods, they may be found coexisting and feeding upon each other with varying interconnections. These technologies deal with (1) the reduction of distance in time (i.e., time and space technologies); (2) the conversion of material things in time (i.e., production technologies); and (3) information-intensive technologies which eliminate certain time–space constraints altogether. The dominant temporal norms I see associated with them are mobility, scarcity, and flexibility. By pulling together several strands of empirical evidence and conceptual approach I hope to illuminate from a social point of view the dialectical processes of timing our minds and minding our time and thereby to enlarge our collective understanding of the societal transition which we find ourselves in right now.

Mobility

Time–space technologies permit the reduction of distance in time. That is the transportation of goods, people, and energy over geographical distances may be effected in potentially less time than before. The bridging of space in less time can fulfill the same function as before, but it alters its efficiency: armies can march on foot against each other, ride on horseback, or operate automatic missile and antimissile systems. New social functions, such as continue to evolve in urban conglomerations, emerge, generating additional infrastructures. These have been the objects of intensive studies of city planners, systems analysts, and geographers. The development of transportation systems belongs to this category with far-reaching spatial and temporal impact on the perception and the division of day and night that systems such as the railway or the electrical power grid have had on societies (Schivelbusch, 1979; Hughes, 1983). The possibility of transporting goods over greater distances or in less time has dramatically altered the size of markets, a consequence which usually is not sufficiently appreciated by economists when they speak about market size. The "timing of space" and "spacing of time" have become a powerful conceptual framework for the study, pioneered by the work of Torsten Hägerstrand and others, of shifting configurations of human activities.

The temporal–spatial norm that has emerged from this set of technologies, simultaneously incorporating a key societal value and a behavioral prerequisite, is *mobility*. It has come to be highly valued not only in economic, but also in cultural terms. Movement through space in less time has become the sine qua non of a system based upon the rapid circulation of goods, people, energy, and information. The pressure to be mobile, to increase the rate of circulation has spread from geographical space to other spaces: mobility in occupational life is inherent in the notion of a career. In a time in which working places themselves become mobile in that they are being displaced by new ones or none at all, *mobility*, not only in geographical terms, has become indispensable for those who want to continue being part of the labor force. The mobility of ideas is one of the mainsprings of scientific productivity. Technical civilization imposes new demands for mobility between different domains, such as work and leisure; high and low culture; the emotional and the rational parts of lives. The rapid succession, or the oscillation between different stages, states (of mind and body), and places of people, things, and ideas has become the dominant time-related norm upholding the rapid circulation of production and consumption of material goods. The appeal of the increasingly stepped-up succession of what is considered to be new, in addition to being a trait inherent in fashions of various kinds, has become the hallmark in our society of material and cultural production alike.

Scarcity

The second major category with a distinctive temporal dimension involves production technologies. The amazing gains that have been achieved in productivity since the beginning of industrialization, consist of production advances which, through division of labor, allow an increased output from a given volume of work and resources, or a given output from a smaller volume of labor and resources. From about 1880 onward, the production increase in the Western economies has been linked by economists to the so-called "rationalization" of production methods; that is, in the rigorous and coherent application of the "economics of time" to the industrial production process (Rosenberg, 1976).[1]

"Saving time" and the continuous exploitation of time resources within the production process have proceeded in twin fashion through technological development and temporal organization of production, its "rationalization" (for recent overviews see Bergman [1983]; Rinderspacher [1985]). For the present purpose it is important to note how the "economics of time," the equation of time with money, have spread from their highly successful application in the production process (a fact that was painfully experienced by the workers) to almost any other segment of social life. From the downtrodden workers who fought for the reduction of working hours to the hurried leisure class for whom having "no time" became a status symbol, the impact of the time dimension of production technologies on all facets of life became pervasive. Based on the economic value that time acquired under industrial capitalism and the convertibility of time and money, time became the ultimately finite, scarce resource. *Scarcity* of time is the temporal norm that has pushed further the efforts to open up additional temporal resources. In the production process this has occurred through further rationalization. By speeding up the work rhythms of machines—and of the humans who operated them—and by improving synchronization and coordination, additional time was "gained." The invention and massive use of the conveyor belt was one example of rationalization methods: by minimizing the time periods of inactivity and rest as well as the slack time for machines and workers, additional time resources were utilized.

Time as a scarce resource and time discipline, for example, punctuality and the general sense of time consciousness, have become the hallmarks of the temporal grid of highly industrialized societies. While temporal flexibility and increased autonomy in the use of one's time have remained the privilege of an elite, strict time discipline and the polarization of social life into work and leisure de facto has been imposed on the majority of working people. Recent information-intensive technologies are continuing to have a strong impact on these patterns.

[1]Sam Macey was right, however, in pointing out that an established clock industry flourished before this date (Personal Communication).

Flexibility

Information-intensive technologies applied to the transmission and processing of information have achieved a new quality of speed, approximating the limits of time open to the human mind. They are able to perform operations in "almost no time": the gain of speed is becoming a factor of marginal utility. Concomitantly, information-intensive technologies often no longer require the simultaneous bodily presence of producer and consumer, of sender and receiver. This, for instance, also goes for the so-called "mental services." This trait has recently been emphasized by Fritz Scharpf who questions the potential for rationalization and the opportunities for lowering production costs in a way similar to corresponding measures in industrial production (Scharpf, 1985). The customer's wish to have a haircut still demands the interaction of hairdresser and customer at the same place and at the same time, but the taping of concerts, soccer games, or language courses no longer involves such a requirement. Production and consumption can now take place independent of each other. Storage and conservation techniques have already made possible a similar temporal independence for the production and consumption of food; biotechnology and genetic engineering are working to accomplish this for living cells and eventually perhaps for human life.

The decoupling of acts of production and consumption which makes possible further rationalization in production, since daily, weekly, or seasonal rhythms in consumer preferences no longer need to be taken into account, is, however, only one aspect of a more general principle of temporal experience which is embedded in the new information-intensive technologies. Just as *mobility* has become the primordial temporal experience in the wake of time and space technologies, *scarcity* and the economic value of time, that of production technologies, so *flexibility* is becoming the temporal norm derived from and buttressing information-intensive technologies. It is also bound to spread to other forms of social organization. Following from the patterns of interaction, work organization, production, and consumption imposed by the new technologies, flexibility is also a prerequisite for the successful implementation of the technologies themselves. Temporal norms are engendered by technologies, yet once they are in place, they become necessary for sustaining the technical system and its social infrastructure. Moreover, they are upheld by specific modes of time discipline which, among other things, are set up to solve conflicts between different time conceptions and norms.

Flexibility, in a way, obliterates the rigidities of time structures which Western industrialized societies have become adjusted to in the course of the past two centuries. The increase of speed, just like the underlying model of mechanical causal linearity has been mastered and superseded by technological systems that are based on cybernetic principles, emphasizing networks, feedback loops, decomposition, and recombination of component elements which follow the organization principles of complexity, rather than those of mere accumulation and output. These developments and the subtle paradigm shifts that have preceded them within physics, biology, and the new cognitive sciences are now becoming more visible in their technological embodiment which also leads to a much more tangible and direct form of interaction with other parts of the social system.

The inherent flexibility of the new technologies manifests itself in an increased availability of possibilities for decentralizing work and consumption in space and time. While this will undoubtedly lead to a continued blurring between work time and leisure time witnessed already now in shadow work and tendencies toward self-service, it opens up new opportunities for individualized time preferences. However, the euphoria with which the new, flexible technologies have been greeted as offering an escape from the iron time cage of the past, is premature. Time flexibility, like decentralization and temporal flexibility attained in a system, necessitates a new level of greater complexity where coordination, synchronization, and centralization takes place. It is, therefore, not to be expected that hierarchies will be abandoned; rather they will become more differentiated and complex. While it remains to be seen how far flexible automation will spread in the organizational principles emphasizing settings for multiskilled workers who are paid for what they know, rather than for how hard they work, will bring about a radical breach with past patterns of work organization and its strict temporal discipline (Hirschhorn, 1984; Ayres, 1984).

The New Time Discipline

Next to work organization there exist cultural orientations that support it. Donald Lowe, in his *History of Bourgeois Perception* (1982), includes among them as a primary constituent, the typographic media, a hierarchy of sensing which emphasizes the primacy of sight, and an epistemic order of development-in-time which provides a temporal connection for observable phenomena beyond their representability in space. Looking back on the past, it is surprising, to cite but one example, how great an importance was attached to punctuality by the older educational practices and how drastic the means had to be for achieving it (Böhme, 1985). This occurred in periods when, judged from today's standards, punctuality was not so much needed, while today, where everything depends on a high level of coordination of individual schedules linked to institutionally imposed schedules, such as public transportation, business hours, work schedules, and so on, punctuality no longer needs to be taught. It has been thoroughly internalized by the technical conditions of our lives.

This thrust toward self-organization is indicative of one direction that corresponds to the idea of smaller, more decentralized, and thus semiautonomous units. Another direction is indicated by the emphasis our society puts on combatting old age. This takes place not only with regard to biological age but also in the realm of technological performance. Industrial and political leaders constantly push for continuous technological innovation, exhorting institutions and corporations to fight against senescence. In some cases, as in that of the United States, firms are promised the possibility of "rebirth" as an ideal to strive for consciously. Instead of accelerating maturity, American corporations are advised to plan strategically for extended product adolescence (Ayres, 1984). Survival and corporate immortality through management of the life cycle of technological processes and products become new goals. A final example is the campaign Mancur Olson has started against the sclerosis of institutions with similar metaphors and aims in mind (1982).

It will be the task of empirical research to carefully scrutinize the evidence for the internal life time cycles of various technological systems of the kind that Cesare Marchetti has pioneered (Nelson and Winter, 1977; Klein, 1977; Marchetti, 1980; Olson, 1982). Looking at diffusion patterns of energy technologies, transportation systems, but also causes of death in a specific human population, or at scientific as well as artistic creativity in terms of the Volterra equations developed for ecological systems, Marchetti finds remarkable invariants in the dynamics of competition between structures capable of multiplication and expansion. If, as Marchetti claims, they become predictable up to a certain point, can the "time discipline" they embody also be "taught" in order to achieve better adaptation between technological and social life cycles? Of course, technologies do not behave like humans, they are generated by human action. The anthropomorphic parallels that emerge when studying technological innovations, are, however, striking. To me, this suggests that cultural orientations that guide the sense of temporal direction and of time discipline in the broadest sense are no longer addressed merely to people, but have to include artifacts. It is not the one, lonely robot or Frankenstein's monster that has come to life and must be controlled. Rather it is an entire sociotechnical system and its interdependencies with society that need guidance and management. The time discipline which has to be learned is no longer one of rigid subordination to clock time or of adjustment to the rhythms of a machine. Rather, it is built on managed growth and obsolescence, on the planning and control of birth, reiteration, and decline. Being part of that system, we are able, perhaps more consciously than ever before, to bring to it our own biological and social knowledge and experience. We may have here a historically unique chance of applying them. Yet it will not be possible to reduce the social costs that every time discipline extracts in its own ways.

Escape from Contradictions

When Joseph A. Schumpeter, the great Austrian economist, equated technological innovation with creative destruction, he was mainly concerned with what he thought to be the driving force behind capitalism: the inventor–entrepreneur. This lonely genius has long since given way to all the Silicon Valleys that have appeared suddenly all over the United States, Japan, and Western Europe.

Today, technological innovation has become science-based, and science itself can no longer proceed without technological innovation. Yet the vision of what once was conceived as more or less unilinear progress, has become punctuated by Kondratieff cycles, long waves, and inherent instabilities. What Harvey Brooks calls "the gradual, incremental unfolding of the world system in a manner that can be described by surprise-free models, with parameters derived from a combination of time series and cross sectional analysis of the existing system" (1986, p. 326) is no longer considered sufficient for describing the intensifying patterns of interaction between technological innovation on the one hand and their impact on the natural environment and the social fabric on the other. The search for new heuristics of thought, of methods, models, and concepts that permit to capture unexpected discrete events, discontinuities in long-term trends, or the sudden emergence of new information in public consciousness and awareness (such as acid rain) is an attempt to come to terms with the perception of new temporal patterns (Clark, 1986). It is part of learning to cope with the new time discipline, of having to manage innovation, repetition, and decline in their multifaceted forms.

Time in social systems, as I stated at the outset, is not independent of "embedded" time, the time found in artifacts and their interaction with the human mind. Hence, it is bound to change with the evolution of societies. Just as the idea that events on earth were but a mirror reflecting celestial happenings in a heaven thought to be inhabited by the gods gave way to the Newtonian time which has, in turn, been superseded by the plurality of temporalities in modern physics, so has social time been undergoing a redefinition. It is structured by the constraints and opportunities of the technological systems, but it also has to find solutions for the temporal conflicts that arise between differently experienced needs for coordination and integration. Temporal asymmetries must be managed through social and institutional mechanisms and the use of explanatory cultural symbols. In a fine analysis the philosopher von Wright arrives at the metaphorical observation that "time is man's escape from contradiction," meaning that time is necessary in order to accept change (1969).

Change in social systems arrives with different faces. In the late twentieth century, change is dominated by scientific and technological developments, by the fast pace in which the industrialized nations press for further technological innovation in their military and economic games of competition. A central contradiction exists in wanting to make the unpredictable occur while trying to predict it before or while it is happening. Western industrialized societies have opted for relentless change, yet they want to control its consequences as well as the process through which it occurs. Choosing futures has become a popular theme in very different circles; its ideological underpinnings range from grassroot political participation to the marriage of market and technocracy where the market creates options of futures and technocracy picks the winner. The answer to these contradictions, the escape route which is opening up, consists in rearranging our relationship with the future.

The Extended Present

My hypothesis is that we are about to abolish the category of the open future as we know it now and to replace it with that of the extended present. We are approaching finiteness in the sense that we have gained sufficient understanding of the problems besetting us in the present while stumbling toward devising corrective policies. This creates awareness of our own limitations and makes us realize the constraints imposed upon our competence. The long-term consequences of human interaction with the natural environment is an example of such understanding, but we can find one in any other policy domain once we start looking for longer-term interconnectedness. This sense of relative mastery and control due to our scientific heritage closes the future as a perspective into which hopes and unresolved contradictions can continue to be projected. Rather, pressure is mounting from many quarters to consider problems in the extended present. Just as science in the nineteenth century was securing a past for nature on which the future of human societies could be built, in the late twentieth century scientific endeavors have increasingly to cope with the problems that beset the present by taking the mortgaged future into account. This in no way contradicts the fact that the touchstone for mature scientific achievements remains the ability to predict, when we extend the present beyond the immediacy of day-to-day concerns, the range of potential consequences which comes into view, demands, under the pressure of time, that action can be taken now if irreversible negative results are to be avoided. This puts heightened demands on the ability of science to predict, if only because the possible negative impacts of scientific and technological interventions may arrive earlier and may be more acute than had been the case before. The quest to predict and to control the future is catching up with us by loading the present with choices that have to be acted upon under the pressure of an often incomplete knowledge and in the face of massive uncertainty (Evers and Nowotny, 1987). The point at issue no longer simply is in which direction the world will be moved through scientific and technological knowledge, but how the various applications of this knowledge, the uses to which they have been put, are interacting with each other, thereby producing a complexity of results which hitherto has not been consciously experienced in the history of humankind (Hägerstrand, 1987). If we are successfully to reach into the future, the price for doing so has partly to be paid in the present. Even the line that separates us from future generations is becoming thinner. Like other generations before them, they will inherit a world they did not make, together with unspecified resources for remaking it. Yet the burdens which we are consciously and knowingly inflicting upon them have become larger and potentially more irreversible. In our still muted concern for their well-being, we find that the future intrudes into the present and that its voices demand some kind of representation now.

The scientific task of coping with our present problems, the boundaries of which have been extended through our dim awareness of the consequences of our scientific and technological advances, is further exacerbated by the fact that much policy- and action-related science has to proceed under novel conditions of uncertainty. Often decisions have to be taken with the knowledge basis still insecure, empirical evidence unavailable, highly controversial, or even contradictory. The right to not knowing-as-yet was granted to science provided it promises a steady advance. Now, as public policy decisions must be made with colliding economic and social interests, a new understanding of the precariousness of scientific knowledge in the extended present becomes necessary. The limits to the growth of our civilization have become internalized and are represented in its knowledge base.

The consequences arising from this diagnosis are manifold. On the technological and social side not only innovations, but also future decline and obsolescence have to be accommodated in the present. We cannot merely make plans for change: plans are needed equally for the orderly discarding of what no longer fits the system. It follows that long-term time perspectives become open to operationalization, however hazy they may still seem. Events in the year 2025 become calculable items on society's global agenda, just as the average manager's desk calendar already includes appointments for the year to come.

Within such an overall time frame, the plurality of times in different segments of the social system from the macro- to the microlevel, also takes on added significance. It is no longer so much the individual's temporal invariables, needs, attitudes, and orientations that have to be ordered in a hierarchy of temporal priorities, but also the time frames of institutions that need better coordination and a place in a nested hierarchy. Beyond coordination on the same functional level of such time schedules as traffic flow, work, or opening hours of shops, it is the time delay of second- and third-order consequences of institutional interactions that need to be considered.

The abolition of the category of the future and its replacement by an extended present is less of a radical break than it may seem at first. Many societies have lived for long stretches of time without considering the future; the idea of an open-ended future oriented toward constant improvement emerged late in Western history. It implied the creation of an ideological distance between what has been experienced and what was to be expected (Koselleck, 1979; Luhmann, 1980). With the help of science and technology this discrepancy became stabilized in the nineteenth century and was identified as the ever-evolving dynamic movement of progress. The future became accessible under the condition of remaining inaccessible. Today, this distance is threatening to collapse. Expectations no longer include the glittering promise of a horizon still to be reached and from which one will be able to extrapolate yet more distant expectations. The category of the future is shrinking into a mere extension of the present, because science and technology have successfully reduced the distance that is needed to integrate their own products into society. While science and technology seemingly are producing a plurality of possible futures, held out for our disposal, there can still be only one present (Nowotny, 1984). It has to be restructured so as to accommodate the choices heaped upon us through the rapid pace of scientific and technological development. It has to come to terms with the new quality of finiteness which arises from the closure of the future.

What about human freedom under such seemingly restrained conditions? I cannot really enter the debate on the freedom of will or the degrees of freedom for individual and collective action under the conditions described, without stating at the outset that I find no ground for either excessive pessimism or optimism. As always, new developments in technology or science are putting hitherto unimaginable tools at society's disposal, thus bringing to the fore hidden value conflicts and divergent views on how societies ought to be managed, and by whom. The very definition of what is to be controlled, and how, opens new areas for the exercise of power. The struggle for who will exert that power in a society whose innovative contours are still fuzzy, has already begun. The more the heated discussions and controversies turn on what will happen in the future, the greater is the concern about who will make decisions in the present.

In my view, preoccupation with the future as though it were really open for choice, is an expression of nostalgia for something which is about to disappear and which is thus prized like an antique object. Under the pressure of having to cope with incessant innovation—a process which at least in its incipient stages, is governed by randomness—an effort at rationalization sets in which is geared toward more control of the innovative present. The investigation of life cycles of technologies, past and present, enjoys great popularity at the moment (Nowotny, 1984). It conveys a deterministic picture of societal life. Yet, as Marchetti points out, some striking self-consistency of structure is found on different levels and in different segments of the social system (Nelson and Winter, 1977; Klein, 1977; Marchetti, 1980). How much freedom this allows, in the end, will depend, as I see it, on our own definition of where the self is to be located in the principle of self-organization and of what the self really stands for.

In the meantime, let me end by approaching what I believe to be the same underlying problem from a slightly different perspective and by phrasing it in more general terms.

Innovation, Repetition, Obsolescence

Reflecting on linked sequences in works of art, George Kubler remarks in *The Shape of Time* (1962) that:

> The occurrence of things is governed by our changing attitudes towards the processes of invention, repetition and discard. Without invention there would only be stale routine. Without copying there would never be enough of any man-made things and without waste or discard too many things would outlast their usefulness. Our attitudes towards these processes are themselves in constant change so that we confront the double difficulty of charting changes together with tracing the change in ideas about change [p.82].

Although Kubler is concerned with aesthetics rather than with what he calls "useful" inventions, there are similarities to be found in both. Kubler sees two inherent tensions: one is between replication, the desire to return to the known patterns, and invention, the desire to escape it by new variation. Society shelters the individual against too much variation by enclosing him or her within an invisible many-layered structure of routine. The other great tension is between retention and discarding. The decision to discard is far from being a simple one; it constitutes a reversal of values since things that once were necessary now become litter or scrap.

As with the elaborate tomb furnishings of many ancient cultures, society also has developed rituals for the retention of things. Today, many people are concerned with saving animals, things, and knowledge which are about to vanish from our civilizing tradition.

Although investigations into the systematics of internal age—the age within one period as opposed to the more external, chronological age of artifacts, ideas, or technologies which appear in a linked system—hold their own fascination, the question of how societies balance their rates of innovation, repetition, and obliteration approaches perhaps the same phenomenon from a different angle. It is not a mere whimsical change of attitudes that tips the balance. With the closure of the category of the future, the present becomes more loaded with all three processes—innovation, repetition, and obsolescence. The denser the rate of innovation, the more attention will have to be given to the problem of waste and waste disposal. Senescent or dying industries, regions, and especially the knowledge and skills of people working and living in them, cannot so easily be discarded as throwaway bottles. The social problems associated with the loss to those who are made redundant, of social identity, self-esteem, social status, and income, make the problem of waste appear in yet another form and one which in the long run cannot be neglected. One strategy for coming to terms with the social costs of obsolescence is to cushion its effects as we do those of old age. The other strategy consists in trying to eliminate waste at the other end; that is, at the beginning of the new cycle. Rather than welcoming innovative activity indiscriminately, the management of the extended present requires order, rationality, and selectivity as well. But how is one to know whether the sprouts of creativity will be weeded out in the right way? Will there remain enough time for time to tell?

Global Finiteness

- My observations have focused on the interaction of time embedded in artifacts, especially the time dimensions of technologies, and the symbolic processes of time structuring which lead to the establishment of specific temporal norms.

- The newcomers among technologies, information-intensive technologies, have approached the limits of speed that can still be exploited through the old means of social organization of time. By decoupling previously existing temporal constraints they generate a new temporal norm, that of flexibility. Flexibility entails a time discipline that differs significantly from that which controlled the age of industrial production.

- Two basic features of this time discipline are discerned on the macro level. One is the pressure of, and the consequent necessity to cope in a more predictable and controlled way with, the processes of innovation, repetition, and obsolescence. Although far-reaching consequences are perhaps most visible in the management of technological change, they undeniably also exist in the social and environmental sphere. The analysis of empirical patterns of duration (life cycles) of technologies is part of a growing scientific effort to discern, in order to control, processes of innovation that appear to be wasteful under the new time discipline. .

- The other feature of the new time discipline involves the abolition of the category of the future and its replacement by the idea of an extended but manageable present. Under such a long-term time perspective leveling-off effects, the idea of limits, of surprise, as well as that of choices, time preferences, and participation in shaping what nostalgically is still called the future, have their place and are compatible with it. The extended present is beginning to be made operational.

- Coming to terms with finiteness does not mean closure in the sense of adopting an apocalyptic or millenarian vision. On the contrary, a new potential for temporal variety and for a multiplicity of individual and collective time schemes is being opened up. Its possibilities, including the cultural dimensions of temporal perception and experience, remain to be explored. It is quite likely, however, that we are about to transcend "bourgeois perception" and the temporality of the past as we enter the global finiteness of the twenty-first century. "Global finiteness" refers to (a) societal awareness reaching the whole globe, i.e., a spatial (as well as ecological, political, economic, and so forth) extension; (b) finiteness in the sense of the extended present, i.e., a temporal concept. Thus, our time horizon shrinks to the extended present, while our spatial horizon extends to the entire globe. In T. S. Eliot's words (1966):

> We shall not cease from exploration
> and the end of all our exploring
> will be to arrive where we started
> And know the place for the first time.

References

Ayres, R. U. (1984),, *The Next Industrial Revolution.* Cambridge, MA: Ballinger.

Bergman, W. (1983), Das Problem der Zeit in der Soziologie. *Kölner Zeitschrift für Soziologie und Sozial-Psychologie,* 35:462–504.

Berman, M. (1982), *All That Is Solid Melts Into Air. The Experience of Modernity.* New York: Simon & Schuster.

Böhme, G. (1985), *Coping with Science: Towards a New Theory of Science.* Theme T Report 9. Linkoping: University of Linkoping.

Brooks, H. (1986), The typology of surprises in technology, institutions and development. In: *Sustainable Development of the Biosphere,* eds., W. C. Clark & R. E. Munn. Cambridge: Cambridge University Press.

Cippola, C. M. (1978), *Clocks and Culture, 1300 to 1700.* New York: Norton.

Clark, W. C. (1986), Sustainable development of the biosphere: Themes for a research program. In: *Sustainable Development of the Biosphere,* eds. W. C. Clark & R. E. Munn. Cambridge: Cambridge University Press.

Dosi, G. (1982), Technological paradigms and technologies trajectories: A suggested interpretation of the determinants and directions of technical change. *Res. Policy*, 11:147–162.

Elias, N. (1984), *Über die Zeit*. Frankfurt: Suhrkamp.

Eliot, T. S. (1944), *Four Quartets*. London: Faber & Faber.

Evers, A., & Nowotny, H. (1987), *Über den Umgang mit Unsicherheit*. Frankfurt: Suhrkamp.

Gould, S. J. (1986a), Review of Martin J. S. Rudwick's *The Great Devonian Controversy: The Shaping of Scientific Knowledge Among Gentlemanly Specialists*. *NY Rev. Books*, February 17:9–15.

—————— (1986b), Evolution and the triumph of homology, or why history matters. *Amer. Sci.*, 7:66–69.

Hägerstrand, T. (1985), Time and culture. Paper presented to the conference on Time Preferences, Wissenschaftszentrum Berlin, December 16–17.

—————— (1987), Presence and absence: A look at conceptual choices and bodily necessities. *Regional Studies*, 18/5:373–380.

Hirschhorn, L. (1984), *Beyond Mechanization: Work and Technology in a Postindustrial Age*. Cambridge: MIT Press.

Hughes, T. H. (1983), *Networks of Power*. Baltimore: Johns Hopkins University Press.

Klein, B. (1977), *Dynamic Economics*. Cambridge: Harvard University Press.

Koselleck, R. (1979), *Vergangene Zukunft*. Frankfurt: Suhrkamp.

Kubler, G. (1962), *The Shape of Time*. New Haven, CT: Yale University Press.

Landes, D. (1983), *Revolution in Time. Clocks and the Making of the Modern World*. Cambridge: Harvard University Press.

Lowe, D.M. (1982), *History of Bourgeois Perception*. Chicago: University of Chicago Press.

Luhmann, N. (1980), *Gesellschaftsstruktur und Semantik*. Frankfurt: Suhrkamp.

Marchetti, C. (1980), Society as a learning system: Discovery, invention and innovation cycles revisited. *Technolog. Forecast. & Soc. Change*, 18:267–282.

Mumford, L. (1934), *Technics and Civilization*. New York: Harcourt, Brace & Co.

Nelson, R. R., & Winter, S. G. (1977), In search of a useful theory of innovation. *Res. Policy*, 6:36–72.

Nowotny, H. (1975), Time structuring and time measurement: On the interrelation between timekeepers and social time. In: *The Study of Time II*, eds. J. T. Fraser & N. Lawrence. New York: Springer.

—————— (1984), On the social ordering of the future. In: *Nineteen Eighty-Four: Science Between Utopia and Dystopia. Yearbook in the Sociology of the Sciences*. Dordrecht: Reidel.

—————— (unpublished), Das Machen der Zeit: Zu Norbert Elias' Entwurf einer Zeittheorie, 1982.

Olson, M. (1982), *The Rise and Fall of Nations*. New Haven, CT: Yale University Press.

Rinderspacher, J. (1985), *Zeit, Arbeit und Belastung*. Frankfurt: Campus.

Rosenberg, N. (1976), *Perspectives on Technology*. Cambridge: Cambridge University Press.

Scharpf, F. (1985), Strukturen der post-industriellen Gesellschaft. *Arbeit und Gesellschaft*, 11/1: 9–34.

Schivelbusch, W. (1979), *Die Geschichte der Eisenbahnreise. Industrialisierung von Raum und Zeit*. Frankfurt: Suhrkamp.

Schumpeter, J. A. (1939), *Business Cycles: A Theoretical, Historical and Statistical Analysis of the Capitalistic Process*. 2 vols. New York: McGraw-Hill.

von Wright, C. H. (1969), *Time, Chance and Contradiction*. Cambridge: Cambridge University Press.

Perspectives

Dr. Nowotny begins by asserting that both time and mind are collective in their nature. Ideas concerning future, past, and present are formed under the guidance of collective time-consciousness which "is echoed in the mind of an individual in a given historical period and concrete societal umwelt" (p. 197). Observing our own age of turmoil, she notes that "we are about to abolish the category of an open [that is, undetermined] future and replace it with an extended present" (p. 207).

If such a change is likely, or even if it is only conceivable, then we have at hand a demonstration in flagrante delicto, *of how society controls what we think about time and mind. Let us see the details.*

Only two of the chapters (those by Fraser and by Michon) attempted to examine, or at least give a working definition of, the concepts of time *and* mind. *The rest of the chapters have addressed such special issues as their authors felt appropriate for a debate on the junction,* time and mind, *leaving a general definition of that theme rather nebulous.*

As I see it, the papers accepted a common, unexamined usage which I would like to represent by verbal imagery.

"Time" has meant that intangible something which may be said to flow—or not to flow—across the immense spaces of the universe and the complex inner spaces of all, or at least certain structures. "Mind" has meant a family of capacities that informed the behavior of a person and somehow related to his or her brain like smoke and steam as they inform the behavior of, and surround, a steam engine.

The words and images of my light-hearted description reflect the character of our age and the nature of the language we speak or, in a more concise expression, our social umwelt. And that, the social relativity of views, is an important part of what Dr. Nowotny had to say.

Psychologists and physicists may decide what the best methods are for searching out the origins of our experience of time's flow; philosophers and philosophically minded scientists may debate the reality or otherwise of a closed past and open future, and the position of mind in the universe. But social scientists—or at least some of them—will question the validity and generality of their conclusions, beyond the particular cultural and social setting where they were reached.

Society is not a passive observer of what individuals discover about the nature of time and mind, but an active contributor to, and censor of, the truth or falsity of those discoveries.

Let me assume that some such profound change as was envisioned by Dr. Nowotny will come about. New conceptualizations of time (and of mind) will then surely be internalized by successive generations of men, women, and children. Future scholars and scientists may then identify the nature of time with the sociotemporality of institutional memory and the collective will, rather than with the noetic temporality of the individual mind and will, tacitly assumed in this book, thus far, as the final arbiter of truth about time and mind.

It is difficult to disagree with Dr. Nowotny's stress on the ferment of collective change in our days. For an understanding of how notions of timing and minding may be changing in that ferment, our best avenues lead not through the precise, analytic methods of scientific inquiry but the intuitive gropings for an understanding of time and mind in the arts and letters. Our sampling begins with an inquiry into the social aspects of the experimental time arts.

12

Social Time in Experimental Music and Art

Albert Mayr

Abstract This chapter adopts the vantage point of the experimental time arts (experimental music, performance art, video art, and experimental film) to formulate a critique of the current standards for the organization of social time in industrialized countries. To that end, the chapter illustrates the contributions made by these forms of art, through their techniques of perception, coding, and communicating human behavior, to the development of a new approach to social time.

I.

Looking North

In 1971 the American composer Christian Wolff wrote a verbal score entitled *Looking North* (unpublished):

> Think of, imagine, devise, a pulse, any you choose, of any design.
> When you hear a sound or see a movement or smell a smell or feel any sensation not seeming to emanate from yourself, whose location in time you can sense, and its occurrence coincides, at some point, with your pulse, make your pulse evident:
> in some degree; for any duration.
> (a) Express all coincidences.
> (b) Express only every tenth one.
> (c) Forget your pulse and play as closely as you can to every second, fifth, twentieth and single expression of pulse of one other player (this can be repeated as in a loop).
> (d) Play a very long, generally low pitched and quiet melody without particular reference to a pulse (once only).
> (e) At any point stop.
> (f) At any point stop, think of another pulse, and proceed as above.

Or: think of, imagine, devise, any number of pulses. . . . and so on, as above. [1]

Wolff's piece sets the framework for the reflections that follow. Their aim is to compare social temporalities in artistic and nonartistic endeavors, and describe some of their observed, and some of their hoped-for, interactions.

I shall restrict my comments to works which, I believe, stand in the tradition of the ontological conception of art, dating to the Pythagoreans, recently and aptly summarized by the postulate of the composer Arnold Schönberg and the architect Adolf Loos, that art has primarily to be true, not beautiful (Waibl, 1985).

The following passage, taken from the writings of the music theorist Eugene Narmour, takes us *in medias res:*

> One reason for the growing complexity of human knowledge was the inescapable empirical conclusion that time is an actively shaping, fundamental variable inherent in all natural and artifactual phenomena—rather than just an idealized, passive medium within which events occur. Nowhere is this more true than in artifactual phenomena where nonrecurrent psychological time must be seen as a virtual property. In a poem, for instance, or a dance or a film or, most tellingly, in a musical composition, the learned and inborn temporal workings of each individual human mind actively participate in the stylistic and idiostructural creation of the art work [1983–1984, p. 130].

It is the temporal workings of both individuals and groups participating in a performance of Wolff's piece that I should like to examine. These temporal workings are "learned and inborn," but, as we shall see, their manifestations are also the product of the macro- and microcontexts in which they are activated and of the procedures by which they are activated.

The socioeconomic and sociocultural context in which pieces such as *Looking North* are performed publicly is far from being of secondary importance. In my view they can be meaningfully played only in off-off-off venues, art galleries and university campuses, collectively known as the "alternate music circuit." The temporal workings called for in *Looking North* are, in fact, in stark contrast with the temporal workings of the institutionalized concert circuit.

The chronometric and chronological articulation of mainstream music events

[1]The term *verbal score* calls perhaps for some explanation: contemporary music has developed a great variety of notational techniques, such as graphic scores, patch diagrams for electroacoustic equipment with instructions for its manipulation, and other forms. In the late sixties several composers—notably those who had been influenced by Cage's aesthetics of indeterminacy—adopted the technique of casting their compositional ideas in the form of verbal directions. These directions define the procedural character of the piece, but leave the choice of its actual sonic manifestations to the performers. Thus, verbal scores may usually be performed by any number of players with any type of sound sources. Among the composers of verbal scores, Wolff has, in my view, made the most stimulating contributions in the field of synchronization procedures.

has to follow rules and procedures which have little to do with making the right music happen at the right moment in the right place. This articulation is controlled, instead, by such matters as the working hours specified in the contracts of musicians and staff, the schedules of conductors and soloists, and transportation and media schedules. At the basis of this heteronomy lies the increased interrelatedness of social activities. A project of any size has to share spatial, temporal, and financial resources and manpower with other projects which may be of a totally different nature. As the demand upon these resources increases, coordination becomes more difficult and the margin of autonomous action diminishes. The required "space–time pockets of local order," to use a felicitous phrase by the time geographer Torsten Hägerstrand (1985, p. 207), become increasingly more rigid and hence more detached from the task for which they had originally been established.

The routines of the institutionalized music of our day bear certain similarities to the hospital routines described by the sociologist Eviatar Zerubavel, with their intricate clockwork scheduling and rotations of shifts—which also bear little, if any, relation to the purpose of a hospital as a place of healing (1979). While the negative repercussions of prevailing scheduling practices for medical care have been recognized and are being critically evaluated, the temporal organization of concert life (as part of the culture industry) has, thus far, been little analyzed for its deleterious effects on music and musicians (Mayr, 1985, 1986).

As I shall try to show, a careful examination of Wolff's score provides several useful elements for such an analysis.

"Think of, imagine, devise, a pulse . . ."

The composer does not ask us to read the pulse from a counter or a meter or a notated score, but to discover and assert our own rhythmic individuality. The anonymous temporal heteronomy that characterizes industrial societies tends to efface this component of our human selves. Machine-paced manual labor (such as in factories), machine-paced intellectual work (such as at computer terminals), and traffic regulations for motorized transportation are among the factors that tend to alienate us from *our* biological and mental rhythms, *our* motor tempos, and *our* cadences. The performing arts—and again, mainly those sectors less constrained by extraneous temporal conditioning—provide some of the rare, remaining opportunities to activate our pulses, tempos, and cadences in a meaningful way.

Wolff generically mentions "a pulse," which therefore may also be a mental construct; other composers refer explicitly to biological or motor pulsations of the performers. In the verbal score of *Heartwhistle*, for example, Richard Hayman gives these instructions: ". . . find and concentrate on . . . the varying pulses of your heartbeat. . . . manifest your pulses by some percussive sound . . . when you feel confident in playing your pulse, whistle a continuous tone . . ." (1975).

In my "Parcours rythmé" (1978) for walking performers, the articulation of the piece results from the relation between the freely chosen individual walking speeds of the players and the preexisting spatial rhythm of the performance area.

J. T. Fraser suggested that for a better understanding of the nature of time as it applies to human affairs, "We should examine, I believe, increasingly more complex clocks instead of increasingly more ideal ones. Instead of oscillating atoms, we should consider evolving genes, feeding fruit flies, and mirgrating elephants" (1978, p. 137).

I believe that we should also start *using* clocks that are more complex than our conventional ones, and that we should readopt, next to the highly predictable, simple periodic clocks, others that are less predictable and exhibit compound periodicities.

With some simplification we could say that in music this has occurred with the shift from the eighteenth-century metronome (occasionally regarded as an ideal clock even by some composers) to such complex, modulated clocks as Hayman's "varying pulse" of our heartbeats. Unlike simple clocks which, so to speak, mainly "do their own thing," complex, modulated clocks link us to a larger rhythmic process. Thus, the heartbeat is modulated by many external and internal factors. What if we considered living not only with, but *by*, the cadence of our heartbeats?[2]

"When you hear a sound . . ."

In *Looking North*, along with the pulse, Wolff asks us to refer to external synchronizers, to events which occur in our personal, variable range of perception. The spatial and sociospatial configuration of the performance area plays an important role here. Conventional concerts take place in halls which exclude, as much as possible, any interference from external sounds; they are often located in majestic buildings that impose a correspondingly majestic behavior and a narrow perceptual focus. Such a situation is hardly conducive to "hearing a sound (any sound), seeing a movement (any movement), or smelling a smell (any smell)," nor does it help us respond to such stimuli in a personal, creative way.

Furthermore, as Wolff tells us, we are to heed events which we perceive directly and which we then relate to our perceptual attitude of the moment. Today, in addition to direct impressions, we are bathed in a torrent of information conveyed to us about events distant in space and time. Our thoughts and actions are based less and less on direct inputs.

The arts may be the only remaining field in which direct, uncoded, medium-specific sensory inputs, and their impact on us, still play an essential role in conception and implementation. These inputs and their impact used to play an almost exclusive role; recently, with conceptual art on the one hand and computer art on the other, things have become a bit foggy. In any case, art, unlike the hard sciences, for example, cannot function without referring, at some level, to direct, uncoded, medium-specific sensory data.

[2]In the Audiographics recording of Hayman's piece an astonishing demonstration of mutual entrainment seems to occur: the two hundred and fifty players, each of whom had begun the performance according to his personal "metronome," at a certain point almost reach rhythmic unison.

In our daily lives we synchronize our activities more and more through indirect, nontemporal signs as opposed to direct, real-time signals. The bells of churches and city halls have lost the battle against appointment calendars and printed timetables. If our civilization has gained in effectiveness in the synchronization of human activities, it has certainly lost in the attractiveness and liveliness of its synchronizers (Mayr, 1988).

"*When you hear a sound . . .*"

Having discussed our perception of internal and external cadences, we may give some thought to our cadences of perception and to the chronosensory ecology in our environments (Schafer, 1973, 1976, 1977). In natural habitats the duration, intensity, and distribution of perceivable stimuli follow an organic score. Furthermore, life in a natural habitat is marked by perceptual macrorhythms that arise from alternating recourse to different sensory channels (that is, such as to vision primarily during the daytime, to hearing, touch, and smell at night time).

In man-made environments this chronosensory ecology is undermined or destroyed by the massive, mostly arhythmic, onslaught of stimuli and the diachronic uniformity of indoor living, where, for example, photoperiodicity has been minimized. On another level, the mass communication media, in their role as an interface between events and perceivers, impose upon us their artificial cadences of indirect perception (Schafer, 1982, 1987).

Such cadences are also widely used in contemporary artistic practice, mainly in the form of fast and slow motion in film. The aesthetic results often remain debatable. As an example in which a stimulating rhythmic interface between the observer and the observed phenomena is created, one may cite Józef Robakowski's *Market* (1970). In this short film the author uses the technique of shooting two frames every five seconds from 7 A.M. to 4 P.M. and succeeds in rendering the human tides at the chosen location in an aesthetically convincing way.

"*At any point stop.*"

Obviously, the performance of *Looking North* may stretch through an indefinite length of time, creating major problems for tightly scheduled, institutionalized concerts, should this work ever be performed in such a setting. The rejection of chronometric conventions is rooted in the aesthetics of indeterminacy; it acquires further significance when considered against the background of readiness with which many composers comply with the prefabricated time slots assigned to them by the culture industry: they do so, for instance, by producing pieces that just fill one or two sides of a long-playing record.

In this context, I wish to speak about pieces that are very long. Leaving aside such precursors as Richard Wagner's *Ring* cycle, length that defies even devoted listeners was introduced into Western music with clear intentions of "épater les bourgeois," by the French composer Erik Satie, in his *Vexations* (1893–1895). Recently the "very long" has lost its polemical overtones and has become a common feature in sound and video installations. The continuity of interaction between such pieces and the audience is inevitably broken up, leading to the need of frequent reestablishment of a linkage between the work's time and the audience's time.

In contemplating his interaction with a sound installation lasting four weeks, the listener will have to devise appropriate temporal strategies for his presence. These might include creative interactions between the work's temporal articulation and the existing social rhythms of the time and place. So far, this opportunity has rarely been taken advantage of, inhibited by the success of the culture industry in severing the links between the temporal arts and the macrotime of society. Historically also, this link has played only a minor role in the West, as compared, for instance, with Chinese music. In ancient Chinese music, writes Lewis Rowell, "the focus was clearly on macro-time and its calendrical significance; the structure of music was viewed as a harmonious reflection of the successive seasonal aspects of cyclical time. Musical time was to be relished in these successive aspects as a resonance to the cosmic scheme of works and days that was prescribed by the ancient classical texts" (1978, p. 585).

Examples of recent Western art that show how the times of long-term art projects can become integrated with social time are the very long, live pieces wherein the artist, while performing, must also engage in other activities in order to survive. One may cite, for instance, Tehching Hsieh's one-year performances in New York City which include: living alone in a cage; living entirely outdoors; punching a clock every hour of the day and night (Tucker, 1986). And, there is the seven-year piece of Linda Montano, at New York's New Museum of Contemporary Art, during which she will be in residence in one of the museum's rooms on the first day of every month, performing various activities and interacting with the public (Tucker, 1986).

Douglas Huebler's *Duration Piece 13* was started on July 1, 1969, with Huebler placing 100 one-dollar bills into circulation in various countries. The serial numbers of the bills were published in the catalogue of the exhibition "Konzeption-Conception," together with the announcement that anyone returning any of these bills to the artist twenty-five years after the beginning of the piece, that is between July 1, 1994, and January 1, 1995, will receive a $1,000 reward (Honnef, 1971, p. 38). Huebler's, and also Montano's pieces bring into play a new temporal relation between art work and art history. In general, the time span required for the performance of a piece is considered an art-historical "now," with the piece becoming art history only after its performance has been completed. Huebler's and Montano's pieces, by expanding the boundaries of the art-historical present (at least as that present is understood in modern Western terms), acquire art-historical depth while they are being performed.

"Before—after."

Next to modifying the temporal relation between art work and art history, contemporary art has developed new types of internal histories in pieces of time art. The possibility of storing in analog form the unfolding of events in time has brought about new relations of the here and now with anticipations and memory.[3]

Some storage-based techniques (which I take to include digital storage with digital-to-analog conversion) have become widely used: flashbacks and flashaheads, tape delay (in audio and video, both in prerecorded and live pieces), and the sampling and real-time processing of sound. There are other techniques, less broadly employed, such as the desynchronization of visual and auditory information. Although postulated by the film directors Eisenstein, Pudovkin, and Aleksandrov as early as 1928, techniques of desynchronization have only been adopted consistently in such recent video works as Dan Graham's video-sound installation *Yesterday/today*, with its constant 24-hour shift between "today's" real-time image and "yesterday's" audio (1973), and Michele Sambin's *Echos*, which is a variable-shift tape piece where the silent gestures of a cello player on video are followed by the corresponding, delayed sounds produced by those gestures (1976).

There are pieces in which the work histories are explicitly built on the experiential aspects of the "before–after" and the "past–present–future" series.

I have in mind Pietro Grossi's computer music program called *Kronos;* when activated it elaborates and plays an irrepeatable sound material based on a combination of parameters selected by the user and a set of there-and-then generated pseudorandom numbers. The program is also able to reconstruct the past history of this unique material time-backward from the present, and construct its future development time-forward. The user may thus instruct the computer to play the piece—as it were, there and then—as it would have been at any arbitrary past or would be at any arbitrary future moment (Grossi, 1985).

Dan Graham's *Past Future Split Attention* (1971) is a live performance piece that requires no hardware but possesses clear links to audiovisual techniques. Its instructions read as follows:

> Two people who know each other are in the same space. While the first person predicts continuously the second person's behavior, the second person recounts (by memory) the first person's past behavior. . . . For one to see the other in terms of the present (attention) there is a mirror reflection or closed figure-eight feedback/feedahead loop of past/future . . . [p. 4].

At least within the circumscribed context of aesthetic activity, pieces such as the two discussed above may be an antidote to the growing tendency in modern civilization to take our pasts and futures away from us, to make us rely on others, on "specialists" to tell us what "really" happened and what is bound to happen.

---

[3]While analog storage is used mainly in the time arts, it has also significance for experimental space arts, which recently have become more time-oriented and are beginning to avail themselves of this possibility.

II.

Centripetal and Centrifugal Forces

In his book, *Art as Experience*, John Dewey defined the "primary task" of the philosophy of art as follows: "This task is to restore continuity between the refined and intensified forms of experience that are works of art and the everyday events, doings and sufferings that are universally recognized to constitute experience" (1934, p. 3).

This is not the place to examine to what extent Dewey's words have been followed in the philosophy of art. Their spirit certainly has characterized, in varying degrees and shades, many avant-garde movements of this century. In these movements the quest for the restoration of continuity between works of art and everyday events manifests itself in strong centripetal and centrifugal forces, as I chose to call them.

By "centripetal" I mean to say that avant-garde and experimental art forms explicitly incorporate procedures, materials, and devices that were regarded until recently as alien to artistic thought and practice. There is hardly any facet of life today, any tool or artifact, any natural or social phenomenon, that has not in one way or another become the object of artistic undertakings.

Early examples in the field of music are Luigi Russolo's futuristic "Arte dei rumori" (1916) and the mastodontic sound event staged by the poets Wladimir Majakowski and Aleksej Gastjeff in Baku in 1926, with the participation of the foghorns of the entire Caspian Fleet, all the sirens of the factories in Baku, two batteries of artillery, a machine-gun unit, several hydroplanes, some choirs, and the audience itself (Fülöp-Miller, 1926, p. 245). In the visual arts we find Marcel Duchamp's famous "Ready mades." Compared to sounds, colors, and shapes, the parameter time has partaken of the centripetal trend only in recent decades, but in manifold ways, as the works discussed in the first part of this chapter show.

"Centrifugal" refers to the way in which many significant manifestations of experimental art forms transcend art's conventional confines and provide perceptual, communicative, and behavioral models for other areas.

Thus, in the early twenties the Bauhaus began the development of graphic, industrial, and urban design on a large scale, thereby inaugurating an irreversible socialization of the visual-spatial arts. Today, the shape and color of even the humblest everyday object are chosen by professional designers. A recent example in the visual arts is the work of the British "Artist Placement Group"; they propose to use "art as a social strategy in institutions and organizations" (1979). The most significant example in the field of organized sound is the "acoustic design" proposed by R. Murray Schafer (1975). According to Schafer, this new form of applied musical composition should extend to all sonic manifestations of human activity. Thanks to his seminal work, musicians are gradually becoming involved in issues concerning our acoustic environment. Music therapy, although not an aesthetic discipline in the strict sense, is an example of how the creative interaction with organized sound may be successfully used in highly problematic social contexts.

No comparable undertakings are under way as far as time is concerned. The organization of social time has not yet been reached by the centrifugal trend of experimental art. The closing section of this chapter is an attempt to open a perspective in this direction.

From the Mechanics of Time to the Aesthetics of Time

In the early twenties Gastjeff addressed the following manifesto to the Soviet revolutionaries:

> First of all, explore the mechanics of time, only afterwards
> begin the reforms!
> To calculate time means to live longer.
> The timetable is:
> a key to the economy of time,
> a key to the planning of work,
> a key to a healthy regime,
> a key to mental hygiene,
> a key to unshakable willpower.
> Once you have the key of time you are armed, you are the
> engineer of your life, the assembler of the time of the others,
> of the factory, of the institution.
> Keep a time budget and you will bring about a revolution of time
> [cited in Fülöp-Miller, 1926, pp. 276–277].

This, to my knowledge, is the strongest literary statement on the organization of social time of that period. However, it contains no ingredients of an aesthetic approach to the organization of time, imbued as it is with the Taylorist euphoria which characterized the early years of the Soviet Union and with the faith in the superiority of a clockwork society (Gorsen and Knödler-Bunte, 1975).

Today, a brief look at the sociotemporal *desiderata* in the industrialized countries shows us that the criteria for the organization of social time have not evolved significantly from Gastjeff's "mechanics of time," even if Taylorist euphoria has evaporated and both the physical world and human society have definitely lost the clockwork character which sometimes has been attributed to them.

In the past sixty years the time-related findings of many sciences have provided us with an impressive store of data on the temporal functions of human beings and the environment. But these findings rarely reach the desks of those who "compose the scores" of the temporal articulation of labor, education, political procedures, health care, communication media, and so forth. Nor has the question of what legal and organizational measures do to, and with, the citizen's time become an issue of general concern—unlike parallel issues regarding spatial or economic resources (Sharp, 1981, p. 20). Left on their own, the uninformed experts resort to the only technique they know: the adding, subtracting, and reshuffling of quantitatively designed time chunks. This technique, combined with the wide-spread obsession with acceleration, has made the mechanics of time organization ever more intricate and, at the same time, ever more banal. Furthermore, the memory of the traditional, more qualitatively designed time orders has been effaced, and the ability of articulating our activities in a rhythmical way has been severely impaired (Hultzsch [1925], cited in Honigswald [1926, p. 85]).[4]

But recently, some of us began to appreciate the richness and beauty of time orders in some non-Western cultures, such as the multilayered cycles of the Mayan calendar. Some of us also began to admire the rhythmic quality permeating even the simplest activities in some other non-Western cultures, as it may be witnessed, for instance, in a performance of African women pounding corn, where an everyday chore is transformed into a complex musical structure. But that appreciation has not yet led to full recognition of the important role of organically developed time orders and rhythmic activity patterns within the totality of our global cultural heritage, or to a resolute stand against their destruction. Nor has that appreciation made us sufficiently receptive of the lessons to be learned from the social temporalities in other cultures. We also need an appropriate experiential frame-work.

I wish to stress that through an active involvement in art projects with, and about, time, we will acquire such a framework. We will also acquire the tools for developing a new discipline, which could be called "time design," devoted to an innovative, coordinated effort for an improvement of our society's temporal "scores." In this discipline it would fall to "artists to collaborate on equal terms with scientists, technologists, and other specialists, in all phases of development," to use the words of UNESCO's *Manila Declaration* (1980, p. 3). In this way it may be possible to overcome the narrowness of existing proposals. Regarding a possible amelioration of our time order, these proposals are confined to simple, purely practical aspects (Joyce, 1954); a broader approach may sometimes be found in the proposals for a less schematic temporal articulation of human activities (Teriet, 1976). What is needed, however, is a truly interdisciplinary perspective seasoned with Utopian overtones, comparable to the perspective underlying the most audacious projects for the organization of social space. For evaluating existing forms of time organization and developing new models, time design would greatly benefit from a generalized theory on the aesthetic value of temporal configurations. Such a theory does not yet exist.

In this chapter I have sketched the features of some ingredients which the experimental time arts may contribute to the recipe for an aesthetic theory of time. Other contributions may come from the experimental aesthetics in the spatial field; I am thinking, for instance, of Le Corbusier's *Modulor*, with its formal grammar, derived from the proportions of the human body (1949), or of the investigations into the aesthetic value of pure shapes, conducted by the psychologist Gustav

[4]Hellmut Hultzsch (1925) states: "Jeder Leistungsvollzug birgt in sich die Möglichkeiten rhythmischer Gestaltung, jeder!"

Theodor Fechner (1872, 1876) and, with a more systematic approach, by the mathematician George David Birkhoff (1950); see also Rauen (1972).

Still other ingredients will have to be sought. In the meantime we should keep in mind Wolff's instruction: "Think of, imagine, devise, a pulse . . ."

References

Artist Placement Group (1979), *Kunst als Soziale Strategie in Institutionen und Organisationen*. Vienna: Galerie nachst St. Stephan.

Birkhoff, G. D. (1950a), Quelques éléments mathématiques de l'art. In: *Collected Mathematical Papers*, Vol. 3. New York: American Mathematical Society, pp. 288–306.

——— (1950b), A mathematical approach to aesthetics. In: *Collected Mathematical Papers*, Vol. 3. New York: American Mathematical Society, pp. 320–333.

——— (1950c), Polygonal forms. In: *Collected Mathematical Papers*, Vol. 3. New York: American Mathematical Society, pp. 334–364.

Dewey, J. (1934), *Art as Experience*. New York: Minton, Balch.

Eisenstein, S. M., Pudovkin, V. I., & Aleksandrov, G. V. (1928), Budustceie Zvukovoj Filmy. *Sovietski ekran*, 32:5.

Fechner, G. T. (1872), *Zur experimentalen Ästhetik*. Hildesheim/Wiesbaden: G. Olms/Breitkopf & Hartel, 1978.

——— (1876), *Vorschule der Asthetik*. Hildesheim/Wiesbaden: G. Olms/Breitkopf & Hartel, 1978.

Fülöp-Miller, R. (1926), *Geist und Gesicht des Bolschewismus*. Vienna: Amalthea Verlag.

Fraser, J. T. (1978), *Time as Conflict*. Basel: Birkhauser.

Gorsen, P., & Knödler-Bunte, E. (1975), *Proletkult 2*. Stuttgart: Frommann/Holzboog.

Graham, D. (1971), Past Future Split Attention. *Flash Art*, 35/36:4.

——— (1973), Yesterday/today. In: *Video-Architecture-Television*. Halifax, Nova Scotia: Press of the Nova Scotia College of Art and Design, 1979, p. 42.

Grossi, P. (1985), Kronos. In: *TAUMUS* (computer music package). Pisa/Florence: Divisione Musicologica CNUCE/C.N.R., in progress.

Hägerstrand, T. (1985), Time-geography: Focus on the corporeality of man, society, and environment. In: *The Science and Praxis of Complexity*. Tokyo and Paris: United Nations University, pp. 193–216.

Hayman, R. I. P. (1975), *Heartwhistle*. Recording and score (excerpts) in: *New Wilderness Audiographics, 8015 A—hearsayseeing*. New York: New Wilderness Foundation, 1980.

Honigswald, R. (1926), *Vom Problem des Rhythmus: Wissenschaftliche Grundlagen*. Leipzig: B. G. Teubner.

Honnef, K. (1971), *Concept Art*. Cologne: Phaidon.

Hultzsch, H. (1925), Eine Studienreise zu Ford. *Sächsische Industrie* No. 19.

Joyce, J. A. (1954), *Economic and Social Advantages of the World Calendar*. London: The World Calendar Association International.

Le Corbusier (1949), *Le Modulor*. Paris: Foundation Le Corbusier.

Mayr, A. (1978), Parcours rythmé. In: *Metafisica del Quotidiano* (catalogue), ed. M. Pasquali. Bologna: Galleria comunale d'arte moderna.

——— (1985), Sketches for a low-frequency solfège. *Music Theory Spectrum*, 7:107–113.

——— (1986), Audible and inaudible musics. In: *Reason, Emotion and Music*, eds. L. Apostel, H. Sabbe, & F. Vandamme. Ghent: Communication & Cognition, pp. 405–412.

——— (1988), Partiture spazio-temporali come parametro di identità socio-culturale. In: *Tempo e Identità*, ed. P. Reale. Milan: Franco Angeli, pp. 201–217.

Narmour, E. (1983–1984), Some major theoretical problems concerning the concept of hierarchy in the analysis of tonal music. *Music Perception*, 1/2:129–199.

Rauen, B. (1972), Breve storia delle estetiche scientifiche. In: *La Scienza e l'Arte,* ed. U. Volli. Milan: G. Mazzotta, pp. 15–44.

Robakowski, J. (1970), *Rynek* (Market). Film directed & produced by J. Robakowski, b/w, 7 min.

Rowell, L. (1978), Time in the musical consciousness of old high civilizations—East and west. In: *The Study of Time III,* eds. J. T. Fraser, N. Lawrence, & D. Park. New York: Springer-Verlag, pp. 578–611.

Russolo, L. (1916), *L'Arte dei rumori.* Milan: Edizioni Futuriste di "Poesia."

Sambin, M. (1976), *Echos.* Videotape. Venice: Galleria del Naviglio.

Satie, E. (1893–1895), Vexations. In: *Pages mystiques.* Paris: Max Eschig, 1969.

Schafer, R. M. (1973), *The Music of the Environment.* Vienna: Universal Edition.

——— (1975), *On Acoustic Design* (with the World Soundscape Project). Record EPN 186,II/2.

——— (1976), *The Tuning of the World.* New York: Alfred A. Knopf.

——— (1977), *Five Village Soundscapes.* Vancouver: A.R.C. Publications.

——— (1982), Radical radio. Lecture at Radio Renaissance, New York.

——— (1987), Radical radio (Excerpts). *Ear,* 11/5, 12/1:18-20.

Sharp, C. (1981), *The Economics of Time.* Oxford, U.K.: Martin Robertson.

Teriet, B. (1976), *Neue Strukturen der Arbeitszeitverteilung.* Göttingen: Otto Schwartz.

Tucker, M. (1986), *Choices: Making an Art of Everyday Life.* New York: The New Museum of Contemporary Art.

UNESCO (1980), *Design for Living—The Manila Declaration.* Paris: UNESCO.

Wolff, C. (unpublished), *Looking North,* 1971.

Waibl, E. (1985), Die Utopie künstlerischer Wahrheit in der Ästhetik von Adolf Loos und Arnold Schönberg. *Conceptus,* 19/46:76-83.

Zerubavel, E. (1979), *Patterns of Time in Hospital Life.* Chicago: University of Chicago Press.

Perspectives

Society, as a collective system, cannot display any of those behavioral and emotional patterns that make the individual into what he or she is. It can show no fear, intuition, empathy, sympathy, sorrow, or joy. Neither can society be concerned with time the way individuals are, because few societies, if any at all, have built into their written or unwritten constitutions a reminder of their certain demise. Societies, even on the tribal levels, always possessed freedoms and potentialities beyond those of their members. But, with the meteoric advance of industrial technology, the possibility that sociotemporal organization would totally, or almost totally, subsume the nootemporal organization of the individual, became a likelihood.

*Alexander Solzhenytsin must have felt this danger for, to oppose it, he advocated the reduction of the scale of life to that of the individual: the economy to mainly manual production, the abandonment of the internal combustion engine, and a return to the intimacy of village life (*Letter to the Soviet Leaders, *trans. Hilary Sternberg. New York: Harper & Row). But for better and also for worse, these are not the ideals that move the governments of our days.*

Developed and developing countries alike, under the thrust of modern science and technology, tend toward ever-larger institutions, ever more artificial goods and services, and ever more homogenized tastes. There is a belief abroad that whatever is large and artificial is likely to be superior to whatever is small and not artificial. This faith is reflected in the current dialectic of musical and artistic life, discussed in its time-related aspects by Professor Mayr.

While many musicians and artists have enlisted the vast and the artificial among their tools and modes of expression, the same and other artists and musicians prefer to stress in their work the organic and the human-sized.

Professor Mayr calls for the reestablishment in music and art of scales and rhythms appropriate in their dimensions to the scales and rhythms of the individual, rather than to those of the large, the inorganic, and the artificial. While such a program may be described as one of scaling down, he also calls for a change that may best be described as one of scaling up. He gives reasons why, in his view, social time scales and rhythms should be selected so as to relate to the processes and moderate dimensions of our bodies, rather than to those of technology, commerce, industry, and artifact.

We observe, I believe, an increasing separation between the sociotemporal and the nootemporal organizations of our lives. The call for redimensioning, sounded by Professor Mayr, is a reaction against that cleavage.

V

Music and Literature

13

Narrative and Narrativity in Music

Jann Pasler

Abstract Recent discussions about narrative have gone well beyond the Greek notion of epic or diegesis, the telling or indirect representation of a story. After years of structural, semiotic, and deconstructive analyses, this special attention to narrative signals a new preoccupation with how meaning can be communicated through a temporal process (as opposed to structural relationships) and how one understands a succession of temporal events. Music, an artform heretofore largely ignored by scholars of narrative and yet the quintessential art of time, offers important clues as to the processes that underlie a narrative and the expectations it creates or with which it plays.

In examining the narrative aspects of music, this chapter will draw on the definitions offered by such scholars as Gérard Genette, A. J. Greimas, Roland Barthes, Mieke Bal, and Paul Ricoeur, but will also point out the limitations of these definitions when applied to music. Moreover it will go beyond the traditional concept of narrative as program music or music with a single dramatic curve and will include a discussion of the narrativity of music, or that which allows narrative expectations to develop in the listener.

In twentieth-century music, the issues of narrative and narrativity are thrown into question and serve as stimuli for significant innovations in how a composition proceeds in time. Antinarratives and nonnarratives develop out of the struggle by composers to avoid narrative and yet rely on the listener's predilection to seek for it. Antinarratives are those works which frustrate the listener's expectation of continuity; nonnarratives are works that use elements of narrative without allowing them to function as they would in a narrative. Works without narrativity shun any organizing principle and try to erase the role of memory. The return by some composers in recent years to genres (such as the opera) and syntaxes (such as tonality) which have traditionally used narrative can only be understood in light of these other developments. The aim of this chapter is to deepen our understanding of narrative in general through an examination of various approaches to the temporal organization of twentieth-century music.

Acknowledgments. I would like to thank the following composers for interviews with them concerning their ideas about narrative and their current projects: John Cage, Tod Machover, Will Ogdon, Bernard Rands, Roger Reynolds, and John Silber.

Time becomes human time to the extent that it is organized after the manner of a narrative; narrative, in turn, is meaningful to the extent that it portrays the features of a temporal experience.   RICOEUR, *TIME AND NARRATIVE*, VOL. 1 (1984)

Reversing decades of neglect and almost complete disinterest, more and more composers are writing operas again. Not only has the number of operas being written increased dramatically in recent years, by comparison with the rest of this century, but the diversity of their styles ranges across the entire field of musical thought. For example, with *Donnerstag aus Licht* in 1981, Stockhausen began a series of seven operas, one for each day of the week. Two years later Messiaen finished his first opera, *Saint Francis of Assisi*. In recent years Philip Glass has completed two operas, *Satyagraha* in 1980 and *Akhnaten* in 1984, in 1986 the English National Opera premiered the second of Harrison Birtwistle's three operas, *The Mask of Orpheus*, and in 1987 the Frankfurt Opera mounted John Cage's first two operas, *Europera I* and *II*. Many other well-known composers have operas in progress: Pierre Boulez, the Pulitzer Prize winners Jacob Druckman (1972), Bernard Rands (1985) and George Rochberg (1986), as well as Morton Subotnik. To celebrate their tenth anniversary in 1987, the Centre Georges Pompidou and the musical research center IRCAM in Paris commissioned a video opera from the young American Tod Machover. What is behind this renewed interest in a genre which fell into disrepute for much of this century? Is it simply opera's commercial appeal, or the fame it brings, or does opera fill a need, felt by both composers and audiences, created by the difficulty of comprehending much contemporary music?

Leaving aside these interesting sociological issues for separate consideration, this chapter explores that significant *aesthetic* force which has led composers to write for the theater again—a renewed concern about narrative in music. *Narrative* has always been one of Western man's primary means of organizing and giving coherence to his experiences and has certainly been the temporal gestalt most broadly used in the arts.[1] After years of structural, semiotic, and deconstructive analyses, the special attention to narrative in recent years by literary theorists (such as Roland Barthes, Seymour Chatman, Gérard Genette, and Mieke Bal), linguists (such as A. J. Greimas), and philosophers (such as Paul Ricoeur) has signaled a new preoccupation with how meaning can be communicated through a temporal process, as opposed to structural relationships, and with how one understands a succession of temporal events. Many scholars of narrative have found the novel and film particularly enlightening, but they have generally ignored music, the quintessential art of time, perhaps because the musical world itself has rarely pondered the nature of a musical narrative. This chapter seeks both (1) to deepen

[1]The theme of this chapter made it necessary to employ a number of concepts, more or less well known in everyday use, but carrying special meanings in literary theory. The Appendix on Terminology (p. 255–257) defines these terms. When they first appear in the text, these terms are italicized.

our understanding of narrative and narrativity in general, and (2) to demonstrate the relevance of narrative concepts to criticism of contemporary music.

First, I will derive a definition of narrative and *narrativity* in music, building on the work of scholars named above while pointing out the limitations of their theories as applied to music. Just as recent analyses of narrative have extended well beyond the Greek notions of epic or diegesis (i.e., the telling or indirect representation of a story), so this discussion will go beyond the conventional notions of a musical narrative as program music and even as music with a single dramatic curve.

Second, with respect to the temporal organization of twentieth-century music, I will suggest that three radical musical innovations developed in part from composers' attempts to play with, manipulate, and abort their listeners' expectation of narrative so that they might nourish understanding of other perceptions of life, which are neither unilinear nor goal-oriented. I call these antinarratives, nonnarratives, and works without any narrativity.

Third, I will propose that the return by some composers in recent years to genres, such as opera, and syntaxes, such as tonality, which have traditionally been thought of as narrative can be understood only in light of these other developments. Moreover, I will show that narrative, as some contemporary composers use it, not only incorporates a multiplicity of perspectives and references, as in some contemporary novels, but also presents events in a kaleidoscopic manner. These two techniques have previously been associated only with works created to deny traditional narrative expectations.

Defining Narrative in Music

Story and Narrative Discourse, Signified and Signifier

For most people, including composers, narrative means story. A narrative is something that tells a story. This concept, however, is not as simple as it may appear, for much rests both on what "story" is and what "tell" may mean. Most literary theorists differentiate between narrative [*récit*] and story [*histoire*]. Because the process of storytelling involves both *signification* and communication, many of them (especially the semioticians) speak of the story as the *signified* or the subject of a discourse, and the narrative (or what some call the narrative text) as the *signifier* or that which communicates the story to the perceiver. From this perspective, a narrative is a kind of discourse, a manifestation of some content in a given medium. Although narratologists disagree as to whether or not this concept of narrative includes the narration of a text, that is, its enuciation or performance before an audience, for present purposes, narrative will refer only to the level of discourse and thereby be considered distinct from both story and narration and capable of entering into various relationships with them. In a later section, I will also distinguish it from narrativity, or what mediates between a narrative discourse and the language structures that inform its production and comprehension.

The very broad notion that contemporary literary theorists have of a narrative's *story* opens the way to a much fuller understanding of narrative than has previously been the case, particularly in music. For Bal (1977), Genette (1972), and Chatman (1978), a story is a series or chain of "events" logically related to one another (i.e., in a temporal and causal order) and caused or undergone by agents, and an event is the passage from one state to another. Depending on how one defines an event in music, this means that a relationship of signifier to signified may exist between a composition and a wide range of extramusical and even musical ideas.

In programmatic pieces such as Berlioz' *Symphonie fantastique*, Strauss' *Till Eulenspiegel*, and Stravinsky's *Petrushka*, what is signified by the music, its "story," can be a series of actions, a given character, or the flux of a character's emotions. The abrupt change from the very slow, frequently broken, chromatic lines and the C minor tonality, to the quick, spiccato, diatonic melody and the C major tonality in the opening of the *Symphonie fantastique* musically embodies the "melancholy reverie, interrupted by a few fits of groundless joy" described in the work's program. The traditional way, especially since Wagner, for a composer to accomplish signification in a composition telling a story, however, is by allying a musical motive—a melodic pattern, harmony, rhythmic shape, and even instrumental timbre—with each character and by transforming them as the story unfolds. In the second tableau of *Petrushka*, for example, Stravinsky uses two superimposed triads in the incompatible relationship of a tritone (F sharp–C) to depict musically the existential state of the puppet Petrushka, who is cursed with a mechanical body together with the human feelings trapped in it. These arpeggiated triads, the clarinets, piano, and then trumpets that play them, and their triplet rhythms return in the third tableau to alternate dramatically with the fierce woodwind and string chords associated with the Moor as Petrushka battles his competitor. Understanding what the "story" is in these examples is thus essential to understanding why the musical events succeed one another as they do.

The musical innovations that Stravinsky developed in working with a story in *Petrushka* (1911) led him to experiment with a second kind of signified in *The Rite of Spring* (1913): stage gestures and actions not dependent on a conventional story for their meaning. In conceiving this ballet, Stravinsky considered the work's organizing principle a certain "choreographic succession" rather than any plot. He states in his *Autobiography* (1936) that he "had imagined the spectacular part of the performance as a series of rhythmic mass movements" (p. 48) (the ordered movement of large groups rather than individual dancers) and sought, as did the choreographer Nijinsky with whom he worked extensively, to create formal structures in the music and the dance that would be intimately linked. In the "Games of the Rival Tribes," for example, Stravinsky juxtaposes two different sets of instruments, two motives, and two rhythmic patterns that alternate constantly throughout the dance to mirror the visual confrontation of the two tribes of dancers on stage. The signified of this kind of music is, therefore, the dance itself. Such a change by Stravinsky from depicting a story, as in *Petrushka*, to incorporating the structural relationship of another artform, as in *The Rite*, marks an important shift of interest in this century away from program music and toward visual and other analogies between the arts not based on or supported by stories (Pasler, 1986, pp. 53–81).

A third type of signified, used throughout history, is reference to, and perhaps elaboration of some aspect of the musical language itself. More than the previous kinds of signifieds, quotation of a tune, a form, a genre, a style, or a performance practice depends on the listener's ability to perceive and understand the reference and its function in the context at hand. In the opening of the last movement of Beethoven's Ninth Symphony, for example, the double basses interrupt the orchestra with a melodic line that recalls eighteenth-century opera recitative. Minutes later Beethoven confirms this allusion by giving the same melody to the baritone soloist and adding the words, "O friends, not these tones; instead let us sing more pleasing and joyful ones." Furthermore, when the text is, "Follow your path with joy, Brothers, like a hero marching to victory," Beethoven composes in the style of "Turkish" music (fifes, triangles, cymbals, and bass drum), which was associated with military groups at the time. By incorporating into this movement such unusual elements as a chorus, fragments of themes from all previous movements, and a theme and variations form, Beethoven played with their function as signifieds in order to stretch conventional notions of the genre and form of a symphony.

With such an open definition of story (as not just the structural support of a composition, but also a parallel structure to it, a source of inspiration for new musical ideas, or merely a referent), clearly all that is necessary to bind signifier and signified is (1) a certain duality—the music and something outside it; (2) a presumed perceptibility of the two; and (3) a relationship linking them. Since the succession of the signified's events often illuminates or reinforces those of the signifier, such a concept helps explain many experimental works wherein composers, to make their meaning clearer or guide their audience to listen in new ways, link pure sound to something external.

Identifying the elements of a narrative discourse is somewhat more difficult. Russian formalists such as Tomashevsky view "the smallest particle of thematic material," the motif, as the primary element of a narrative (Tomashevsky [1925] cited in Martin [1986, p.112]). This thematic approach is appropriate in analyzing much eighteenth- and nineteenth-century music, and, if one construes a theme as more than merely a melodic line or sequence of pitches, it may also be extended to some contemporary music. In Roger Reynolds's *Vertigo* (1986), for example, the elements treated thematically are microcompositions, not only composed but also performed in certain ways and recorded in advance. Two other theories— Chatman's idea of narrative as "a connected sequence of narrative statements," with the statements as being the expression of either dynamic events or static existents, and Metz' notion of the sentence, "or at least some segment similar in magnitude to the sentence," as the proper unit of narrative—suggest the complete phrase as the narrative unit of music, but do not necessarily account for the relationship between the parts and the whole (Metz, 1974, p.25; Chatman, 1978, p. 31). Others approach the narrative as the amplification of a verb. Thus Propp and Barthes (in

Barthes [1977, pp. 88–91]) refer to the narrative units as functions, Bremond as elementary sequences, and Greimas as narrative programs (Greimas and Courtés, 1979). In his analysis of the Chopin Polonaise-Fantasy Opus 61, Eero Tarasti (1984) shows how ten Greimasian narrative programs (i.e., diving in and recovering; topological disengagement; the various dances; fulfillment) function to advance or to frustrate movement to a final resolution. The decision to consider static entities or functional processes as the basic elements of a musical narrative should probably depend on the work at hand, whether its signified is a static entity or dynamic process, and exactly what undergoes transformation in the composition.

Given this distinction between story and narrative then, two important interrelated issues of debate arise. First, whether in the Aristotelian sense, the narrative describes a story through indirect means (diegesis) or it presents or acts out the story dramatically (mimesis). What otherwise might differentiate the former, used in epic, from the latter, used in tragedy, is not as clear-cut in music as it is in literature (Aristotle, *Poetics*). Obviously, opera exploits mimetic devices, but in his song "Erlkönig," for example, Schubert, respecting Goethe's text, uses both diegesis for the narrator who describes the action in the first and last stanzas, and mimesis for the three characters—father, son, and erlking—who enact it in the middle stanzas (Cone, 1974, pp. 1–19). The second issue is whether or not the narrative, independent of the story, can contain meaning. Ricoeur takes a helpful stance in this regard in that he characterizes narrative not by its "mode," but by its "object." For him, diegesis and mimesis are both subcategories of a more general Aristotelian concept called muthos, or the organization of events. He writes, "The essential thing is that the poet—whether narrator or dramatist—be a 'maker of plots'" (Ricoeur, 1984, pp. 36, 41). He furthermore defines mimesis not merely as representation, but as creative imitation, involving an ordering, or reordering, of a story's elements. Unlike Bremond and Genette for whom a narrative cannot contain but only carry meaning, Ricoeur posits meaning in the construction of the narrative itself. In discussing music, Ricoeur's interpretation is preferable because music can both tell or convey the meaning of something extramusical (such as a program or a text) and present a strictly musical meaning all its own.

A number of relationships between narrative and story can be manipulated when both are seen as inherently meaningful. Metz (1974) and Genette (1972) discuss at length the numerous possibilities of aspect, the way the narrator perceives the story; mood, the type of discourse used by the narrator; voice, the characters or personas he assumes in the telling; and especially tense, the time of the narrative in relation to that of the story. Concordances and discordances, or what Genette calls anachronies, may be constructed between the temporal order of events in the story and the pseudotemporal order of their arrangement in the discourse, the duration of events in the story and in the telling, as well as the frequency of repetition in both. If one views the standard idea of a sonata form as a work's underlying signified, then any rearrangement of parts, such as placing a final cadence at a work's beginning, can be discussed in this regard. Although these notions could be greatly elaborated, further discussion must be relegated to future articles.

Narrative Structure and Narrative Logic

A narrative is also a kind of structure. As a structure, considered by some as independent of any medium, it must have wholeness (in that its events must be related or mutually entailing), transformation, and self-regulation (i.e., self-maintenance and closure, that is, all transformations must engender only elements already within the system) (Chatman [1978, pp. 20–21] cites Piaget's conception of a structure; see Piaget [1971, pp. 3–16].) Most literary theorists view narrative as an object more than as a process and thereby emphasize its closed, finite nature. They point to the stability of the boundaries that separate it from the real world (and physical time), and to the order, or temporal sequence, in which its events are presented, namely, its beginning, middle, and end. (All these issues have close correlates in music and Rowell [1981] Kramer [1978, 1981], and Clifton [1983] have studied them extensively.) Ricoeur focuses instead on how the configurational dimension of narrative structures its episodic or chronological dimension. In other words, how the succession of events is integrated, using repetition and relying on the listener's recollection, into a significant whole. Ricoeur calls this the invention of a plot, and herein lies an explanation for the claim cited at the beginning of this chapter: in the narrative's organization and retelling of the events of a story, "time becomes human time." The beginning of a narrative, as Ricoeur sees it then, involves "the absence of necessity in the succession" rather than merely "the absence of some antecedent." The "sense of an ending," from his perspective, also differs from the "openendness of mere succession" because of the shape imposed by the plot's configuration (Ricoeur, 1980, p. 179; 1984, pp. 3, 38, 67).

Only in conversation theory and in music do people speak of a very specific kind of configuration as narrative. In his studies of stories told by black American adolescents, Labov describes a fully formed narrative as having the following: a summary clause (abstract), an orientation of who, when, and where placed anywhere in the text, a complicating action, an evaluation of the point of the narrative, a result or resolution, and a coda, often returning the listener to the present time (Labov, 1972, pp. 363–370). Childs calls a similar pattern in music a "narrative curve" and describes it as an introduction (involving some question or tension), a statement, a development (possibly of relationships increasing irregularly in complexity and intensity), a climax, a resolution or relaxation or "falling action," and a concluding gesture (possibly a restatement and the renewal of cosmic order). Childs finds this curve to be the most "basic structural organization of a work of time art" and sees it as a way of representing life (Childs, 1977). Other musicians have defined narrative in a like manner. Edward Cone calls it "introduction, statement, development, climax, restatement, peroration" (1967, p. 37), of which the sonata allegro form is the best example in eighteenth- and nineteenth-century music. In a recent interview with the author (May 19, 1986), Roger Reynolds spoke of it as proposition, elaboration, and conclusion.[2] Interest-

---

[2] In his *Recent Theories of Narrative* (1986, pp. 81–82), Wallace Martin cites a diagram of the "normal plot" (as developed by the German critic Gustav Freytag) whose inverted V shape

ingly, Childs and Kramer (whom Childs quotes) suggest that listeners endeavor to hear such a curve in a composition even when it demonstrably does not exist. Unless some manner of this "narrative dramatism" (Childs, 1977, p. 116) exists, it is feared, listeners may not be able to understand the music.

This concentration on the structure of a narrative and on the order of its events, however, says little about the logic of the movement from one event to another. Unfortunately, most literary theorists give little attention to this, the truly temporal aspect of a narrative. Those who do discuss a narrative's temporality, such as Metz and Genette, speak of it in relationship to that of the story, which it refigures, and thus skirt the issue. The notion of a narrative curve, found in conversation theory and music, may be somewhat constricting, but it offers some insight into the most primary characteristic of a narrative's movement; that is, the inherent directedness of the succession of its events. A narrative must go somewhere. Circularity as well as stasis is disturbing to its dynamic nature. Something propels the story and the perceiver's interest, even though the answer to the question of "so what?" is neither predictable nor deducible (were it so, the story might not be worth telling, that is, narratable). Some, such as Ricoeur, view the story's conclusion as the "pole of attraction of the entire development" (Ricoeur, 1980, p. 174). In his studies of oral narratives, Labov found the speaker's evaluation of the story to be the crux of the narrative, for without it, the story could be perceived as pointless.

In music, the few theorists who have analyzed narrative (Stoianova [1976], Childs [1977], and Kramer [1978, 1981]) define goal-orientation as central to a musical narrative. Stoianova refers to the existence of not only an "end-goal," but also an "initial impetus" (1976, p. 16). The now celebrated early twentieth-century Austrian music theorist, Heinrich Schenker, has demonstrated the extent to which most tonal works begin in a tonality, modulate to some alternative one, usually its fifth, and return to the opening tonality at the piece's end. In her analysis of Boulez' *Rituel in Memoriam Maderna*, a nontonal work, Stoianova shows a similar kind of teleological movement. Just as in Stravinsky's *Symphonies of Wind Instruments* (from which Boulez borrows the idea), the initial impetus, E flat, is also the end-goal of the piece, the last note, as well as the center of a symmetrical system based on the tritone, A-E flat-A, Stoianova even goes so far to add unidirectionality to her definition of narrative—although contemporary composers and other theorists may disagree. The point being that a narrative must have a fundamental point of reference, and its events must progress, not just succeed one another.

Most people generally think of a narrative as linear, or consisting of events that are dependent on immediately preceding events and following the irreversible order of time. For Ricoeur, however, this "then and then" structure characterizes only the episodic dimension of a narrative, not the configurational one (1984, p. 67).[3] Those

resembles in great part the narrative curve of many musical compositions. The trouble with this diagram, as Martin points out, is that it doesn't describe most plots, except perhaps those of short stories.

[3]In his "Introduction to the Structural Analysis of Narratives" (1977), Roland Barthes

literary theorists who tie the temporal progression of a narrative to that of a story would also argue that ellipses, summaries, flashbacks, and flashforwards interrupt any linearity a narrative might have. Chatman, moreover, believes that the author "selects those events he feels are sufficient to elicit the necessary sense of continuum" and finds "inference-drawing," or the listener's filling in of the gaps left by these temporal condensations or reorderings, to be an important aspect of narrative and that which differentiates it from lyric, expository, and other genres (Chatman, 1978, pp. 30–31). In music, likewise, a work may or may not have linearity, as Kramer has shown, on a number of hierarchic levels (i.e., from one section to the next), within an individual section but not beyond it, or from one section to other "previous but not immediately adjacent" ones (1981, p. 554). For a narrative to be connected, it is not necessary that the movement from one moment to the next be linear, but that linearity exist on the structural level of the piece.

Narrative Transformation

The ultimate reason narrative events are directed and connected is that they undergo or cause transformation, which is probably the narrative's most important and most illusive characteristic. Some change, or what Aristotle in his *Poetics* calls peripety, must take place in the middle of a narrative text. The narrative situation itself calls for it, as Miller (1981) points out, in that narrative arises from some disequilibrium, suspense, or general insufficiency. Reynolds adds that a musical narrative must also start with something which is incomplete and enticing so that the listener is interested in its future possibilities (Interview with the author, May 19, 1986).

   Most analyses of narrative largely ignore this aspect of a narrative because they emphasize structural relationships rather than their transformation in time, and static rather than dynamic relationships between the parts of a narrative. Even Piaget, who claims that all structures are "systems of transformations," adds that "transformation need not be a temporal process" (1971, p. 11). In defining a narrative event as a narrative program, "an utterance of doing governing an utterance of state," and narrative as a string of presupposed and presupposing narrative programs, or a narrative trajectory leading from an initial state to a final state (Greimas and Courtes, 1979, pp. 207, 245), Greimas comes to grips with the dynamic nature of a narrative; but his use of f (x), a mathematical symbol borrowed from calculus, to describe a narrative program as a function that operates in a given way on an object or state over time implies that the transformations in a narrative are continuous in the mathematical sense (that is, that there are no interruptions or points of discontinuity), that they are therefore consistent and predictable according to the formula, and that they belong to a set of preexistent codes, none of which is necessarily the case in musical transformations. As Stoianova points out, detours along the way are more the rule than the exception in music.

posits that the "confusion between consecution and consequence, temporality and logic" is the central problem of narrative syntax (pp. 98–104).

Only Tzvetan Todorov (1978) proposes a typology of narrative transformations and for him they are the essence of narrative. Those expressible as simple sentences—changes of status (positive to negative), of mode (necessity, possibility), of intention, manner, or aspect—he calls simple transformations; those requiring a dependent clause—changes of supposition (prediction—realization) and of knowledge (problem—solution, deformed presentation—correct presentation)—he calls complex transformations. What is critical about these transformations in his view is that they help explain the tension that exists in narratives between difference and similarity. Transformation, as he explains it, represents a synthesis of differences and resemblance; that is, it links two similar things without allowing them to be identified with one another. The exclusive presence of one or the other would result in a discourse which is no longer narrative.

While it is difficult to translate these notions into ways of thinking about music, they do suggest a fundamental difference between two kinds of transformation in music. The first, thematic transformation—"the process of modifying a theme so that in a new context it is different yet manifestly made of the same elements" (Macdonald, 1980, pp. 117–118)—was perhaps the most widely used developmental technique in nineteenth-century music, especially that of Liszt, Berlioz, and Wagner. It allowed a composer to suggest different programmatic intentions, such as those effected by Todorov's simple transformations (i.e., despair–joy; aggressive–lyrical), while insuring a composition's unity.

A second kind of musical transformation characteristic of narratives does not necessarily depend on any recurrent material, but rather on a certain kind of relationship between events which are in themselves complex states of being. One example is tension–resolution. Very often in tonal works, this has meant extending a dissonance structurally through modulation into and elaboration of a new harmony, then returning to the opening tonality. But tension and resolution may be created by other musical means as well. In Debussy's *Jeux*, for example, tension results at rehearsal number *16* from the superimposition of six different rhythmic divisions of the measure and numerous melodic lines moving in different directions, the increasingly loud dynamics, and the dominant seventh harmony. The sense of resolution which follows results not only from the cadence, but also from the sudden stasis and rhythmic regularity, the reduction to one melodic line, and the molto diminuendo. This excerpt also exemplifies what Leonard Meyer (1984) and Eugene Narmour call an "implication—realization model of communication" of which narratives are special cases. Like other syntactical or "script-based" implications (antecedent–consequent phrases, etc.), the dominant seventh chord inherently suggests the cadence which follows. Perhaps not prospectively but certainly retrospectively, the rhythm, timbre, and melody also call out for what follows— simplicity after extreme complexity, the reestablishment of balance and equilibrium—only in a different way. These fall into Meyer's category of statistical or "plan-based" implications because they lead to a climax by virtue of their increasing intensity and to resolution through abating processes.[4] Narrative

---

[4]I wish to thank Leonard Meyer for providing me with a copy of his lecture, "Music and

transformations thus depend on mutually entailing implications within the events themselves.

Transformation, particularly in music, also involves a creative manipulation and integration of the three senses of time—past, present, and future. Ricoeur calls this the "threefold present" and defines it as "distention" or "extension," borrowing the concepts from Augustine. "The soul 'distends' itself as it 'engages' itself," he explains, or alternatively, one can only really experience distention "if the mind acts, that is, expects, attends, and remembers" (1984, p. 21). The shape that narrative gives to distention involves expectation, memory, and attention, not in isolation but in interaction with one another. To follow a narrative in music as in literature, one must develop expectations from the work's implications, use one's "accumulated memory" of its events to comprehend or, as Ricoeur puts it, "grasp together in a single mental act things which are not experienced together" and pay attention to understand what comes next (Ricoeur, 1984, p. 159). (Ricoeur borrows this idea of comprehension as a "grasping together" from Louis O. Mink [1972, pp. 735–737].)

Narrativity

Narrativity is that which allows a perceiver to develop expectations, to grasp together events, and to comprehend their implications. Greimas describes it as the organizing principle of all discourse, whether narrative or nonnarrative. Such a concept mediates between what Saussure (1976) called "langue," the semionarrative structures of the language itself, and "parole," the discursive structures in which language is manifested. Narrativity governs the production of a discourse by an author as well as its reading by a perceiver, and relies on the author's and perceiver's narrative competence, or their culturally engrained ability to apprehend how such structures normally behave as well as how they might behave in the narrative at hand. Lyotard defines this competence as threefold: "know-how, knowing how to speak, and knowing how to hear" (1984, p. 21); but one should add that this competence is not only prospective, but also retrospective, allowing the perceiver to understand what it means to have followed a narrative. From this definition, it is evident narrativity is based on the temporal archetypes known and understood by a given culture, perhaps even those "presignified at the level of human acting," as Ricoeur puts it (1984, p. 81). As such, it is clearly much more than the generic word for narrative, more than what Metz loosely defines as that which makes a narrative recognizable and what Ricoeur calls the referential capacity of narrative works; it is what permits a categorical understanding of a narrative's plot, its configuration, and its semantics.

The narrativity of a composition, or the presence of some organizing principle, some macrostructure and syntax characteristic of a certain period and place, presents the listener with a set of probability relationships concerning, for example, where

Ideology in the Nineteenth Century," presented to Stanford University, May 17 and 21, 1984, and for bringing these categories to my attention.

to expect a climax, or how opposing ideas may be brought into reconciliation. The more familiar he is with them, the more definite will be the order he seeks in the work, and the more occasion the composer has to play with expectation and surprise (Childs, 1977, p. 117). It is in fact the "arousal and subsequent inhibition of expectant tendencies in the shaping of musical experience" (through delay, ambiguity, and improbability), as Meyer points out, that gives rise to musical meaning (Meyer, 1967, pp. 5–11). A work's narrativity then sets the stage for the communication of meaning.

Alternatives to Narrative in This Century

In the twentieth century, many composers have rejected the paramountcy of narrative or narrativity in music. Their attempts to thwart listeners' expectation of narrative have stimulated three significant innovations with respect to how a composition proceeds through time. The first two innovations—antinarratives and nonnarratives—both challenge important aspects of narrative, but still have narrativity (i.e., some organizing principle). The third—works without narrativity—try to eliminate completely the listeners' predilection to seek for narrativity. My discussion does not intend to reduce composers' search for deeper or less constricting ways of expressing man's relationship to sound and time to merely a rejection of narrative or narrativity. Rather, it seeks to show the relationship of these widely divergent styles, whatever their other intentions might be, to narrative concepts.

Antinarrative

Antinarratives are works which rely on the listener's expectation of narrative, but frustrate it through continual interruption of a work's temporal processes and proceed by change without narrative transformation. Stravinsky's (and indeed even Debussy's) abrupt juxtaposition of contrasting and often unrelated ideas exhibits antinarrative tendencies in the occasional discontinuity of their music's moment-to-moment motion, although the overall structure of their works is not necessarily antinarrative. In literature, Chatman finds such forms dependent on "antistories," or stories in which all choices are equally valid. As in the definition I give to the term, they call into question the logic of narrative that "one thing leads to one and only one other, the second to a third and so on to the finale" (1978, pp. 56–57). Music which leaves "open" to the performer the exact realization of a given set of notes, chords, or rhythms, without giving up some overall organizing principle, may achieve a similar effect. However, it is Stockhausen's experiments with moment form in the late 1950s and 1960s that constitute perhaps the clearest example of antinarrative in music.

Explaining his *Carré* (1958–1959) in the program notes for its first performance, Stockhausen first asserts about the form he is developing, "This piece tells no story. Every moment can exist for itself" (composer's note on record jacket for

Gruppen and *Carré*, Deutsche Grammophon 137 002). In this work, he both eliminates any signification a text may have through using phonemes composed according to purely musical criteria; and he defines the units of these forms as moments—quasi-independent sections that neither depend on one another nor are necessarily interrelated.

Stockhausen further explained the intent of his moment forms in an interview with the West German Radio in Cologne on January 12, 1961:

> During the last years there have been forms composed in music which are far removed from the form of a dramatic finale; they lead up to no climax, nor do they have prepared, and thus expected, climaxes, nor the usual introductory, intensifying, transitional, and cadential stages which are related to the curve of development in a whole work [Liner note for Stockhausen's *Kontakte*, Wergo WER 60009].

This statement reveals that the "story" Stockhausen is rejecting is the narrative curve discussed by Childs. Moment forms, he continues, "are rather immediately intense and—permanently present—endeavor to maintain the level of continued 'peaks' up to the end." By thus refusing to make a hierarchy of the events in such pieces, he shuns any structural configuration of his moments, narrative or otherwise. Without configuration, the precise order of events as well as the beginning and end are more arbitrary. Stockhausen also points out that "at any moment one may expect a maximum or a minimum" and "one is unable to predict with certainty the direction of the movement from any given point," thereby denying any explicit directedness from one moment to the next and any goal-orientation in the work as a whole. Such a focus on individual sections that do not rely on one's accumulated memory from one to the next aims to engage the listener in the "now," a "malleable Now" as Kramer observes (1978, p. 194), that is a key to escaping our otherwise conventional concept of time as horizontal.

To create a moment form, Stockhausen turned in many of his works to the technique of juxtaposition and the use and integration of noise. In his *Stop* (1965), twenty-eight sections of notated pitches, with only general indications as to the manner in which these notes are to be played, alternate with fourteen sections of "noises," also to be played in certain tempi and with certain dynamic properties. Changes between sections can be abrupt from one of the six instrumental groups to the next, or involving some manner of overlap of either groups of instruments or individual ones. In the middle of the piece, there is even a quote from a work Kramer considers the first moment form, Stravinsky's *Symphonies of Wind Instruments*. The noises which, by definition, have no functional implications, "stop" the pitched sections and prevent one from anticipating what will come next.

While there might not be a story, connectedness, mutually entailing implications, or even hierarchical configuration in *Stop*, there is, however, narrativity. The piece consists not only of a continuous metamorphosis of tones and noises, but also of a particular organizing principle: the presentation of a twelve-tone row, the gradual interpenetration of noises with pitches, and the noises' gradual increase in dynamic intensity from being very soft to very loud. *Stop*, moreover, begins and ends with a single pitch, played forte, the work's highest and lowest notes and the first and last notes of the twelve-tone row.[5] The second section, the longest in the work, is in a sense the kernal of the work in that it presents all the twelve tones "to be read upwards and downwards, several times, with different beginnings and endings," the four intervals of a fifth in the tone row,[6] and all the work's dynamic levels, from the loudest to the softest, to be played irregularly and by different instruments. Each note of the row is then presented in its own sections, and at the exact middle of the work, section 21, the three middle notes of the row occur simultaneously, drawing attention to this structural point. In a typical twelve-tone manner, all eleven notes of the row except the last one return in the next to last section, giving a sense of arrival to the final low C when it comes at the very end.[7]

Nonnarrative

Nonnarratives are works that may use elements of narrative but without allowing them to function as they would in a narrative. Much minimal music falls into this category.[8] It consists largely of traditional tonal triads and their inversions; however, the triads are not used as structural means of establishing, departing from, and returning to a tonal center, nor are they incidental references to the tonal system. Operas composed in the minimal style may likewise employ traditional operatic means—singers, stage events, and so on—but they are usually not signifiers of some drama nor the signifieds of the music. Stage activity and sound in the Glass operas, for example, are linked only in that they occur at the same time. Most singing in *Akhnaten* is by choruses that, by their nature, do not attempt any characterization.

   Minimal works are usually also well-defined structures in that their elements are mutually related and derive from one another; however, there is no tension inherent in their openings, no peripety in the middle, and the transformation these works undergo is little other than the gradual unfolding of an objective process. Many consist of the constant recycling of a limited number of notes (six in Reich's

[5]The row is B, B flat, G, A, G sharp, D sharp, E, A, F, C sharp, F sharp, C.

[6]That is, F sharp, C sharp, G sharp, D sharp.

[7]Interestingly, as in other moments forms Kramer (1978) has analyzed, Stockhausen uses the Fibonacci number series in *Stop* to determine the duration of each of his moments. Each of the sections lasts the duration of one of the Fibonacci numbers between 3 and 55: 8, 55, 5, 5, 5, 13, 5, 5, 13, 8, 8, 13, 8, 5, 13, 5, 21, 34, 3, . . . except immediately before and after the middle point when two sections last 32 and 27 × 2 = 54 beats respectively. I wish to thank Eduardo Larin for bringing this piece to my attention.

[8]In an interview with Cole Gagne and Tracy Caras on November 13, 1980 (1982), Glass specifically calls his music non-narrative and remarks, "because it is non-narrative, we don't hear it within the usual time frame of most musical experiences . . . we don't hear the music as narrative or a model of colloquial time. What we're hearing then is music in another time system" (p. 214).

Piano Phase [1967] and five in Glass' *Two Pages* [1968]) whose order, combination, and accentual pattern may change, but without implying any hierarchy either between the notes of the pattern or from one pattern to the next. Lacking any tonal or thematic dialectic, they proceed continuously through repetition, addition, and subtraction of the pattern, but without conflict or interruption, direction or goals. The particular succession of patterns and the number of times one may be repeated is unpredictable. Beginning and end merely frame the processes, articulate the work's boundaries, and separate it from real time; they do not serve to unify the whole.

Although several minimal pieces return to their original material at the end, such as Reich's *Clapping Music* or his *Piano Phase* that begins and ends on a unison after a series of phase shifts, memory does not function in them as it does in narrative music.[9] As Mertens points out, one has to forget or move away from something to remember or return to it, and the repetition in this music is constant. In minimal music, repetition, therefore, does not require a backward glancing, the "existential endeepening" of time; it does not require us to recollect (see Ricoeur [1980, pp. 183–189] for a fuller discussion of "narrative repetition"). Instead of mediating past, present, and future, it forces us to concentrate fully on an extended present. Time appears to stand still as the work turns in place. Indeed the object here is not time, but eternity.

Contrary to what one might expect, nonnarrative works can have narrativity. Reich's *Music for 18 Musicians* (1974–1976) has a clear organizing principle. The piece is built on a type of "cantus firmus," a series of eleven chords, first presented in the opening section and then serving as the basis of a chain of successive compositions (either in an arch form ABCDCBA or a phase process), one for each of the chords. The way that certain elements return in the piece from one section to another, even though often in new roles and instrumentations, gives the work an arch shape. For example, not only do the opening chords return at the end of the piece, but also the women's voices and bass clarinets that play them. The musical material characterizing section two, that is, the canon or phase relation between the two xylophones and the two pianos, also returns in section nine, although in a different harmonic context. And so forth. Wesley York (1985) has shown how the alternation between two basic processes and their integration in Glass' *Two Pages* also results in an arch form; however, the exposition, development, and varied return he hears in this piece is not obvious and remains for this author inaudible.

Nonnarrativity

A third type of innovation constitutes works without narrativity, those that shun any organizing principle, whether an overall structure or preordained syntax, and

---

[9]My research assistant Toshie Kakinuma's unpublished paper, "Minimal Music and Narrativity— Reich's *Piano Phase*," presents a penetrating analysis of *Piano Phase* as nonnarrative. I am grateful to her for help in researching this article.

thereby try to erase the role of memory.[10] In their search for more ambiguous kinds of meaning they cannot or do not wish to clarify, composers of these works renounce and refuse to mediate between the sounds they produce or call for and all inherited, specific, and codified musical signification.

John Cage has said that syntax in language is like the army in society; to rid ourselves of it, we must demilitarize language.[11] Since the 1940s, he has turned to chance procedures for generating his notes in order to use only "sounds free of [his] intentions" and to insure a complete absence of repetition, redundancy, and patterns. Such a compositional method emphasizes not the choices a composer makes, but the questions he asks. Cage explains, "It is, in fact, my taste and my memory that I wish to be free of" (Shoemaker, 1984, p. 27). In composing the *Freeman Etudes* for solo violin (1977–1980), for example, as well as the *Etudes Australes* for piano and the *Etudes Boreales* for piano and cello from the same period, Cage superimposed a transparent sheet on a map of the stars and derived his sound aggregates from a one centimeter wide grid drawn on the sheet. After determining which of the twelve tones on his grid each star was nearest, he then used chance operations to select in which octave the note would be played, with which duration and dynamic intensity, which microtonal inflections would be added to it, and so on. Only bowing and fingering were left to the performer's discretion.[12] The composer refers to this piece as "all process" and to the variety that arises from the different etudes as being "like changes in the weather."[13] Constant dynamic changes between each note give the work great fluidity, but perhaps the most striking effect of this music (whose every note is determined independently of the surrounding notes) is like that of the stars which, on a clear night, appear singular, independent of one another, and of varying densities while at the same time nonhierarchical and undifferentiated within the larger picture of the whole.

As with viewing the stars, whatever shape the perceiver might hear in a *Freeman Etude* derives more from what he is seeking in it than from the work itself. The extreme registral leaps from virtually inaudible notes four octaves above middle C to those in the middle register, and occasional extraordinarily long silences such as the nine-second one followed by the twenty-one-second one in the fifteenth etude, mitigate strongly against any narrativity being read into the work. It is a strange coincidence then when, in the fifth etude, the first nine notes—probably the most regular rhythmic succession of notes in the set—sound like a phrase when they end with a falling fourth and a diminuendo to ppp, and when they are followed by another quasi-phrase of fifteen notes that ends with a falling fifth and a large crescendo.

[10]Metz discusses the many forms in which the "breakdown of narrativity" has been argued in modern film (1974, pp. 185–227).

[11]Cage borrows this notion from Norman O. Brown (Cage, 1973, p. ii; 1979, p. 183).

[12]From a telephone interview with the author, October 21, 1986. (For more details on how Cage used the star maps to generate his *Freeman Etudes*, see Zukofsky [1982, pp. 103–105].)

[13]See note 12. In his *Empty Words*, Cage furthermore explains how a process is like the weather: "In the case of weather, though we notice changes in it, we have no clear knowledge of its beginning or ending. At a given moment, we are when we are" (p. 178).

Other composers, like Jean-Charles François and John Silber in the improvisatory group *Kiva*, are investigating means of getting away from "collective memory" by doing away with notation systems and traditional instruments, both of which in their view severely limit the "information content" of music. Their interest is in sound, prelinguistic sound which is essentially nonrepeatable and cannot be fully notated, and in composing with color, or timbre, rather than with notes, lines, or counterpoint. To free themselves of automatic reflexes and knowledge of semantic and syntactic musical systems, over the past twelve years John Silber explains that they developed a series of movement exercises for the body and the voice ranging from placing the body in certain positions to produce different vocal expressions to experimenting with "nasal projections very high in the head," "sounds that are chest driven," and others that are "almost abdominal in their projection" (from an interview with the author, May 22, 1986). In three recent essay-performances, Jean-Charles François describes their search for a "music of no memory, yet presence" that derives from sound itself rather than any "belief systems embedded in our ears" (François, 1986a,b,c).

The result is a music of constant change in which sounds are explored rather than exploited, sometimes collectively by the performer–composers, sometimes by only one of them, and in which silence plays a preeminent role, shaping the sounds that move into and out of it, usually almost imperceptibly. Many of *Kiva*'s sounds derive from mundane gestures, such as moving objects on a table or parts of an instrument, others from using the voice and playing traditional instruments—keyboard, percussion, winds, and the violin—in nontraditional, at times electronically altered ways. Their incorporation of media, ranging from dance to silent film to video, serves to increase the variety and complexity of the expression and its meaning.

New Forms of Narrative in Contemporary Music

In recent years, there has developed a gap between music whose organizational principles or lack thereof are used to stretch the limits of our perceptions (such as totally serialized works and some chance-determined ones), and music whose experience is easily perceptible but vaguely structured (such as some minimal music and Pauline Oliveros' meditation music). Both have risks—the intricate complexity of the former may be imperceptible, while the utter simplicity of the latter may appear without meaning. Some composers are using narrative again as an explicit form of communication in order to bridge that gap.

First, the signification process is returning in music. In the mid-1960s, George Rochberg began to quote tonal music of the past; later he composed sections of movements or whole movements in the language of tonality. The variation movement of his Third String Quartet (1971–1972), for example, is not only unambiguously in A Major and thematic, but in each variation the rhythmic values become increasingly quick—from eighth notes, to sixteenths and triplet sixteenths, to thirty-second notes, to trills—as in variation movements of late Beethoven works. Penderecki's Second Symphony (1979–1980) uses a tonal form, the sonata allegro, as well as a Brucknerian orchestra. In pieces such as these, tonality and other references to music of the past are as much the subjects of the discourse as operatic recitative was for Beethoven in his Ninth Symphony.

John Cage's two operas, *Europera I* and *II* (premiered at the Frankfurt Opera, November 1987) consist entirely of quotations. The ten singers in the first opera and nine in the second perform a collage of sixty-four opera arias of their choice, ranging from Gluck to Puccini, interspersed by instrumentalists who play fragments from the same arias. Chance determines the order of the arias and both operas end when their time is up—one and one-half hours for the first and forty-five minutes for the second. Unlike most operas, there is no story, although the stories of the various operas are printed in the program notes, and no relationship between the music and the costumes, lighting, singers' actions, or decor (from an interview with the author, October 21, 1986).

Composers are also increasingly linking their music to other art forms, and using them to reinforce a composition's meaning or make it more apparent. Roger Reynolds's music and Ed Emshwiller's video for *Eclipse* (1979–1981) treat images analogously to suggest an analogous content. Both communicate the idea of emerging and going beyond traditional boundaries by taking an abstract outline (whether synthesized sounds with vowel-like properties or a circle) and then continuously transform it, first into something representational (standard speech or faces), and then into something suprareal (represented by the juxtaposition of six or eight fragmented texts and three different voices behaving in three different ways, together with the image of the face whose various aspects are in constant metamorphosis). After alternating between only sound and only image, the modes only combine when both are attempting to exceed their boundaries.

In a number of works which resemble dramatic cantatas, composers are even turning to the use of a story in the traditional sense of the word. Frederic Rzewski's setting of Brecht's epic poem *Antigone-Legend* (1983), for soprano and piano, is literally programmatic, using musical means such as register, rhythm, dynamics, and timbre to differentiate the personas and recount the drama. The first two times Antigone speaks, the singer uses sprechstimme (speak-singing) to distinguish her from the narrator. Many descriptions and introductions of her and occasionally her vocal line are characteristically marked by syncopated rhythms, sometimes simultaneously in both the piano and the voice (such as at rehearsal numbers *46–50, 51–52, 55, 57–59, 64,* and *74*). At one point (from rehearsal number *103* to *111*), the singer (as narrator) describes a conversation between Kreon and his son, while the piano interrupts the tale after each sentence as if to act out their dialogue. "To avoid the risk of losing the element of action in the sterile ritual of the concert hall," the composer indicates that the music should be accompanied by either hand-held puppets who represent the play's action or by screens on which the most important scenes are painted. Harrison Birtwistle's *Nenia: the Death of Orpheus* (1970) also uses one singer in three roles (Orpheus, Eurydice, and the narrator), has each sing in a different manner, and rapidly changes from one to the next to suggest several simultaneous perspectives on the action.

Bernard Rands' two recent song cycles, *Canti Lunatici* (1981) and *Canti del Sol* (1983), embody four signifieds—a story, another artform (the poetry), other musical compositions, and tonality, but without representing characters or actions with specific musical material. In *Canti Lunatici*, the chosen order in which the fifteen poems appear tells a three-tiered story, a mythical one of the waxing and waning of the moon, a stellar one of the seasons, and a psychological one of man's responses to the moon's phases. The poems of the second cycle tell a similar story of the sun's cycle. The composer ensures the accessibility of these texts to English-speaking audiences by providing translations of those sung in Italian, Spanish, German, and French, and by having the lights on during performances so they can be read. He moreover differentiates the two cycles by setting the moon poems in a melismatic or florid manner (to suggest a kind of lunacy) and the sun poems with quickly moving syllables, particularly at the beginning when the work gathers momentum rapidly like the sun rises.

In the middle of *Canti Lunatici*, wherein the composer sets the eighth poem of the set (7 + 1 + 7) describing the moon at its fullest, Rands quotes Debussy's *Clair de lune* in the piano, changing it somewhat (such as the intervals of a fifth to tritones) but maintaining exactly the same rhythms, gestures, melodic contours, and registral changes. The singer meanwhile occasionally repeats the same notes and rhythms as the piano part, but most of the time reads the text, drawing the listener's attention to the surreal images (white moons with diamond navels, with weeping black tears, etc.) of the Hans Arp poem. The instrumentalists, quiet at first, gradually overwhelm both stanzas of the poem with aggressively loud oscillating figures in the winds and xylophones, reiterating the tritone on which the piece is based, A–E flat. At the end of *Canti del Sol*, Rands also quotes the contour and rhythms of the vocal line of Debussy's setting of Baudelaire's *Harmonie du soir* in his vocal setting of the same poem. Although quite fitting references, these quotations depend on the listener's familiarity with what is being quoted in order that the meaning of these sections be truly multiple.

This extensive use of signifieds and even story in Rands' pieces raises the question of whether their structure and logic are those of a narrative. Other than the return to the opening, middle register A in the vocal part of *Canti Lunatici* at the end of the piece, and the return at the end of *Canti del Sol* to the words that began *Canti Lunatici*, "Ognuno sta solo . . . ed subito sera" (Each one stands alone . . . and in no time it's evening), thus marking the end of a twenty-four-hour cycle, there is no repetition or return in the two works. But the order in which the poems are arranged gives an arch shape to the first cycle as well as to the two cycles as a whole. And, even though there are two tonal centers in *Canti Lunatici*, A and E flat, the continual elaboration of these tonalities throughout the work gives it great coherence. The opening melisma that introduces the tritone between the A and E flat is furthermore a classic "narrative situation," posing the musical question of how the two tonalities will be brought into a satisfying relationship.

Moreover, while the organization of *Canti Lunatici* is not that of a narrative curve, the work does generally follow the story. In addition, though each poem, surrounded by some silence, seems almost self-sufficient, the work's events do progress, not just succeed one another. They are connected by a configuration the composer calls "labyrinthine," which he compares to that of Joyce's *Ulysses* (from an interview with the author, May 15, 1986). Sometimes the story is in evidence and the musical phrases develop linearly; other times, the composer digresses, the music moves tangentially to explore myriad possibilities suggested in the musical ideas themselves, before returning to the story and picking up the thread again. Because the musical events are not primarily dependent on previous ones and are implied only ultimately, they do not occur in the traditional narrative order wherein if one leaves out one aspect of the story, then one cannot continue and one is lost. Narrative in this music results instead from the kaleidoscopic presentation of elements of a story whose *cumulative* impact, rather than moment to moment logic, is that of a narrative.

In conclusion, I am suggesting that a new kind of narrative is arising in some contemporary works. These narratives borrow the most important attributes of traditional narratives—the use of signifieds, well-defined structures, configuration, unifying reference points, transformation, and memory. But they continue to respond to the modern desire for expressing the multiplicity of existence, fragmentary and seemingly irrational orders, and meanings that go beyond those that are known. They may use many signifieds—complementary ones (as in *Canti Lunatici*) or contradictory ones (as in Cage's *Europera I* and *II*)—that reinforce each other's meaning or inspire new meanings. Even if their configuration is not that of a dramatic curve, their structures generally have clearly defined beginnings and endings and they reach closure of one sort or another. They often progress to and from what Machover calls "nodal points," points of departure and arrival provided by the story (from an interview with the author June 4, 1986). But perhaps most importantly, such works may incorporate more than one narrative, either successively or simultaneously. Birtwistle, for example, presents four versions of Eurydice's death in *The Mask of Orpheus,* and intersperses six related myths that comment on the Orpheus myth. By contrast, in his opera *Valis,* Machover develops four narrative strands at the same time—the main character's normal life, his connection to the narrator, his double, his relation to a woman trying to commit suicide, and his mental world as reflected in the journal he is writing.

The logic of these narratives is often that of the kaleidoscope. Rands says he felt no compunction about reordering the events of Van Gogh's life to present them in a kaleidoscopic manner in his opera *Le Tambourin*. Such a method of composition places emphasis on the whole, rather than the precise movement of one section to another. Transformation in these works thus does not depend on immediate connections from one section to the next, but rather on some overall connectivity. The goal, as in *Canti Lunatici*, is to make a cumulative impact. From this perspective then, narrative is the sense that one has of a certain kind of a whole when one has reached the end, not necessarily while one is listening to each and every part in its middle.

Time and Mind

As it reflects the mind's search for making sense and for order, narrative is not just a mode of perception and cognition, but also a mode of thinking. With time as its material and its ultimate reference, it differs in a significant way from that involving abstract logic.[14] The mental process Ricoeur calls configuration, or the "grasping together" of events that are not simultaneous into one thought he calls plot, is a critical characteristic of narrative thinking, that which makes possible the conception and construction of temporal wholes. As Ricoeur points out, "it is only in virtue of poetic composition that something counts as a beginning, middle, and end" (1984, p. 38). The fact that we tend to impose narrative or try to perceive it, especially when listening to music, even when it is clearly not in evidence, suggests that narrative has come to dominate the way we think of the processes of life and nature. As such then, it provides us with a way of understanding our predecessors and of communicating not only with each other, but also our successors.

However, because man's experience and understanding of time has changed in this century, artists of all kinds, particularly composers, have sought to give form to other, not necessarily goal-oriented, or dramatic, or organic processes. One cannot develop expectations about these processes or resolve their inexplicable but inherent contradictions; one cannot grasp them into one thought; one can only endure them. Antinarratives, nonnarratives, and works without narrativity particularly in music reveal how inadequate the idea of basing a narrative on ordinary time has become. The return to using narrative concepts, perhaps in response to the crisis over a lack of norms in this century,[15] signals a renewed desire on the part of composers to have their audiences participate in the aesthetic experience by bringing their own knowledge of life's processes to the music; however, as life has changed, the events signified and organized by those narratives have changed. Postmodern narratives, if one dares to call them that, do create an order—what Lyotard calls an "internal equilibrium"—but at the same time, unlike their predecessors, they "tolerate the incommensurable."[16]

[14]As Claude Bremond points out in his *Logique du récit* (1973), the minimal condition for narrative's existence is that something happen to a subject between a time t and a time $t + n$ (pp. 99–100).

[15]Jürgen Habermas calls this century's "legitimation crisis" (1975) and Lyotard borrows and expands on this concept (1984, pp. 6–9).

[16]In his *The Postmodern Condition*, Lyotard writes: "Postmodern knowledge is not simply a tool of the authorities; it refines our sensitivity to differences and reinforces our ability to tolerate the incommensurable. Its principle is not the expert's homology, but the inventor's paralogy" (pp. xxv, 7).

References

Aristotle, Poetics. *Introduction to Aristotle*, ed. R. McKeon. New York: Modern Library, 1947.

Bal, M. (1977), *Narratologie*. Paris: Klincksieck.

Barthes, R. (1967), *Elements of Semiology*, trans. A. Lavers & C. Smith. Boston: Beacon Press. Originally published in 1964 as *Éléments de sémiologie*.

———— (1977), Introduction to the structural analysis of narratives. In: *Image, Music, Text*, trans. S. Heath. New York: Hill & Wang, pp. 79–124.

Bremond, C. (1973), *Logique du récit*. Paris: Editions du Seuil.

Cage, J. (1973), *M*. Middletown, CT: Wesleyan University Press.

———— (1979), *Empty Words*. Middletown, CT: Wesleyan University Press.

Carr, D. (1986), *Time, Narrative, and History*. Bloomington: Indiana University Press.

Chatman, S. (1978), *Story and Discourse*. Ithaca, NY: Cornell University Press.

Childs, B. (1977), Time and music: A composer's view. *Perspect. of New Music*, 2/15 (Spring/Summer): 194–219.

Clifton, T. (1983), *Music as Heard*. New Haven, CT: Yale University Press.

Cone, E. (1967), Beyond analysis. *Perspect. of New Music*, 6/1(Fall-Winter):37.

———— (1974), *The Composer's Voice*. Berkeley: University of California Press.

Culler, J. (1981), *The Pursuit of Signs*. Ithaca: Cornell University Press.

Doležel, (1976), A scheme of narrative time. In: *Semiotics of Art*, eds. L. Matejka & I. Titunik. Cambridge: MIT Press, pp. 209–217.

Epstein, D. (1981), On musical continuity. In: *The Study of Time*, Vol. IV , eds. J. T. Fraser, N. Lawrence, & D. Park. New York: Springer Verlag, pp. 180–197.

François, J.-C. (1986a), Music without representation and unreadable notation. Paper presented at the Departmental Seminar of the Music Department, University of California, San Diego, October 2.

———— (1986b), Trigger timbre, dynamic timbre. Paper presented at the Departmental Seminar of the Music Department, University of California, San Diego, October 9.

———— (1986c), Entanglements, networks, and knots. Paper presented at the Departmental Seminar of the Music Department, University of California, San Diego, October 10.

Gagne, C., & Caras, T. (1982), Interview with Philip Glass on November 13, 1980. In: *Soundpieces*. Metuchen, NJ: Scarecrow Press.

Genette, G. (1972), *Narrative Discourse*, trans. J. E. Lewin. Ithaca, NY: Cornell University Press, 1980. Orginally published as *Discours du récit*.

Greimas, A. J., & Courtés, J. (1979), *Semiotics and Language*, trans. L. Crist et al. Bloomington: Indiana University Press, 1982. Originally published as *Sémiotique*.

Habermas, J. (1975), *The Legitimation Crisis*, trans. T. McCarthy. Boston: Beacon Press.

Kakinuma, T. (unpublished), Minimal music and narrativity—Reich's piano phase.

Kermode, F. (1967), *The Sense of an Ending*. New York: Oxford University Press.

Kramer, J. (1978), Moment form in twentieth-century music. *Mus. Quart.*, 2/64:177–194.

———— (1981), New temporalities in music. *Crit. Inquiry*, 3/7(Spring):539–556.

Labov, W. (1972), *Language in the Inner City*. Philadelphia: University of Pennsylvania Press.

Lyotard, J.-F. (1984), *The Postmodern Condition: A Report on Knowledge*, trans. G. Bennington & B. Massumi. Minneapolis: University of Minnesota Press. Originally published in 1979 as *La Condition postmoderne: rapport sur le savoir*.

Macdonald, H. (1980), Thematic transformation. In: *The New Grove Dictionary of Music and Musicians*, ed. S. Sadie, Vol. 19. London: Macmillan, pp. 117–118.

Machover, T. (1986), A stubborn search for artistic unity. In: *The Language of Electro-Acoustic Music*, ed. S. Emmerson. London: Macmillan, pp. 185–209.

Martin, W. (1986), *Recent Theories of Narrative*. Ithaca, NY: Cornell University Press.

Mertens, W. (1983), *American Minimal Music*, trans. J. Hautekiet. New York: Alexander Broude. Originally published in 1980 as *Amerikaanse repetitieve muziek*.

Metz, C. (1974), *Film Language*, trans. M. Taylor. New York: Oxford University Press. Originally published in 1967 as *Essais sur la signification au cinema*.

Meyer, L. (1967), *Music, the Arts, and Ideas*. Chicago: University of Chicago Press.

——— (1984), Music and ideology in the nineteenth century. Tanner Lectures on Human Values, delivered at Stanford University, May 17 and 21.

Miller, D. A. (1981), *Narrative and Its Discontents*. Princeton, NJ: Princeton University Press.

Mink, L. O. (1972), Interpretation and narrative understanding. *J. Philos.*, 9/69:735–737.

Pasler, J. (1986), Music and spectacle in *Petrushka* and *The Rite of Spring*. In: *Confronting Stravinsky*, ed. J. Pasler. Berkeley: University of California Press.

Piaget, J. (1971), *Structuralism*, trans. C. Maschler. New York: Harper & Row.

Ricoeur, P. (1980), Narrative time. *Crit. Inquiry*, 1/7:169–190.

——— (1984), *Time and Narrative*, Vol. 1, trans. K. McLaughlin & D. Pellauer. Chicago: University of Chicago Press. Originally published in 1983 as *Temps et récit*, Vol. I.

——— (1985), *Time and Narrative*, Vol. 2. trans. K. McLaughlin & D. Pellauer. Chicago: University of Chicago Press. Originally published in 1984 as *Temps et récit*, Vol. 2.

Rowell, L. (1981), The creation of audible time. *The Study of Time*, Vol. IV. eds. J. T. Fraser, N. Lawrence, & D. Park. New York: Springer-Verlag, pp. 198–210.

Saussure, F. de, (1976), *Cours de linguistique générale*. Paris: Payot.

Scholes, R. (1980), Language, narrative, and anti-narrative. *Crit. Inquiry*, 1/7:204–212.

———, Kellogg, R. (1966), *The Nature of Narrative*. New York: Oxford University Press.

Shoemaker, W. (1984), The age of Cage. *Downbeat*, December:27.

Stoianova, I. (1976), Narrativisme, téléologie et invariance dans l'oeuvre musicale. *Musique en jeu*, 25:15–31.

Stravinsky, I. (1936), *An Autobiography*. New York: Simon & Schuster.

Tarasti, E. (1984), Pour une narratologie de Chopin. *IRASM*, 15:53–75.

Todorov, T. (1978), *Poétique de la prose*. Paris: Seuil.

Tomashevsky, B. (1925), Thematics. In: *Russian Formalist Criticism: Four Essays*, eds. L. Lemon & M. Reis. Lincoln: University of Nebraska, 1965, pp. 61–95.

White, H. (1980), The value of narrativity in the representation of reality. *Crit. Inquiry*, 1/7:5–27.

York, W. (1985), Form and process. In: *Contiguous Lines*, ed. T. DeLio. Lanham: University Press of America, pp. 81–106.

Zukofsky, P. (1982), John Cage's recent violin music. In: *A John Cage Reader*, eds. P. Gena & J. Brent. New York: C. F. Peters, pp. 103–105.

Appendix 1: TERMINOLOGY, Adapted from That of Selected Authors

Discourse: "Is language being performed" (Metz, 1974, p. 25).

Discourse is "the means by which the content is communicated"; its manifestation in a medium, involving order and selection (Chatman, 1978, p. 19).

Narratable: Means "worthy of telling" (Culler, 1981, p. 184).

"The narratable: the instances of disequilibrium, suspense, and general insufficiency from which a narrative appears to arise. This term is meant to cover the various incitements to narrative, as well as the dynamic ensuing from such incitements" (Miller, 1981, p. ix).

Narrative [récit]: "Narrative is a closed discourse of unclosed events that proceeds by unrealizing a temporal sequence of events" (Metz, 1974, p. 28).

Narrative is a "discourse that undertakes to tell of an event or series of events" (Genette, 1972, p. 25).

"Narrative discourse consists of a connected sequence of narrative statements" (i.e., expression of events or existents) (Chatman, 1978, p. 31).

Narrative discourse is "a locus of the figurative representations of different forms of human communication produced from tension and of returns to equilibrium." A narrative schema is "the narrative organization of discourses," the series of establishments, breaks, reestablishments of contractual obligations between sender and receiver. A narrative strategy orders the arrangements and intertwinings of narrative trajectories, or the series of simple or complex narrative programs (i.e. the elements of narrative syntax "composed of an utterance of doing governing an utterance of state") (Greimas and Courtés, 1979, pp. 203–208, 245).

Narrative is a way of interpreting, valuing, and presenting in a certain order a series of events chosen for their appropriateness to a thematic structure (Culler, 1981).

Narrative is "one method of recapitulating past experiences by matching a verbal sequence of clauses to the sequence of events which (it is inferred) actually occurred" (Labov, 1972, pp. 359–360).

Narrative time mediates between two dimensions. The episodic dimension draws narrative time in the direction of the linear representation of time, constituting an open series of events which follow one another in the irreversible order of time; the configurational dimension transforms the succession of events into one meaningful whole and, through this reflective act, translates the plot into one "thought," which is its point or theme. To make a narrative, that is, concretely to lead a situation and characters from some beginning to some ending, requires the mediation of recognized cultural configurations; that is, plot-types handed down by tradition (Ricoeur, 1980, 1984).

   Narrativity: "The organizing principle of all discourse, whether narrative or non-narrative"; narrativity governs the production and reading of this kind of discourse and depends on the perceiver's narrative competence (i.e., syntagmatic intelligence) (Greimas and Courtes, 1979, p. 209).

"The narrativity of a text is the manner by which a text is decoded as narrative" (Bal, 1977, p. 5).

One law of narrativity is "the ability or rather the necessity of proceeding like a series of options directed by the narrator" (Bremond, 1973, p. 99).

Narrativity is "the language structure that has temporality as its ultimate reference" (Ricoeur, 1980, p. 169).

   Signification: A process, "the act which binds the signifier and the signified, an act whose product is the sign" (Barthes, 1967, p. 48).

"The minimum structure any signification requires is the presence of two terms and a relationship linking them" (Greimas, cited by Metz [1974, p. 16]).

"Signification presupposes perception (of the terms and their relation)" (Greimas, cited by Metz [1974, p. 16]).

Signified: The succession of events that are subjects of this discourse and its series of internal relations (Genette, 1972).

The signified is the narrative content, or story [histoire] (Genette, 1972; Bal, 1977).

Signifier: The material mediator of the signified (Barthes, 1967).

The signifier signifies the signified by means of connotation (i.e., using style, genre, symbol, poetic atmosphere) or denotation (i.e, by diegesis, or reciting of the facts) (Metz, 1974).

Story [histoire]: "A series of events" (the passage from one state to another) "which are logically related" (i.e., ordered in time and space) "and caused or undergone by actors" (something which acts) (Bal, 1977, p. 4).

A story is "the content of the narrative expression," a chain of events (actions and happenings) and existents (characters and setting) (Chatman, 1978, pp. 19, 23).

Perspectives

The common meaning of narration as story-telling through words overlooks the many channels through which people communicate. A picture, it is said, is worth a thousand words. When words and moving pictures are combined, for instance, then the eye helps interpret the ear—to paraphrase Shakespeare's Rape of Lucrece—*and we have the recipe of that powerful means of communication which put Hollywood in business.*

One may next think of musicals and of opera, for they combine words, moving images, and music. Dr. Pasler does indeed mention opera in the introduction to her chapter. But she goes much beyond this obvious step. Following the work of literary scholars and music theorists, she extends the meaning of narration and narrativity to include the conveyance of meaning through music.

The power and flexibility of spoken language are necessary tools for the definition of reasoned personal and collective identities. If a schematic generalization is permitted, to help make an important point, then music may be thought to do the same for feeling as language does for reasoning. It helps define the emotive self both in its individual and its social dimensions.

Narration, Professor Pasler tells us, is "not just a mode of perception and cognition but also a mode of thinking." Music, in the musical present, creates musical memories and musical expectations, the very stuff of narration. Story-telling leads to story thinking and to the consequent enlargement of nootemporal horizons. Music making leads to music feeling which when modulated, played on, soothed, and shaken up by the power of sound, leads to the enlargement of our emotive horizons. Our minds integrate the new expectations and memories into the structure of the mental present where they become intricately intertwined with all the other elements that contribute to the human knowledge of time. Together, they help the mind in its continuous scanning of the hierarchy of its temporalities and make possible the universal magic we recognize in the musical creation of meaning and time.

From music, we turn to words said, written, or only half-formed in the mind as hazy images, signifying the features of both possible and impossible worlds. By putting such representations out to pasture on the fields of hope, fear, joy, and regret, language and language-thinking help create and maintain the open horizons of noetic time.

The position of humans beneath those horizons is described by the first aphorism of Hippocrates: "Life is short, the Art is long, opportunity fleeting, experiment treacherous, judgment difficult."

Recognizing that our lives are short is a part of the price we pay for the advantages of being able to think in terms of distant futures and pasts. Art is "long" because human knowledge, though it derives from the mental skills of the individual, always involves futures and pasts beyond the reach of a single life. The recognition that opportunity is fleeting is one of the double-edged swords of knowing time. It is a powerful weapon, for it enables humans to prepare for unique instants of future contingencies. But it is also a heavy burden, for it can fill the mind with regrets for past opportunities missed, whether for love and kindness or for power and glory. Finally, the purpose of judgment is to identify permanent patterns among our impressions so as to decrease the treacherous aspects of experimentation: it enables us to learn.

The experimentation that Hippocrates speaks about is conducted, by each and every one of us on the bio-, noo-, and sociotemporal worlds, simultaneously. It is the self-appointed task of the literary arts to survey the infinite variety of these experiments. But a writer's survey is not a passive report. By pursuing his or her task, a writer creates new domains of experience.

The chapter that follows tells us about such new realities, with special focus on the issues of time and mind.

14

Mind and Time: A Comparative Reading of Haiku, Kafka, and Le Guin

Marlene Pilarcik Soulsby

Abstract Literature, by its very nature, involves the mind in a temporal process: the reader experiences a literary work in time as word follows word, sentence follows sentence in sequential fashion. During the reading process, the moving present of the reader's mind as it follows the text also becomes the means by which a fictive experience of temporality is generated in the mind. The mind actualizes the fluctuations, leaps, regressions, and anticipations that constitute the temporal dynamics of the literary work. Thus literature has its life, and indeed its very existence, from the simultaneous interaction of the mind in time and the creation of a temporal reality in the mind. This accounts for the different kinds of temporal experiences we have each time we read a text. As Wolfgang Iser points out, different time sequences exist during a first reading and during subsequent readings of the same text because the process of anticipation and retrospection changes with acquired knowledge of the whole.

In my study, I examine the temporal experience of reading selections from the works of three writers who approach the mind–time problematic from quite different perspectives. The Japanese haiku, consisting of only seventeen syllables, is the shortest form in world literature, yet the brevity of the reading duration is essential to the temporal effect it induces. Basho's famous frog plopping into an old pond generates the simultaneous experience of being and becoming. Much of Franz Kafka's work involves the reader in disruption and contradiction, leading to a frustrating attempt to find order in a chaotic universe. His creation of dreamlike realities in some of the shorter parables and in "Der Landarzt" thrusts the reader into a time frame experience that is at once eerily familiar and yet unfamiliar. Ursula Le Guin's novel, *The Lathe of Heaven*, though linear and chronological, simultaneously disrupts chronology. The protagonist is caught in a nightmarish relativity in which his consciousness is the only constant and dreams irrevocably alter time and reality.

By examining these works experientially as well as thematically we are of course confronted with the inevitable paradox—how do we examine the flow after it has stopped flowing? But then,

261

aren't we irresistibly drawn to the paradoxical? Isn't that what entices us again and again to look at this thing called time?

> Footfalls echo in the memory
> Down the passage which we did not take
> Towards the door we never opened
> Into the rose-garden. My words echo
> Thus, in your mind.

Reading this passage from T. S. Eliot's "Burnt Norton" (1943, p. 13), we experience a movement down a passage, toward a door, and into a rose garden—none of which really happens but all of which comes alive in our minds as we follow the sequence of words on the page. This is the power of literature—the power to make even a memory of what did not happen a part of our immediate and present experience. The words of the text and the reader's mind interact through time to produce an experience that *is* the literary work of art. Without a reader in whose mind the words can echo, texts remain static, lifeless objects sitting on someone's bookshelf. Poulet (1969) says, "They wait for someone to come and deliver them from their materiality, from their immobility. . . . Are they aware that an act of man might suddenly transform their existence?" (p. 53).

Literary critics have focused increased attention on this "act of man" that can transform a static object into a dynamic temporal happening. Rosenblatt describes a poem as "an event in time" (1964; p. 126; 1978). Iser claims that a text only exists potentially until the mind of a reader interacts with it, re-creates it, and thus actualizes it in time (1974, 1978). Fish challenges the self-sufficiency of the text by arguing that meaning itself is what a text does to the reader as he reads in time (1980).

Studies which emphasize the dynamic, temporal, and affective dimensions of the literary text remind us that literature, like life itself, must be grasped on the move, in the flux and movement of the mind as it builds a world from the sequence of words and images. Literature, by its very nature, is a re-creation in time, generating movement from stillness, change from constancy. Its meaning, therefore, does not exist independently in the text but involves both the textual structures and the process of change and transition that occurs in the mind while reading.

At the 1979 International Society for the Study of Time (ISST) conference, Torgovnick discussed the significance of endings and closures in the experience of the reader. Knowledge of endings gives a vantage point from which one can organize events and give them coherent meaning (Torgovnick, 1981). Thus, during subsequent readings of a text we recognize connections and patterns which were not obvious at a first reading (Torgovnick, 1981, p. 184). For this reason, a reading experience is repeatable but inevitably different. As Iser points out, in each new reading all that changes is the time dimension of the reader but this change significantly alters how a reader differentiates and combines images along the time axis of the text (1978, p. 149). During a first reading, memory and expectation interact and modify each other in a way which is not possible during subsequent readings when the text as a whole is part of memory. If we consider the reader's position in a text as a moving point or intersection between memory and anticipation, we see that as anticipations are fulfilled, frustrated, or modified, they fall into the realm of memory. This newly acquired knowledge now also has a retroactive effect on what has already been read. In other words, "reading does not merely flow forward"; it is a dialectical process involving a continual modification of memory and expectation (Iser, 1978, pp. 114, 118).

If we approach a text from the vantage point of knowing its beginning, middle, and ending, we are no longer immersed in it. With a retrospective point of view, we stand outside and analyze it as an organic whole. In my discussion of Hesse's *Das Glasperlenspiel* and Kawabata's *Meijin* at that same conference, I argued that the demands and expectations of narrative causality in those works give way to a lyrical simultaneity. The endings are implicit in the beginnings; progressive movement is illusory. Although this becomes evident in retrospect, the initial readings generate a variety of temporal experiences. In order to appreciate the dialectical tensions and the paradoxical unity of movement and stillness which enliven those works, we must also consider what happens to the time sense of the reader while reading (Pilarcik, 1981, pp. 119–135).

A literary work can so affect the reader's sense of presence that a minute might expand well beyond its actual dimensions, years might speed by, linear causality might loosen, fall back on itself, or disintegrate into isolated fragments. A text once opened can use the moving present of the reader's mind to fashion a fictive present, an illusory present, with its own time-frame, by stimulating a wide range of human temporal experience. The text prestructures an experience which the mind can actualize if the textual signals stimulate a response that is familiar to the reader, that is, within the realm of meaningful possibility. According to Fraser's model of a nested hierarchy of mental umwelts, the human experience of time can range from the highest level of noetic functioning to the increasing disorganization of more primitive umwelts: from past–present–future consciousness to the "creature present" of biotemporality, the *nunc stance* of eotemporality, the fragmentation of prototemporality, and even to the chaos of atemporality. Each of these levels, when thought of as a world in which we might exist, evokes different feelings or moods (Fraser, 1978, p. 284).

The very act of reading is in itself a noetic function of the mind, in that the literary event takes shape where memory and anticipation meet in a moving present. This process, however, is also the means by which a complexity of other temporal umwelts, including those associated with the break-up or absence of temporal ordering, is activated. To illustrate how literary meaning is shaped by the interaction of the mind in time and the generation of temporal experience in the mind, I have chosen to discuss three very different literary events. These examples by no means exhaust all possibilities, which are as varied as life itself, but they reveal the significance of the reader's moment to moment participation in understanding what literature *is* because of what it *does*.

The Eternal Moment

The old pond.
  A frog jumps in—
    Plop!

Furuike (ya)
kawazu tobikomu
mizu no oto

R. H. Blyth's translation of Basho's best-known haiku is only one of over a hundred translations and adaptations collected by Hiroaki Sato (1985). Literally translated, the poem reads:

> Old pond ya
> frog(s) jumps in
> water's sound

It may seem curious that such a short poem of merely seventeen syllables about a frog jumping into an old pond inspires so much interest even in translation, where the nuances and allusions of the original language are lost. Yet readers have responded to the poem even if they know nothing of Japanese sensibility and aesthetics, even if they know nothing of zen and the poetics of haiku. The poem has a concrete immediacy that can be felt without intellectual explanation.

What happens in the brief duration of the reading, a reading which can be completed in one breath-length? (Yasuda, 1957, p. 31). Essentially, the image of a frog appears in our consciousness and then disappears. There is no explanation, no discussion; it just happens, triggering an instant of surprise, as when something takes us off-guard. This subtle, inner jolt *is* the poem. In other words, the poem is not about ponds or frogs or any *thing;* it is what it does to us before we have time to think about it.

As we begin to read, the poem brings to mind the image of an old pond. This is followed by the particle, "ya," which Blyth translates with a period. The "ya," known as a *kireji* or cutting word, has no particular meaning here but cuts the poem, interrupts its flow, and suggests that a contrast, illustration, or description of some sort will follow. Very often the particle "ya" is indicated by a colon in translations (Henderson, 1958, p. 189). The "ya" or period signals a pause and allows the first image time to take hold in the imagination. The pond suggested by the poem could take a variety of forms depending on the reader's past experience and memory. It could appear in any number of states, ranging from stillness to agitation, as in a storm. The absence of detail and description gives the image an openness and indeterminacy which the visual perception of an actual pond could not have. The poem, therefore, relies on the participation of the reader, not to complete the picture, but rather to experience what is being communicated through it.

The range of possibilities becomes more focused by the appearance of a frog jumping in. This sudden movement evokes a sense of contrast to the pond, determining that it is still and has been still, absolutely still—until this moment. Significantly, the two images have no causal relationship and no intellectual connection; they merely coexist, each in its own right (Blyth, 1964, p. 11). Yet their juxtaposition creates a dynamic response in the mind of the reader. As the image of the pond falls into memory, it creates a background against which the image of the frog appears. At the same time, the image of the pond is retrospectively modified by the new image. The heightened sense of undisturbed stillness is evoked at the instant that motion disrupts it. In addition, the awareness of motion awakens a sense of expectation, projecting the mind forward. The poem ends with a sound that is over as soon as the words that signal it are read. The frog and the sound disappear in virtually the same instant that they appear in our awareness. The sound of water is subtle and undramatic, yet it jars the absolute silence that precedes and follows it. By its very existence, it calls forth the silence, just as the motion of the frog evokes the motionless tranquility of the old pond. Blyth says that "the silence of the old pond continues timelessly, whereas the sound of the water is as a bubble upon that river of silence" (Blyth, 1964, p. 12).

The experience of the poem results from the changes or shifts that occur in the mind while reading. That is to say, the haiku does not cumulatively build up the image, but rather engages the reader's mind in a two-way relationship, where the past affects the present and the present modifies the past. The movement, therefore, is not linear, but flows simultaneously backward and forward. After we have read the poem, the pond, the frog, and the sound all live simultaneously in our memory so that when thinking of the old pond, we are on the verge of waiting for the frog that has already jumped in, and the sound makes us aware that a frog has been there in the first place. Thus, the poem is an experience of simultaneity in sequentiality, timelessness in time: an eternal moment that exists in the brevity of the reading experience.

Kenkichi Yamamoto suggests that haiku by its very nature rests in a contradiction—the tension between the temporality of its poetic form and the atemporality of the experience it evokes:

> As long as a haiku is made up of the interlocking of words to a total length of seventeen syllables in its structure, it is inevitable that it be subject to the laws of time progression; however, I think the fact that it is a characteristic of haiku to echo back as a totality when one reaches its end—i.e., to echo back from the end to its beginning—seems to show that in its inner nature a haiku tends to deny in itself the temporal element inherent in its poetic form. That is to say, on one hand the words are arranged by the poet within the seventeen syllables in a temporal order; on the other hand, through the grasping insight of the reader, they must attain meaning simultaneously [1952, pp. 69–70].

The poetic form, the concreteness of the images, even the sequential order of the words, all are used as stategies to force the mind for an instant to bypass its tendency to understand in terms of causal order and connectivity. Pond, frog, and sound, although apprehended sequentially, involve the consciousness on a different level, one which does not look for causal order. On this level of biotemporal, consciousness, phenomena are perceived directly as sensory stimuli without the imposition of symbolic or logical meaning.

Basho said that what makes a *hokku*[1] is "the mind that goes off and returns" (quoted in Sato [1983, p. 128]). The mind, which Basho says "goes off" while reading the poem, returns to itself to "grasp" the message, but in returning it activates a developmentally older faculty than that of discursive reasoning, a faculty without abstract tensions, a faculty highly responsive to direct and concrete stimuli, a faculty focused on the present. The aesthetic value of such an experience lies in the free and spontaneous associations triggered by the words in the reader's mind. Because the familiar is perceived in an unfamiliar way, the reader makes the discovery of seeing something ordinary as though for the first time. For an instant, we see a commonplace phenomenon of nature as it flashes in our minds, and we are struck by the poignant beauty of the fleeting moment.

The Fragmented Moment

Basho's haiku uses the temporality of its literary form to overcome temporality, but the prose pieces we will examine by Kafka use our expectations of narrative linearity to subvert and fragment our sense of time. They appear to guide us through a sequence of events but in actuality they confound our attempts to build a coherent causal order, creating feelings of frustration and confusion. Kafka's work engages the noetic tendencies of mind in self-contradictory efforts, forcing the reader to become aware of more primitive levels of experience.

For example, in the parable, "A Common Confusion" (1931), A travels to H in ten minutes and returns back in the same amount of time, but the next day the same trip takes ten hours. Because A arrives late, he fails to keep his appointment with B and returns home, but this time he covers the same distance in an instant. Meanwhile, B, who had left a half hour before to go to A's village, arrived immediately after A's departure and had even met A on the threshold while A was leaving. By the time we have tried to untangle exactly what happened in terms of a linear sequence, A stumbles on the stairs in his rush to meet B who is still waiting for him, and B, either near or far, we can't be sure, stamps down the stairs in a rage, (Kafka, 1931). We could say that the text is illogical, but actually the text is consistently inconsistent within its own temporal and spatial configurations. Within the framework of this fictive reality, B can leave hours after A and meet him before A leaves. The common experience which results in a common confusion has nothing to do with trying to keep business appointments, but rather with the process of trying to make this reality conform to our preconceptions of space–time relationships. The tangled sequential order and A's repeated inability to connect with B contradict our memory and frustrate our logical expectations. On one hand, the text invites us to use our powers of logical reasoning to solve the puzzle of this dilemma, but on the other hand, the more we use logic, the more we get enmeshed in contradiction. This is no arithmetic problem for which a solution can be found, even though its language gives that impression. The meaning of the piece lies in the

[1]*Hokku* is the opening part of a *renga* or linked poem. It became dissociated with the *renga* and was the forerunner of *haiku*.

build-up of confusion from common cognitive processes. The reconciliation of A and B, though apparently close at hand, is infinitely far in time and space.

Likewise, the parable, "Give It Up" (1936), thrusts us into an unsettling relativity and contradiction. At first, however, the sequence of images encourages a sense of security by providing a concrete time, place, goal, and direction for the protagonist. It is morning, he is in a city; he is walking to the train station. This security begins to collapse with the discovery in the second sentence that a discrepancy exists between the tower clock and the protagonist's watch. Thrown in a panic because he is behind time, he no longer knows where to go; the city is unfamiliar; and he begins running without a direction. The situation may evoke familiar memories and feelings in the reader: we know how it feels to be late, to sleep in, to forget to set our clocks, to be behind schedule. Yes, it can throw us temporarily out of sorts to learn that things are not the way we had assumed or had come to expect. But here the incongruous clocks totally disrupt the familiarity of the world suggested by the first sentence. Now the empty streets have an eerie, unreal quality, and the feeling of security fades further into the background as the desire to find some certainty in this world intensifies. Like the protagonist, we feel ourselves rushing to finish the lengthy sentence in the hope that this expectation will be fulfilled. The sight of a policeman calms the mental frenzy of the protagonist and the shorter sentences slow down the reading flow. Surely this figure of authority, whose job it is to maintain order, will set things straight. We begin to anticipate a resolution and return to normal. We wait for the two worlds to come together, for personal time to be reconciled to clock time, for the inner turmoil to dissolve and give us that calm sense of purpose again with which we started the story. But our anticipations and our hope collapse as the policeman turns away with a laugh. The text has led us to believe that order can be restored. Kafka uses words which suggest a positive turn of events: "fortunately" he sees a *Schutzmann*, a word for policeman that is derived from *Schutz*, protection. In addition, the policeman is smiling. But this momentary build-up of hope quickly degenerates as we realize that they are not communicating on the same level. The sense of unease and disruption that began with a discrepancy in time returns now with even greater force. The protagonist is attempting to use ordinary references of time, space, and language in an out of the ordinary situation. He expects to respond to this new situation as he has done in the past and does not realize the futility of such an effort. Wrenched from the comfortable security of his past existence, he rushes in a panic to try to recapture it. Since he persists in hanging on to an illusory past, he is doomed. The policeman turns away with a laugh—and the protagonist stares bewildered into the emptiness that follows.

As we read this text, we have certain expectations; we expect a progression, a conclusion, an explanation of some sort, but are left with ambiguity and a bewildering lack of communication. The ending is so unexpected that we may be inclined to reread or to go back to the beginning to see if there is something we have overlooked. The text, however, provides as little direction for us as the policeman does for the protagonist. The burden of understanding falls on the reader, who cannot rely on his accustomed way of thinking. The noetic mind, that discovers meaningful patterns and causal order, flounders here in a self-contradictory text. For the reader, as well as for the protagonist, there is no "way" to have order imposed on the disjointed reality that confronts him. The reader must come to grips with the futility of expecting that the text will reconcile its own internal contradictions. Instead, it invites us to fill in the gaps and then loses us in those very gaps. The "meaning" of the work lies in the shock of discovering that our attempts to rely on the authority of the text to structure a coherent whole are doomed from the start (see Politzer [1966, pp. 1–22] for another reading of this parable).

Kafka's work typically confounds the reader's efforts to fit events into a unidirectional, past–present–future continuum. In "The Country Doctor" (1919), for example, the steady dissolution of temporal and spatial order creates an increasingly uncomfortable feeling of internal disruption and impotency. The reader follows the protagonist, not through events in time, but rather through a hierarchy of temporal experiences ranging from the expectations of noetic order to the anxiety-ridden fragmentation of the prototemporal.

The story is related as a first-person narrative, beginning with the statement, "I was in great perplexity [Verlegenheit]: . . ." (Kafka, 1919, p. 74). The word, *Verlegenheit*, which also connotes embarrassment or confusion, and the colon that follows suggest that we can expect to learn the nature, causes, and consequences of a dilemma from a protagonist who is viewing events from a retrospective point of view (see Canning [1984, pp. 187–212] for a discussion of the semantic and thematic implications of *Verlegenheit*). At first it seems that the cause of the difficulty was that his horse had died in the night, and he had no means to reach a seriously ill patient ten miles away, but in fact, the images of immobility that follow one another indicate an underlying paralysis, the cause of which is not clear. As the doctor stands paralyzed in the ever-deepening snow, his servant girl initiates action to find other horses; she beckons him toward the courtyard, where, in "confused" distress, he kicks open the door of an uninhabited pigsty. This action causes two enormous horses and an unearthly groom to emerge from the low space; all of which contradicts our normal expectations and brings an unsettling element into the immediacy of the reading experience. Although both the doctor and the girl accept this turn of events with easy familiarity, the reader feels a tension between his desire to fit the elements of this narrative into noetic logic and the voice of the protagonist. If we identify with the protagonist, and allow his thoughts to become our thoughts, we become aware that he triggers primitive emotions and responses in our minds. The vibrant, powerful horses and the sensual groom demand present-centeredness to satisfy the immediate demands of sensation and instinct. This is the "creature present" of biotemporal consciousness (Fraser, 1981, p. 5). To force us into this mode of thought, the verb tense shifts suddenly from past to present: "'Give him a hand,' I said, and the willing girl hurried to help the groom with the harnessing. Yet hardly was she beside him when the groom [clips] hold of her and [pushes] his face against hers" (Kafka, 1919, p. 221).[2]

[2]*The Complete Stories*, p. 221. Since Willa and Edwin Muir do not maintain the tense shift, I have altered their translation to conform to the original.

Dorrit Cohn, who has given considerable attention to the use of narrative tense in this story, suggests that the shift to present eliminates the "temporal distance between the narrating and experiencing self, momentarily giving the illusion that the speaker recounts his tale as it unfolds, with no foreknowledge of the future" (1968, p. 148). The reader, therefore, can no longer expect the insight of a retrospective point of view, but rather feels caught up in the flux of events as they happen. At the beginning of the story, the narrator indicated that he was relating his dilemma, explaining his embarrassment with knowledge of the whole from beginning to end, but the change to the present denies this knowledge and presumes an innocence about the future consequences of his actions.

The change from past to present occurs at the instant that the groom lays hold of Rose and bites her, leaving two red marks in her cheek. The doctor responds to this attack by yelling in a fury, but he does nothing because, as he says: "I . . . [reflect] that the man [is] a stranger; that I [do] not know where he [comes] from, and that of his own free will he [is] helping me out when everyone else [refuses]" (p. 221). These are not the thoughts of hindsight, but rather a paralyzing rationalization resulting from the conflict between primitive desire and the demands of responsibility, a present-centered consciousness and one that takes memory and future consequences into account. The doctor's thoughts are too easily diverted from Rose to the exhilarating prospect of driving the magnificent horses. We begin to doubt that he is genuinely concerned about her welfare or even thinking about possible danger that might befall her, so wrapped up is he in the presentness of these events. And yet, when Rose runs shrieking into the house, he indicates that she has "a justified presentiment that her fate [is] inescapable." This prediction, which indicates future knowledge, could serve as an excuse for the doctor not to take direct action against the groom, but it also conflicts with the doctor's stance of innocence. His verbal protests ring then insincere and even deceptive: " 'You're coming with me,' I [say] to the Groom, 'or I won't go, urgent as my journey is. I'm not thinking of paying for it by handing the girl over to you' " (p. 221).

The groom, ignoring all protests because he "knows" the thoughts of the doctor, finishes harnessing the horses. As readers, therefore, we do not have the privilege of knowing the doctor's real thoughts. We must speculate: perhaps the doctor himself is unaware of them; perhaps he is suppressing them; perhaps he is making excuses for them. In any case, we have great cause to suspect the truth of the surface narrative, namely, that perspective presented to us by the conscious voice of the narrator. If an attitude of distrust grows between protagonist and reader, this will inevitably affect how we understand the *Verlegenheit* which is the focal point of the story. Each reader brings to this story elements of his or her own unconscious self, and therefore, responses can be quite varied.

When the rape of Rose is imminent, the doctor is swept away by the horses and images of brutal passion are juxtaposed to the dissolution of time and space: "as if my patient's farmyard [opens] out just before my courtyard gate, I [am] already there" (p. 221). The narrative now moves the reader into another level of temporal experience, the dreamlike abiding present of eotemporal consciousness, where the unidirectional quality of cause and effect dissolves. The voice of the protagonist moves back and forth in time and space, in and out of mind and world. Events are interwoven with interior monologue, with memories, with speculation about Rose, with general observations about himself and the condition of the times. Although still in the present tense, the narrative flow is repeatedly stopped, reversed, and then brought back to the present.

With the sick boy in front of him, the doctor "only now" remembers Rose and thinks of rescuing her, but he reminds us of the present state of affairs: he is ten miles away. Of course, he could leave the boy and return home, but he allows his coat to be taken from him. He could confront the immediate problem and examine the boy, but he hunts for instruments, examines his tweezers, and thinks about Rose, a situation over which he now has no control. This intermingling of the memory of Rose and the immediate reality of the sick boy makes the two situations cotemporal in his mind and in ours. Thus, the fate of Rose and of the boy are linked in the mental present.

When the doctor is finally cajoled toward the bed, he confirms what he *already knows*—the boy is quite sound, just bad circulation and too much coffee. This pronouncement is followed by a rush of thoughts ranging from the difficulties of performing his duty as doctor to the expectations and lack of understanding from society, to Rose, to the boy, and to the horses dwelling in his dilapidated pigsty. One thought follows another, not in sequential order, but in associative leaps:

> I am no world reformer and so I let him lie. I [am] the district doctor and [do] my duty to the uttermost, to the point where it [becomes] almost too much. I [am] badly paid and yet generous and helpful to the poor. I [must] still see that Rose [is] all right, and then the boy might have his way and I [want] to die too. What [am] I doing [here] in [this] endless winter! My horse [is] dead, and not a single person in the village [will] lend me another. I [have] to get my team out of the pigsty; if they [weren't by chance] horses, I [would have] to travel with swine. That [is] how it [is] [pp. 222–223].

We also learn that Rose, the "pretty" girl whom he says he must sacrifice to the demands of duty, has lived in his house for years without his noticing her. These thoughts so preoccupy his mind that his attention is only forced back to the boy when the sister flutters a blood-soaked towel before him. Now he acknowledges that the boy may be ill and discovers the existence of a horrible wound, rose-red, infested with thick, blood-spotted wriggling worms. Was the wound there all along but unnoticed, just as Rose had lived unnoticed in his house until she was violated? Or did it just open during the examination? Was the wound the cause for the doctor's being called from his bed in the middle of the night or did the doctor himself cause the wound to blossom? Did he "already know" about the wound with the retrospective knowledge of a different temporal point of view, or does he discover it at the same time that we do? These questions present difficulties for the reader who is attempting to fit the narration into a linear continuum with causal connections. Associatively and experientially, cause and effect, Rose, boy, and wound are simultaneous in the mental present of doctor and reader.

The doctor, unable to anticipate any action beyond this present dilemma, thinks the boy is "past helping," and therefore fails to act toward a resolution, a hope for healing. Others strip his clothes and take him to the bed where he is laid next to the boy. Now he tells the boy his wound is not so serious and merely a matter of perspective: "your mistake is: you have not a wide enough view" (p. 225). With these words of "honor" from the "official doctor," who does his duty and writes prescriptions, he performs the external ritual of human compassion but not with the genuine intent of healing, not with the willingness to risk himself for the welfare of another.

As the boy takes these words to heart, the doctor becomes focused on his own future course of action—escape, and the verb tense changes again to the narrative past, thus countering any suggestion of possible forward progression in time. Without wasting time to dress, the doctor rushed from the house, hurried into the gig, and expected to return home with the same instantaneous speed with which he arrived. Instead, the horses moved slowly, "like old men" crawling through the snowy waste.

Again the tense changes to the present as space and time expand infinitely, thrusting the naked doctor into an endless night, where he is lost forever. The present of this prototemporal umwelt consumes all of the past and the future in an eternal, frozen moment, where return is impossible and progression nullified, where his hopeless fate is caused by the meaningless sequence of events and the events result again and again from his already doomed existence. He is already old, his practice already done for, a successor already robbing him, and the groom still raging in his house with Rose as his victim.

The doctor is doomed to tell and retell his story in exactly the same way because he has made no progress out of it or learned anything from it. He fails to see the empty repetitive functionalism of his life, which is the cause of his *Verlegenheit*. Whenever he is called upon to act with authentic human self-extension, he hesitates and suffers from the torment and impotency of internal conflict. This is the wound that he cannot exorcise and heal, because he does not even recognize it festering on his own side.

In the end, he wants to return home, not to help Rose, but to spring back into his bed, to try to regain a lost sense of security by reliving the past. But he is doomed only to relive his past mistakes with no insight into their cause or consequences. No wonder there is no real progression or forward movement in the story. The consciousness of the speaker has undergone no change, has achieved no understanding, is trapped forever in the lower reaches of the human consciousness. Thus, he becomes the victim of his own fragmented self and is doomed to live in empty meaninglessness with no hope of escape, only a cyclic repetition of the same.

He says he feels betrayed, but in fact who has betrayed whom? Don't we as readers also feel betrayed by the unreliability of the text we have just read—a text which sets up expectations and then undermines them, a text whose point of view we come to distrust, a text that confounds our rational ability to make sense of its reality? Isn't this part of the unsettling experience of reading the text? Thus, the experience of the protagonist and that of the reader are very similar. As Frye says, the real torment for both "lies less in searching for sense than in believing one is finding it along the way" (1983, p. 322).

The Moment of Chaos

Unlike Kafka, the popular writer of fantasy and science fiction, Ursula Le Guin, creates texts which use, rather than frustrate, the tendency of the noetic mind to find order and connectivity. She relies on scientific fact, the expectations of causal narrativity, and the immediate power of imagery to evoke unrealities; that is, thought-experiments in the reader's imagination. In *The Lathe of Heaven* (1973), for example, the reader follows a constantly shifting continuum, which eventually disintegrates into chaotic meaninglessness and then rebuilds or re-creates itself into new order. The affective impact of the shifting continuum and the tension generated by the efforts of the mind to maintain coherence are known to the reader well before any discussion of the ideas takes place.

The protagonist, George Orr, has the uncanny ability to affect reality with his dreams. When he dreams effectively, present reality is altered in accordance with his dream, but not in a miraculous or dreamlike way. As he says, "Each dream covers its tracks completely" (p. 50). In other words, past history also changes in order to fit the new circumstance naturally into a linear, causal scheme of things. Therefore, when he dreams of a world free of the problems of overpopulation, a carcinogenic plague results in the past in order to give logical, causal explanation for the new present reality. Paradoxically, each change simultaneously maintains and reverses the directional linearity of the causal chain.

The experience of reading this work, therefore, involves the mind in quite a different way from that of Basho's haiku or Kafka's stories. From beginning to end, the reader must actively employ logic and reason to assemble a growing complexity of causal relationships and simultaneously existing temporal continuums. On one level, we follow a linear moving present, but we must continually alter the past retrospectively as changes occur in the present. If any confusion exists, it is because we have failed to make all the logical and necessary adaptations.

Only George, and any one who happens to be with him at the instant of the change, has simultaneous memory of both temporal continuums. The reader, like George, is aware of each shift as it occurs, but whereas George has immediate awareness of the new present and all that has led up to it, the reader is repeatedly involved in a process of comparing and revising his memory to accommodate the shift. For example, on page 11, Dr. Haber's office is an interior, windowless efficiency suite on the sixty-third floor. Space is cramped and one can hear noise from the elevator, doors, typewriters and toilets. On page 53, however, the office is on the first floor of a research institute, is air-conditioned, serene, and has a large corner window with a sweeping view of the city and river. On page 132, his suite covers half an acre and includes seven rooms.

With each new shift in the time continuum, numerous unanticipated changes also occur. Even George must remind himself at times that causality is not a simple linear path, but a complex network of coexisting related factors. Sturgeon commented that the novel demands an attentive and concentrated reading (1972, p. 106). This concentration is not only necessary to adjust to a new present, but to see this new present in light of a new past compared to all other pasts. In addition, the reader must be ever ready to alter anticipations of the future. For example, in one continuum, Heather is a lawyer; in another, a legal secretary; in one she is black; in another, gray; in one she is aggressive, like a spider eyeing her prey; in another, quiet and submissive; in one she is George's wife; in another she does not exist at all. She is always herself but different. The changing present not only affects her past but also our expectations of her future role in the novel.

As a result of the continual reordering of the temporal dimension of the text, the integrity of chronological sequentiality is upheld but coexistent with cyclic repetitiveness. A recurrent leitmotif is the phrase, "to go is to return." For the reader, the experience of progressive reading is simultaneously a return, a continual return to and modification of what was. Each new change necessitates new endings and new beginnings. The result is ever different; the process is ever the same. Thus, being and becoming are not paradoxical opposites but one unity in the realm of human experience.

For Le Guin, the force of sequentiality and causality is directly related to questions of ethics and human responsibility because the future is driven by actions in the present, and the present bears the weight of all the past. Therefore, both future and past converge in the now with human consciousness and responsibility. Dr. Haber, the faustian psychiatric dream specialist, learns how to manipulate George's dreams to alter reality for what he believes to be the betterment of mankind. In order to accomplish these ends and also to gain more and more power for himself, he hypnotizes George and implants suggestions for his dreams. But he has no control over how George's unconscious will interprets and responds to the suggestion. For example, he wants George to solve the race problem, and George does, in a very primal and direct manner—he dreams everyone gray. The illogic of the dream reality pops into waking reality and becomes logical, commonplace, ordinary. Everything, even the most bizarre, fits.

Eventually, however, as the changes occur more and more frequently, George and the reader begin to feel the weight of a reality that has lost its equilibrium. This culminates in a scene where dream and reality merge into a nightmarish dissolution of all space and time, the chaos of atemporality. George enters the chaos and restores balance to the universe. On the story level, Haber has developed a method to imitate the reality-changing dream patterns of George's mind, but his attempt at effective dreaming results in chaos. George selflessly fights against the chaos to reach the dream augmentor and shut it off.

For the reader, the experience of dissolution begins gradually as image follows image with ever-loosening connections and space begins to merge with time. The sequence of George's actions provides the only sense of stability in a world that is falling apart:

The car swung wild in the abyss, between the unforming city and the form-less sky.

"Nothing seems to go quite right today," said a woman farther back in the car, in a loud, quivering voice.

The light of the eruption was terrible and gorgeous. Its huge, material, geological vigor was reassuring, compared to the hollow area that now lay ahead of the car, at the upper end of the line.

The presentiment which had seized Heather as she looked down from the jade sky was now a presence. It was there. It was an area, or perhaps a time period, of a sort of emptiness. It was the presence of absence: an unquantifiable entity without qualities, into which all things fell and from which nothing came forth. . . . He walked forward, while his eyes informed him that he walked on mist, on mud, on decayed corpses, on innumerable tiny toads. It was very cold, yet there was a smell of hot metal and burning hair or flesh. He crossed the lobby; gold letters from the aphorism around the dome leapt about him momentarily, MAN MANKIND M N A A A. The A's tried to trip his feet. . . .

Up on the top story, the floor was ice. It was about a finger's width thick, and quite clear. Through it could be seen the stars of the Southern Hemisphere. Orr stepped out onto it and all the stars rang loud and false, like cracked bells. The foul smell was much worse, making him gag. He went forward, holding out his hand. The panel of the door of Haber's office was there to meet it; he could not see it but he touched it. A wolf howled. The lava moved toward the city [p. 166].

In this passage the tension builds from the interweaving of two contradictory temporal moods: one generated by unrelated images in a fragmented sequence and one resulting from the progressive movement of George, who struggles against the widening chaos. Human consciousness of the highest order pulls against the threat of total annihilation. After George enters the "eye of the nightmare" and turns off the augmentor, the narrative returns to a unified linear progression of events. A new reality, a new time begins, different, but still the same. Out of chaos, the world is restored. Out of nonbeing, space and time separate to actualize creation from destruction.

At one point in the novel Haber says to George, "Life—evolution—the whole universe of spacetime, matterenergy—existence itself—is essentially change." The novel intensifies our awareness of existence as change by forcing the mind into the process of change over and over again. But, as George replies, "That is one aspect of it. . . . The other is stillness" (p. 135). In the character and perspective of George we have this stillness, a point of stability where becoming and being, creation and duration are one. Even though he does not recognize it himself until the end, the reader identifies him as "the still point of the turning world." Despite all change, George is constant. His point of view is certain in the total relativity of space and time around him. All temporal continuities converge with him at the center. Unlike Haber who tries to stand outside of time and manipulate it, George realizes that, "We're in the world, not against it" (p. 136). Just let it be. By being in the world, we affect change in it. He says, "I walk on the ground and the ground's walked on by me, I breathe the air and change it, I am entirely interconnected with the world" (p. 150). The process of self and world interacting and changing in time is dynamic, creative; it is life itself. But change alone is meaningless without continuity and the promise of endurance. George is free of Haber's influence and the fear of change when he accepts the freedom and the responsibility to work within the flow of time, making choices, entering into commitments which bind together past, present, and future into a unified whole.

Each of the works we have examined uses the moving present of the mind in time, the linear temporality of the reading process to generate various experiences or feelings of temporality in the mind. Basho's haiku jolts the mind into overcoming the sequentiality of language and of time itself to experience a moment in which all is simultaneous. Yet the very temporality of the literary form and the process of making connections between the elements as they appear in the consciousness of the reader are the means by which this experience is realized. The process *is* the experience. The unfolding of the text is its unity. Kafka's work, on the other hand, forces the mind again and again into frustrating contradiction and temporal incongruities. The apparent linear progression of the narrative form is an illusion. The invitation to use intellect and causal logic to connect the sequence of events is undermined and rendered useless. The build-up of his dreamlike realities generates an increasingly uneasy experience of disruption at the core of things. In haiku the moving present, the memory of the past, and the anticipation of the future function together in unity. In Kafka's work they are all wrenched asunder and pull the mind in a confusing tangle. Le Guin's novel relies on the interaction of memory and anticipation in the moving present of the reader's mind to actualize the thought experiment: what if causality were reversible? What if reality were absolutely relative to the consciousness of the individual? What if dream and reality were not opposing states of being? We may be reminded of the Taoist anecdote about Chuang Tsu who dreamed he was a butterfly and then woke only to wonder if he were Chuang Tsu who had dreamed he was a butterfly or a butterfly dreaming he was a man. Le Guin manipulates our temporal experience but in such a way that apparent opposites of sequentiality and simultaneity, change and duration, form a whole with human consciousness at the center.

In the works of all three writers, the reader is drawn toward different kinds of temporal experience on a variety of levels. The affective impact of this experience not only supports the thematic "meaning," it is the meaning. The reader lives the tensions and the moods of each work and feels drawn again and again to ponder about, to shudder at, to delight in this thing called time.

References

Blyth, R. H. (1964),, A History of Haiku. Hokuseido. .

Canning, P. (1984), Kafka's hierogram: The trauma of the "Landarzt." Germ. Quart., 57/2:197–212.

Cohn, D. (1968), Kafka's eternal present: Narrative tense in "Ein Landarzt" and other first-person stories. PMLA, 83:144–150.

Eliot, T. S. (1943), Four Quartets. New York: Harcourt Brace Jovanovich, 1971.

Fish, S. (1980), Is There a Text in This Class: The Authority of Interpretive Communities. Cambridge, MA: Harvard University Press.

Fraser, J. T. (1978), Time as Conflict: A Scientific and Humanistic Study. Basel: Birkhauser.

———— (1981), Temporal levels and reality testing. Internat. J. Psycho-Anal., 62/3:3–26.

Frye, L. O. (1983), Reconstructions: Kafka's "Ein Landarzt." Colloquia Germanica, 16/4:321–336.

Henderson, H. G. (1958), An Introduction to Haiku. Garden City, NY: Doubleday.

Iser, W. (1974), The Implied Reader: Patterns of Communication in Prose Fiction From Bunyan to Beckett. Baltimore: Johns Hopkins University Press.

———— (1978), The Act of Reading: A Theory of Aesthetic Response. Baltimore: Johns Hopkins University Press.

Kafka, F. (1919), The country doctor. In: The Complete Stories, ed. N. N. Glatzer. New York: Schocken, 1971

———— (1931), A common confusion. In: The Complete Stories, ed. N. N. Glatzer. New York: Schocken, 1971.

———— (1936), Give it up. In: The Complete Stories, ed. N. N. Glatzer. New York: Schocken, 1971.

Le Guin, U. K. (1973), The Lathe of Heaven. New York: Avon.

Pilarcik, M. A. (1981), Beginnings and endings: Hesse and Kawabata. In: The Study of Time, Vol. IV, eds. J. T. Fraser, N. Lawrence, & D. Park. New York: Springer.

Politzer, H. (1966), Franz Kafka: Parable and Paradox. Ithaca, NY: Cornell University Press.

Poulet, G. (1969), Phenomenology of reading. New Lit. Hist. 1:53–68.

Rosenblatt, L. (1964), The poem as event. College English, 1/26:123–127.

———— (1978), The Reader, the Text, the Poem: The Transactional Theory of the Literary Work. Carbondale, IL: Southern Illinois University Press.

Sato, H. (1983), One Hundred Frogs: From Renga to Haiku to English. New York: Weatherhill.

Sturgeon, T. (1972), Of Mars and reality. Nat. Rev., February:106–107.

Torgovnick, M. (1981), Closure and the shape of fictions: The example of "Women in Love." In: The Study of Time, Vol. IV., eds. J. T. Fraser, N. Lawrence, & D. Park. New York: Springer.

Yasuda, K. (1957), The Japanese Haiku. Rutland: Tuttle.

Yamamoto, K. (1952), Junsui Haiku. Tokyo: Sogen-Sha.

VI

Philosophy and Natural Philosophy

15

Res Cogitans: The Time of Mind

Charles M. Sherover

Abstract By common consent, most modern thought has ensued from the work of René Descartes. In order to provide a philosophic foundation for the new sciences, Descartes developed a metaphysics which provided for only two kinds of substance in the world: (1) body or physical existence and (2) mind or mental existence. As he posed it, the philosophic task was to explain how the latter could attain some degrees of certain systematic knowledge of the former.

Descartes had described physical or corporeal things as essentially spatial, and knowable to the extent that they are mathematically describable. But, aside from entitling mind as *res cogitans* (= thinking entity), he left its essential nature in the dark. The object of this chapter is not to do an analysis of the Cartesian work, but rather to take his sole positive description of mind as the point of departure for rethinking the nature of mind.

The argument here is that we only experience our own minds in that thinking-activity which constitutes experience—and that our experiences of mind are thereby pervasively temporal: in its own activity, in its references to objects of thought, and its grounding presupposition of the continuity of the self that persists through and unifies the flow of its pervasively temporal experience. Rather than analyze the Cartesian legacy, the chapter seeks to execute what in the "jargon" of existential phenomenology would be termed a *retrieve* of the Cartesian problematic; that is, attempt to develop the philosophic possibilities which it presents to us in its description of mind but which it itself neglected or failed to exhibit.

The conclusion is that the concept of mind as "thinking entity" (*res cogitans*) properly suggests the examination of mind solely in that nonspatial set of terms, those of time-and-temporality, a concept which Descartes, himself, did not seem to understand. As such the chapter utilizes the Leibnizian and Kantian critiques of this phase of Cartesianism and implicitly presumes the analysis of temporality which Heidegger advanced and which the chapter seeks to develop in terms of our experience of mind.

Modern philosophy, it is generally agreed, takes its point of departure from the work of René Descartes (1596–1650). Whatever else this genesis provided, at least we can say that it made the conception of the thinking mind central to all subsequent philosophical thought.

The first known certainty, Descartes insisted, is not the nature of the physical things perceived as external to consciousness; rather, it is the thinking mind itself in which consciousness of such perceptions arise. Systematic introspection becomes the new path to scientific or systematically grounded knowledge. Its function is to ground cognitive thinking in the thinking mind—which lodges all true knowledge and must certify all knowledge-claims; the nature of the individual thinking mind thus sets out, in advance of any specific use, the grounds of legitimacy for the admission of knowledge-claims and thereby the legitimatization of certainty for those knowledge-claims it deems to be properly admitted. Descartes' *"Cogito ergo sum"* ("I think therefore I am") becomes the first principle of modern thought, the necessary presupposition of any individual cognitive thinking, and the irreducible evidence of individual existence.[1]

Descartes' fundamental concern, however, was not to elucidate the nature of mind as such but rather to validate Galileo's new mathematical physics; to do this he needed to justify the applications of the mathematical concepts he found as innate qualities of the thinking mind to the objects comprising the experienced physical world.[2] In order to ground this, he posited the thesis that the world is composed of two radically different kinds of substances: of physical things that occupy space and are thereby subject to the mathematical descriptions of size, weight, resistance, and place—later enumerated as the "primary qualities" characteristic of space-occupying entities with which science deals—and of "mental substance," essentially describable by the *negations* of these spatializing predicates.

But what kind of an entity is this "mental substance"? Mind, as an existent functioning entity, is only described by negations of the predicates rightfully attributable to physical objects.[3] Although mind is portrayed as a kind of "substance," the only *positive* description we have of mind is that it is *res cogitans*, the thinking entity, a nonspatial substance characterizable only by the *activity* of think*ing*.[4] This formulation bequeathed to what followed the notion of mind as

[1]This, I think, still stands even as we accept the thesis (implied by both Leibniz and Rousseau and explicitly developed by Royce and Heidegger) that the individuality of thought presupposes the sociality of human be-ing; i.e., the "I" always and necessarily presupposes the "we." To demonstrate this thesis together with its basic compatibility with the Cartesian principle, would, however, in the context of this chapter, take us far afield.

[2]Note Descartes' statement at the end of his Fifth Meditation together with the opening of the Sixth, which limits our knowledge of "material things . . . [only] in so far as they are considered as the objects of pure mathematics" in *Works*, Vol. I, p. 185. *N.B.:* This proposal, that we can only understand the world of things to the extent that they meet (mathematical) ideas within our own minds which we necessarily use to think about them, does indeed foreshadow Kant's Copernican Revolution: we can only come to know things insofar as they can appear to and meet the categorial structuring of our human modes of sensibility and understanding.

[3]In view of the subsequent description of God as a transcendent mind beyond our understanding, we may well ask whether this is not but a secularization of the medieval doctrine of "negative theology."

[4]Important to note is the comprehensive nature of thinking as encompassing virtually any act of consciousness as one that ". . . doubts, affirms, denies, that knows a few things, that is ignorant of many, that wishes, that desires, that also imagines and perceives." See "Meditation on the First Philosophy" in *Works*, Vol. I, p. 157.

grounding all experience—but, aside from specifying it as our source of mathematics, its nonspatiality and its nature *qua* activity, Descartes left its inherent nature in the dark.

Some Ensuing Questions

Subsequent philosophic thought carried these general theses in diverse directions. Some philosophers have taken as seriously fundamental the stated Cartesian thesis that mind and body are actually two radically different kinds of substances: body as inherently spatial and mind as inherently nonspatial. Pursuing this they are enveloped by the question of *what kind of thing* mind, as a nonspatial entity, might really be. And they have been concerned to pursue some of the questions this twofold ontology suggests: If mind and body are so different, how can one communicate with the other? Can mind justifiably be reduced to body? Is the mind then merely an epiphenomenon of the brain? And if Descartes is correctly read as having suggested that we are each enclosed within our own individual thinking, how can we truly face the question, not so much of "other bodies," but of "other minds"?

I want to propose an alternate route from this Cartesian genesis because I think it one more fruitful to explore. It seems to offer greater developmental possibilities and to suggest more sophisticated responses to that kind of inquiry.

I am rather entranced by at least this somewhat paradoxical consideration: Descartes (1) refused to reduce mind to the mathematically describable spatial; (2) and he only described mind by what it does: as *"res cogitans,"* as "the thinking entity." But, (3) this is an activity description and any activity requires a real temporal spread of continuity so that it may function; (4) yet Descartes attributed neither temporal predicates nor continuity to mind. (5) Indeed, he seems to have had problems with the very idea of temporal continuity, epitomized in his conviction that each moment is a somehow irreducible real self-enclosed atomic point in the structure of this universe, and is devoid of any sustaining continuity with any other moment.[5] Mind is described only as an activity; yet no temporal predicates are ascribed to it! If mind is knowable by us only as the "think*ing* entity," whatever else mind might conceivably be, it can only be understood by us as pervasively temporal.

Consequent Philosophic Development

It was not long before this kind of thought seems to have been taken up in somewhat different ways by both Locke (1632–1704) and Leibniz (1646–1716).

[5]See *Works*, "Meditations," III, Vol. I, p. 168; "Arguments Demonstrating the Existence of God (Addendum to Reply to Objection II)," Axiom II, Vol. II, p. 56; and "Reply to Objections, V," Vol. II, p. 219, Sec. 9.

Despite their historic controversy—which sets out the still-contemporary divide in all subsequent Western philosophy—they each effectively set aside the notion of "substance" as the prime characteristic of mind; for both insisted that mind is known by us as a temporal activity.

John Locke, in his famous *Essay Concerning the Human Understanding* (1690), pointed out that even the most systematic introspection presents not the thinking mind itself, but rather a "train of ideas" which succeed each other in consciousness (II, XIV, p. 3). Each idea as momentary object of thought is transitional, progressively disappearing into the past as it is pushed on by a new idea (or altered object of mental focus) seemingly coming into present attention out of the future.

Leibniz, in his *New Essays*, epitomized and carried forward this view of mind as a dynamic processing of ideas when he explicitly argued that "to think and to be thinking are the same" (Leibniz, 1949, IV, vii, p. 7). This conscious thinking, he had said, is "not only of my thinking self, but also of my thoughts, and it is no more certain that I think than that I think this or that" (Leibniz, 1965, p. 25). (This consideration clearly suggests itself as pointing to a phenomenological notion of intentionality.) Just because these ideas, which are the content of my thinking activity, are immediately reflective of the world within which I find myself, Leibniz transcended the Cartesian problem of an isolated mind; for mind now is not only in cognitive contact with the world; it discovers its own inherent structure only as it functions by thinking about the things in the world reflected within its thinking activity.

This intellectual development reached its full expression in Immanuel Kant's *Critique of Pure Reason* (1781, 1787) which, to this point, argued that time, as the form of consciousness—which Kant (1724–1804), following Augustine (354–430) in *On the Free Choice of the Will* (1984), called "inner sense"—is the form of all of our thinking. This, he went on to point out, means that our cognitive thinking must be organized by time-structured categories, that it can only generate knowledge, as distinct from conjecture and speculation, when it is concerned with time-bound sensory presentations (Kant, 1781, 1787, A146-7=B186-7).

This Kantian thesis brings us into main currents of modern philosophic thought. Taken up by prime movements of nineteenth-century thinking, it has molded prime schools of contemporary thought. American contextualistic pragmatism, announced by Charles Peirce and William James, made the pervasive temporality of all thinking its central point of departure; Josiah Royce, in terms of philosophic idealism, and John Dewey, in terms of philosophic naturalism, gave it further development by carrying it forward into every area of intellectual consideration. In our own local epoch, the centrality of time in human thinking, and thereby the essential temporality of mind, was underscored by Henri Bergson's *Time and Free Will* (1889) and Edmund Husserl's *The Phenomenology of Inner Time Consciousness* (1905–1910); their thrust has been most forcefully developed in the work of existential phenomenologists, particularly Martin Heidegger's *Being and Time* (1927) and Maurice Merleau-Ponty's *The Phenomenology of Perception* (1962).

The Historicity of Our Thinking

This historical overview might be regarded by some as perhaps interesting but essentially extraneous. I do not think so. For I am aware of no thinking that starts from "scratch" and transpires in an ideational vacuum. Any act of thought starts by taking up a given ideational heritage. Any act of thought arises in response to questions we have been asked, experiences we have undergone, and the ensuing hopes and fears we have set out to realize or avoid. Any act of thought incorporates into its central structure a set of originally unexamined valuational judgments regarding what is important or unimportant, and proceeds by a logic which it accepts as legitimate.

Your thinking and mine both arise in this present historic context of ideational social development. Our thinking picks up some inherited theses concerning both doctrine and method we accept as "obviously true," calls some of the ideas handed to us as questionable, and openly challenges others. The cultural context in which each finds personhood is essentially historical. Often taken as something of an allegedly temporally transcendent "God's-eye view," any act of thinking is nevertheless culturally bound: its present formulations are initially framed in accord with the particular parochial culture within which it finds itself and which is but one contemporary distilled version of an entire civilization's current legacy. The landmarks of a culture's development, can be pinpointed, in an oversimplified way, as I have just done in terms of one theme, by pointing to key thinkers along the way. However, we need to recognize, if not always take the time to acknowledge, that each of these landmark thinkers was himself responding to an ideational complex of ideas which was itself developing while he was encountering them and which would not have been recognized at any stage of development in precisely the same form by his grandparents.

The content of any individual's thinking is thus a present individual response to his own historic inheritance. This inheritance provides the parameters we each use to guide our own thinking: the valuational standards and distinctions we invoke, often without question or conscious awareness; the questions which we raise in the face of proffered answers; the problematics we see in what members of an earlier generation may have taken as assured doctrine. Royce once suggested that each of us is born with an overwhelming debt, a debt to the entire historically still developing civilization which has received us into its currently expressed localized form. All thinking, I think we will all agree, is contextually bound. But the context is first of all a dynamically historic one, which is to say that it is the temporal context of our inherently historical sociality.

Any individual thinking is thus historically situated. The immediate context within which it finds itself is a complex of individual interactions which have arisen out of a developing history that presents itself as a contemporary environment—our understandings of sociological and political and economic structures, family mores, and religious or ideological allegiances, many of which are never articulated but nevertheless heedlessly taken for granted. Its historicity is thus not only grandly political. For the family setting within which each individual develops is itself a particular historical ongoing process within the larger continuously developing social world.

Our conscious thinking utilizes a language, let us not forget, as an instrument of thought. And this too, historically developed, imposes a set of canons and procedures and presuppositions which only come into view when deliberately compared with other languages, particularly those of radically different cultures. Any individual's thinking activity thus reflects the historical milieu which is continually nourishing him even while he is developing his own distinctive judgmental outlook from it. No individual's thinking can then be "objective" beyond those culturally induced categories which are transcendentally operative in his thinking.[6] No matter how dispassionate one may seek to be, one can but express a particular kind of outlook on the historically developing world within which he finds himself functioning.

As social beings, any individual thinking thus necessarily incorporates particularized time predicates, as particular differentiating descriptions of the historically developed social milieu out of which whatever individuality we each manifest has arisen. Because each individuality is idiosyncratically reflective of the nourishing culture, it is historical, thereby temporal, from the outset.

Time and Thought

As we progressively narrow the societal area of consideration, we finally come to the individual who reflects, even in his most strident individuality, the entire historical ethos which, in his own biographical development, he had absorbed into himself—and of which he must always remain an, even if critical, expression. However important this sociohistorical ethos may be in structuring the process and context of individual thinking, however pervasively our thoughts may be socially stimulated and socially directed, thinking ultimately is an individual matter. For each individual finds his own bond with, and differentiation from, his social context, in his own self, in his perception of his own identity and individuality, in his own evaluative outlook and his relations with the other people and things that comprise the world in which he lives his own activity of being within which he develops his own perspectival understanding of his world—the content that he attaches to *his* verb "I think."

For, let us not forget, as Leibniz pointed out, that one cannot merely think. Any act of thinking is not only in a context of thought; it is *about* something—an idea, representation, desire, or thing—that is the object of the verb that itself but names an activity of being. Any act of thinking is other-directed. My thinking is the activity of relating myself conceptually to whatever it is that I am thinking

---

[6]The term *transcendentally* is meant in a generally Kantian sense—as those interpretive categories which are employed, even when unexplicated but implicitly present while unwittingly presumed, in one's particular thinkings—as founding the possibility of the particular thoughts one develops to understand his own perceptions.

about. "I think" always means "I am thinking some-thing"; "I am thinking x—chair, enemy, friend." This is clearly recognized by each one of us: when you confront me sitting like Rodin's statue, buried in thought, you ask, "what are you doing?"; when I reply, "I am thinking," your immediate response is: "but what are you thinking about?" One cannot think without reaching out from the act of thinking to the object of one's thought. Conceivably, one can think about the nature of thinking itself, as Aristotle's God was eternally supposed to be doing, but—even here, one is thinking about something other than one's immediate thinking self. The verb phrase "I think," like the verb "I eat" or "I want," has a transitive verb and requires an object, even if it may on occasion be reflexive. One cannot think without thinking about something, even if that something, as in the case of some mystics, is about the presumed nothingness of all being.

Whatever it is that one thinks about is itself time-bound, an event or happening that itself consumes duration—whether it be an idea demanding attention in consciousness or an event or durational entity in the world presumably beyond individual consciousness.

It is not only the object of thought that is inherently temporal. Regardless of what one is thinking about, the activity of thinking itself "takes time." It may be momentary or leisurely, but no matter how fleeting, it incorporates duration. Thinking does not only occur in a historic setting; it takes up into itself historically developed parameters of thought, and refers to conceptual objects that themselves incorporate temporal predicates. Thinking itself necessarily consumes time. It incorporates time into itself. It is spread over those so-called moments—seconds, minutes, or hours—we use as a convenient externalizing metric for comparing experiential durations with each other.

Any specific act of thinking transpires in culturally developed, thereby historical, situations, thus incorporating and thereby expressing a temporally framed orientation. It refers to ideas, notions, or representations that are themselves durationally constituted as the objects of its referential intentions. And it does all this, as a process or activity, by itself utilizing spreads of time in order to do so.

The Temporal Structure of Our Thinking

Some of these observations do require development, but I would find it strange to find them regarded as particularly controversial. However, let us now proceed one step more—to a brief consideration of just *how* our thinking uses time for its own process of activity. What I want to suggest is that no kind of conscious thinking is devoid of temporal constituents, that all types of conscious thinking embody the integration of the thinker's past, present, and future into the thinker's outlook, and that this integration usually functions under guidance by what, in the standpoint of the present, is conceived as future.

Conscious thought may, I think, be roughly discriminated into at least three kinds, each with temporal characteristics peculiar to itself—while yet embracing crucial similarities with the others:

1. When I just stop, perhaps in awe or wonder, to gaze at a beautiful sunset or a beautiful painting, I am not usually conscious of the continuing pulse of time. I am, as it were, caught up in a seemingly temporally seamless duration of esthetic response or religious awe. My attention is fully consumed by the object that commands my gaze.

But is this truly a nontemporal experience—as many estheticians and mystics have often claimed? Doesn't my present experiential moment connect what I see with what I have seen before? Doesn't it *press* to maintain its continuing present against distraction from future interruption? And if, while enthralled, I am conscious that this experience must itself terminate, isn't my continuing entrance-ment itself something of a protest against its impending presently future ending? Most crucially, doesn't the meaning I read into this presently consuming presentation represent my projected integration of past experiences which I immediately find either similar or dissimilar, the present activation of my esthetic education, the esthetic norms I have been taught to value, and my hope for its continuity into at least the immediate future? And, when the esthetic experience—which must be durational in order to be experiential—has itself ended, don't I note its termination and yet carry the memory of the experience with me? Don't I regard the experience itself as a discontinuity within the continuum of that experiential flow in which I find my own being? Esthetic, as mystic, experience, it would seem, is an experience of a durational present which is imbued with meaning by the past I bring with me and the future I either anticipate or fear (Gadamer, 1975, pp. 107ff).

2. When I am faced with a problematic situation, a task to be undertaken, a conflict of desire or obligation to be resolved, I face what we generally term a practical problem. I face myself facing the question "what should I do?" That "should" directly refers to the future, to what is not yet but is shortly to be judged within the area of feasibility. The past we say is over and done with and the immediate present is what is now actual—and neither is subject to any decision I might feel called upon to make. But a problematic situation defines itself in the guise of the future presenting itself to me as somewhat open, as presenting a finite range of alternate possibilities. Between these possibilities which I judge as viable, I must select a course of action bridging the temporal interim between the immediately present moment and the state of resolution which I seek to achieve. Any action that is not a mere reflexive reaction is a deliberative practical action that is responsive to, and thereby guided by, a present vision of the possibilities for the future, for the not-yet but the yet-may-be. In forming my decision, I bring into thought those aspects of the past which seem pertinent to the problematic I see before me. But their selection, out of all my uncountably myriad past experiences, is of those few that strike me as presently germane to my task at hand.

Practical action situations most clearly present a future-orientation. They project one out of the actuality of one's present and past into what is, in the most literal sense, presently unknown and unknowable. They are guided by a judgment of possibility which may be secure or merely hopeful in its outlook. But it is this reading of possibly alternative future actualities that brings me to commit myself to one specific course of action. If this were all, it would be enough to support the argument that all thinking is inherently temporal.

But something more is crucial. The meaning which I read into my present problematic situation does not come out of the past and is certainly not dictated by the immediate present. For I read my present as itself closing off some possibilities I might like to pursue and as opening up those other possible courses of action which I regard as viable. My interpretation of any problematic situation, the very way in which I define it to myself, is by means of those possibilities for the "henceforth" which, for whatever reasons, I see it as offering. My present vision of possibility is not only an invitation which calls me to action. The problematic meaning I see in my present situation is itself essentially structured by these conceived possibilities— encapsuled in the question "what should I do about this?"

Any situation which I comprehend as demanding a response on my part is imbued by me with the meaning I interpret it to embody— not by an ambiguously indefinite past and not by the immediate present, but by those specific alternative possibilities of futurity I see it as commanding me to decide between.

3. At first blush, the cognitive situation might seem somewhat different. Like the esthetic, it is focused on the content of the present presentation; for, in contrast to the practical, it is focused on the content of the present presentation; it is focused *not* on "what *I* should do?" but on the content of my awareness. It calls for a suspension of the personal, a call to depersonalized acknowledgment of the cold truth of factuality before me. But, let me suggest, it cannot avoid the strictures of practical reason just because it presents any momentary choice before me by means of the question "if anything, what should I do about it?" My answer to this question structures the meaning I read into the presented situation. Does the panorama I look at call for a response by me? If so what kind of response should it be? My answers to these questions delineate the meaning I read into the situation and structure the way I interpret and thereby understand what I am seeing. This is to say that no conscious perception of mine is devoid of judgmental factors I bring into it. No perception of mine is devoid of my projection of my subjective outlook. No perception of mine is then devoid of questioning in terms of possibilities of the future.

As epitomized in the popular picture of scientific objectivity, science eschews all subjectivity and asks us merely to recognize "the facts." Which facts? Not the myriad details in the panorama before us, but those which are selectively judged to be relevant or important. Judged by what criteria? Only by invoking evaluative norms can I regard some aspects of the panorama as trivial, recognize others as important, and respond accordingly. But this is an interpretive procedure; I am not merely reporting the myriad details before me; I am selecting some for interpretive attention and read them in terms of the meaning I see them as bearing according to canons I accept; without this deliberate intrusion by me as the committed investigator into the situation of the factualities of what I am trying to discover, I could discover nothing. We are asked to recognize the actual facts of the case, not by a passive unresponsive gaze, but by an active procedure of deliberative investigation. One need but consider that a physicist, chemist, biologist, and poet, looking at the same oak tree in the yard will provide radically different descriptions of their common object of attention—just because each description is a response to the differently framed specific questions each chooses to ask. Or I may set out to learn "the facts" of the case by an attentive concentration on learning—which is to say, by an active course of temporal commitment into what, in the standpoint of the momentary present, is a choice of possibilities not yet actualized.

And again, one should ask about the motivation for undertaking such a course of action. Is it not to attain a knowledge that one does not yet have, to attain or avoid a possibility of a future state of accomplishments, reward, or chastisement? Is the activity of the most dispassionate student or investigator comprehensible without cognizance of the goal he foresees? This is to ask for the evaluative criteria to which he has committed himself as the justification of the procedure he chooses to follow. One of the more thoughtless clichés of our time is that the scientific endeavor is value-free. Without a high evaluation of depersonalized truth, without the approbative evaluation of specified judgmental criteria, indeed, without an existential commitment to very specific investigatory procedures, modern scientific objectivity could not be.

And let us note, as something of a footnote, that the procedure of any investigation or of any learning procedure, invariably involves the investigator's handling and manipulation of aspects of the physical environment—be it a microscope, a pencil and paper, a piece of chalk on a blackboard—and thereby of practical skills in deliberately manipulating selected components of the physical environment, for a purpose. The entire procedure of following out a commitment to pursuing a goal constitutes itself by a series of smaller steps: to use that test tube I must first walk over to get it; to insure that the experiment is not besmirched by unwanted input, I must first clean the test tube. As Dewey once pointed out, every course of action, which we first grandly sketch out as a set of intelligently chosen means to a desired end, is itself but a continuum of interim means and ends—each one, let us note, futurally oriented. And the end itself—learning the multiplication table, discovering the atomic structure of this pencil, cooking something to eat—each step in the necessary process is itself an interim goal that is yet a means to something later, while the possibility of the realization of which is the goal of the action—being able to use the multiplication table, comprehending the atomic structure of this pencil, actually cooking an edible meal—is not intrinsically treasured for itself but for some still further end, goal, or value even more temporally remote.

These three kinds of thinking are not only durational; each involves some kind of unification of memory-selection from the past, selective sensory awareness of the immediately actual present, and the anticipation of possible futurity. Each necessarily seeks to recollect only what is deemed relevant to the present task—by selective acts of memory-recall which but bring selective aspects of my past into my present awareness. Each takes its stance in the immediacy of the focused present presentation. Each interprets the meaning of what is presently seen as possibilities of continuance into the future or imperatives for action-commitments to possibility-realization in the future.[7]

This interpretive function of the human understanding—taking time, structured by time, oriented to temporally presented actualities and temporal possibilities—enables us to be ourselves as beings who operate into the future. For our primary mode of evaluative judgment is directed to what-may-yet-be but is-not-yet; our primary mode of evaluative judgment is directed to what appears to us as possibilities for development which are dependent on what we decide. This futural orientation of all human thinking allows us, indeed requires us, to project our own evaluative judgments into the "what-is-not-yet"; it requires us to project ourselves into the future, and to bring futurity into the constitution of the lived present. No action that is not commensurate with this description would appear to be experientially comprehensible. As Leibniz once said, we are like "little gods": by virtue of our interpretive judgments which determine all our responses and actions, we are creators, each in his own domain, of what is not yet but yet shall be. In the activity of thinking, we each project ourselves into the future that is now literally unknown and thereby make and form the oncoming future present that will yet be known.

The Essential Temporality of Mind

These phenomenological considerations do, I think, demonstrate the essentially temporal structure of human thinking. They show that any kind of thought integrates the three temporal modes of pastness, presence, and futurity into the interpretations of meaning seen as embodied in the living present; they also suggest that of the three, most kinds of conscious human thinking are primarily oriented to what-is-not-yet, to what-yet-can-be, to the possibilities of futurity which the present situation is judged to present as its crucial meaning.

All thinking, then, is not only a time-durational process. Thinking is not merely concerned with temporally defined objects—whether they be things in the world as such or thoughts in our thinking. The thinking process itself is the continual interpretive integration of the three temporal modes of the thinking activity that is the self; it provides the meanings that are developed in the commitments brought forth as imperatives for action. It is this continuing process of continually integrating the continuity of temporally framed and temporally structured experiencing that enables each to find his own selfhood in the continuity of the "I" who does the thinking.

Mind then appears to us as essentially temporal in every way that it manifests

---

[7]This meaning will differ as it involves moral or prudential judgment—but such differentiations, important as they are intrinsically, are not germane to the present discussion. For some further discussion of this, see Sherover (1975, pp. 215–230). For a discussion of some of the sociopolitical inferences to be drawn from this phenomenological description, see my "The Temporality of the Common Good: Futurity and Freedom" (1984, pp. 475–497).

its activity of being. Its activity is thinking which, as any process or activity, "takes time"; it is oriented to objects, whether events in the so-called "external world" or to ideas or notions that are the fleeting objects of thinking itself; in its thinking it but incorporates its continual synthesizing or integration of the temporal modes of pastness, presentness, and futurity, which essentially characterize every experiential awareness. Mind, as *res cogitans*, then appears to us as a temporally structured ideationalizing activity—revealing selfhood to the self while it is continually incorporating temporal predicates in every aspect that it is presenting for our discernment.

Some Philosophic Implications

I began with Descartes who is generally credited as having provided the innovative force—almost five hundred years ago—that impelled the development of a new way of philosophic thinking, the thinking out of which our contemporary views have evolved.

What has been repudiated in the preceding discussions is not only the Cartesian notion of mind as a self-enclosed entity, but also the claim of the Platonistic thesis that mind finds truth only by escaping temporality.[8] The notion of timelessness is not experiential; it can be reconciled with neither the temporal objects of experience nor the temporal structure of thinking itself. We may, indeed, legitimately claim to know truths that stretch across the expanse of human temporality and are thus for us "transtemporal"—but we know of no way to experience truths which relate neither to the temporally constituted objects that provide the content of our experience nor to the temporal constitution of the experiencing process itself; we have no way of relating to truths which are incapable of temporal instantiation and thereby of temporal predicates. The laws of arithmetic, for example, are deemed by us to be applicable to every "moment" of experiential time; thereby, they are to us transtemporal as they are continuously validated by temporal predicates and find their meaning for us revealed in every temporal moment in which they are tested. Like any other "necessary truth" that may find instantiation throughout our particular experiences, they are (transcendentally) presupposed by us as universally necessary conditions of *our* experiences; nothing, however, is thereby said about their ontological status beyond the constitution of our possible experiences (Kant, 1781, 1787, A218 = B265–A225 = B273). Whatever an allegedly timeless truth may be in itself, it is, as such, only available *to us* as a possible object of temporally constituted experience, and is thereby, within the range of possible human experience, inherently time-bound.

Insofar as any allegedly transcendent truth-claim needs to be tested by us

---

[8]The continuing allure of Platonism may well be, as Heidegger once suggested, a sign of a continuing attempt to escape from temporality. On any kind of Platonism, it is hard to see how one can explain why or how a completely atemporal realm of true "reality" could or should bring a temporal order into being. Even Plato could only do so by invoking a demiurgic myth.

within a temporal context, we have no experiential basis for claiming an insight into any truths to which time-predicates are irrelevant. What has then been affirmed is the thesis that any truth within the possible human ken, as the thinking that develops it, is inherently temporal in every aspect of its knowable being.

I have side-stepped Descartes' thesis that mind is some kind of nonmaterial substance, but I have explored the meaning of his only positive description of mind: that whatever it may conceivably be in itself, it only manifests itself to us as a thinking-activity (*res cogitans*). In propounding this thesis, Descartes had seen, I think, further than his own historically time-bound thought could carry him; indeed, he has provided us with a way of thinking about the nature of mind that stretches beyond his own historically bound finite vision. In a nutshell, he has provided us with the most succinct description of mind we have; when we explore its meaning we come to focus not on what mind "is" but on what it "does," on the ways it manifests its presence to us in everything we do and think. Only in its continuing particularized functioning do we find awareness of the biographical particularities that constitute our own individual being.

Were it now possible to continue this discussion, I would like to develop some of the wider philosophical implications of what I think has been established. For philosophy, as I see it, does not look to any final answers. Rather it seeks out the further questions which any resolution of earlier inquiries opens up for further exploration.

In this vein, let me conclude by suggesting that if this general argument is deemed to be experientially valid, a number of questions immediately present themselves for further discussion:

1. The activity of mind appears to be essentially a continuity of interpretational activity that is temporally structured; if so, is it really legitimate to understand mind in any mechanistic sense of efficacious causal determinism? For such causality reduces the present to the past—while this phenomenological description sees a mind as an activity that is rooted, not in its past which it only *uses* for its own discriminative evaluations, but in its future *qua* conceived possibilities which it necessarily faces as somewhat open.

The modern claim of universal legitimacy for explanation by means of efficacious causality is generally traced back to Descartes. But Descartes himself never universalized such explanation; he demanded it merely for explanation of the things of nature, physical things that are spatially describable.

It was not long before Leibniz denominated such efficacious causal explanation as but one species of the Principle of Sufficient Reason, reason sufficient for explanation of an event. Entirely appropriate for the study of physical nature, it hardly begins to explain the reasoning activity of mind—which is more generally explicable in terms of purposes and motives which, in contrast, do not seek to reduce the present to the past, but look to visions of the future as a means of explaining present deliberation and action.

2. If so, this temporalist conception of mind provides a defense of the notion

of evaluative or interpretive freedom as crucial to the explanation of all mental activity.

Indeed, in his Fourth Meditation, Descartes himself suggested this by arguing that our differentiation of truth from error depends upon the ability or capacity of the mind to freely suspend final judgment until it has rightfully judged that all the relevant evidence was in. Descartes was apparently careful to maintain the distinction between: (1) the mechanism he saw as tied to the spatiality of the physical, and (2) the freedom of judgment he reserved to *res cogitans*. Unfortunately, much of modern philosophy has focused on the mechanism and made it more pervasive than even Descartes ever appears to have suggested; it has thus, without any explicit justification, resolutely come to read the functioning of mind in terms that Descartes himself had reserved to what he called "body."

The Leibnizian protest against this was taken up and developed by Kant, who is the first modern philosopher to have faced this distinction with utmost seriousness. His own adaptation of the Leibnizian distinction between the phenomenal (as the physical order of sequential mechanism) and the noumenal (as the governing reality of rational freedom) argues that they are but distinctive *aspects* of the one real world—in which both the necessitarian determinism of physical matter and the freedom intrinsic to the rationality of mind inhere. For the world as one whole *includes* in its unitary wholeness our own thoughts and acts initiated by our own minds' rationally grounded interpretive decisions about what is yet to be done.

However one may find this Kantian development, the portrayal of mental activity as a continuity of interpretive integration—of futural possibilities (which are necessarily understood as presently open) with consequently selected aspects of present perception and selected retrieval of the past—reopens the contemporary discussion of freedom-and-determination on a new level; that discussion has been largely conducted by presuming the *universal* legitimacy of the model of efficacious causality, a conceptual model which this present discussion urges is severely limited in justifiable application.

3. If this interpretive perspective has any merit, then another area of speculative thought is opened up: for if mind is not only continuously temporal, but is largely oriented to futural possibilities—rather than being chained to determination by the past or pinned onto the fleeting actuality of the present moment—then our growing knowledge and directive control of the things constituting the world presumes the possibility of a free temporally structured mind to attain true degrees of understanding of the world itself.

One of the most ancient of Western philosophic theses is that "like knows like." If so, then mind can only attain any understandings of the world to the extent that the world as it appears to human consciousness is somehow accordant with the structures and categories of the knowing mind itself. The world as such, at least insofar as we may come to understand it, cannot then be a completely determined system, every detail of which was inherently set out on the "first day of creation." If the human mind, *as an activity within the world*, is a continuity of interpretive thinking that continually operates on principles of temporally open possibilities which are subject to somewhat free interpretive decisions of rational intelligence, then we can begin to understand how the human mind can indeed attain degrees of insight into the world of nature. For, if this human mind's intrusions into physical processes can indeed redirect aspects of their development, then at least some particulars of the world's developmental being are still open, and the limits of free human decisions define temporally operable limits of temporally bound real alternative possibilities.

4. Although I have gone beyond Descartes—bypassing his notion of mind as a kind of "thing" and postulating the essential temporality and thereby the essential continuity of the thinking mind—this consideration takes us right back to the original Cartesian postulate, if with a difference. Mind is somehow different from the physicality of the things of the world we seek to understand, but we can only understand the things of the world insofar as they correlate with conceptual categories found intrinsic to the thinking mind itself.

If mind is somehow a transtemporal continuity; if it uses time in its activity of thinking to seek comprehension of the temporally constituted objects which appear to its outlook by using temporal predicates for its understanding of their relationships to each other and to itself; then mind is a "thinking entity" that continually uses time, continually functions by means of temporal terms, and cannot find its own being except by means of the continuity of time. In short, mind must find temporality not only intrinsic to its own self but also intrinsic to any external intelligibility with which it can deal.

We may then face Descartes' opening query: "what" is mind? We find that we can only know it, as he originally declared, as the "thinking entity" (*res cogitans*), as the thinking activity in which each of us finds awareness of his own being. Whether we can attain any insight into *what it is* beyond *what and how it does* is a question which must still remain open.

5. However, this last speculation may go, whatever *kind* of thing an individual mind may inherently be—a question Kant had set aside as inherently unanswerable by us except as possibly revealed in the continuing experience of rational freedom—we do know that each of us only experiences his own mind, his own self, as a self-conscious being who is a socially rooted individual, and who is pervasively temporal while facing all the vicissitudes of being free. This inherent time-bound freedom of individual minds then becomes primordial.

This primordiality does suggest some important rethinking for the systematic study of the individual psyche. This primordiality also proposes some crucial theses for valuational priorities when theorizing about the moral obligations of citizens of organized societies—about the criteria for intelligent judgments concerning those policy decisions that are appropriate rational procedures for the political organizations in which every contemporary individual, as an activity of finite freedom, finds its own individual being.

Each of these questions would take us far afield. Each requires a separate and detailed treatment on its own. I mention them only to indicate that examining the essentially free temporality of the "thinking entity" that each finds himself to be, is no pedantic exercise; rather it is an inquiry which has importantly pervasive implications for myriad questions beyond itself.

References

St. Augustine (1984), *On the Free Choice of the Will*, trans. A. S. Benjamin & L. H. Hackstaff. Indianapolis: Bobbs-Merrill Educational.

Bergson, H. (1889), *Time and Free Will*, trans. F.L. Pogson. London: George Allen & Unwin.

Descartes, R. (1968), *The Philosophical Works of Descartes*, trans. E. S. Haldane & G. R. T. Ross. 2 vols. Cambridge: Cambridge University Press.

Gadamer, H.-G. (1975), *Truth and Method*. New York: The Seabury Press.

Heidegger, M. (1927), *Being and Time*, trans. J. Macquarrie & E. Robinson. New York: Harper & Row, 1962.

Husserl, E. (1905–1910), *The Phenomenology of Internal Time-Consciousness*, ed. M. Heidegger, trans. J. S. Churchill. Bloomington: Indiana University Press, 1964.

Kant, I. (1781, 1787), *Critique of Pure Reason*, trans. N. K. Smith. New York: St. Martin's Press, 1968.

Leibniz, G. W. (1949), *New Essays on the Human Understanding*, trans. A. G. Langley. LaSalle: Open Court.

——— (1965), Critical Remarks Concerning the General Part of Descartes' Principles (1.7.). In: *Monadology and Other Philosophical Essays*, eds. P. & A. Schrecker. Indianapolis: The Bobbs-Merrill Company.

Locke, J. (1690), *Essay Concerning the Human Understanding*, ed. A. C. Fraser. 2 vols. New York: Dover, 1894.

Merleau-Ponty, M. (1962), *The Phenomenology of Perception*, trans. C. Smith. London: Routledge & Kegan Paul.

Sherover, C. M. (1975), Time and ethics: How is morality possible? In: *The Study of Time II*, eds. J. T. Fraser & N. Lawrence. New York: Springer-Verlag.

——— (1984), The temporality of the common good: Futurity and freedom. *Rev. Metaphys.*, 37/3:475–497.

16

Man and Time: Some Historical and Critical Reflections

G. J. Whitrow

The subject of time has long been associated with paradox, no less so today than in previous ages. This is seen not only at the philosophical level but also in the contemporary general attitude to time. For, whereas modern industrial civilization is dependent on time to a far greater extent than any previous civilization, except possibly that of the Mayans of Mesoamerica, there is a peculiar ambivalence in this dependence. Although our knowledge of the past of both man and the universe is far greater than that possessed by our ancestors, our feeling of continuity with the past has tended to diminish because of the many rapid changes that now influence our lives. As a result, time has tended to become so fragmented that for many people only the present appears to be significant. The past is widely regarded as "out-of date" and therefore useless, and the future appears to be increasingly unpredictable. Moreover, because the present differs so much from the past, it is becoming more and more difficult to realize what the past was actually like.

Despite this diminution of temporal perspective in our daily lives, the opposite influence prevails when we seek to investigate the nature of society and of the physical world. Nowadays, more than ever before, we believe that only by studying the past can we hope to understand the present. We are consequently confronted with the paradoxical situation that the past is simultaneously devalued and enhanced in value. This is due to the dynamic nature of our civilization. In former times society was more static. Despite conquests and upheavals, the nature of civilization changed far less rapidly than it has recently. Even for historians the concept of time was less significant than it is for their successors today. For example, we regard it as one of the first duties of the historian to date events precisely, the date being regarded by us as an essential feature. This attitude, however, is comparatively modern.

Indeed, it was not until the nineteenth century that the fundamental significance of temporal perspective came to be generally recognized. This was several hundred years after the theory and practice of spatial perspective had been developed by painters and others. It is perhaps not surprising that Descartes in his new science of *mathesis universalis* had no place for the historical form of thought, because of the primitive state in his day of the historical sciences compared with the mathematical. His devaluation of history was accompanied by the promotion of space as the basic concept in his philosophy of nature. The key figure in the development of the mechanistic concept of the universe, he was greatly influenced by the analogy of the clock, but despite this time played a secondary role in his system.

The Cartesian belief that space is a more fundamental category than time had a long history going back to antiquity and has had a continuing appeal to many right down to the present day. For example, even so empirically minded a thinker as Bertrand Russell, in his essay on "Mysticism and Logic," declared that time is an unimportant and superficial characteristic of reality, and he went on to claim that "a certain emancipation from slavery to time is essential to philosophic thought" (Russell, 1917, p. 21). Alas, even philosophers are men like the rest of us. The Russian philosopher Nicolas Berdyaev is said once to have broken off his impassioned plea for the insignificance and unreality of time by suddenly looking at his watch with genuine anxiety, fearing that he was a few minutes late for taking his medicine.

It is well known that many philosophers with their stern faith in logic and precise reasoning have regarded time as a thoroughly unsatisfactory concept. As the psychologist Pierre Janet remarked in his book on time and memory, whenever stress is laid on logic and reason time tends to be unpopular (1928, chapter 20). Philosophers often have a particular horror of the concept and many have done all they can to suppress it. It is therefore perhaps not surprising that, as the Cambridge philosopher C. D. Broad admitted, "Our knowledge of time as of space owes more to the labours of mathematicians and physicists than to those of professed philosophers" (1921, p. 343). Nevertheless, it must be pointed out that many mathematicians and physicists too have been skeptical about the ultimate signifi-cance of time and have been far more favorably inclined to spatial concepts. To some extent this may be because space seems to be presented to us all of a piece, whereas time comes to us only bit by bit. The past can be recalled only by the dubious aid of memory, the future is unknown, and only the present is directly experienced. There is also a notable difference between space and time in the case of measurement. Freedom to move about in space leads to the idea of the transportable measuring rod, but the absence of any corresponding freedom to rove about in time makes it impossible for us to compare *directly* the duration of a particular process with its duration when repeated.

It is a remarkable fact that even Einstein, who made the greatest contribution since the seventeenth century to our understanding of physical time when he formulated the special theory of relativity, later became decidedly wary of the concept. Indeed, an indication of this was already given in the course of his famous 1905 paper on that theory where he stated that "all our judgments in which time plays a part are always judgments of *simultaneous events*" (p. 39). By some curious oversight he seems to have forgotten that many of our judgments concerning time are to do with temporal order or sequence; for example, judging that one event occurs after another. Simultaneity is a symmetrical concept and so is therefore more "spacelike" than is the concept of temporal order or precedence. Einstein's tendency to assign a less important role to time than to space became quite explicit later in his life. For example, in 1952, in expressing his views on the formation of our concepts of space and time he declared that "it is characteristic of thought in natural science generally that it endeavours in principle to make do with 'space-like' concepts *alone*, and strives to express with their aid all relations having the form of laws" (pp. 141–142). It is true that in this same passage he argued that "the formation of the concept of the material object must precede our concepts of time and space," but he made no mention of processes in the external world and it would seem that he regarded "objects" as more fundamental than "processes."

Einstein's bias in favor of the concept of space had deep roots in the history of physics. Indeed, the idea of time as a quasi-geometrical locus that can be represented by a straight line can be traced back to the Greeks. The idea was successfully exploited by Galileo in his pioneer researches on the science of motion early in the seventeenth century[1] and culminated in the theory of dynamics developed toward the end of the eighteenth century by Lagrange, who regarded time as a kind of fourth dimension of space. This idea was carried further as a result of the theory of relativity, for Einstein eventually concluded that the objective world of physics is essentially a four-dimensional structure, its resolution into space and time depending on the observer. "It appears therefore more natural," he wrote, "to think of physical reality as a four-dimensional existence, instead of, as hitherto, the *evolution* of a three-dimensional existence" (1952, p. 150).

The idea that time and space are closely associated concepts has long been entertained by philosophers. For example, John Locke in his *Essay Concerning Human Understanding* after discussing space and time separately devoted a chapter to their joint consideration, and concluded by pointing out that "expansion and duration do mutually embrace and comprehend each other; every part of space being in every part of duration, and every part of duration in every part of expansion" (1690, p. 121). Also in both Newton's and Leibniz's very different views, space and time are each treated similarly, and in Kant's writings too the arguments presented in favor of his theory of time correspond point by point to the arguments presented for his theory of space. Kant believed that both are parts of our mental apparatus for imagining or visualizing the world, space being the basis for the coordination of our external perceptions, whereas time is the basis for the coordination of our internal perceptions. He goes on to say that since time is nothing but the intuition of ourselves and of our inner state it has nothing to do with either shape or appearances, and because of this deficiency we have to make use of analogies. "We represent the time-sequence by a line progressing to infinity, in which the manifold constitutes a series of one dimension only; and we reason from

---

[1]No similar development took place, however, in the Indian, Chinese, or Mayan civilizations.

the properties of this line to all the properties of time, with this one exception, that while the parts of the line are simultaneous the parts of time are always successive" (1781, p. 50).

The representation of time by a straight line, which is often referred to as the "spatialization of time," involves the assumption that, regarded mathematically, time is one-dimensional. Should we attribute the origin of this idea to the fact that, strictly speaking, we can attend to only one thing at a time, and thereby conclude that our idea of unidimensional time is a consequence of our manner of thinking having the form of a linear sequence? I think that there is more to it than that, since I believe that the one-dimensional nature of time can be associated with another, and no less significant fact that, whereas there exists free mobility in space, there is no such possibility in time. For, we can express this difference by noting that, although it is possible to describe a closed circuit in space, so that we return to the same place as before, it is impossible to describe a closed circuit in time. This is easily seen by imagining a clock to be set at zero at a particular event. Let it continue to tick as it describes the circuit. Then at each instant it will record a time different from zero and this will still be the case on its return to the initial event. But this contradicts the assumption that it is, in fact, the same event as before, since the clock thereat now reads a different time. Only in the case of a one-dimensional space is there anything that at all corresponds to the absence of free mobility in time. For in the case of a set of distinct objects arranged in a one-dimensional space (e.g. like beads strung on a wire), we cannot alter the order in which they occur merely by moving them about, at least so long as no two of them can occupy the same place or jump over each other. Although this analogy does not provide a logically conclusive argument, I believe that it helps us to understand why any spatial representation of time is restricted to a one-dimensional form.

In considering a line as representing temporal duration we assume that temporal instants correspond to geometrical points. Although the mental present cannot be regarded as durationless, the instant of mathematical time is assumed to have this property. However convenient this idea and the associated concept of the continuity of time may be for the development of mathematical physics, it is natural to ask whether there is anything corresponding to them in the physical world. Some civilizations in the past, for example medieval Islam, have regarded time as atomic rather than continuous. More recently, Galileo's pupil Torricelli also thought of time as "granular," and a similar concept was advocated by Descartes. He believed that a material body has only the property of spatial extension and no inherent capacity for endurance. This was because, in his view, a self-conserving being requires nothing but itself in order to exist and self-conservation must therefore be the unique prerogative of God. Consequently, a material body can only continue to exist if it is re-created by God from instant to instant. Because of this, Descartes felt compelled to assume that the instants at which material things exist must be discontinuous, or atomic.

The idea of temporal atomicity does not necessarily imply that there must be gaps between successive instants, but rather that there is a limit to the division of any duration into successive parts. It would mean that as far as time is concerned there are minimal processes in nature, i.e. processes of shortest duration. So far, modern physicists have felt no need to adopt the concept of *temporal* atomicity. Nevertheless, although the concept of continuous time is a useful mathematical device, it does not follow that it necessarily corresponds to anything in the natural world. Similarly, although the associated concept of the durationless instant is a useful aid to the mathematical physicist, it has its conceptual limitations. For, as Whitehead has argued, "There is no nature apart from transition, and there is no transition apart from temporal duration. This is why an instant of time, conceived as a primary single fact, is nonsense" (Whitehead, 1938, p. 207). In other words, times can consist only of parts of time and there are no parts of time that are not temporal. The concept of the instant is, in fact, a purely static concept, like that of the geometrical point, and hence it omits the most characteristic features of time.

Similarly, as M. Čapek has pointed out, "the geometrical line that is *already drawn* to symbolize 'the course of time' tends to hide the most essential character of becoming—its incompleteness" (1971, p. 131). For, even if we imagine the line representing time to be incomplete and continually extending itself into the future, the idea presupposes unoccupied points beyond the end of the line symbolizing the present, and these points suggest the preexistence of the future. In other words, the use of the straight line to represent a temporal sequence should not, in my opinion, lead us to overlook the important consideration that *the act of drawing the line*, rather than the line itself, provides the more complete analogy. At a given instant the moving end of the line corresponds to the present, the part of the line already drawn corresponds to the past, and the part not yet drawn corresponds to the future. We must, therefore, not overlook the fact that the geometrical representation of time, useful though it is, does not correspond to all the essential features of the concept. In particular, the usefulness of the four-dimensional space–time of relativity theory does not rule out the possibility that we live in an evolving universe.

If we survey the ideas that have been held about time down the centuries we find a continually increasing emphasis on the historical aspects of both social and physical reality. Belief in the concept of cyclical time—that is to say in the cyclical nature of the social and the physical world—has been replaced in recent centuries by a growing awareness of the evolutionary nature of man and of his environment. In every age there has been an underlying analogy between the prevailing concepts of society and of the universe. Each of these analogies can be associated with a different view of the nature and significance of time. From the ancient Greeks to the seventeenth century the dominant analogy was that of macrocosm and microcosm based on the belief that the world is a kind of organism, both alive and intelligent, and the concept of time was dominated by teleology. This analogy was eventually supplanted by the mechanistic analogy, which originated in the later Middle Ages and Renaissance and was not finally discarded until the present century. This analogy not only gave rise to the idea of the clocklike universe created by an external intelligence, but also to a quasi-mechanical concept of society that is perhaps most explicitly described in the Introduction to Hobbes's *Leviathan* (1651), where the state is regarded as an artificial man and man himself is regarded mechanistically.

Finally, we have the historical analogy that originated in the eighteenth century, according to which both the universe and society are regarded as evolving in time.

Indeed, it is only in the last two centuries that belief in the unchanging character of the universe has been seriously undermined. Until the nineteenth century the concept of evolution made little impact on man's way of thinking about the world. Astronomy, the oldest and most advanced science, did not indicate any evidence of trend in the universe. For, although it had long been realized that time itself could be measured by the motion of the heavenly bodies and that the accuracy of man-made clocks could be controlled by reference to astronomical observations, the pattern of celestial motions, like that of a system of wheels, appeared to be the same whether it was read forwards or backwards, and the future was regarded as essentially a repetition of the past. Consequently, centuries ago it was natural for man to lay primary emphasis on the cyclical aspects of time and the universe. During the course of the eighteenth century, however, the belief began to spread that the idea of time is an essential part of the idea of nature. Just as acceptance of the Copernican theory had shattered the tightly knit confines of the world in space, similarly the tendency to look at things historically led to a correspondingly vast extension of the world in time.

The idea of time's arrow as an essential characteristic of the universe arose when men first began to question the age-old belief that the general state of the physical world remains more or less the same indefinitely. The concept of evolution was introduced in the eighteenth and nineteenth centuries into the study of both living organisms and the physical world in general. The idea of the irreversibility of organic evolution has been called Dollo's law after the Belgian paleontologist who, in 1893, drew attention to the evidence for it in the fossil record. Although some small-scale reversals have been reported, generally speaking evolution is the result of many variations occurring in a definite order. Consequently, for it to be reversible there would have to be an extremely improbable recurrence of specific variations acting in the reverse sense to those that produced the original transformations. Moreover, evolution necessarily occurs on the basis of what has already happened, that is of previous evolution. If there is an evolutionary sequence of species A, B, and C, such that B evolved from A and C evolved from B, the fact that C differs from A makes it most unlikely that B could at some later stage result from C. Hence, the overall evolutionary process would appear to be essentially irreversible, and so, as H. F. Blum has remarked, "the Ammonites, the Dinosaur, and the *Lepidodendron* are gone beyond recall" (1962, p. 201).

Among the evolutionary processes occurring in the world of inorganic phenomena, much attention has been devoted this century to radioactivity. In 1902 Rutherford and Soddy announced their famous law that the rate of decay of a given amount of a radioactive element is proportional to the number of atoms of the element that are present. This law is based on the fact that the probability of an atom breaking up is independent of its age and also of the temperature, pressure, and other physical characteristics of the environment. It depends only on the particular element concerned, because radioactivity is essentially a nuclear phenomenon that is independent of the external influences to which the element might be subjected. As a consequence of the Rutherford–Soddy law it can easily be shown that radioactive decay is not only an indicator of time's arrow but can also be used as a means of measuring time. In other words, radioactive deposits can be regarded as noncyclic or evolutionary clocks. A well-known example is the carbon-14 clock that has proved so useful for archaeologists.

In recent years much attention has been devoted by astrophysicists to the subject of stellar evolution. Here again we are confronted by one-way processes. We now believe that nuclear processes deep in the interiors of stars are responsible for stellar radiation. Whereas it is thought that a star like the sun can continue to radiate steadily for thousands of millions of years, highly luminous stars are comparatively short-lived. All stars are believed to have only a finite period of time as radiating bodies and consequently have a definite life-history. Moreover, galaxies—vast stellar systems like our own that is dominated by the Milky Way—also are thought to have evolutionary histories. Thus, both on the terrestrial scale and on the celestial scale there is abundant evidence of trend in the universe when sufficiently long scales of time are considered.

As regards the evolution of the universe as a whole, many cosmologists now believe that it began with matter and radiation in an extremely dense high-temperature state following an initial "explosion." As the universe expanded, the temperature decreased. In the first three minutes or so it fell sufficiently for the principal elementary particles and the simplest atomic nuclei to be generated (Weinberg, 1977). These were followed much later by the creation of stable atoms and in due course by the formation of stars and galaxies. The expansion of the universe thus provided the time-direction signpost of inorganic evolution (including that of radioactive decay) and this ultimately gave rise to that of biological evolution and of all organic processes, culminating in our conscious awareness of time's arrow.

.What particularly distinguishes man in contemporary society is that he has become increasingly time-conscious. The moment we rouse ourselves from sleep we usually wonder what time it is. During our daily routine we are continually concerned about time and are forever consulting our clocks and watches. In previous ages most men worked hard but worried less about time than we do. Until the rise of modern industrial civilization men's lives were far less consciously dominated by time than they have been since. The development and continual improvement of the mechanical clock and, more recently, of portable watches has had a profound influence on the way we live.

Today it is difficult for us to realize what life was like when people had no clocks and watches. Even after the invention of the mechanical clock most people were little affected by its steady clank. For a public clock, whether installed in a church or a town square, was only an intermittent reminder of the passage of time, but a domestic clock or a watch was a continually visible indicator. Long after they were invented, domestic clocks and watches were restricted to the wealthy and their possession was looked upon as a sign of affluence rather than as a social necessity. When ordinary folk encountered a watch they were often puzzled by it and inclined to regard it as something evil and dangerous. An amusing instance of this is related by John Aubrey, in the late seventeenth century, concerning an Oxford don, Thomas Allen (1542–1632), who owned many mathematical and other scientific instruments. When staying one Long Vacation with a friend "at Hom Lacey in Herefordshire," he happened to leave his watch on the windowsill of his chamber. According to Aubrey,

> The maydes came in to make the bed, and hearing a thing in a vase cry *Tick, Tick, Tick*, presently concluded that it was his Devill, and took it by the string with the tongues, and threw it out of the windowe into the mote (to drown the Devill). It so happened that the string hung on a sprig of an elder that grew out of the mote, and this confirmed them that 'twas the Devill. [So] the good old gentleman got his watch back [1949, p. 133].

As late as the middle of the seventeenth century we find, for example, that even at the age of thirty Samuel Pepys (1633–1703), already an important government official, did not possess a watch. Instead, he lived by the church bells of London and occasionally a sundial, as did almost everyone else there. Consequently, very few specific appointments were made. Pepys moved around from public places to coffee houses and taverns hoping to do business. He often went to discuss matters with the Lord High Admiral, James, Duke of York, only to find that the Duke had gone hunting. Pepys never expresses surprise or resentment. Time had a different meaning for him and his contemporaries than it has for us.

Not only do most workers nowadays have to clock in and clock out when they begin and end their working day, but time-keeping applies no less generally to sporting activities. Indeed, anything, however idiotic, can now be regarded as a sport so long as it can be timed and can be used to set up a "record." Kevin Sheenan, of Limerick, acquired a kind of fame by talking nonstop for 127 hours, and in the United States a preacher established another record by delivering a sermon that lasted forty-eight hours.[2] In these and many other ways most of us have become more and more subservient to the tyranny of time. As Lewis Mumford has so pertinently remarked, "The clock, not the steam-engine, is the key machine of the modern industrial age" (1934, p. 14). The popularization of time-keeping that followed the mass production of cheap watches in the nineteenth century has accentuated the tendency for even the most basic functions of living to be regulated chronometrically: "One ate, not upon feeling hungry, but when prompted by the clock; one slept, not when one was tired, but when the clock sanctioned it" (Mumford, 1934, p. 17). A good example of how strange our modern preoccupation with time seemed to someone used to a very different way of life is provided by the diary kept by the Nepalese ruler Jang Bahadur on his visit to Britain in 1850. According to the translation by John Whelpton of a biography of him in Nepali published in Katmandu in 1957 and containing excerpts from this diary, he remarked that "Getting dressed, eating, keeping appointments, sleeping, getting

---

[2]This achievement would not have amused Queen Victoria who is said to have had placed conspicuously in all the pulpits used by her chaplains a sand-clock that ran for only ten minutes!

up—everything is determined by the clock . . . where you look, there you see a clock" (Gellner, 1983, p. 1438).

In contrast with our modern preoccupation with time, it appears from our knowledge of surviving primitive races that man, like other animals, has a natural tendency to live in a continual present. For example, although the children of Australian aborigines are of a similar mental capacity to white children, they have great difficulty in telling the time by the clock. They can read off the time as a memory exercise, but they are quite unable to relate it to the time of day. There is a cultural gap between their idea of time and ours which they find difficult to cross. It is surely significant that Rousseau, who extolled the noble savage, detested time and clocks and threw away his watch!

Kant believed that our concept of time is a prior condition of our experience of the world, but this does not explain why earlier peoples and civilizations have regarded time differently from us. Indeed, it is coming to be increasingly recognized that, instead of being a prior condition, our idea of time should be regarded as a consequence of our experience of the world, the result of a long evolution. The human mind has the power, apparently not possessed by animals, to construct the idea of time from our awareness of certain features characterizing the data of our experience. Although Kant threw no light on the origin of this power, he realized that it was a peculiarity of the human mind. In recent years it has become clear that all our mental abilities are potential capacities which we can only realize in practice by learning how to use them. For, whereas animals inherit various particular patterns of sensory awareness known as "releasers" (because they automatically initiate certain types of action), man has to learn to construct all his patterns of awareness from his own experience. Consequently, our ideas of time and space, which according to Kant function as if they were releasers, must instead be regarded as mental constructs which have to be learned.

The continuing evolution of our sense of time is revealed by the increasing importance of tense in the development of language. Greater knowledge of the universe has thus been accompanied by a greater appreciation of the distinctions between past, present, and future as man has learnt to transcend the limitations of "the eternal present." It is these distinctions that differentiate time most strikingly from space. Although our awareness of time involves psychological and cultural factors, as well as physiological processes below the level of consciousness, it is based on an external factor which we call physical time. None of the attempts that have been made to reduce this to some allegedly more fundamental concept has been successful. Some concepts must be taken as fundamental and it would seem that time itself should be so regarded. Nevertheless, this does not mean that it is "absolute," existing in its own right independently of everything else. Time is the essential concomitant of activity, for without time there can be no activity and without activity there can be no time.

References

Aubrey, J. (1949), *Brief Lives and Other Selected Writings*, ed. A. Powell. London: Cresset Press.

Blum, H. F. (1962), *Time's Arrow and Evolution*. New York: Harper.

Broad, C. D. (1921), Time. In: *Encyclopedia of Religion and Ethics,* Vol. 12. Edinburgh: Clark.

Čapek, M. (1971), *Bergson and Modern Physics: A Reinterpretation and Re-evaluation*. Dordrecht: Reidel.

Einstein, A. (1905), On the electrodynamics of moving bodies. In: *The Principle of Relativity*, trans. W. Perett & G. B. Jeffery. London: Methuen, 1923.

———— (1952), *Relativity: The Special and the General Theory*, 15th ed., trans. R. W. Lawson. London: Methuen, 1955.

Gellner, E. (1983), Book review. *Times Literary Supplement*, 23 December: 1438.

Hobbes, T. (1651), *Leviathan*. New York: Macmillan, 1986.

Janet, P. (1928), *L'évolution de la mémoire et de la notion du temps*. Paris: Cahine.

Kant, I. (1781), *Critique of Pure Reason*, trans. N. Kemp Smith. London: Macmillan, 1934.

Locke, J. (1690), *An Essay Concerning Human Understanding*, ed. A. S. Pringle-Pattison. Oxford: Clarendon Press, 1934.

Mumford, L. (1934), *Technics and Civilization*. London: Routledge & Kegan Paul.

Russell, B. (1917), *Mysticism and Logic*. London: Allen & Unwin.

Weinberg, S. (1977), *The First Three Minutes: A Modern View of the Origin of the Universe*. London: Andre Deutsch.

Whitehead, A. N. (1938), *Modes of Thought*. Cambridge: Cambridge University Press.

The Elusiveness of the Mind

J. T. Fraser

What kind of patterns may be recognized in our epistemic jigsaw puzzle, with its figures of thought on the nature of time and mind? What kind of permanent, defensible patterns emerge—if any?

A regularity, lawfulness, or principle is what it is, by virtue of being permanent for extended periods of time. Perhaps the most important function of the mind is to distinguish processes or structures that appear permanent from those temporal and spatial patterns that appear contingent and unpredictable. Whenever we attempt to describe the permanent features of minding, we are employing the skills of the mind to describe those skills.

Reading the chapters of this volume—cerebral, scholarly, analytic—leaves one (left me) with the feeling that the self-examining mind eluded those who intended to discover what it is exactly that they are examining. And, that it did so by demanding for such a discovery the logic and language of a temporal level which the searchers could not have possibly possessed. The idea suggests itself: perhaps the nature of the human mind includes among its essential ingredients the capacity to frustrate all intellectual inquiries into its precise nature, so as to retain its integrity, freedom, and creative potential.

This kind of open-endedness would not be unique to the mind. Organic evolution maintains its freedom by analogous means. It creates new life forms whose structures and functions are unpredictable before they actually appear. The mind may be doing the same in the domain of symbolic transformations of experience. Neither is the idea of identifying the mind with a sophisticated skill of elusiveness into self-inquiries in itself new. It was suggested well over twenty years ago and elaborated in many books and public lectures by the late Professor Donald MacKay (1966).

Nor was Professor MacKay the first one to suggest it. Dostoyevsky did so in his *Notes from the Underground* when he wrote that man will retain his dream that he is not a "piano key," a passive device, a predictable actor. Though his actions may be partly governed by the precise laws of nature, he will never "be controlled so completely that soon one will be able to desire nothing but by the calendar" (1864, p. 145).

> And . . . even if man really were nothing but a piano key, even if this were proved to him by natural science and mathematics, even then he would not become reasonable, but purposely do something perverse . . . to have his own way. [H]e will devise destruction and chaos, will devise suffering of all sorts [to] have his own way. . . . He will launch a curse upon the world [to] convince himself that he is not a piano key! If you say that all this, too, can be calculated and tabulated . . . then man would purposely go mad [in order to prove] to himself continually that he is a man and not an organ stop [1864, pp. 145–146].

> Consciousness . . . is infinitely superior to two times two makes four. Once you have two times two makes four, there is nothing left to do or understand. . . . While if you stick with consciousness, even though you attain the same result, you can at least flog yourself at times, and that will, at any rate, liven you up [1864, p. 149].

It is the creative chaos of the elusive mind that is being slowly colonized by reason, using the idea of time as its main organizing principle.

The direction in which our understanding of time and mind may develop cannot even be guessed without first guessing the direction of social change. The blending of technology with biology, the constantly narrowing global present, the increasing communication density, the interpenetration of ideological, commercial and military empires, the graying of the calendar, all of them being hallmarks of the time-compact globe will alter the questions regarding time and mind that will have to be answered, as well as the languages and logics to be used in the answers.

For now, from the point of view of this contributor to the volume, the "some day," the "long ago," and the "far away" will remain the true home of man. For, these are regions of reality that cannot be visited by members of any other species. It is the yearning for such nonpresent homes that made the crazy quilt of civilizations possible, and spurred us on along an uneasy path.

References

Dostoyevsky, F. (1864), *Notes from the Underground*. In: *Short Novels of the Masters*, trans. B. G. Gourney. New York: Holt, Rinehart.

MacKay, D. (1966), Conscious control of action. In: *Brain and Conscious Experience*, ed. J. C. Eccles. Berlin: Springer Verlag, pp. 422–445.

Index